D1228644

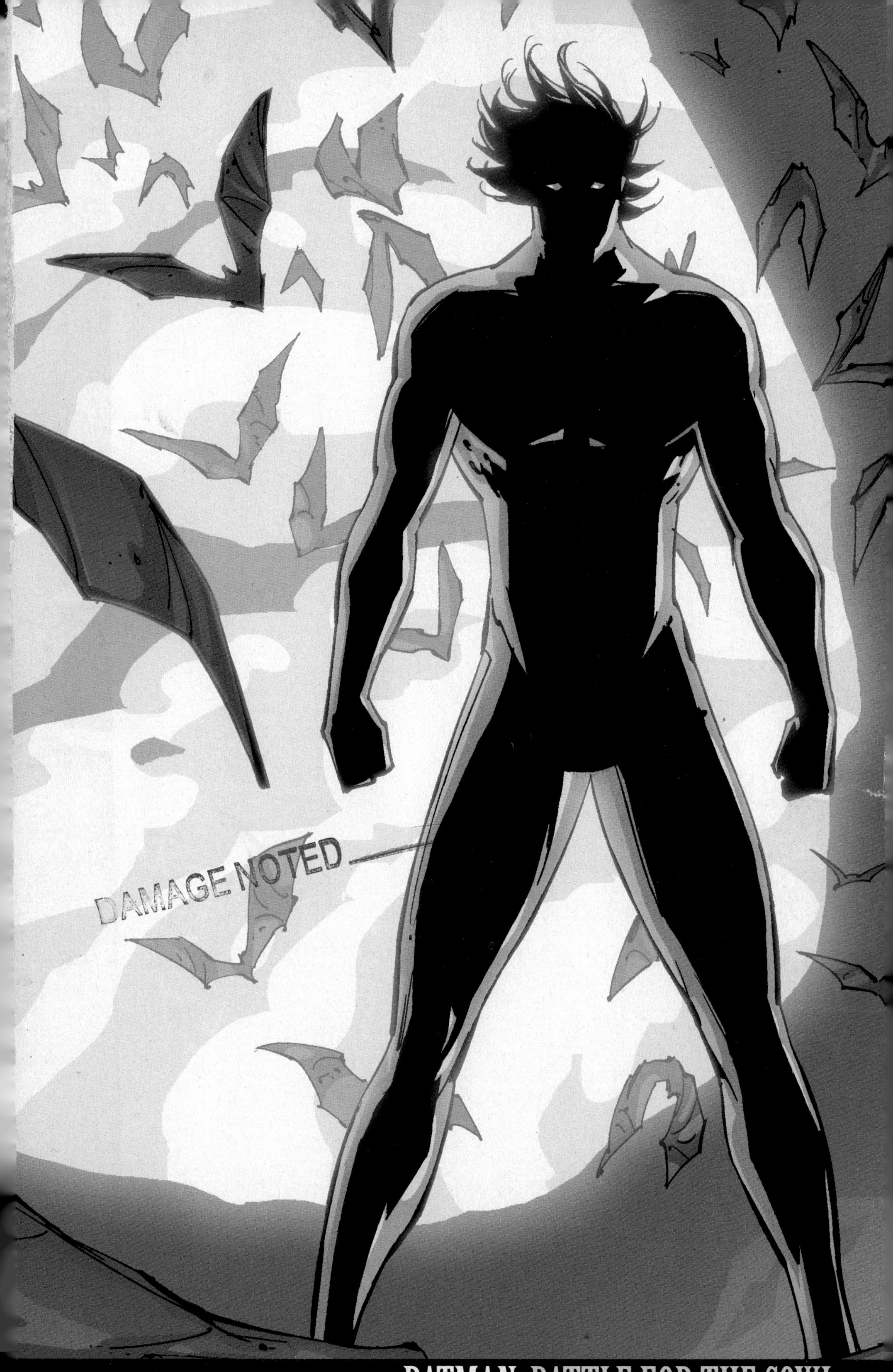

BATMAN: BATTLE FOR THE COWL

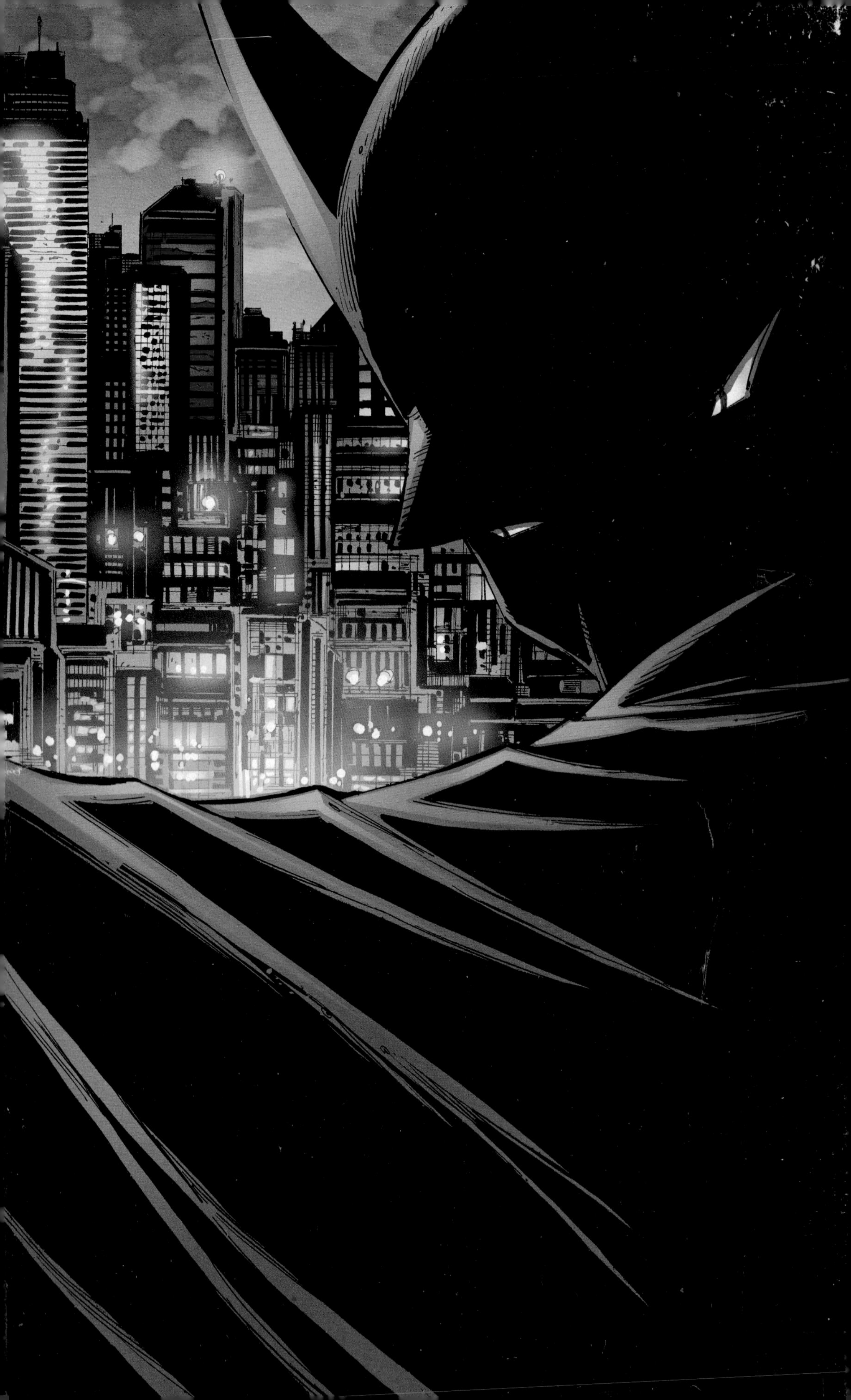

BATMAN: BATTLE FOR THE COWL

BATTLE FOR THE COWL

Tony S. Daniel Writer and Penciller

Sandu Florea Inker

Ian Hannin Colorist

Jared K. Fletcher Letterer

Tony S. Daniel Original Series Covers

GOTHAM GAZETTE

Fabian Nicieza Writer

**Dustin Nguyen   Guillem March   ChrisCross
Jamie McKelvie   Alex Konat   Mark McKenna** Artists

Guy Major   Guillem March Colorists

Steve Wands Letterer

Dustin Nguyen Original Series Covers

BATMAN created by Bob Kane

Dan DiDio SVP – Executive Editor
Mike Marts Editor – Original Series
Janelle Siegel Assistant Editor – Original Series
Georg Brewer VP – Design & DC Direct Creative
Bob Harras Group Editor – Collected Editions
Scott Nybakken Editor
Robbin Brosterman Design Director – Books
Louis Prandi Art Director

DC COMICS
Paul Levitz President & Publisher
Richard Bruning SVP – Creative Director
Patrick Caldon EVP – Finance & Operations
Amy Genkins SVP – Business & Legal Affairs
Jim Lee Editorial Director – WildStorm
Gregory Noveck SVP – Creative Affairs
Steve Rotterdam SVP – Sales & Marketing
Cheryl Rubin SVP – Brand Management

Cover art by Tony S. Daniel.
Cover color by Ian Hannin.

BATMAN: BATTLE FOR THE COWL

DC Comics, 1700 Broadway, New York, NY 10019
A Warner Bros. Entertainment Company
Printed by RR Donnelley, Salem, VA, USA 10/21/09.
First Printing.
HC ISBN: 978-1-4012-2416-5
SC ISBN: 978-1-4012-2417-2

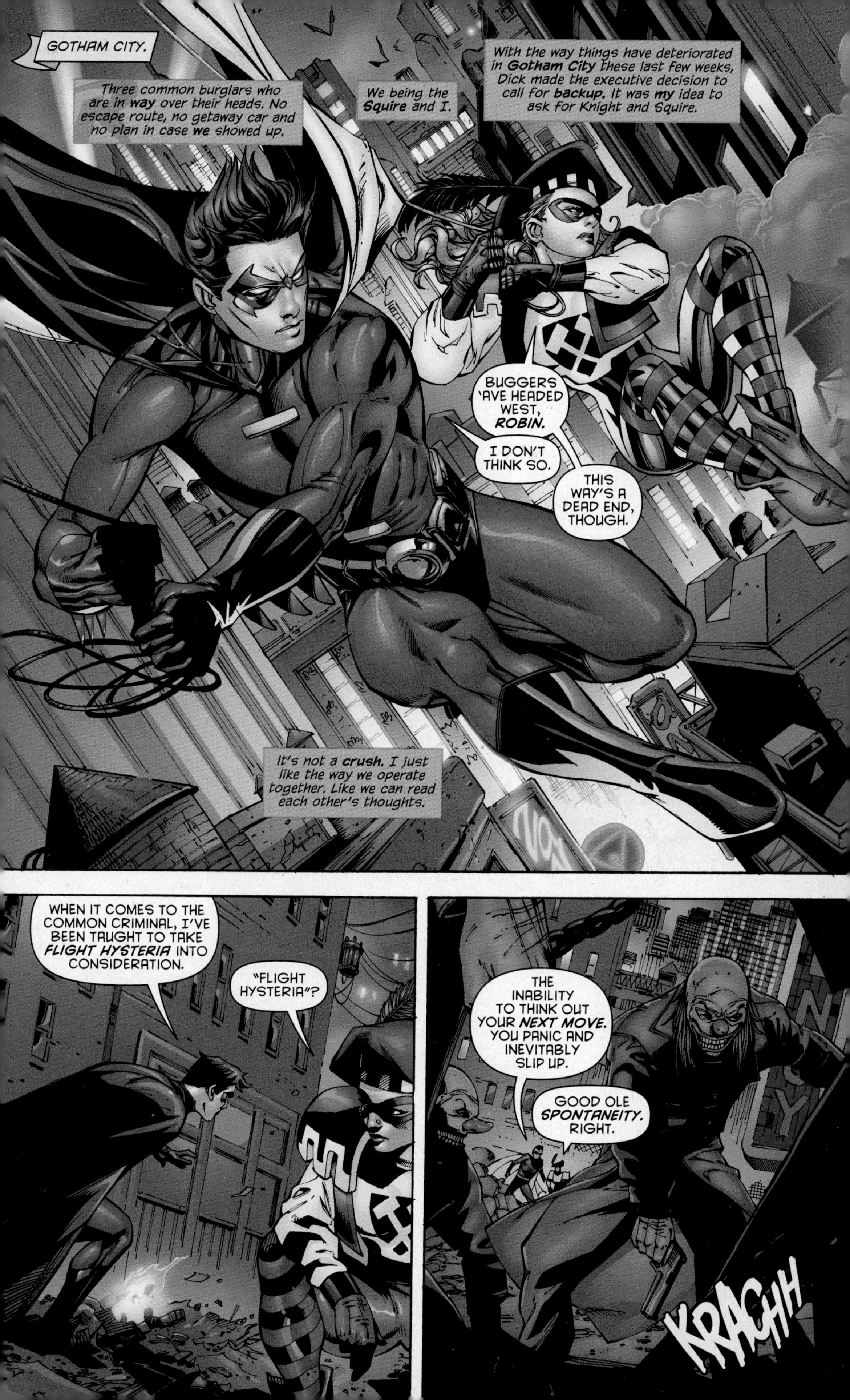
GOTHAM CITY.
Three common burglars who are in way over their heads. No escape route, no getaway car and no plan in case we showed up.
We being the Squire and I.
With the way things have deteriorated in Gotham City these last few weeks, Dick made the executive decision to call for backup. It was my idea to ask for Knight and Squire.
BUGGERS 'AVE HEADED WEST, ROBIN.
I DON'T THINK SO.
THIS WAY'S A DEAD END, THOUGH.
It's not a crush. I just like the way we operate together. Like we can read each other's thoughts.
WHEN IT COMES TO THE COMMON CRIMINAL, I'VE BEEN TAUGHT TO TAKE FLIGHT HYSTERIA INTO CONSIDERATION.
"FLIGHT HYSTERIA"?
THE INABILITY TO THINK OUT YOUR NEXT MOVE. YOU PANIC AND INEVITABLY SLIP UP.
GOOD OLE SPONTANEITY. RIGHT.
KRACHH

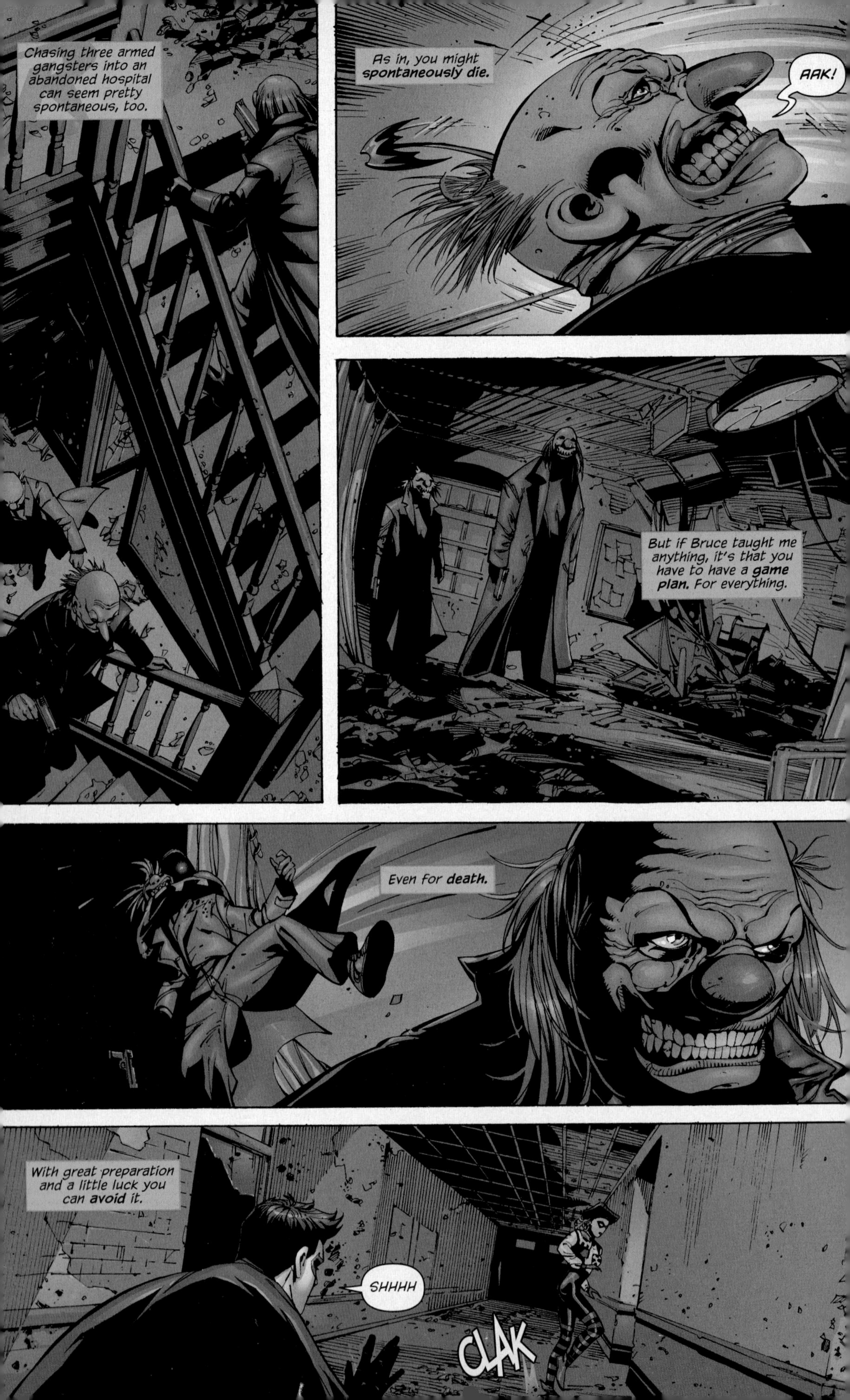
Chasing three armed gangsters into an abandoned hospital can seem pretty spontaneous, too.
As in, you might spontaneously die.
AAK!
But if Bruce taught me anything, it's that you have to have a game plan. For everything.
Even for death.
With great preparation and a little luck you can avoid it.
SHHHH
CLAK

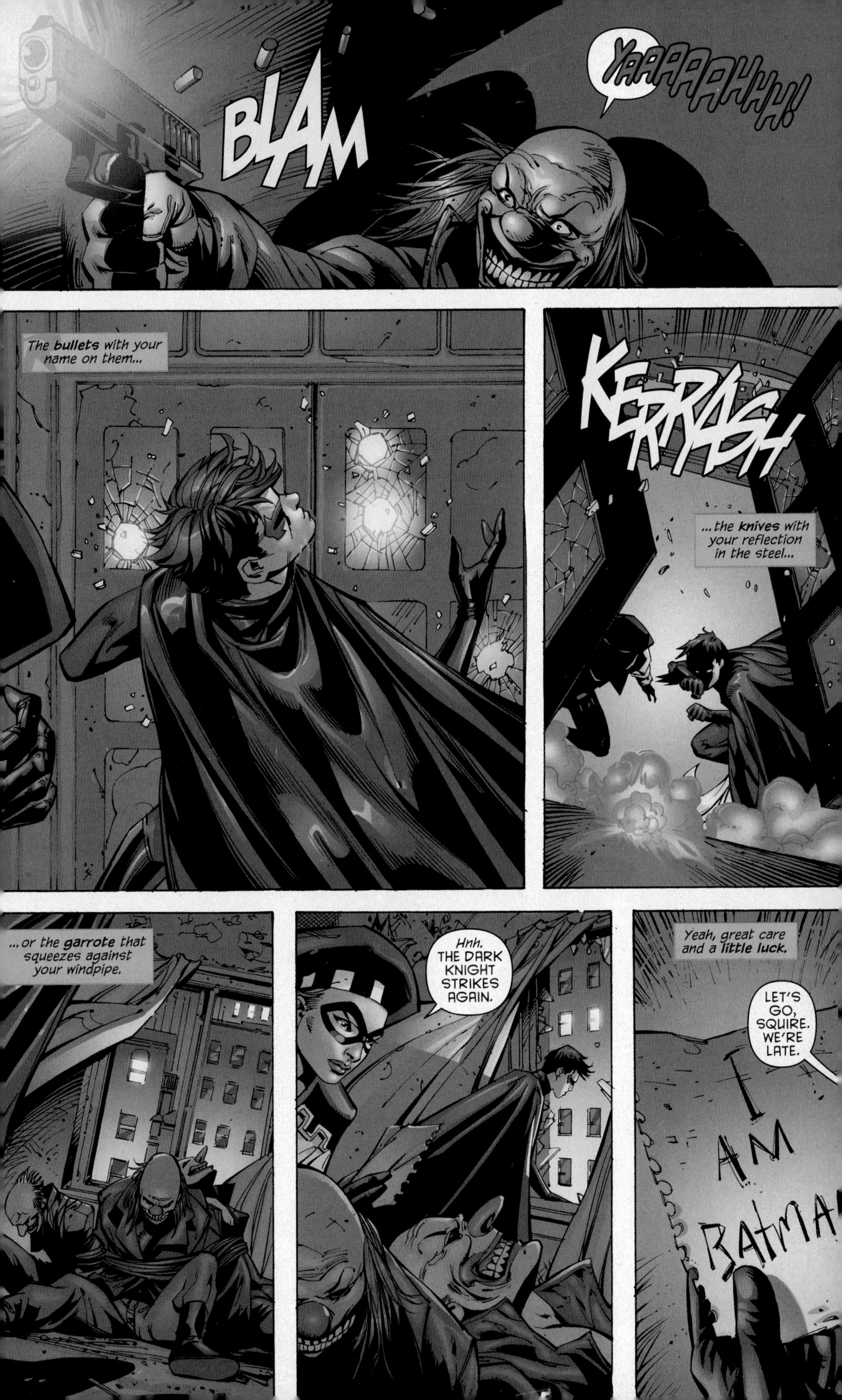
BLAM
YAAAAAHHHH!
The bullets with your name on them...
KERRASH
...the knives with your reflection in the steel...
...or the garrote that squeezes against your windpipe.
Hnh. THE DARK KNIGHT STRIKES AGAIN.
Yeah, great care and a little luck.
LET'S GO, SQUIRE. WE'RE LATE.
I AM BATMA

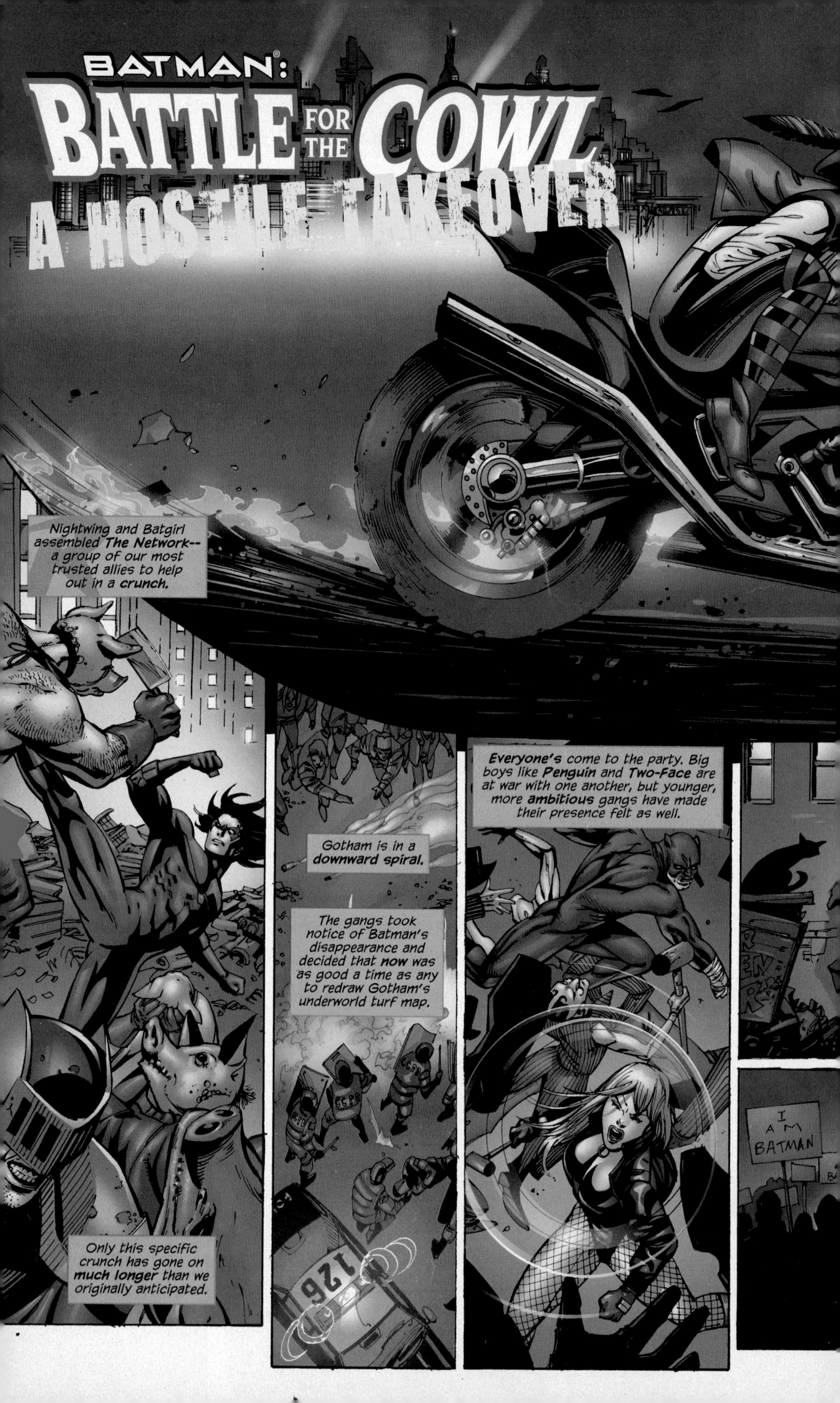
BATMAN®:
BATTLE FOR THE COWL
A HOSTILE TAKEOVER
Nightwing and Batgirl assembled The Network-- a group of our most trusted allies to help out in a crunch.
Only this specific crunch has gone on much longer than we originally anticipated.
Gotham is in a downward spiral.
The gangs took notice of Batman's disappearance and decided that now was as good a time as any to redraw Gotham's underworld turf map.
Everyone's come to the party. Big boys like Penguin and Two-Face are at war with one another, but younger, more ambitious gangs have made their presence felt as well.
I AM BATMAN

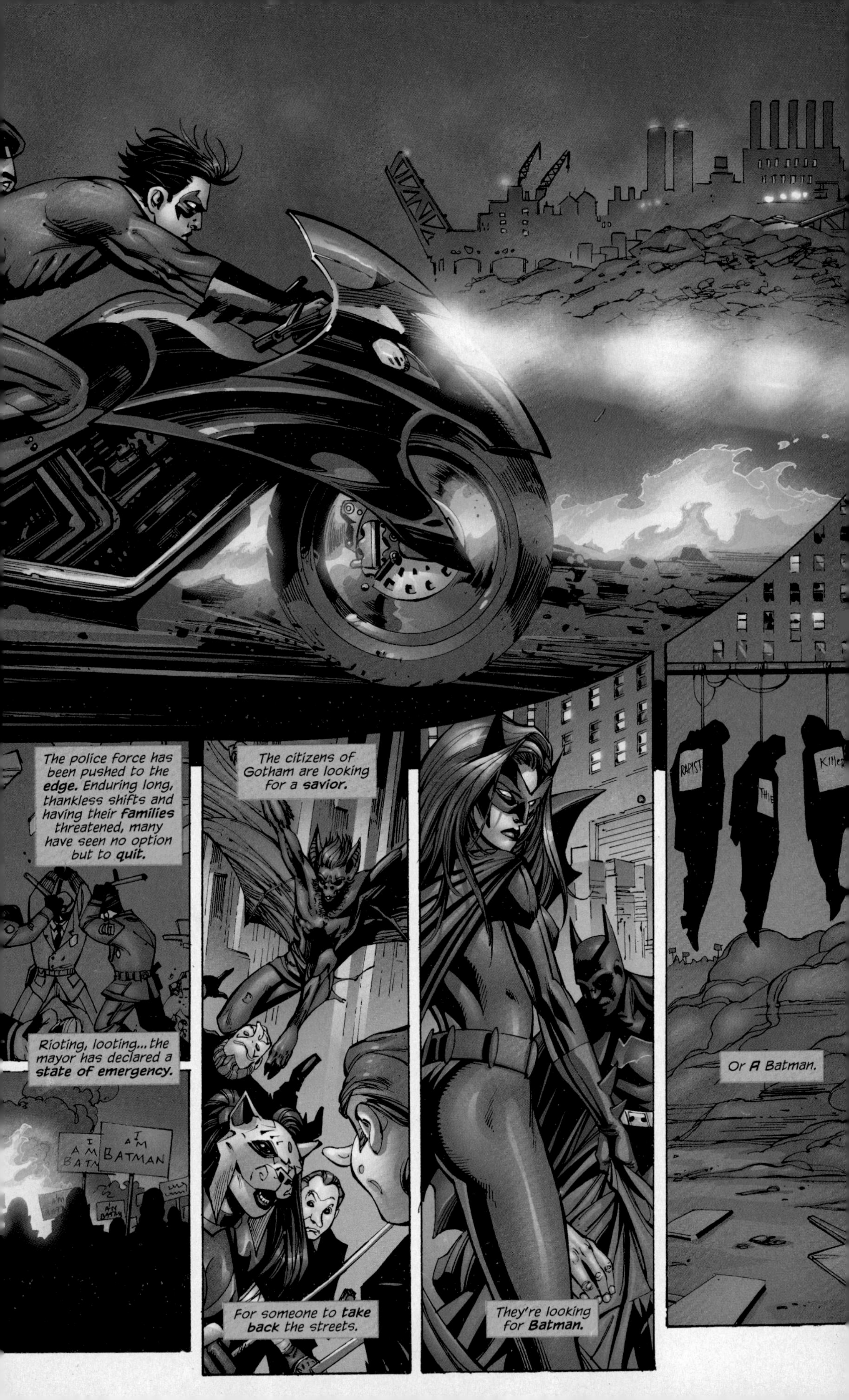
The police force has been pushed to the **edge.** Enduring long, thankless shifts and having their **families** threatened, many have seen no option but to **quit.**
Rioting, looting... the mayor has declared a **state of emergency.**
I AM BATMAN
The citizens of Gotham are looking for a **savior.**
For someone to **take back** the streets.
They're looking for **Batman.**
RAPIST
Killer
Or **A** Batman.

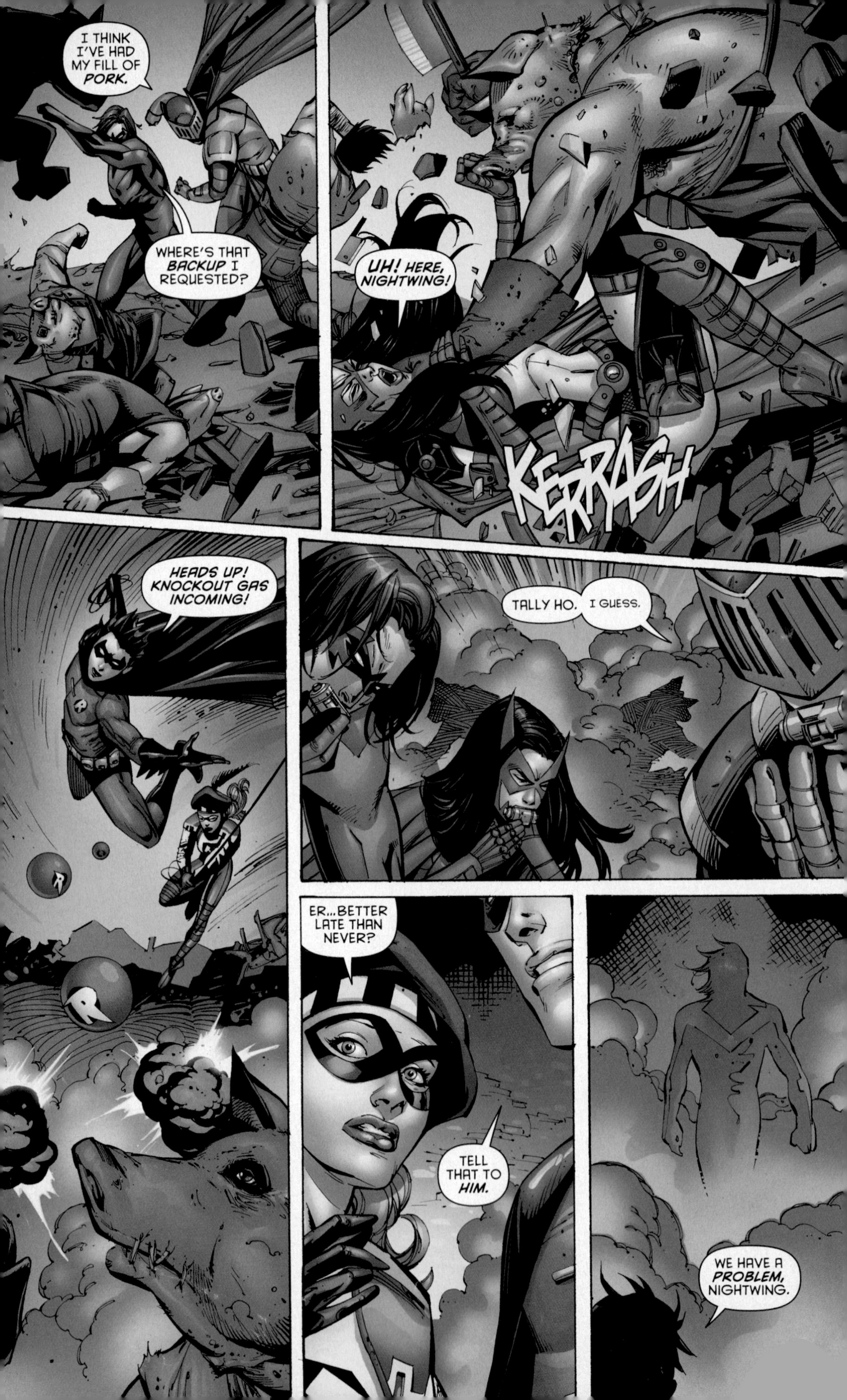
I THINK I'VE HAD MY FILL OF PORK.
WHERE'S THAT BACKUP I REQUESTED?
UH! HERE, NIGHTWING!
KERRASH
HEADS UP! KNOCKOUT GAS INCOMING!
TALLY HO.
I GUESS.
ER...BETTER LATE THAN NEVER?
TELL THAT TO HIM.
WE HAVE A PROBLEM, NIGHTWING.

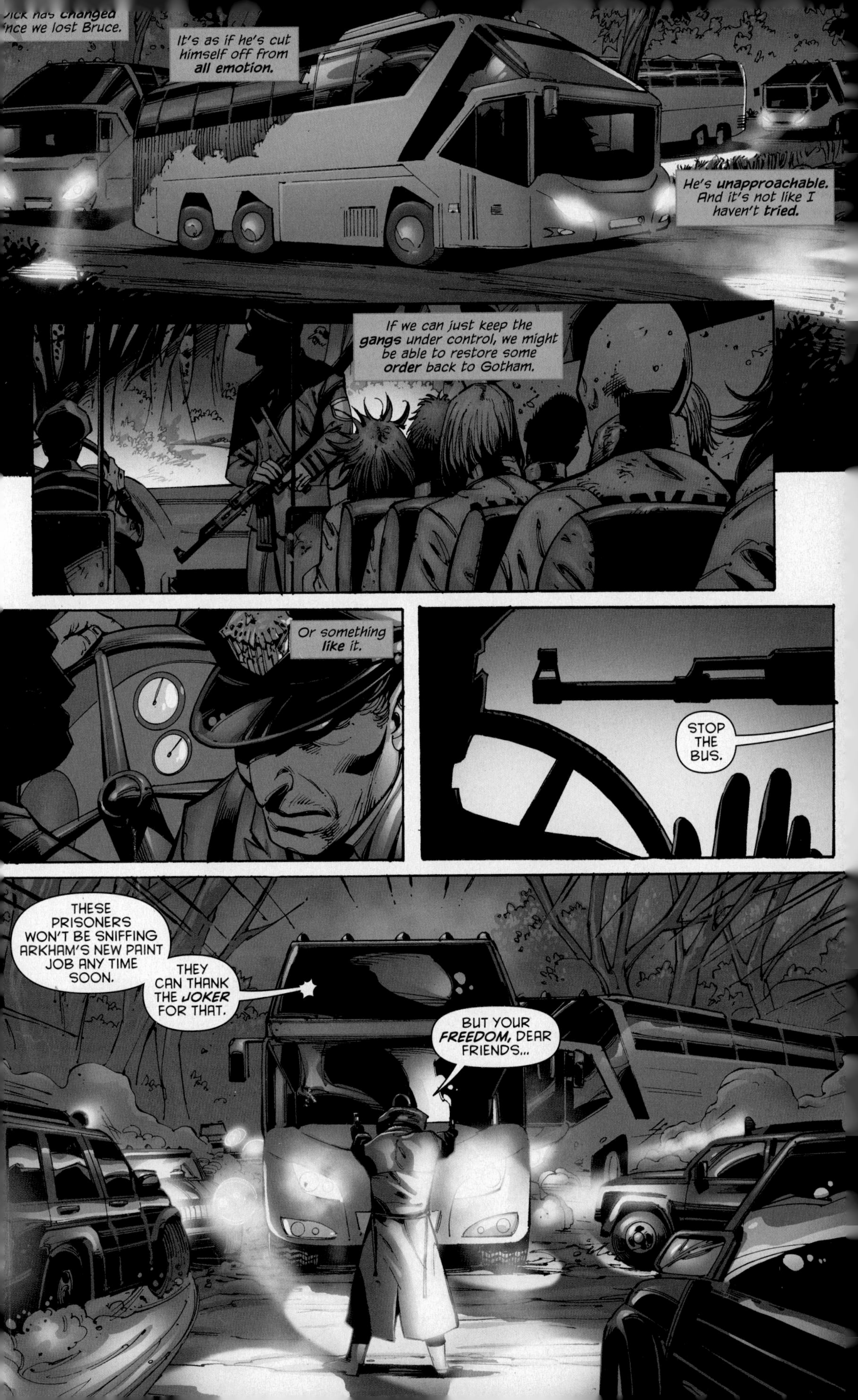

Dick has changed since we lost Bruce.
It's as if he's cut himself off from all emotion.
He's unapproachable. And it's not like I haven't tried.
If we can just keep the gangs under control, we might be able to restore some order back to Gotham.
Or something like it.
STOP THE BUS.
THESE PRISONERS WON'T BE SNIFFING ARKHAM'S NEW PAINT JOB ANY TIME SOON.
THEY CAN THANK THE JOKER FOR THAT.
BUT YOUR FREEDOM, DEAR FRIENDS...

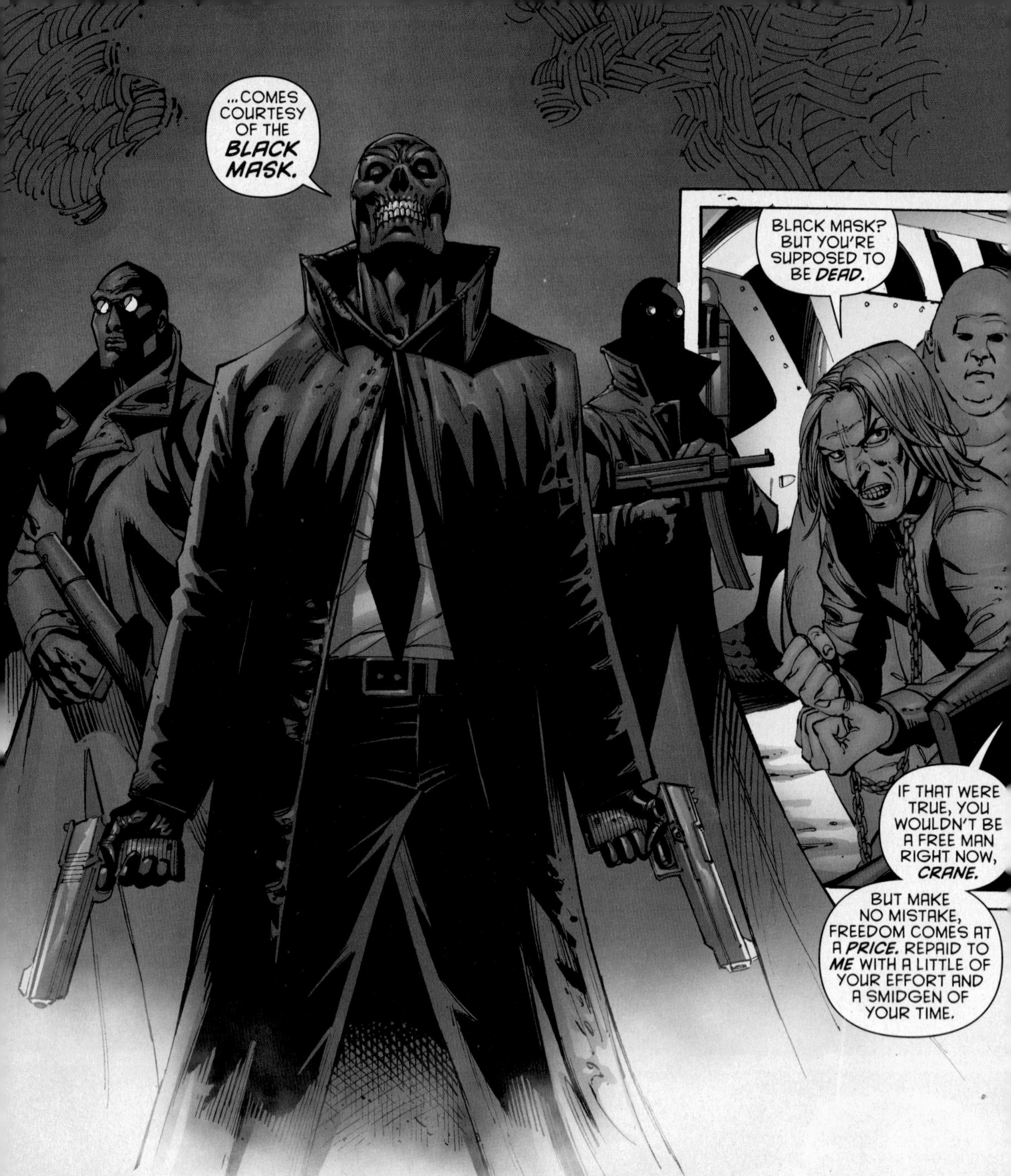
...COMES COURTESY OF THE BLACK MASK.
BLACK MASK? BUT YOU'RE SUPPOSED TO BE DEAD.
IF THAT WERE TRUE, YOU WOULDN'T BE A FREE MAN RIGHT NOW, CRANE.
BUT MAKE NO MISTAKE, FREEDOM COMES AT A PRICE. REPAID TO ME WITH A LITTLE OF YOUR EFFORT AND A SMIDGEN OF YOUR TIME.

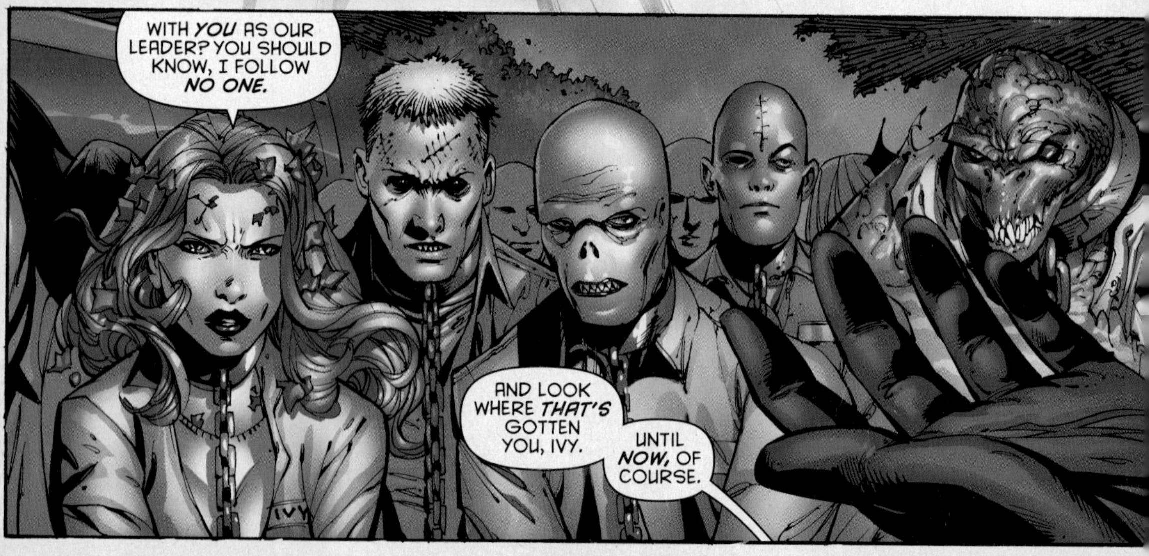
WITH YOU AS OUR LEADER? YOU SHOULD KNOW, I FOLLOW NO ONE.
AND LOOK WHERE THAT'S GOTTEN YOU, IVY.
UNTIL NOW, OF COURSE.
IVY

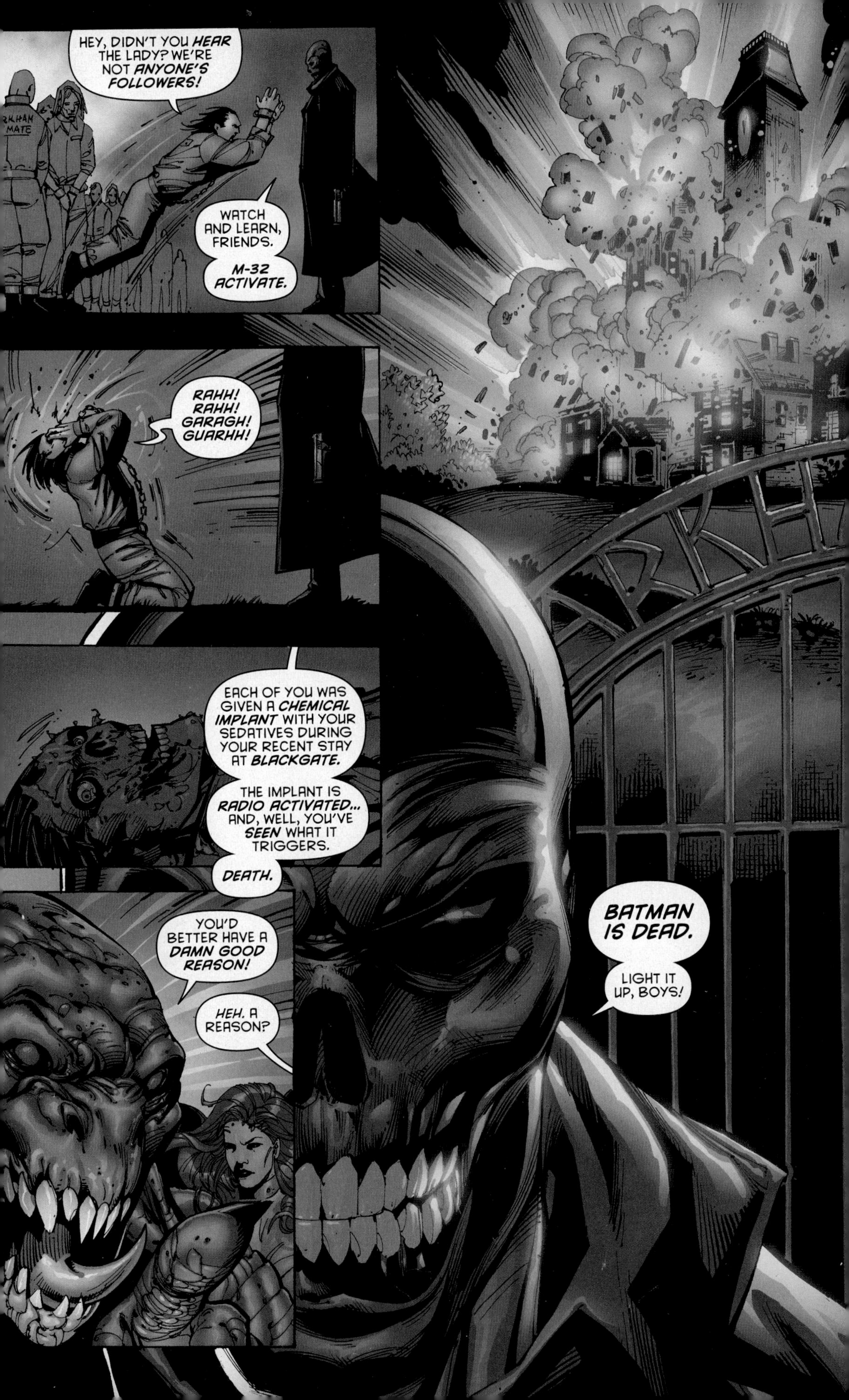
HEY, DIDN'T YOU HEAR THE LADY? WE'RE NOT ANYONE'S FOLLOWERS!
RKHAM MATE
WATCH AND LEARN, FRIENDS.
M-32 ACTIVATE.
RAHH! RAHH! GARAGH! GUARHH!
EACH OF YOU WAS GIVEN A CHEMICAL IMPLANT WITH YOUR SEDATIVES DURING YOUR RECENT STAY AT BLACKGATE.
THE IMPLANT IS RADIO ACTIVATED... AND, WELL, YOU'VE SEEN WHAT IT TRIGGERS.
DEATH.
YOU'D BETTER HAVE A DAMN GOOD REASON!
HEH. A REASON?
BATMAN IS DEAD.
LIGHT IT UP, BOYS!

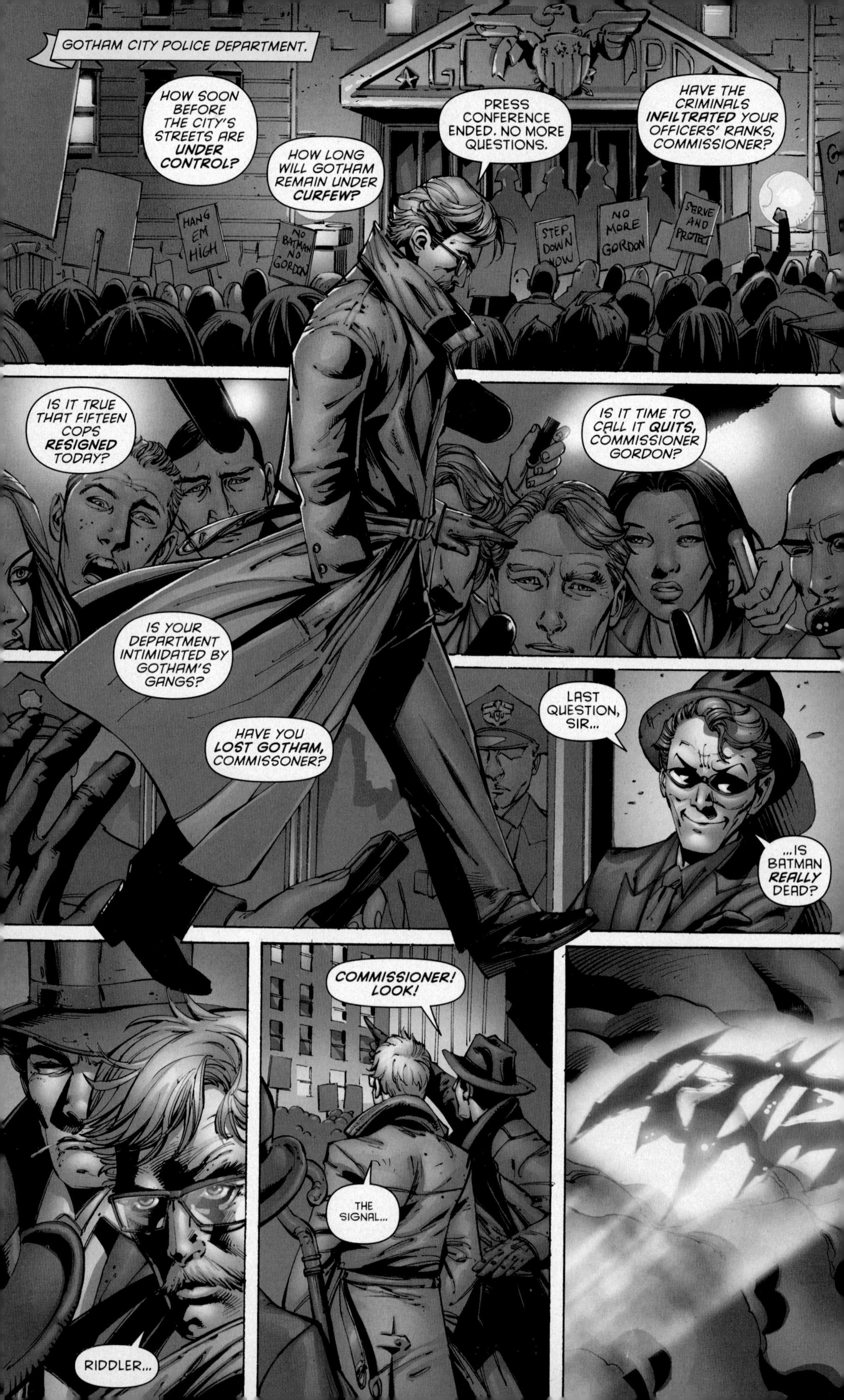
GOTHAM CITY POLICE DEPARTMENT.
HOW SOON BEFORE THE CITY'S STREETS ARE UNDER CONTROL?
HOW LONG WILL GOTHAM REMAIN UNDER CURFEW?
PRESS CONFERENCE ENDED. NO MORE QUESTIONS.
HAVE THE CRIMINALS INFILTRATED YOUR OFFICERS' RANKS, COMMISSIONER?
HANG EM HIGH
NO BATMAN NO GORDON
STEP DOWN NOW
NO MORE GORDON
SERVE AND PROTECT
IS IT TRUE THAT FIFTEEN COPS RESIGNED TODAY?
IS IT TIME TO CALL IT QUITS, COMMISSIONER GORDON?
IS YOUR DEPARTMENT INTIMIDATED BY GOTHAM'S GANGS?
HAVE YOU LOST GOTHAM, COMMISSONER?
LAST QUESTION, SIR...
...IS BATMAN REALLY DEAD?
RIDDLER...
COMMISSIONER! LOOK!
THE SIGNAL...

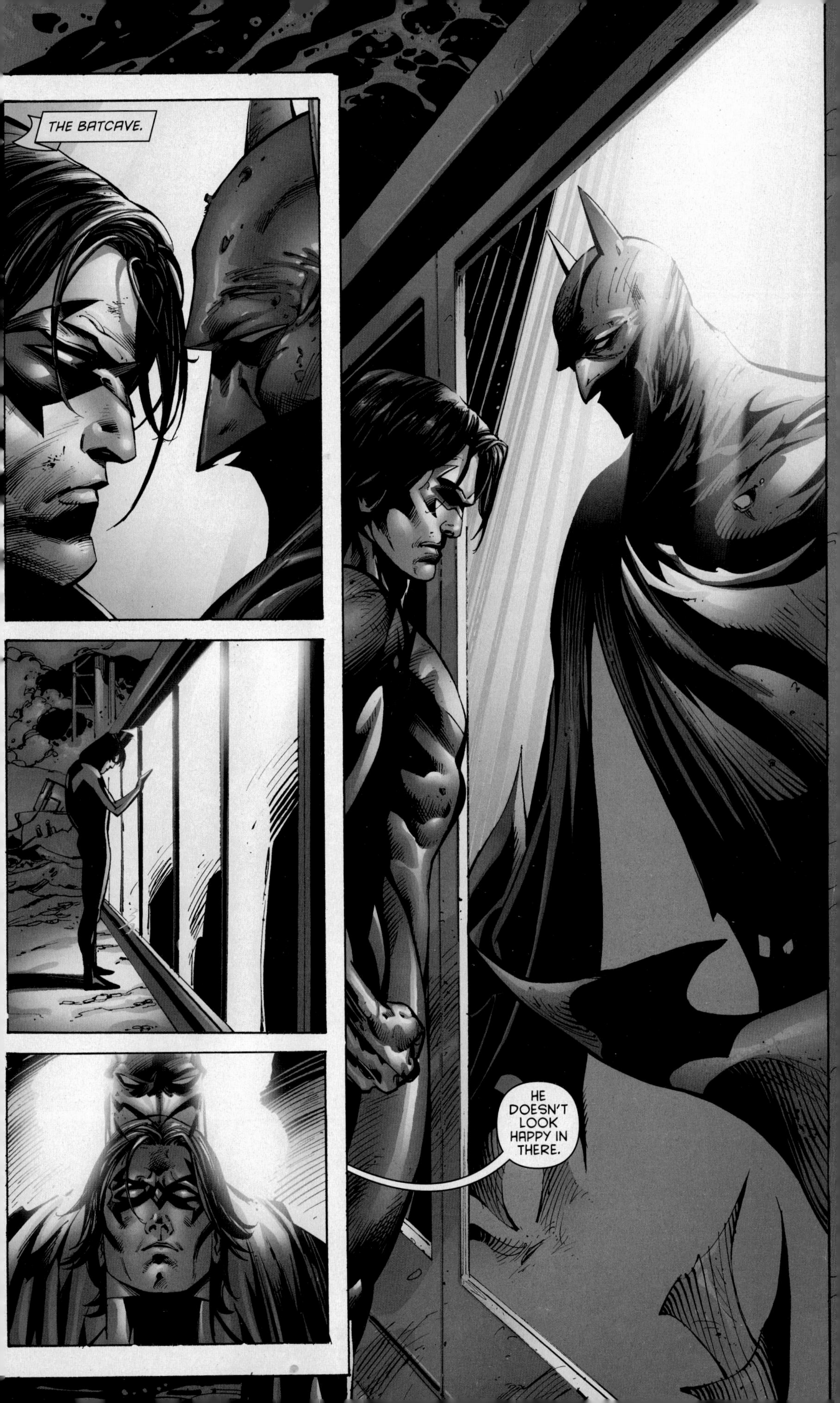
THE BATCAVE.
HE DOESN'T LOOK HAPPY IN THERE.

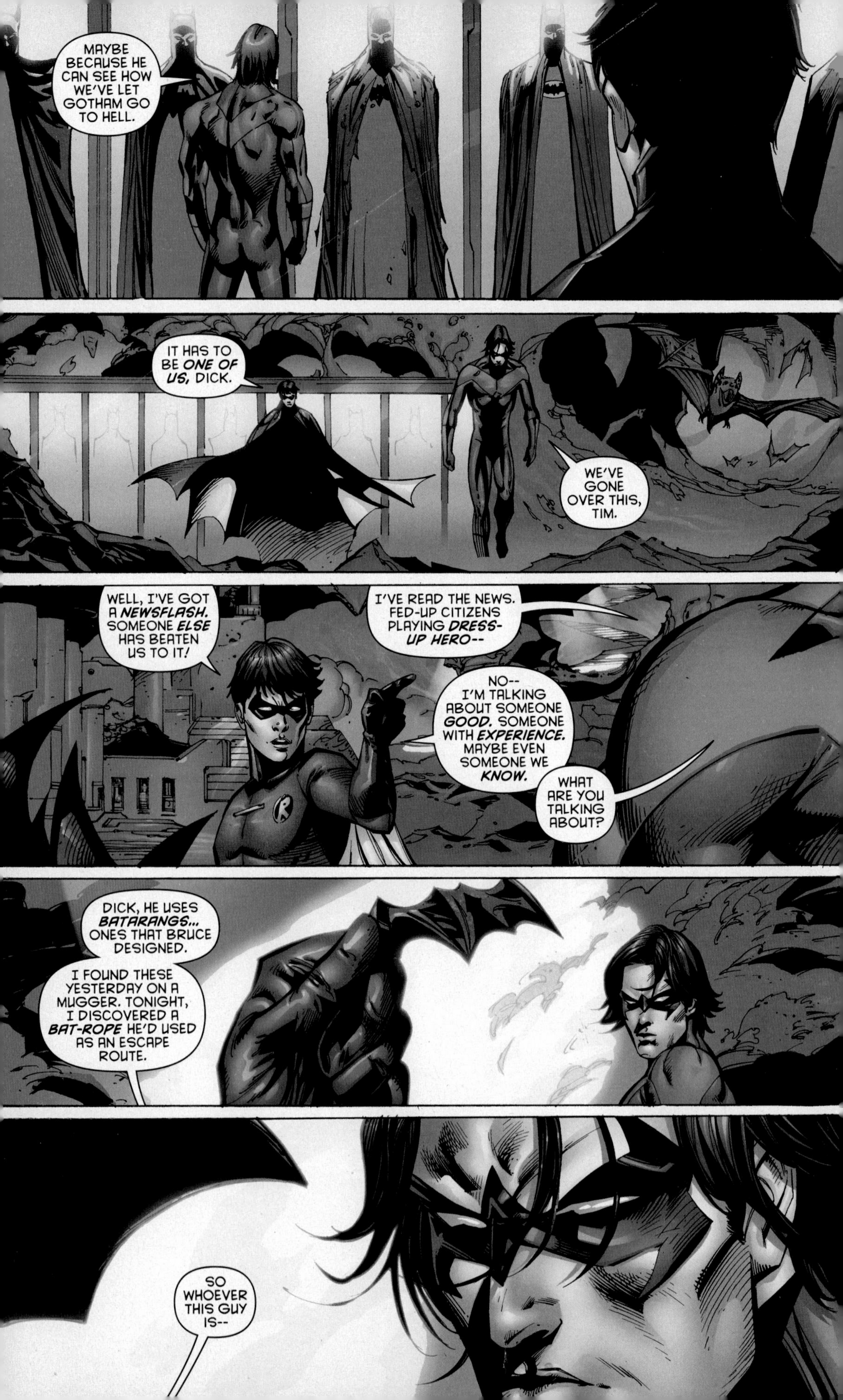
MAYBE BECAUSE HE CAN SEE HOW WE'VE LET GOTHAM GO TO HELL.
IT HAS TO BE ONE OF US, DICK.
WE'VE GONE OVER THIS, TIM.
WELL, I'VE GOT A NEWSFLASH. SOMEONE ELSE HAS BEATEN US TO IT!
I'VE READ THE NEWS. FED-UP CITIZENS PLAYING DRESS-UP HERO--
NO-- I'M TALKING ABOUT SOMEONE GOOD. SOMEONE WITH EXPERIENCE. MAYBE EVEN SOMEONE WE KNOW.
WHAT ARE YOU TALKING ABOUT?
DICK, HE USES BATARANGS... ONES THAT BRUCE DESIGNED.
I FOUND THESE YESTERDAY ON A MUGGER. TONIGHT, I DISCOVERED A BAT-ROPE HE'D USED AS AN ESCAPE ROUTE.
SO WHOEVER THIS GUY IS--

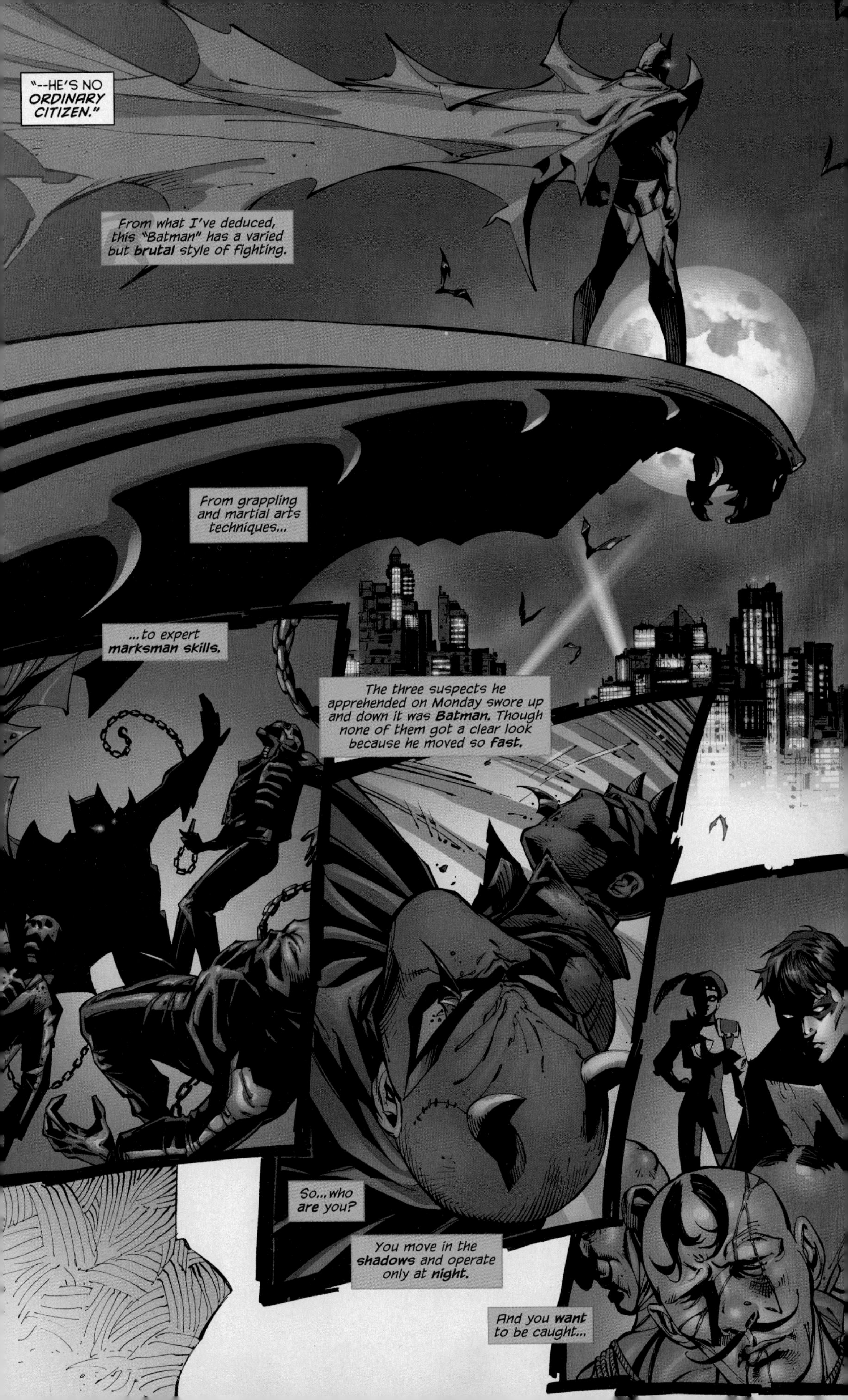
"--HE'S NO ORDINARY CITIZEN."
From what I've deduced, this "Batman" has a varied but brutal style of fighting.
From grappling and martial arts techniques...
...to expert marksman skills.
The three suspects he apprehended on Monday swore up and down it was Batman. Though none of them got a clear look because he moved so fast.
So...who are you?
You move in the shadows and operate only at night.
And you want to be caught...

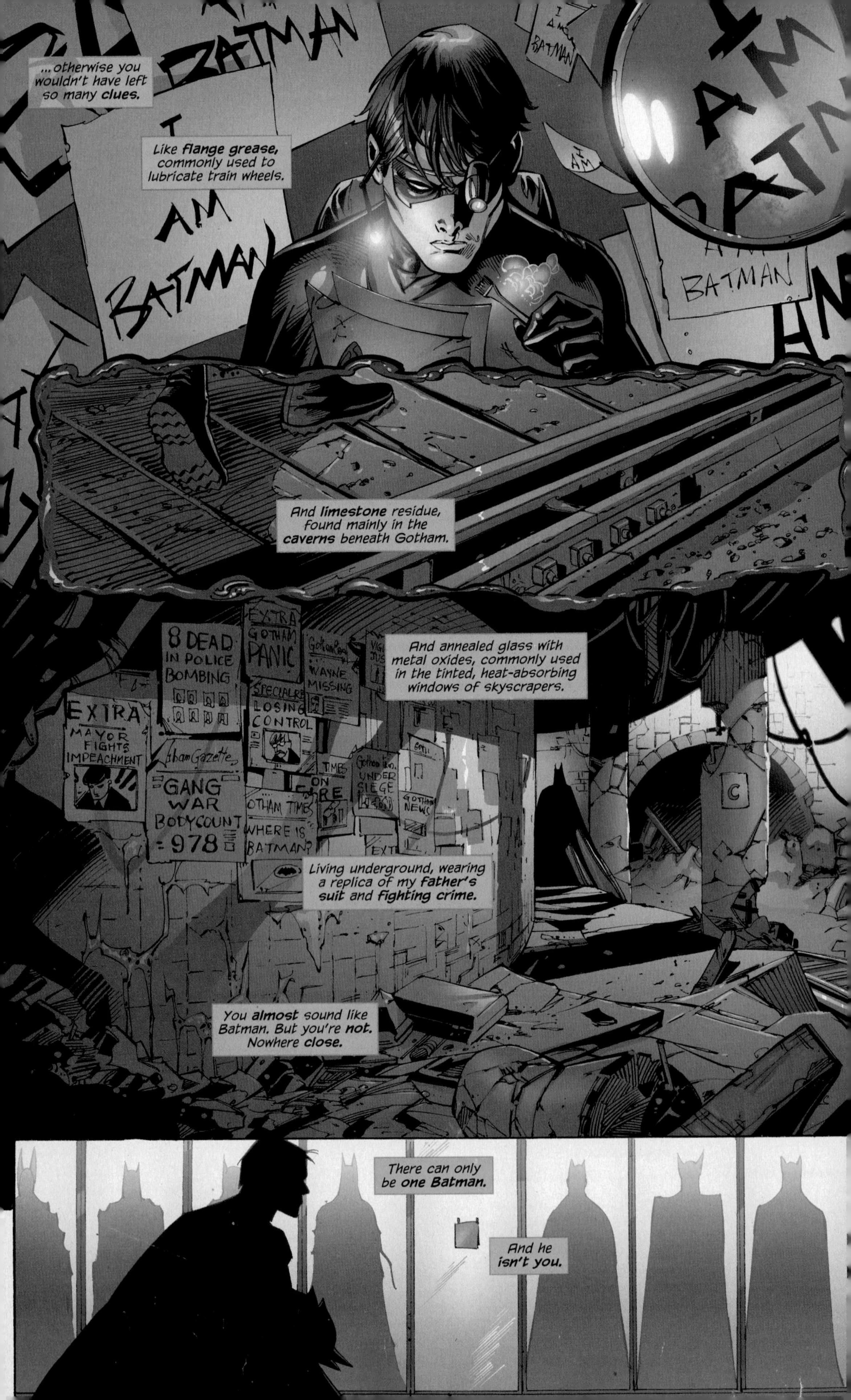

...otherwise you wouldn't have left so many clues.
Like flange grease, commonly used to lubricate train wheels.
I AM BATMAN
And limestone residue, found mainly in the caverns beneath Gotham.
8 DEAD IN POLICE BOMBING
EXTRA GOTHAM PANIC
WAYNE MISSING
LOSING CONTROL
EXTRA MAYOR FIGHTS IMPEACHMENT
GANG WAR BODYCOUNT = 978
WHERE IS BATMAN?
UNDER SIEGE
And annealed glass with metal oxides, commonly used in the tinted, heat-absorbing windows of skyscrapers.
Living underground, wearing a replica of my father's suit and fighting crime.
You almost sound like Batman. But you're not. Nowhere close.
There can only be one Batman.
And he isn't you.

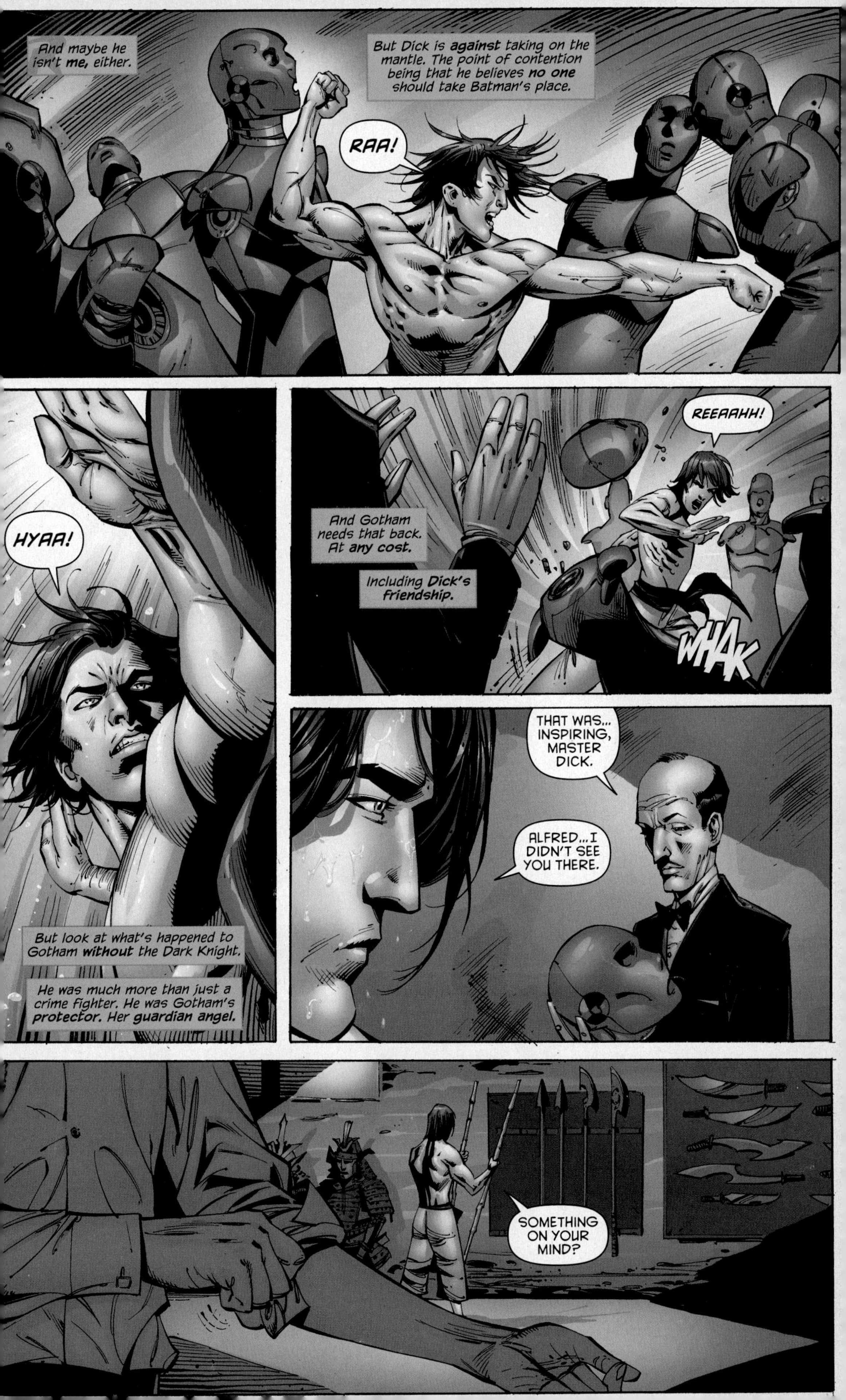
And maybe he isn't **me,** either.
But Dick is **against** taking on the mantle. The point of contention being that he believes **no one** should take Batman's place.
RAA!
HYAA!
And Gotham needs that back. At **any cost.**
Including **Dick's friendship.**
REEAAHH!
WHAK
But look at what's happened to Gotham **without** the Dark Knight.
He was much more than just a crime fighter. He was Gotham's **protector.** Her **guardian angel.**
THAT WAS... INSPIRING, MASTER DICK.
ALFRED...I DIDN'T SEE YOU THERE.
SOMETHING ON YOUR MIND?

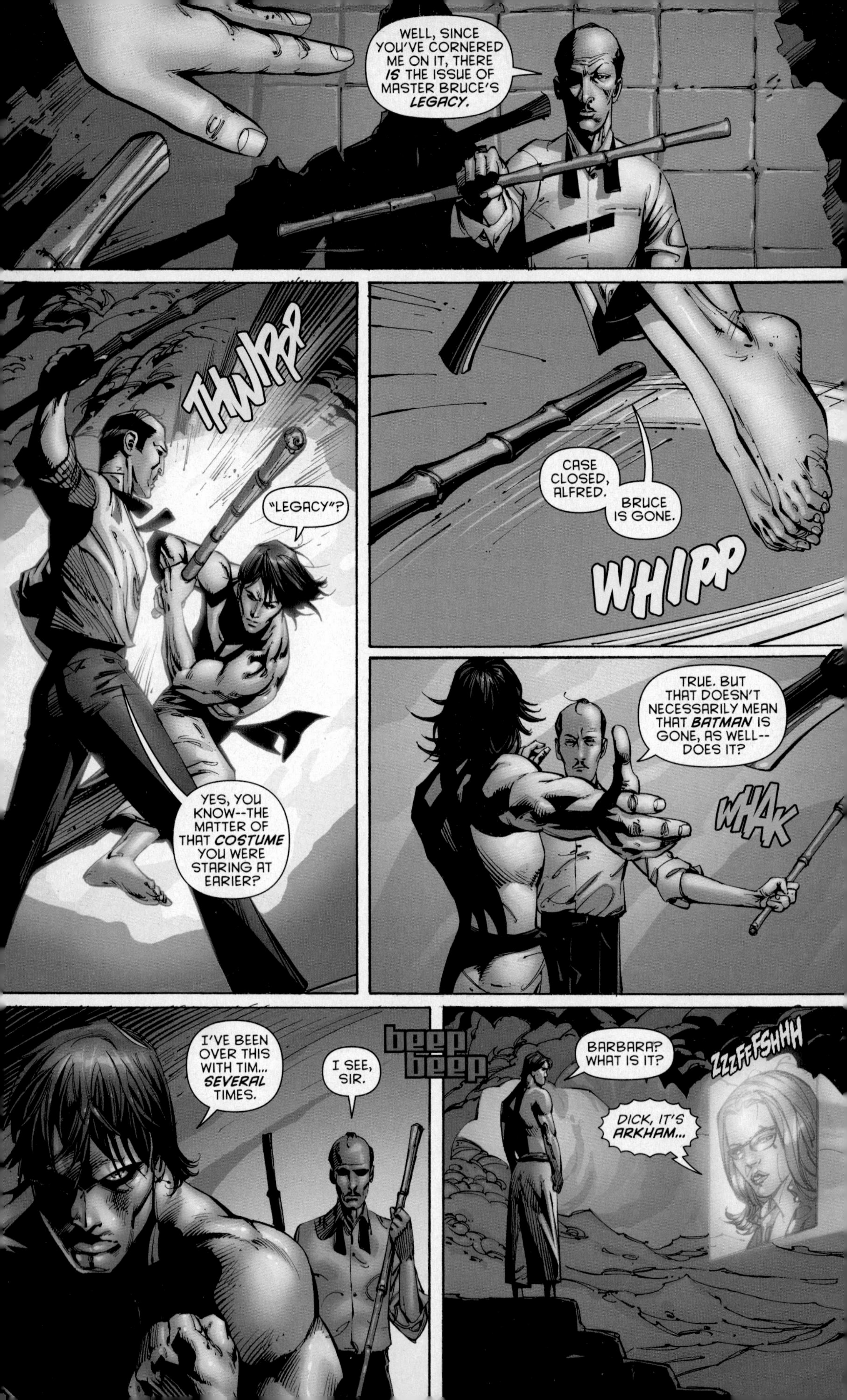

WELL, SINCE YOU'VE CORNERED ME ON IT, THERE *IS* THE ISSUE OF MASTER BRUCE'S *LEGACY.*
THWIPP
"LEGACY"?
YES, YOU KNOW--THE MATTER OF THAT *COSTUME* YOU WERE STARING AT EARIER?
CASE CLOSED, ALFRED.
BRUCE IS GONE.
WHIPP
TRUE. BUT THAT DOESN'T NECESSARILY MEAN THAT *BATMAN* IS GONE, AS WELL--DOES IT?
WHAK
I'VE BEEN OVER THIS WITH TIM... *SEVERAL* TIMES.
I SEE, SIR.
beep beep
BARBARA? WHAT IS IT?
ZZZFFFSHHH
DICK, IT'S *ARKHAM...*

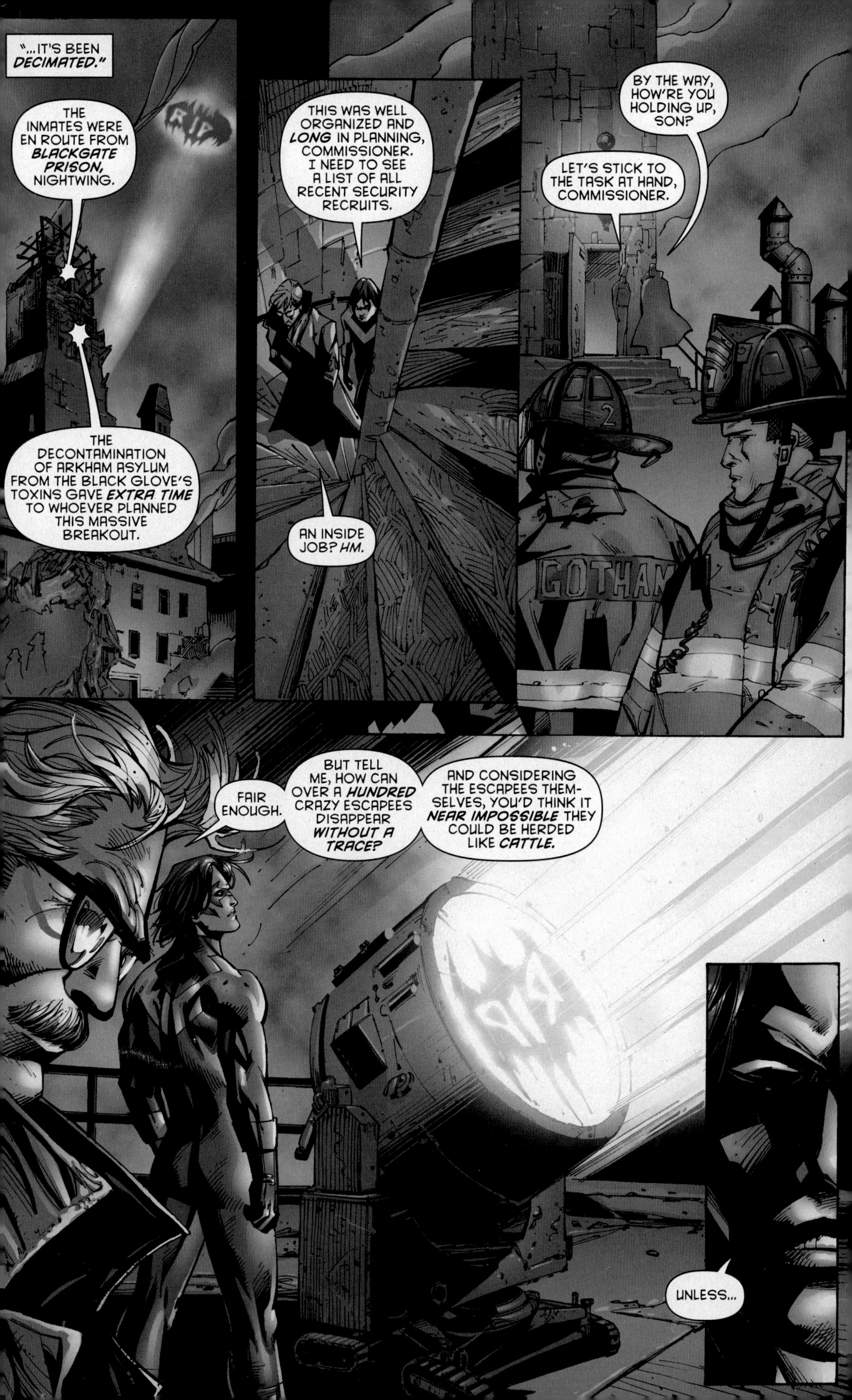
"...IT'S BEEN DECIMATED."
THE INMATES WERE EN ROUTE FROM BLACKGATE PRISON, NIGHTWING.
THE DECONTAMINATION OF ARKHAM ASYLUM FROM THE BLACK GLOVE'S TOXINS GAVE EXTRA TIME TO WHOEVER PLANNED THIS MASSIVE BREAKOUT.
R.I.P.
THIS WAS WELL ORGANIZED AND LONG IN PLANNING, COMMISSIONER. I NEED TO SEE A LIST OF ALL RECENT SECURITY RECRUITS.
AN INSIDE JOB? HM.
BY THE WAY, HOW'RE YOU HOLDING UP, SON?
LET'S STICK TO THE TASK AT HAND, COMMISSIONER.
GOTHAM
FAIR ENOUGH.
BUT TELL ME, HOW CAN OVER A HUNDRED CRAZY ESCAPEES DISAPPEAR WITHOUT A TRACE?
AND CONSIDERING THE ESCAPEES THEMSELVES, YOU'D THINK IT NEAR IMPOSSIBLE THEY COULD BE HERDED LIKE CATTLE.
UNLESS...

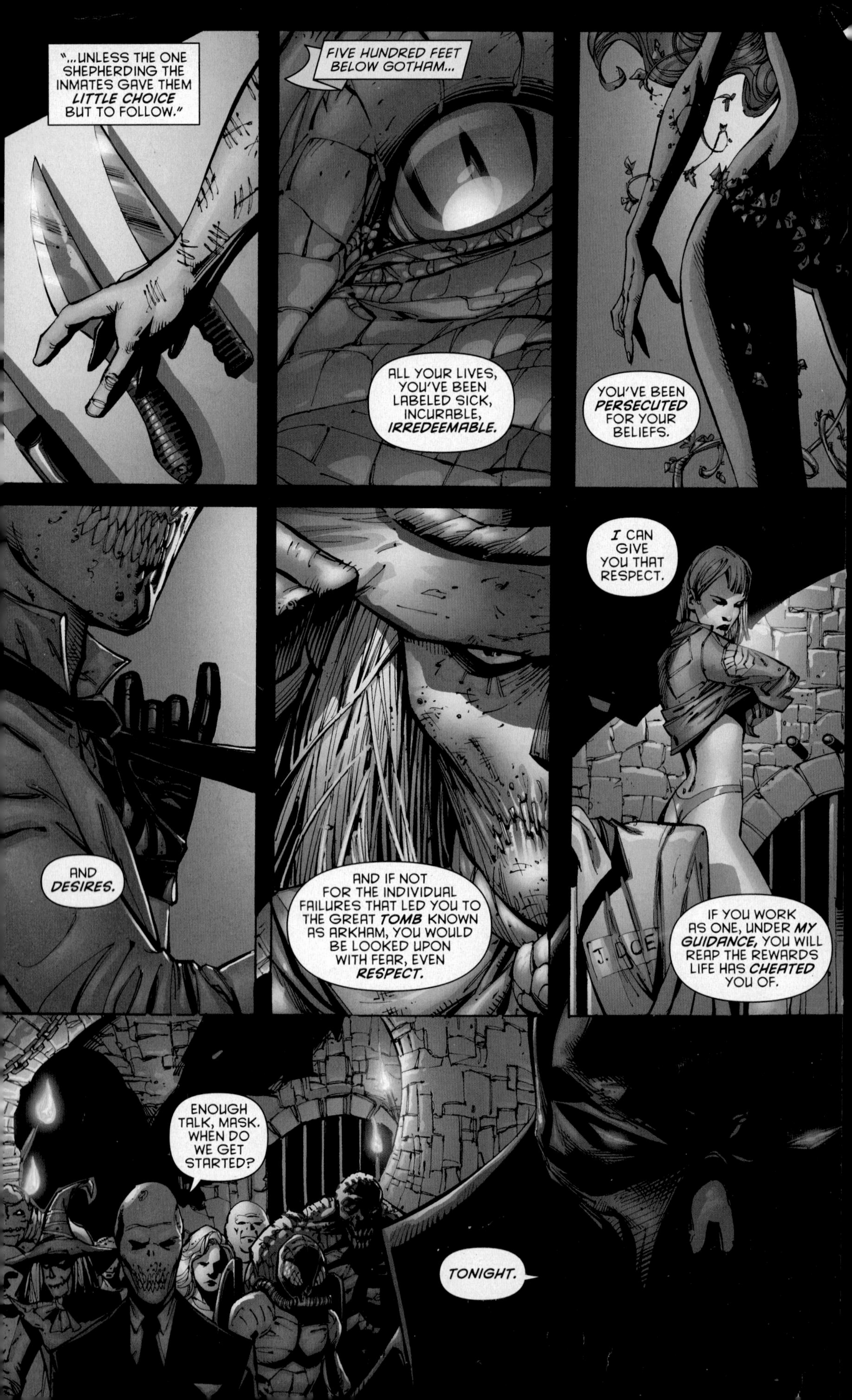

"...UNLESS THE ONE SHEPHERDING THE INMATES GAVE THEM *LITTLE CHOICE* BUT TO FOLLOW."
FIVE HUNDRED FEET BELOW GOTHAM...
ALL YOUR LIVES, YOU'VE BEEN LABELED SICK, INCURABLE, ***IRREDEEMABLE.***
YOU'VE BEEN ***PERSECUTED*** FOR YOUR BELIEFS.
AND ***DESIRES.***
AND IF NOT FOR THE INDIVIDUAL FAILURES THAT LED YOU TO THE GREAT ***TOMB*** KNOWN AS ARKHAM, YOU WOULD BE LOOKED UPON WITH FEAR, EVEN ***RESPECT.***
I CAN GIVE YOU THAT RESPECT.
J. DOE
IF YOU WORK AS ONE, UNDER ***MY GUIDANCE,*** YOU WILL REAP THE REWARDS LIFE HAS ***CHEATED*** YOU OF.
ENOUGH TALK, MASK. WHEN DO WE GET STARTED?
TONIGHT.

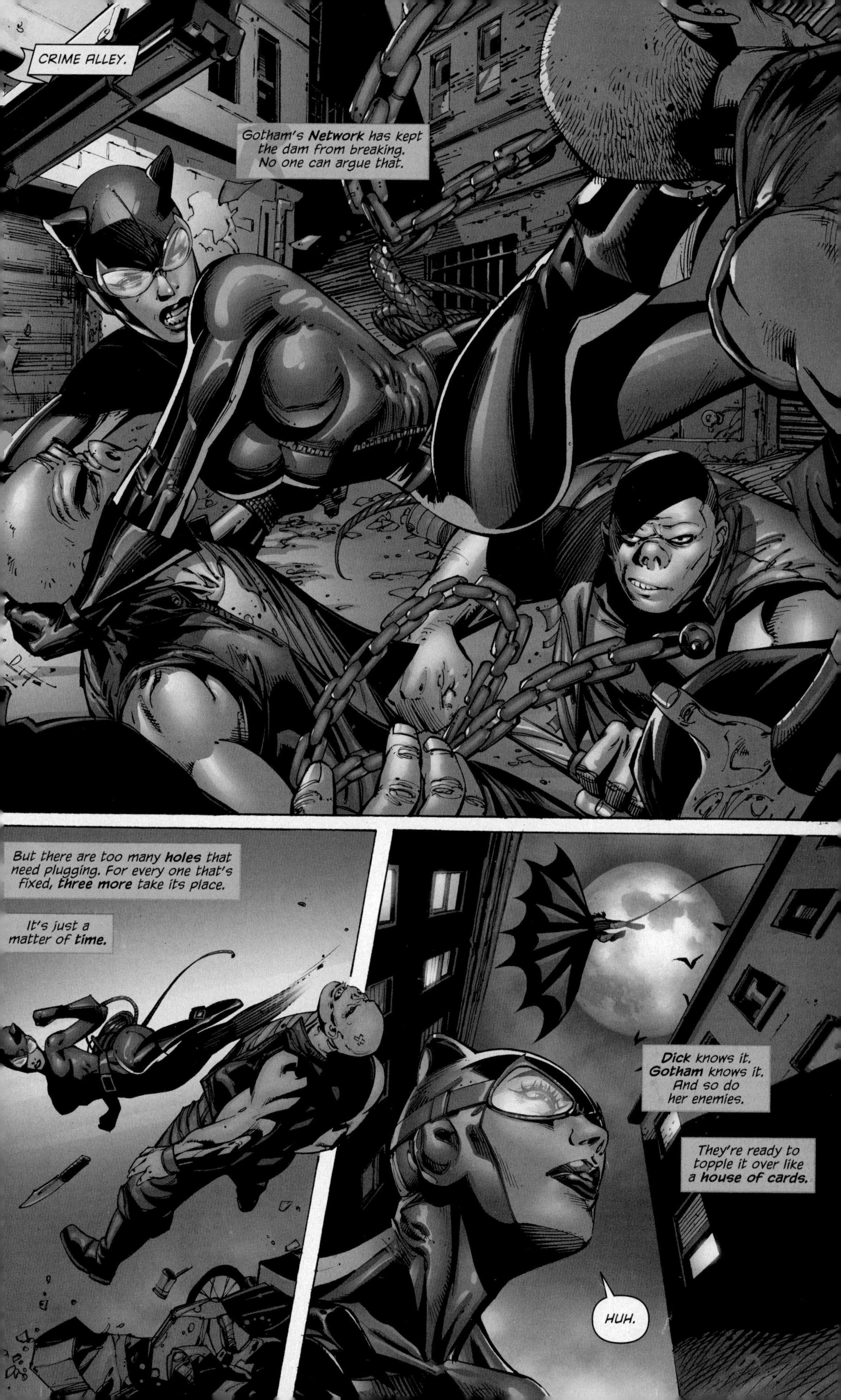
CRIME ALLEY.
Gotham's **Network** has kept the dam from breaking. No one can argue that.
But there are too many **holes** that need plugging. For every one that's fixed, **three more** take its place.
It's just a matter of **time.**
Dick knows it. **Gotham** knows it. And so do her enemies.
They're ready to topple it over like a **house of cards.**
HUH.

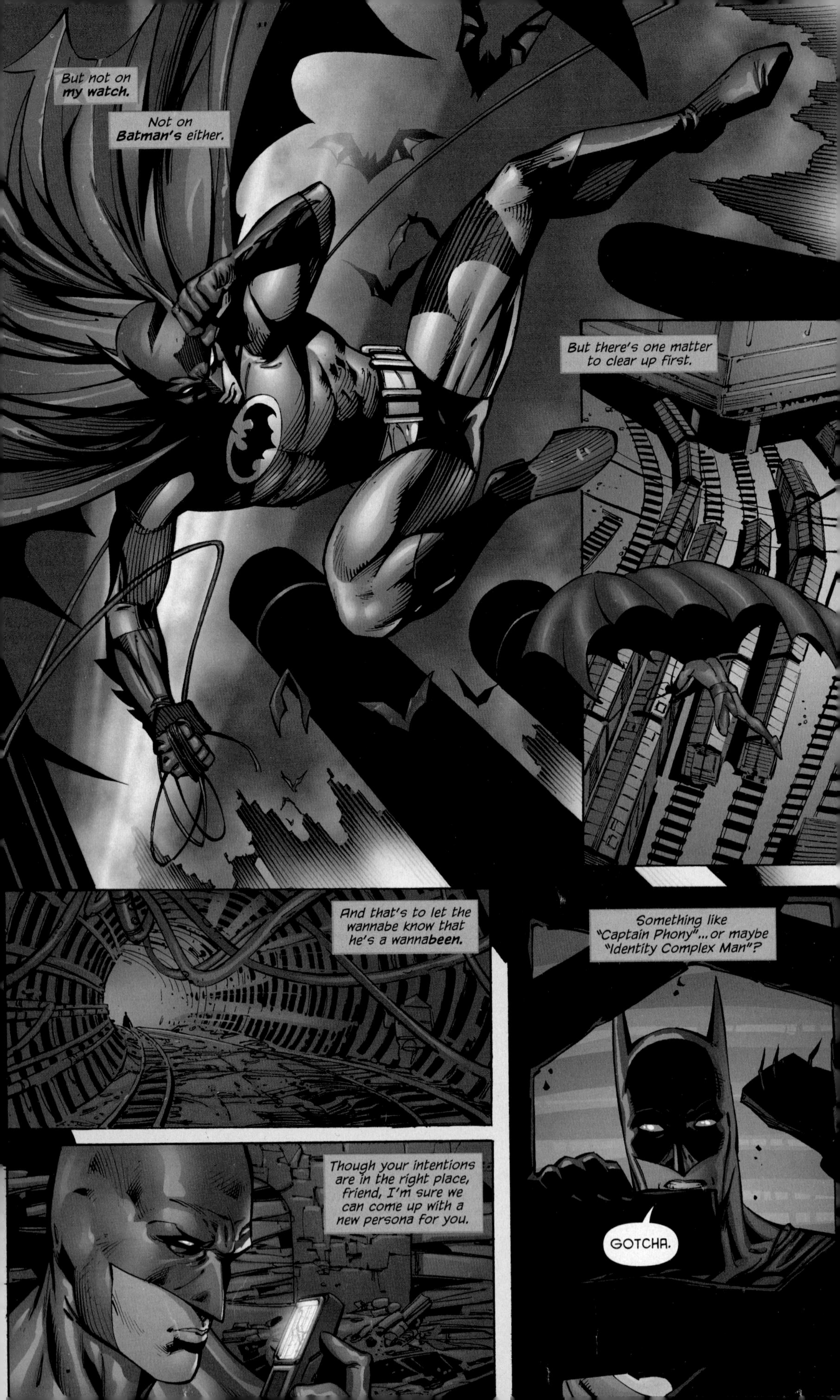
But not on my watch.
Not on Batman's either.
But there's one matter to clear up first.
And that's to let the wannabe know that he's a wannabeen.
Though your intentions are in the right place, friend, I'm sure we can come up with a new persona for you.
Something like "Captain Phony"...or maybe "Identity Complex Man"?
GOTCHA.

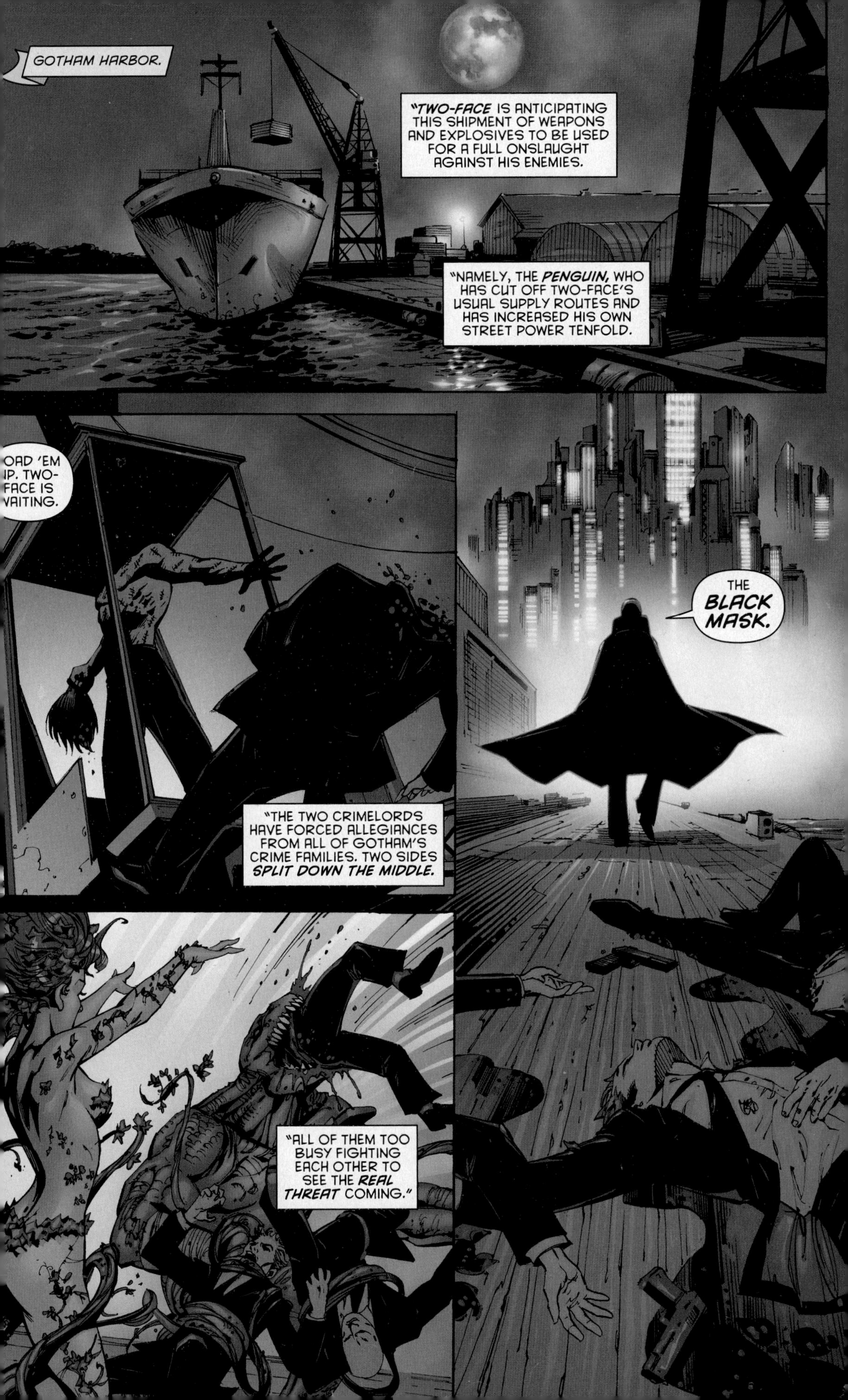
GOTHAM HARBOR.
"TWO-FACE IS ANTICIPATING THIS SHIPMENT OF WEAPONS AND EXPLOSIVES TO BE USED FOR A FULL ONSLAUGHT AGAINST HIS ENEMIES.
"NAMELY, THE PENGUIN, WHO HAS CUT OFF TWO-FACE'S USUAL SUPPLY ROUTES AND HAS INCREASED HIS OWN STREET POWER TENFOLD.
OAD 'EM IP. TWO-FACE IS VAITING.
"THE TWO CRIMELORDS HAVE FORCED ALLEGIANCES FROM ALL OF GOTHAM'S CRIME FAMILIES. TWO SIDES SPLIT DOWN THE MIDDLE.
THE BLACK MASK.
"ALL OF THEM TOO BUSY FIGHTING EACH OTHER TO SEE THE REAL THREAT COMING."

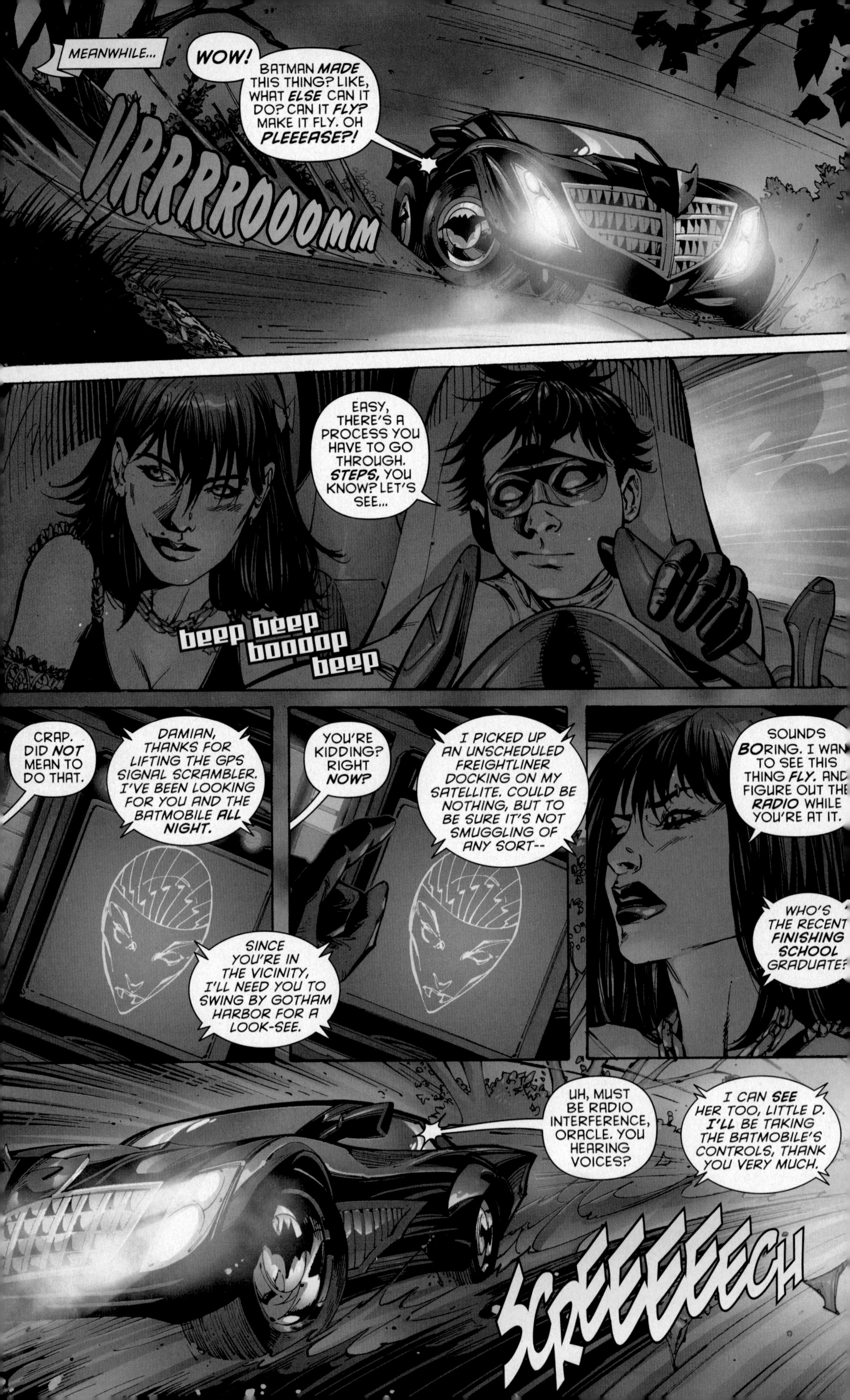
MEANWHILE...
VRRRROOOOMM
WOW! BATMAN MADE THIS THING? LIKE, WHAT ELSE CAN IT DO? CAN IT FLY? MAKE IT FLY. OH PLEEEASE?!
EASY, THERE'S A PROCESS YOU HAVE TO GO THROUGH. STEPS, YOU KNOW? LET'S SEE...
beep beep booooop beep
CRAP. DID NOT MEAN TO DO THAT.
DAMIAN, THANKS FOR LIFTING THE GPS SIGNAL SCRAMBLER. I'VE BEEN LOOKING FOR YOU AND THE BATMOBILE ALL NIGHT.
SINCE YOU'RE IN THE VICINITY, I'LL NEED YOU TO SWING BY GOTHAM HARBOR FOR A LOOK-SEE.
YOU'RE KIDDING? RIGHT NOW?
I PICKED UP AN UNSCHEDULED FREIGHTLINER DOCKING ON MY SATELLITE. COULD BE NOTHING, BUT TO BE SURE IT'S NOT SMUGGLING OF ANY SORT--
SOUNDS BORING. I WAN TO SEE THIS THING FLY. AND FIGURE OUT THE RADIO WHILE YOU'RE AT IT.
WHO'S THE RECENT FINISHING SCHOOL GRADUATE?
UH, MUST BE RADIO INTERFERENCE, ORACLE. YOU HEARING VOICES?
I CAN SEE HER TOO, LITTLE D. I'LL BE TAKING THE BATMOBILE'S CONTROLS, THANK YOU VERY MUCH.
SCREEEEECH

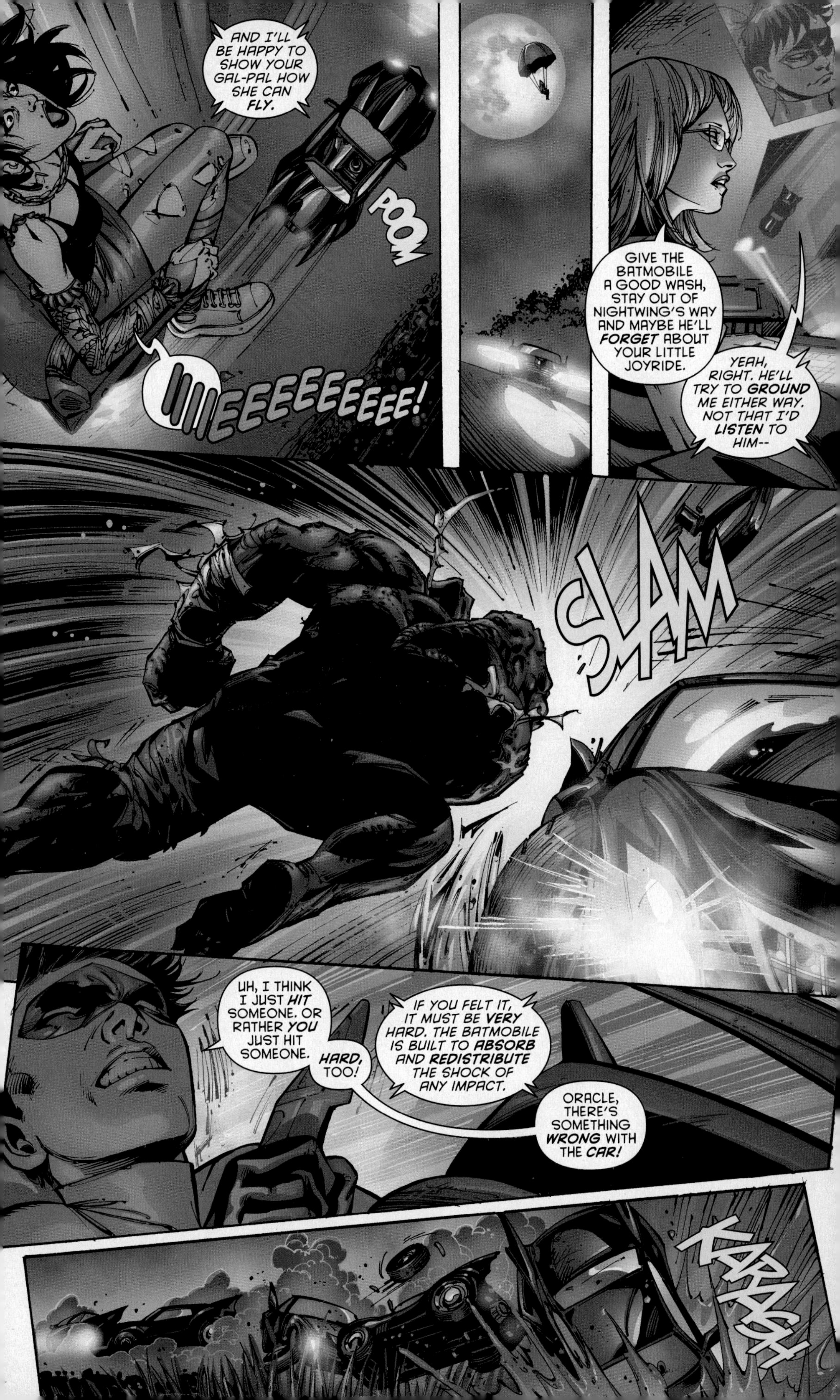

AND I'LL BE HAPPY TO SHOW YOUR GAL-PAL HOW SHE CAN FLY.
POOM
WEEEEEEEEEEE!
GIVE THE BATMOBILE A GOOD WASH, STAY OUT OF NIGHTWING'S WAY AND MAYBE HE'LL FORGET ABOUT YOUR LITTLE JOYRIDE.
YEAH, RIGHT. HE'LL TRY TO GROUND ME EITHER WAY. NOT THAT I'D LISTEN TO HIM--
SLAM
UH, I THINK I JUST HIT SOMEONE. OR RATHER YOU JUST HIT SOMEONE.
HARD, TOO!
IF YOU FELT IT, IT MUST BE VERY HARD. THE BATMOBILE IS BUILT TO ABSORB AND REDISTRIBUTE THE SHOCK OF ANY IMPACT.
ORACLE, THERE'S SOMETHING WRONG WITH THE CAR!
KARASH

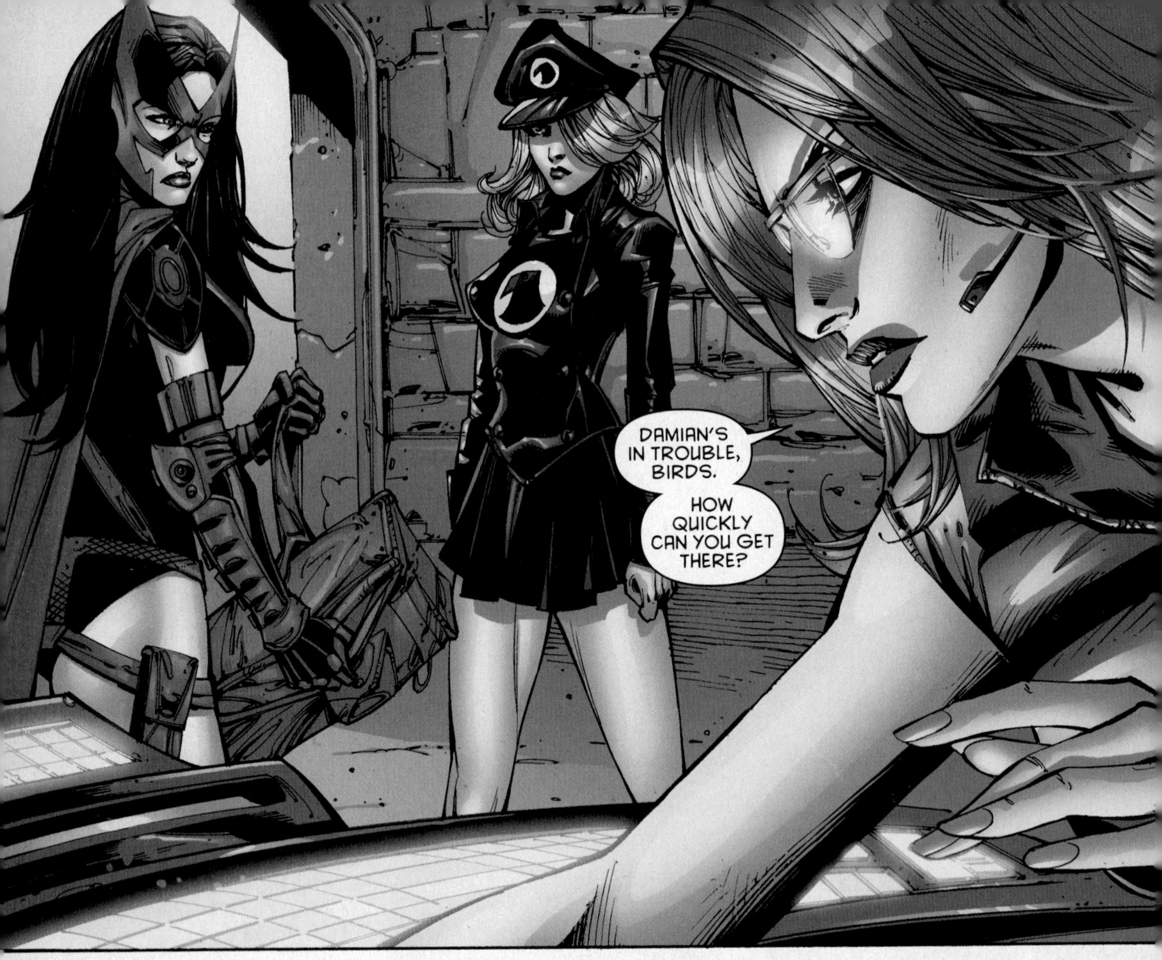
DAMIAN'S IN TROUBLE, BIRDS.
HOW QUICKLY CAN YOU GET THERE?

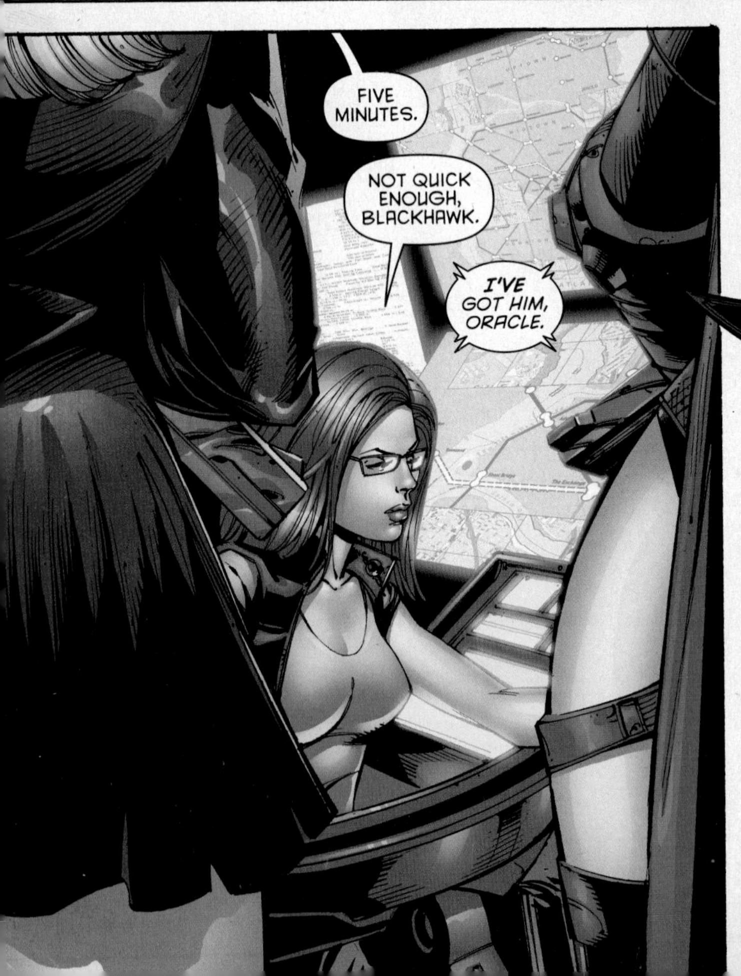
FIVE MINUTES.
NOT QUICK ENOUGH, BLACKHAWK.
I'VE GOT HIM, ORACLE.

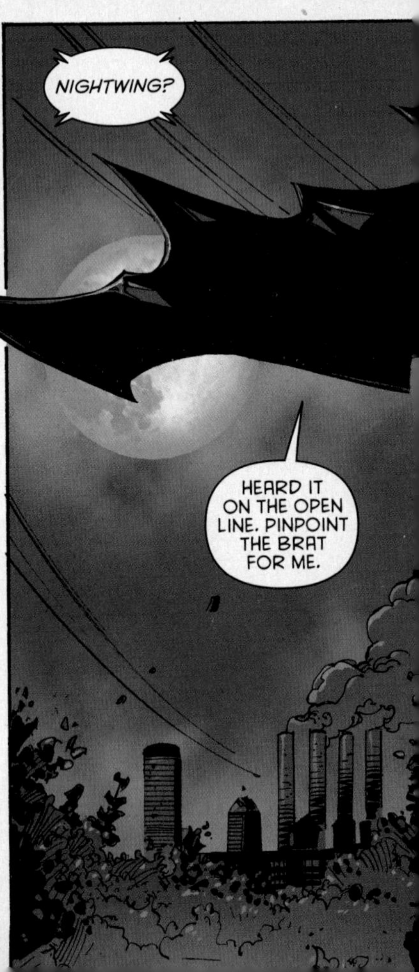
NIGHTWING?
HEARD IT ON THE OPEN LINE. PINPOINT THE BRAT FOR ME.

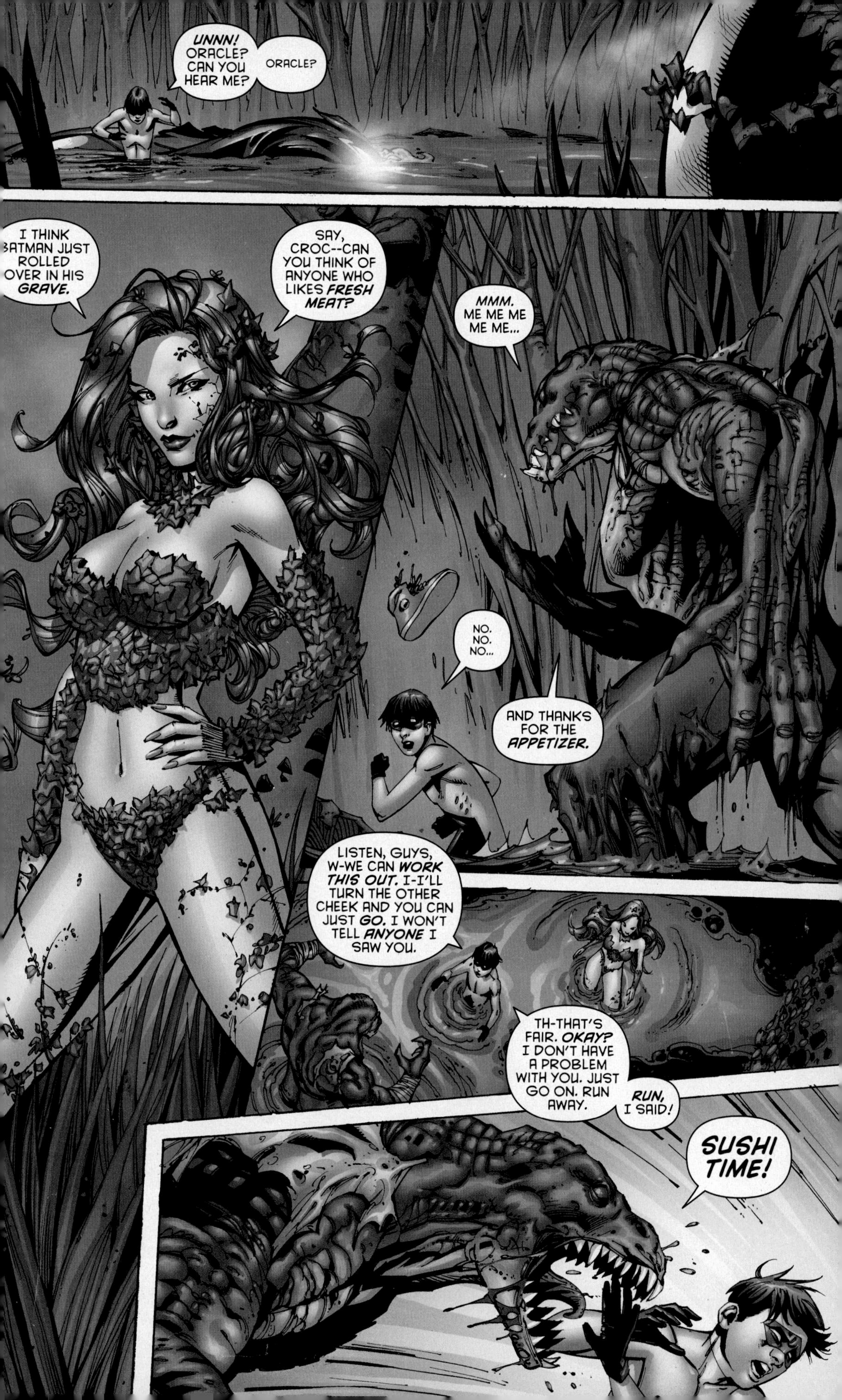
UNNN! ORACLE? CAN YOU HEAR ME?
ORACLE?
I THINK BATMAN JUST ROLLED OVER IN HIS GRAVE.
SAY, CROC--CAN YOU THINK OF ANYONE WHO LIKES FRESH MEAT?
MMM. ME ME ME ME ME...
NO. NO. NO...
AND THANKS FOR THE APPETIZER.
LISTEN, GUYS, W-WE CAN WORK THIS OUT. I-I'LL TURN THE OTHER CHEEK AND YOU CAN JUST GO. I WON'T TELL ANYONE I SAW YOU.
TH-THAT'S FAIR. OKAY? I DON'T HAVE A PROBLEM WITH YOU. JUST GO ON. RUN AWAY.
RUN, I SAID!
SUSHI TIME!

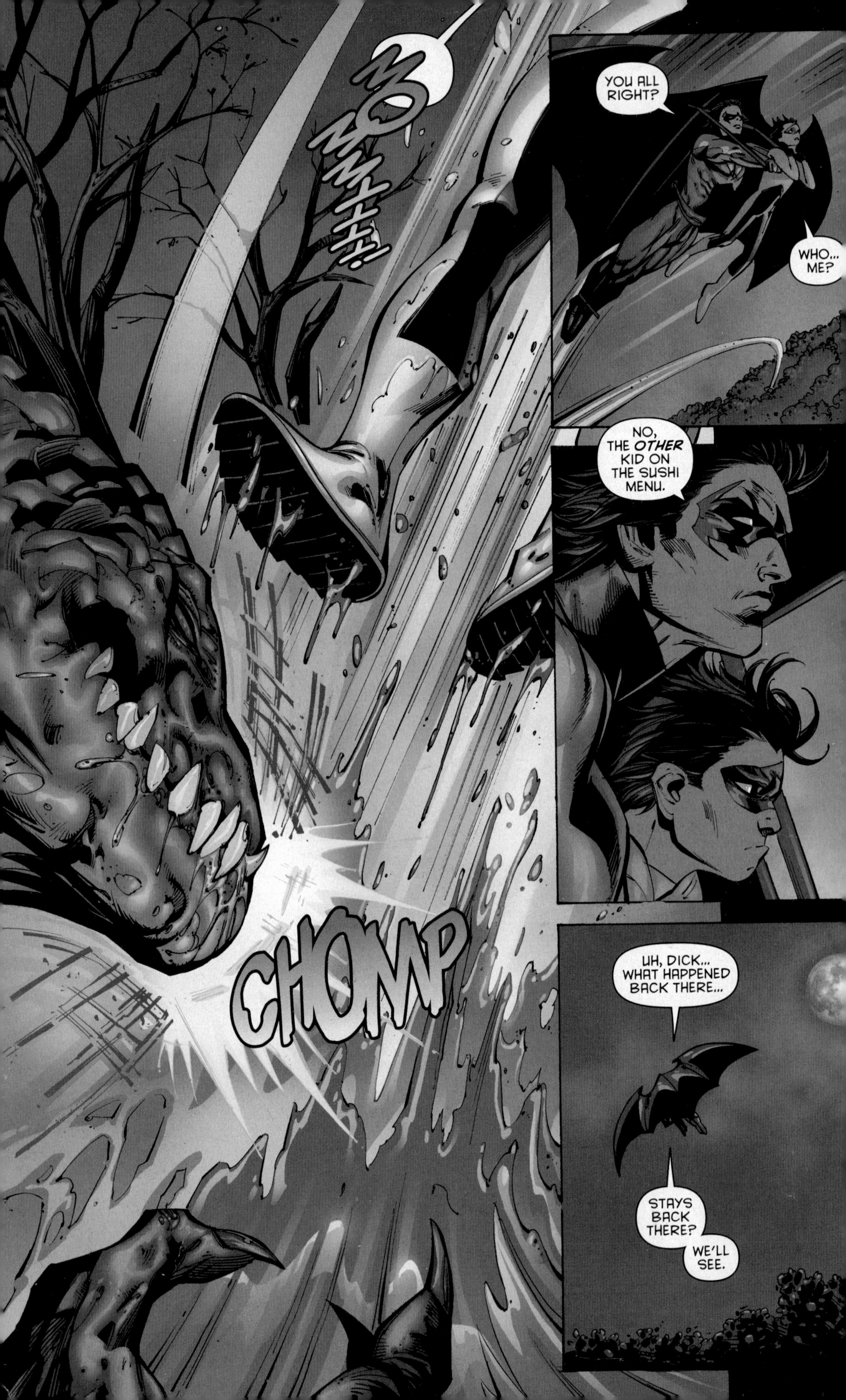
MOMMYYY!!
YOU ALL RIGHT?
WHO... ME?
NO, THE OTHER KID ON THE SUSHI MENU.
CHOMP
UH, DICK... WHAT HAPPENED BACK THERE...
STAYS BACK THERE?
WE'LL SEE.

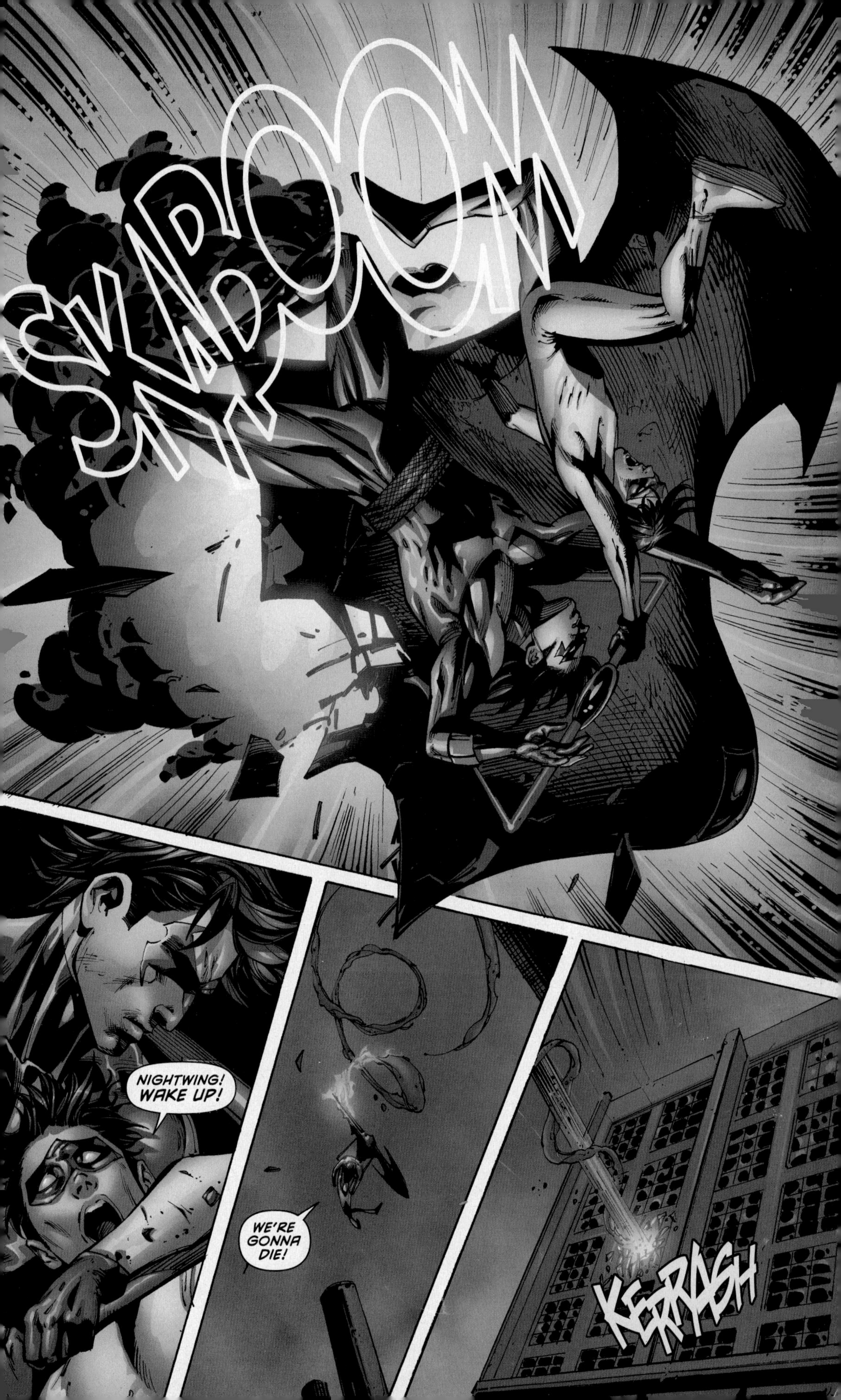
SKADOOM
NIGHTWING! WAKE UP!
WE'RE GONNA DIE!
KERRASH

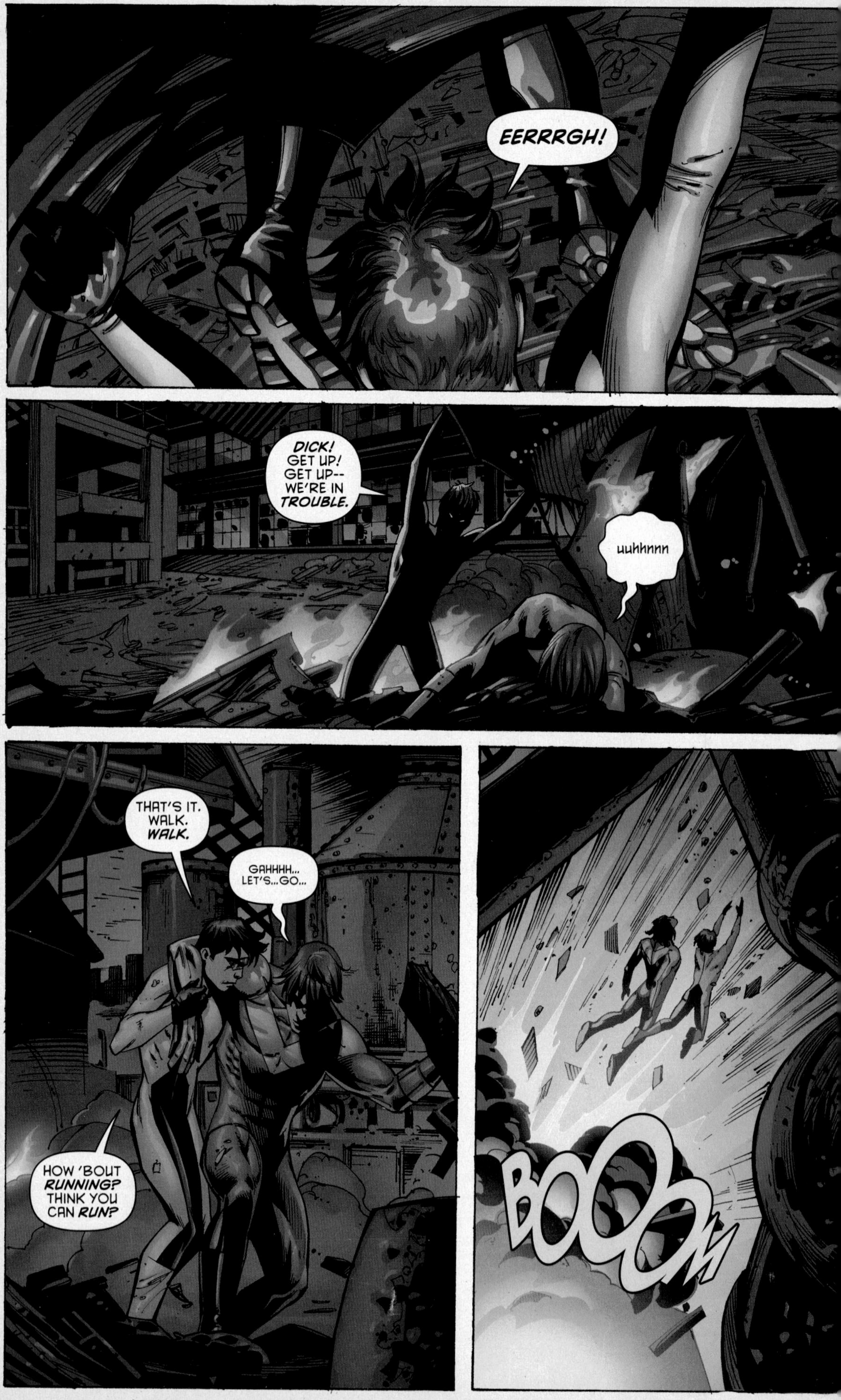
EERRRGH!
DICK! GET UP! GET UP-- WE'RE IN TROUBLE.
uuhhnnn
THAT'S IT. WALK. WALK.
GAHHHH... LET'S...GO...
HOW 'BOUT RUNNING? THINK YOU CAN RUN?
BOOOM

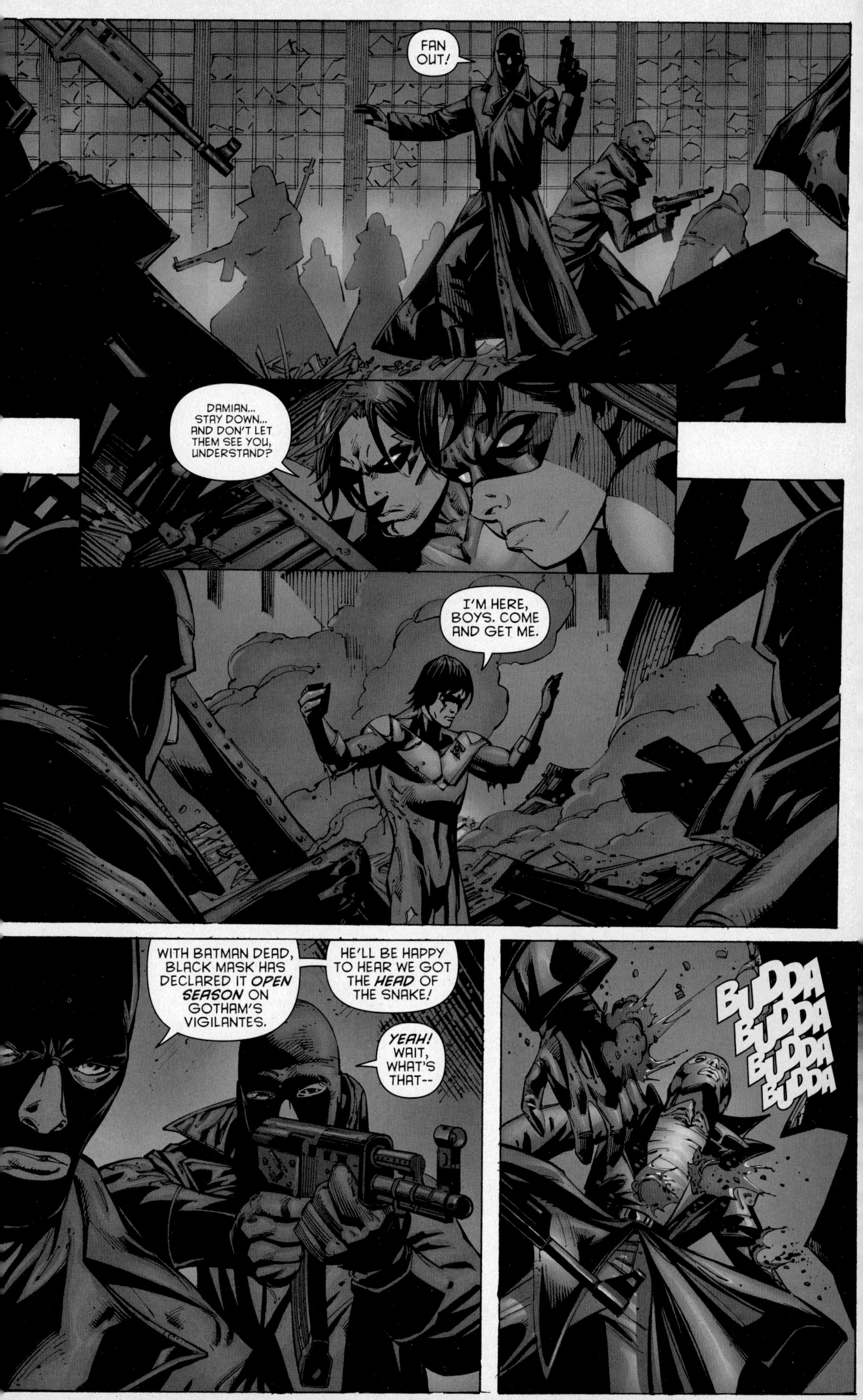
FAN OUT!
DAMIAN... STAY DOWN... AND DON'T LET THEM SEE YOU, UNDERSTAND?
I'M HERE, BOYS. COME AND GET ME.
WITH BATMAN DEAD, BLACK MASK HAS DECLARED IT *OPEN SEASON* ON GOTHAM'S VIGILANTES.
HE'LL BE HAPPY TO HEAR WE GOT THE *HEAD* OF THE SNAKE!
YEAH! WAIT, WHAT'S THAT--
BUDDA BUDDA BUDDA BUDDA

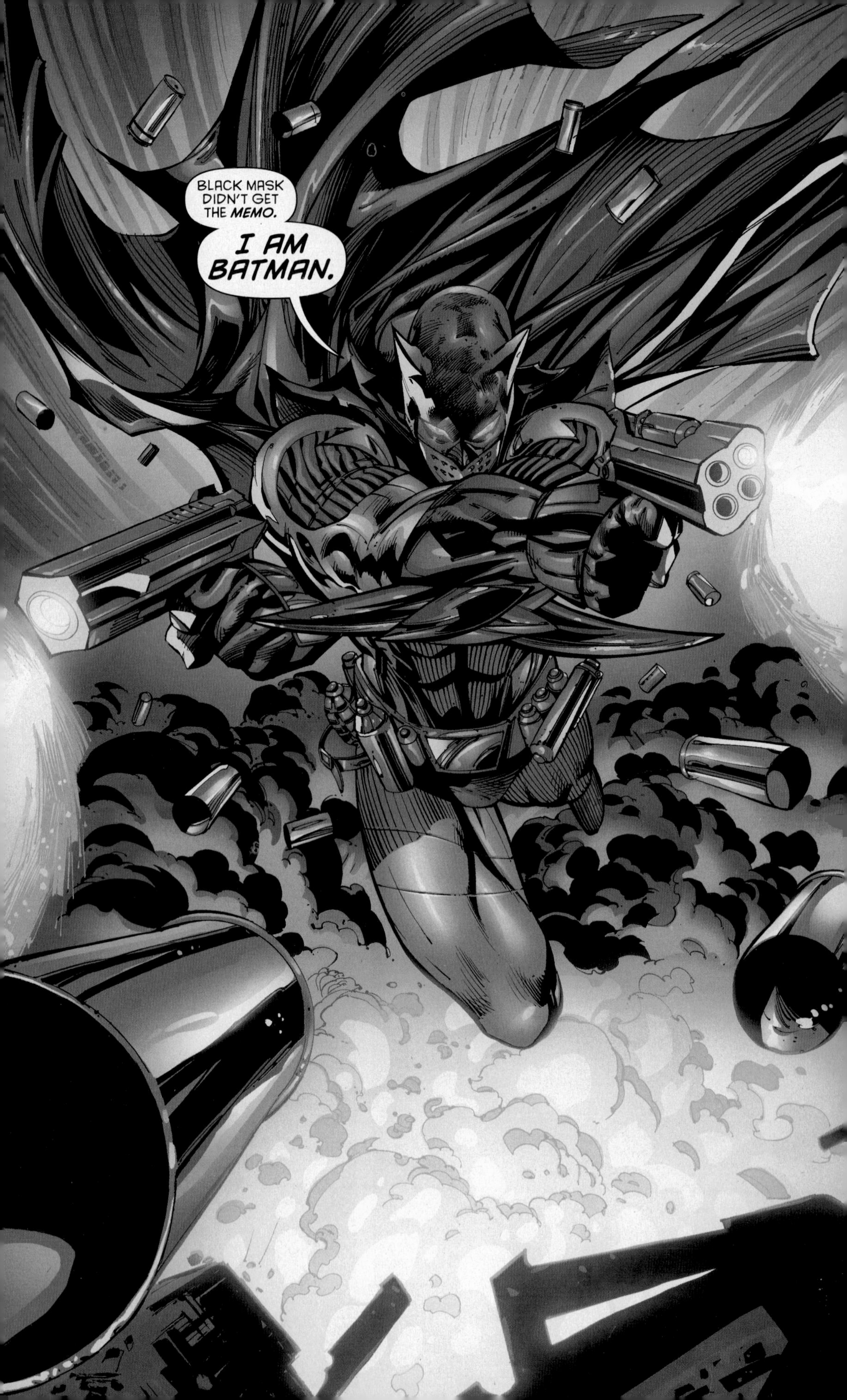
BLACK MASK DIDN'T GET THE MEMO.
I AM BATMAN.

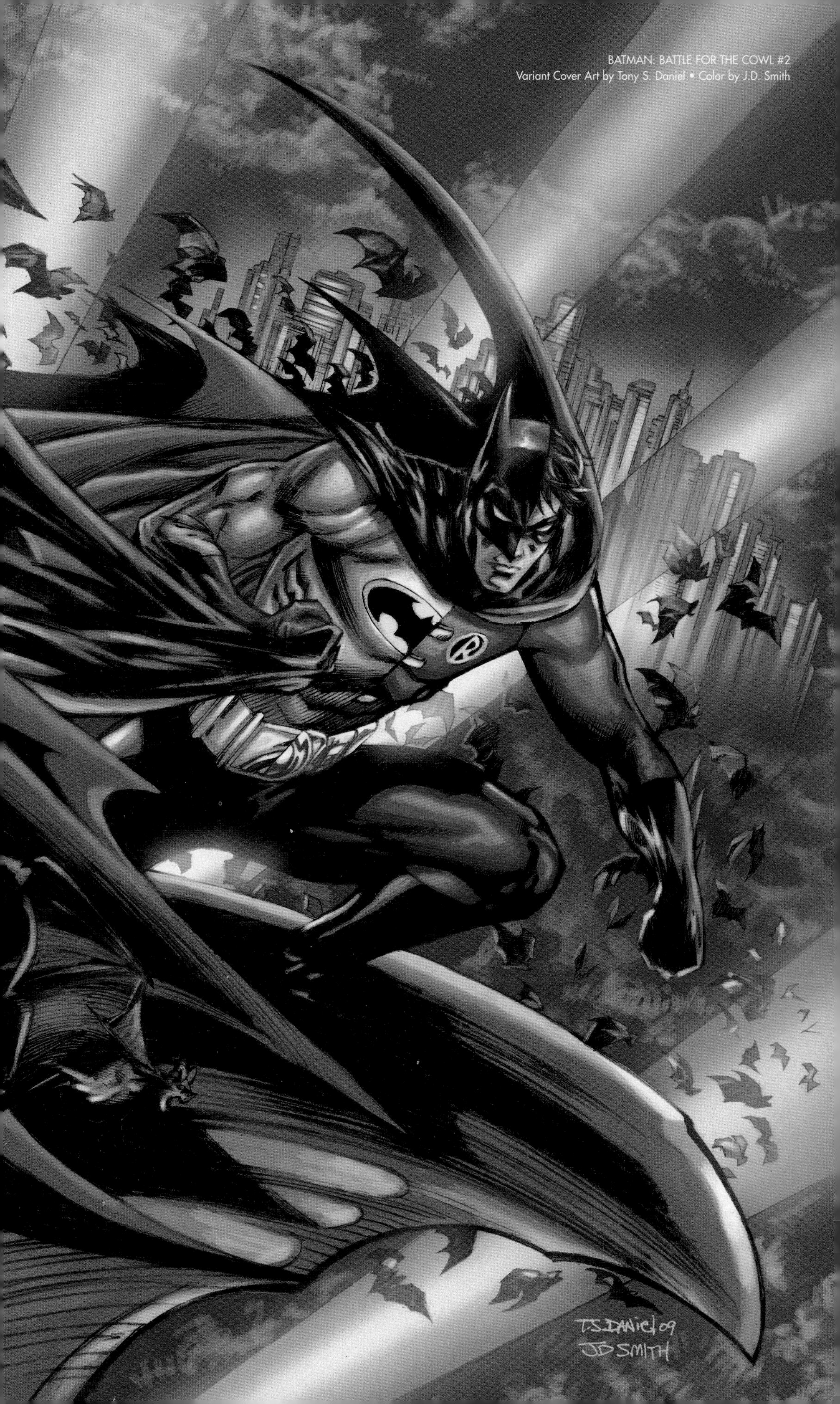
T.S.Daniel 09
JD SMITH

BATMAN: BATTLE FOR THE COWL #2
Variant Cover Art by Tony S. Daniel • Color by J.D. Smith

"Look at me. Do you see **terror**?
Do you see **fear**?
Or is it just your **own reflection**?"

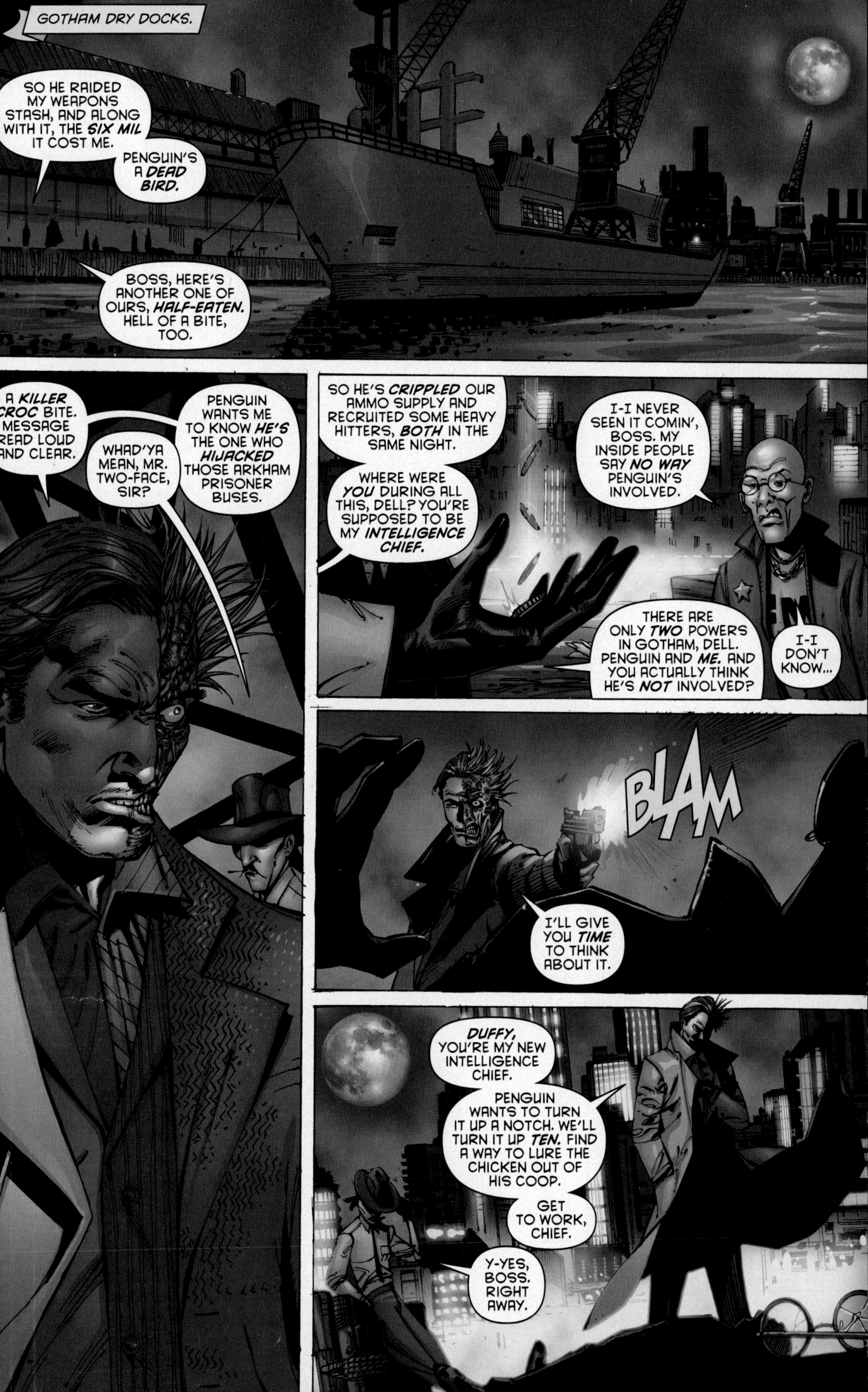
GOTHAM DRY DOCKS.
SO HE RAIDED MY WEAPONS STASH, AND ALONG WITH IT, THE SIX MIL IT COST ME.
PENGUIN'S A DEAD BIRD.
BOSS, HERE'S ANOTHER ONE OF OURS, HALF-EATEN. HELL OF A BITE, TOO.
A KILLER CROC BITE. MESSAGE READ LOUD AND CLEAR.
PENGUIN WANTS ME TO KNOW HE'S THE ONE WHO HIJACKED THOSE ARKHAM PRISONER BUSES.
WHAD'YA MEAN, MR. TWO-FACE, SIR?
SO HE'S CRIPPLED OUR AMMO SUPPLY AND RECRUITED SOME HEAVY HITTERS, BOTH IN THE SAME NIGHT.
WHERE WERE YOU DURING ALL THIS, DELL? YOU'RE SUPPOSED TO BE MY INTELLIGENCE CHIEF.
I-I NEVER SEEN IT COMIN', BOSS. MY INSIDE PEOPLE SAY NO WAY PENGUIN'S INVOLVED.
THERE ARE ONLY TWO POWERS IN GOTHAM, DELL. PENGUIN AND ME. AND YOU ACTUALLY THINK HE'S NOT INVOLVED?
I-I DON'T KNOW...
BLAM
I'LL GIVE YOU TIME TO THINK ABOUT IT.
DUFFY, YOU'RE MY NEW INTELLIGENCE CHIEF.
PENGUIN WANTS TO TURN IT UP A NOTCH. WE'LL TURN IT UP TEN. FIND A WAY TO LURE THE CHICKEN OUT OF HIS COOP.
GET TO WORK, CHIEF.
Y-YES, BOSS. RIGHT AWAY.

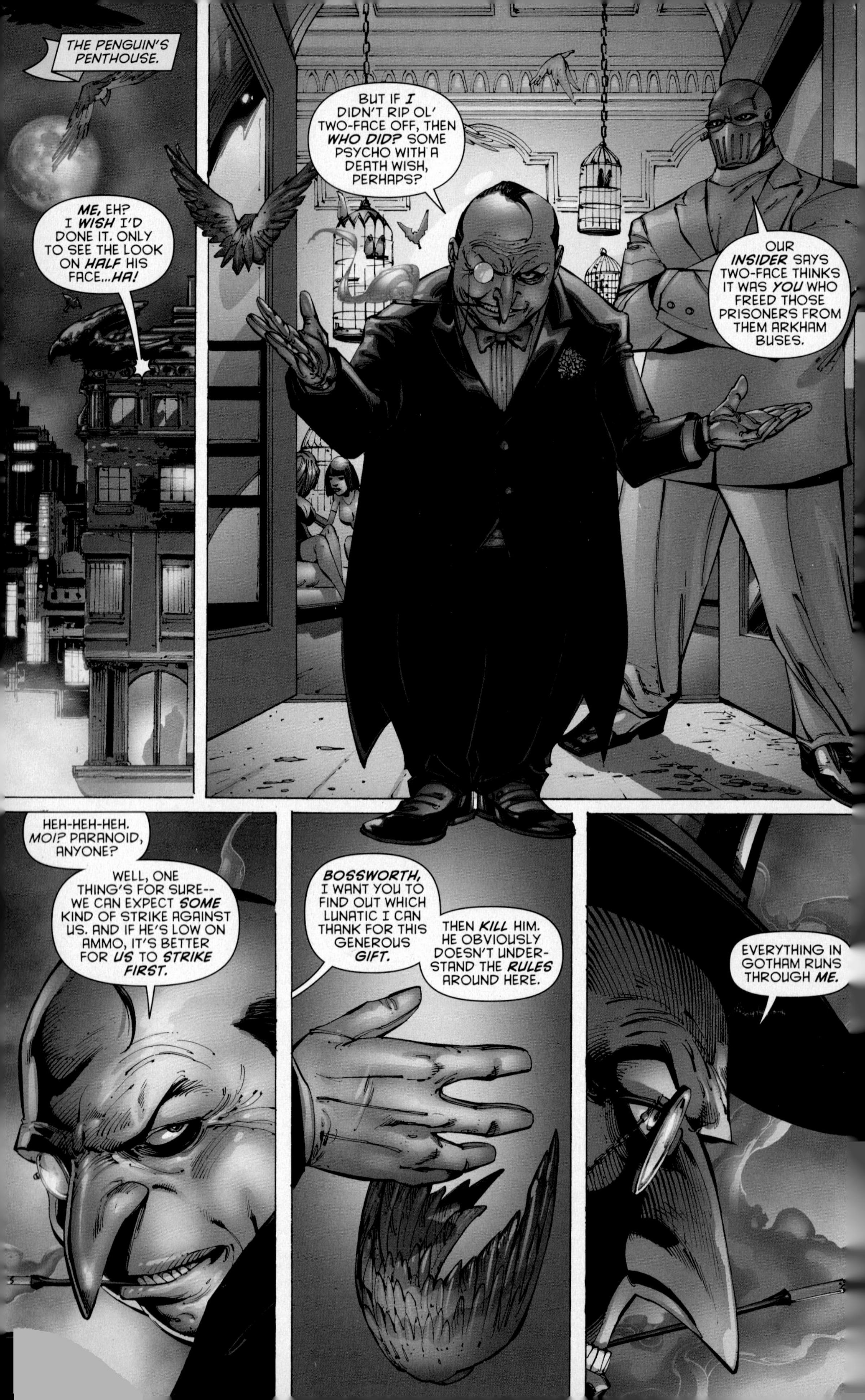
THE PENGUIN'S PENTHOUSE.
ME, EH? I WISH I'D DONE IT. ONLY TO SEE THE LOOK ON HALF HIS FACE...HA!
BUT IF I DIDN'T RIP OL' TWO-FACE OFF, THEN WHO DID? SOME PSYCHO WITH A DEATH WISH, PERHAPS?
OUR INSIDER SAYS TWO-FACE THINKS IT WAS YOU WHO FREED THOSE PRISONERS FROM THEM ARKHAM BUSES.
HEH-HEH-HEH. MOI? PARANOID, ANYONE?
WELL, ONE THING'S FOR SURE-- WE CAN EXPECT SOME KIND OF STRIKE AGAINST US. AND IF HE'S LOW ON AMMO, IT'S BETTER FOR US TO STRIKE FIRST.
BOSSWORTH, I WANT YOU TO FIND OUT WHICH LUNATIC I CAN THANK FOR THIS GENEROUS GIFT.
THEN KILL HIM. HE OBVIOUSLY DOESN'T UNDERSTAND THE RULES AROUND HERE.
EVERYTHING IN GOTHAM RUNS THROUGH ME.

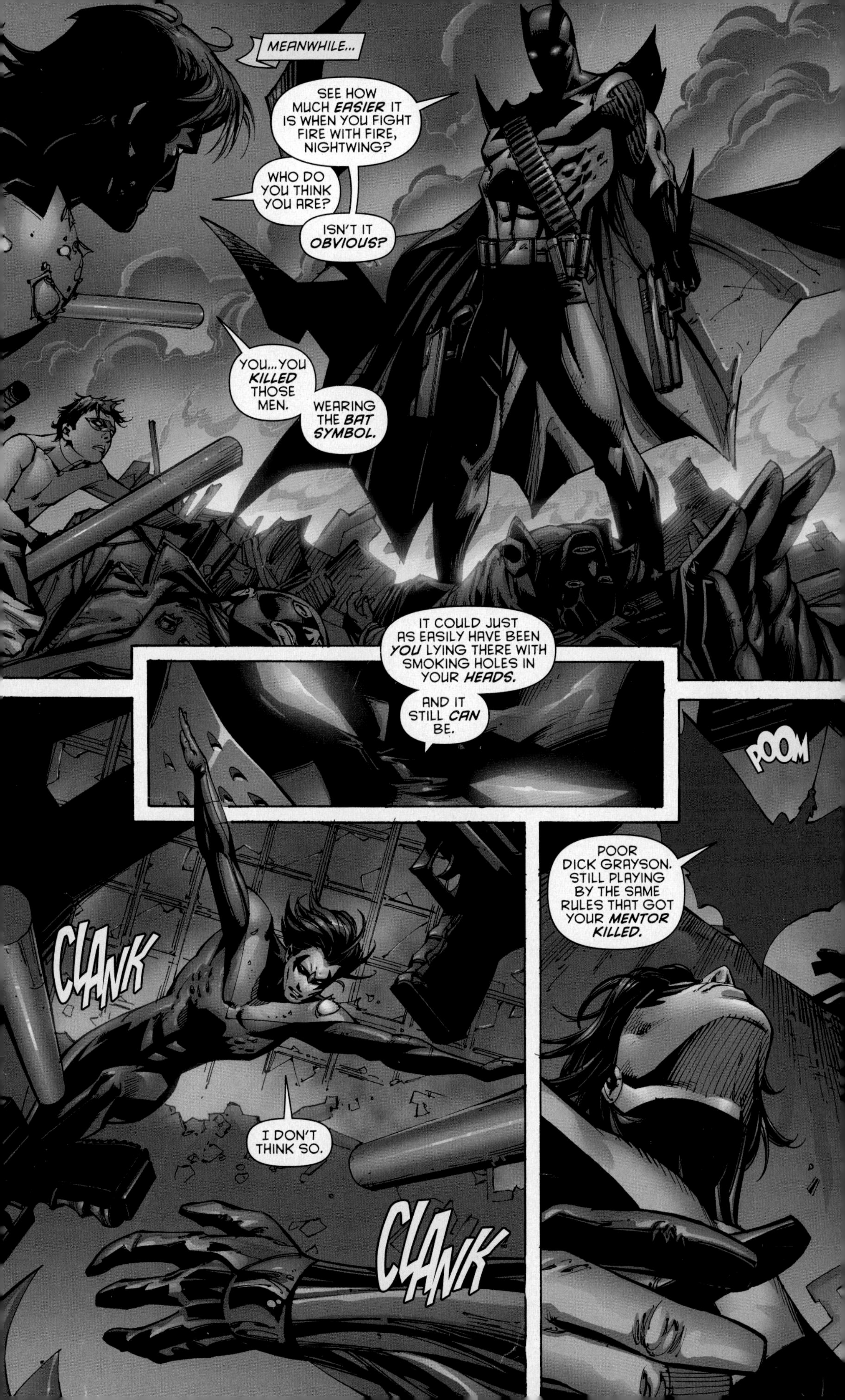
MEANWHILE...
SEE HOW MUCH EASIER IT IS WHEN YOU FIGHT FIRE WITH FIRE, NIGHTWING?
WHO DO YOU THINK YOU ARE?
ISN'T IT OBVIOUS?
YOU...YOU KILLED THOSE MEN.
WEARING THE BAT SYMBOL.
IT COULD JUST AS EASILY HAVE BEEN YOU LYING THERE WITH SMOKING HOLES IN YOUR HEADS.
AND IT STILL CAN BE.
POOM
CLANK
I DON'T THINK SO.
CLANK
POOR DICK GRAYSON. STILL PLAYING BY THE SAME RULES THAT GOT YOUR MENTOR KILLED.

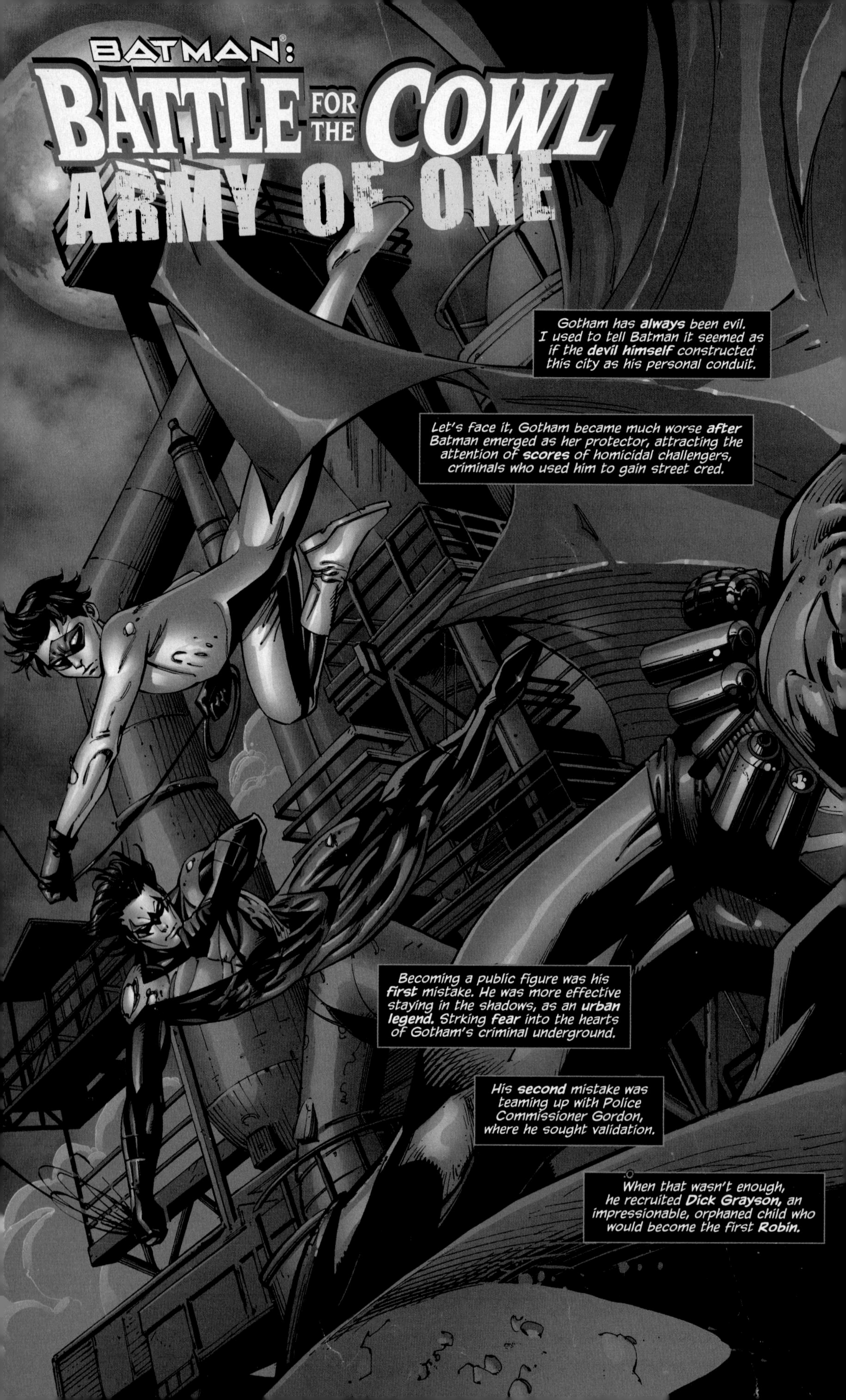
BATMAN®:
BATTLE FOR THE COWL
ARMY OF ONE
Gotham has always been evil. I used to tell Batman it seemed as if the devil himself constructed this city as his personal conduit.
Let's face it, Gotham became much worse after Batman emerged as her protector, attracting the attention of scores of homicidal challengers, criminals who used him to gain street cred.
Becoming a public figure was his first mistake. He was more effective staying in the shadows, as an urban legend. Strking fear into the hearts of Gotham's criminal underground.
His second mistake was teaming up with Police Commissioner Gordon, where he sought validation.
When that wasn't enough, he recruited Dick Grayson, an impressionable, orphaned child who would become the first Robin.

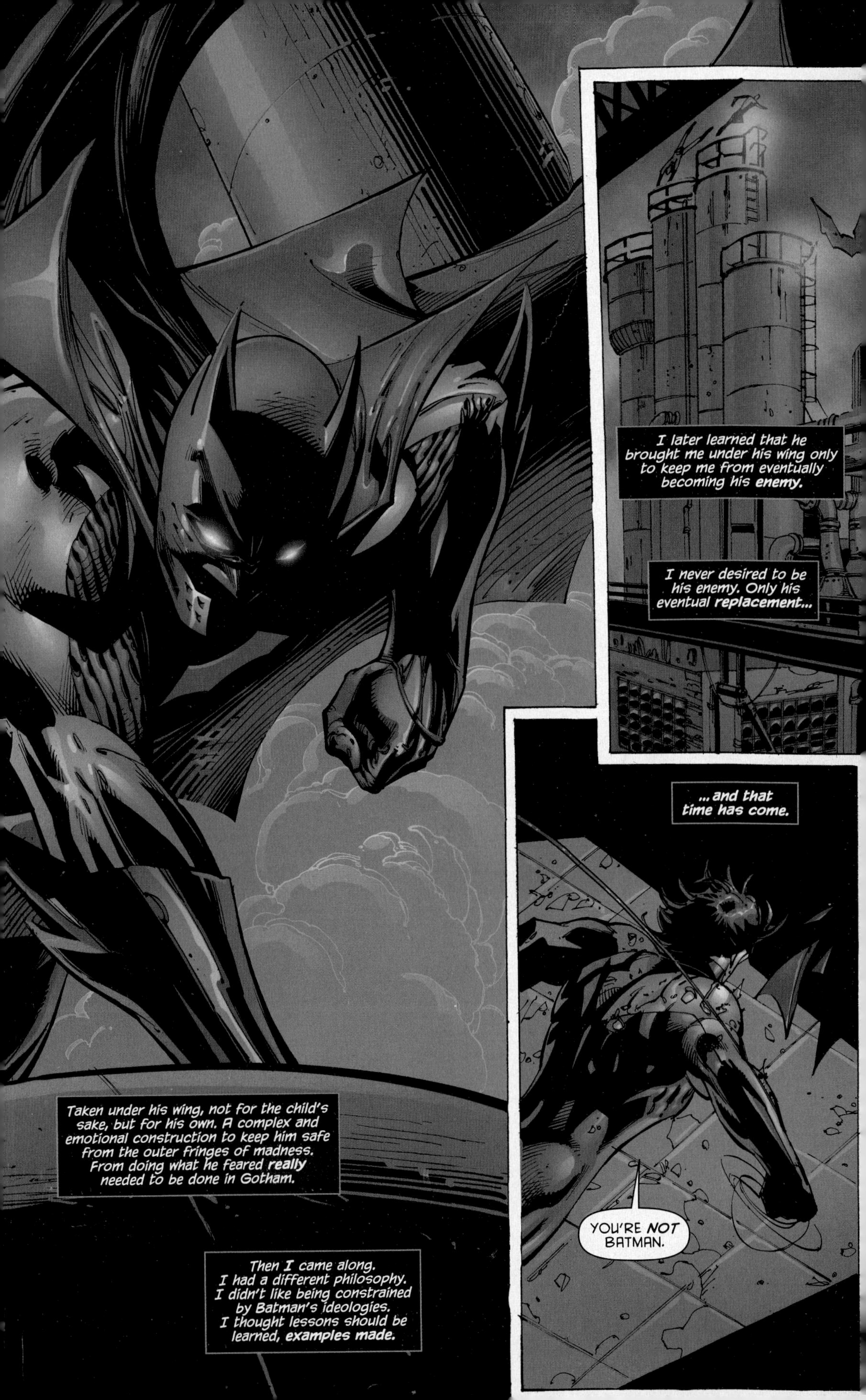
Taken under his wing, not for the child's sake, but for his own. A complex and emotional construction to keep him safe from the outer fringes of madness. From doing what he feared really needed to be done in Gotham.
Then I came along. I had a different philosophy. I didn't like being constrained by Batman's ideologies. I thought lessons should be learned, examples made.
I later learned that he brought me under his wing only to keep me from eventually becoming his enemy.
I never desired to be his enemy. Only his eventual replacement...
...and that time has come.
YOU'RE NOT BATMAN.

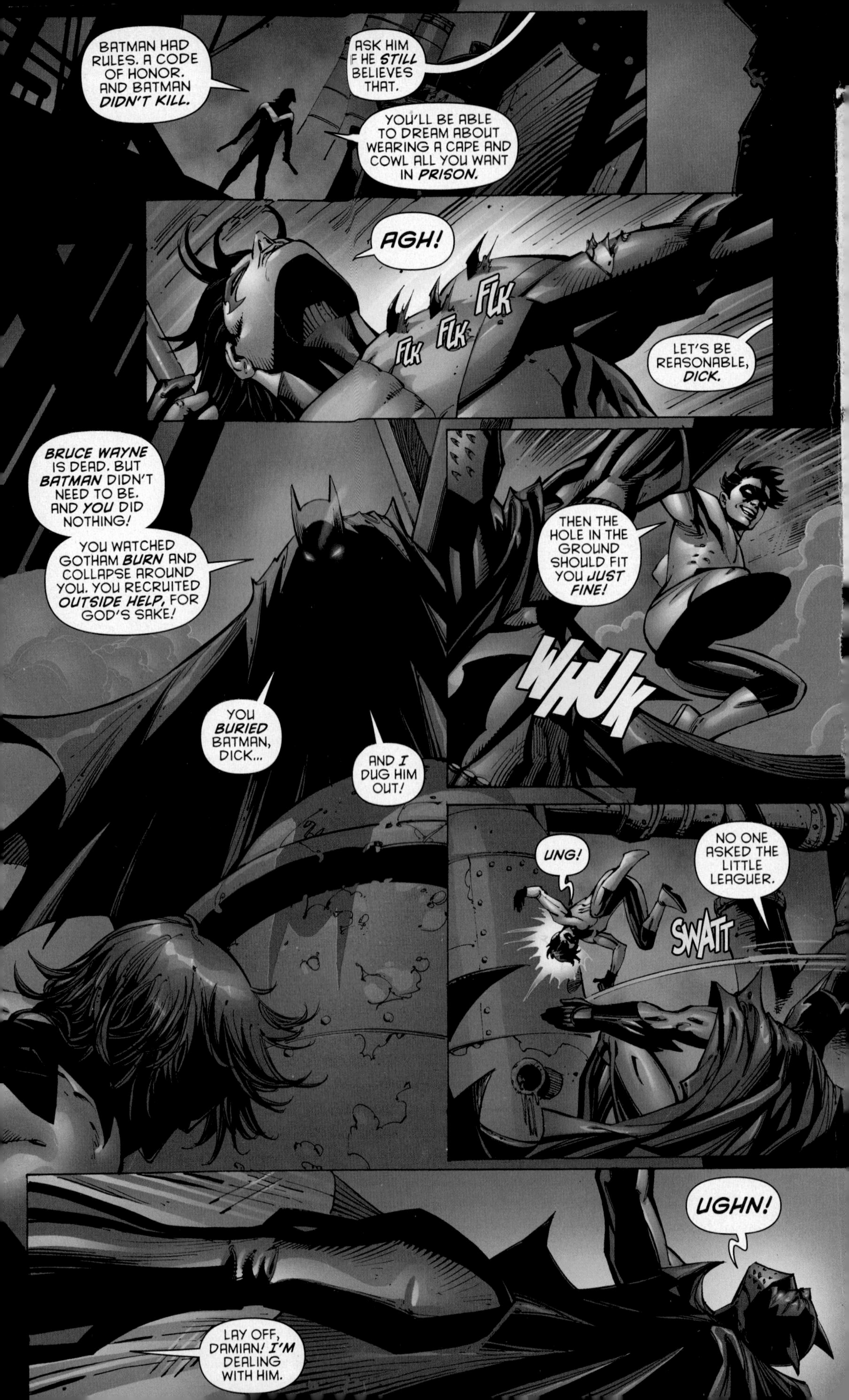
BATMAN HAD RULES. A CODE OF HONOR. AND BATMAN DIDN'T KILL.
ASK HIM IF HE STILL BELIEVES THAT.
YOU'LL BE ABLE TO DREAM ABOUT WEARING A CAPE AND COWL ALL YOU WANT IN PRISON.
AGH!
FLK
FLK
FLK
LET'S BE REASONABLE, DICK.
BRUCE WAYNE IS DEAD. BUT BATMAN DIDN'T NEED TO BE. AND YOU DID NOTHING!
YOU WATCHED GOTHAM BURN AND COLLAPSE AROUND YOU. YOU RECRUITED OUTSIDE HELP, FOR GOD'S SAKE!
YOU BURIED BATMAN, DICK...
AND I DUG HIM OUT!
THEN THE HOLE IN THE GROUND SHOULD FIT YOU JUST FINE!
WHUK
UNG!
NO ONE ASKED THE LITTLE LEAGUER.
SWATT
UGHN!
LAY OFF, DAMIAN! I'M DEALING WITH HIM.

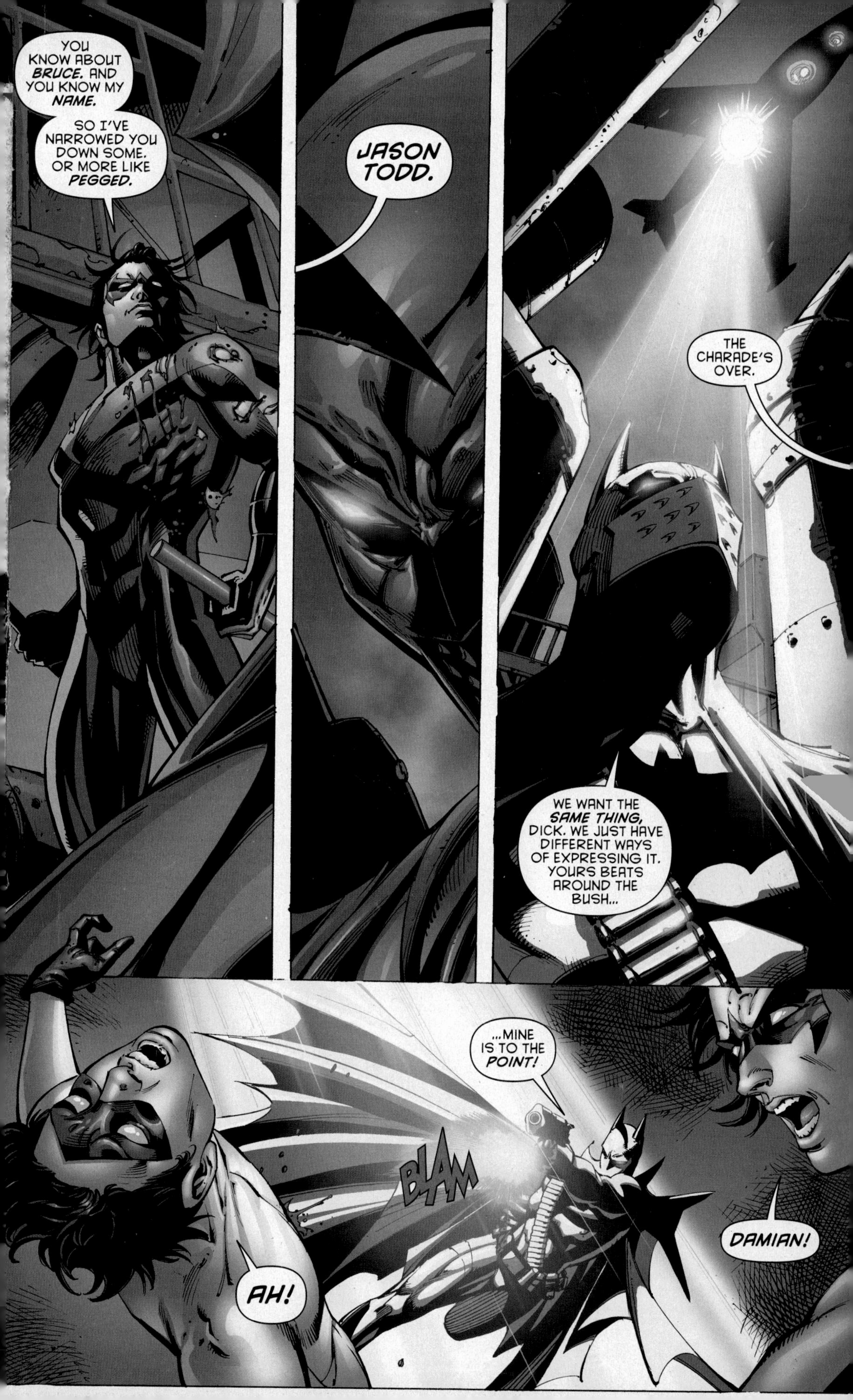
YOU KNOW ABOUT BRUCE. AND YOU KNOW MY NAME.
SO I'VE NARROWED YOU DOWN SOME. OR MORE LIKE PEGGED.
JASON TODD.
THE CHARADE'S OVER.
WE WANT THE SAME THING, DICK. WE JUST HAVE DIFFERENT WAYS OF EXPRESSING IT. YOURS BEATS AROUND THE BUSH...
...MINE IS TO THE POINT!
BLAM
AH!
DAMIAN!

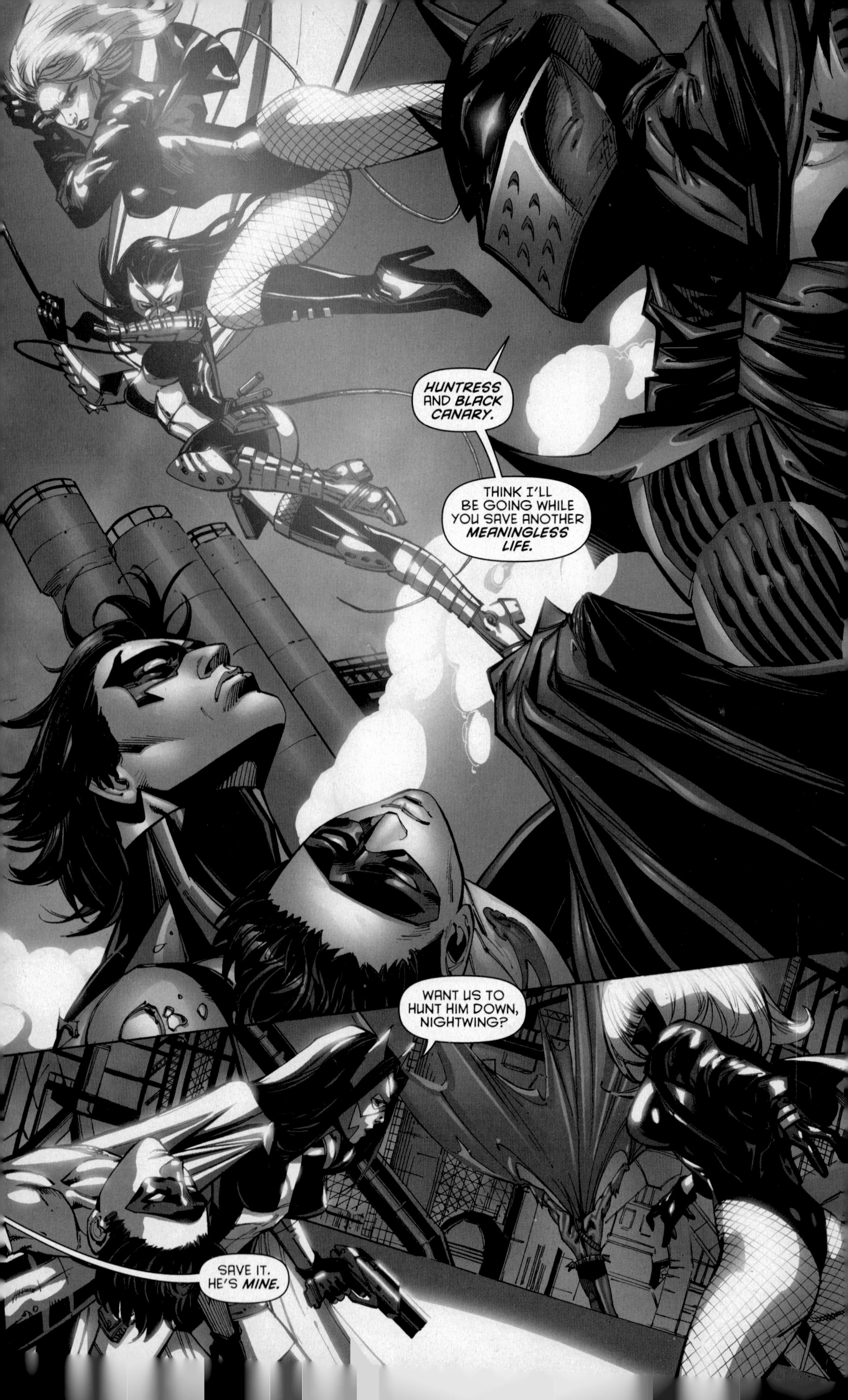
HUNTRESS AND BLACK CANARY.
THINK I'LL BE GOING WHILE YOU SAVE ANOTHER MEANINGLESS LIFE.
WANT US TO HUNT HIM DOWN, NIGHTWING?
SAVE IT. HE'S MINE.

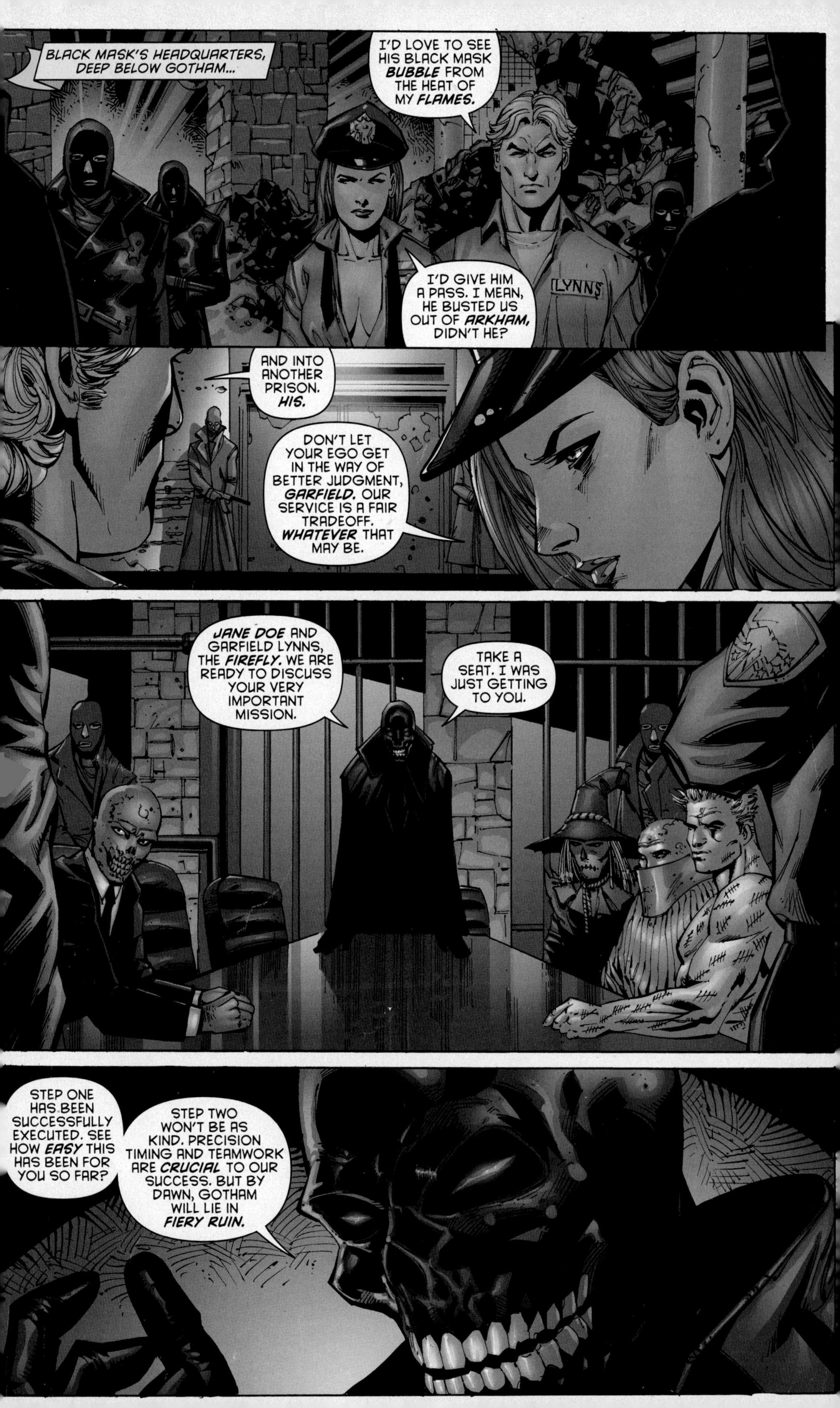
BLACK MASK'S HEADQUARTERS, DEEP BELOW GOTHAM...
I'D LOVE TO SEE HIS BLACK MASK BUBBLE FROM THE HEAT OF MY FLAMES.
I'D GIVE HIM A PASS. I MEAN, HE BUSTED US OUT OF ARKHAM, DIDN'T HE?
LYNNS
AND INTO ANOTHER PRISON. HIS.
DON'T LET YOUR EGO GET IN THE WAY OF BETTER JUDGMENT, GARFIELD. OUR SERVICE IS A FAIR TRADEOFF. WHATEVER THAT MAY BE.
JANE DOE AND GARFIELD LYNNS, THE FIREFLY. WE ARE READY TO DISCUSS YOUR VERY IMPORTANT MISSION.
TAKE A SEAT. I WAS JUST GETTING TO YOU.
STEP ONE HAS BEEN SUCCESSFULLY EXECUTED. SEE HOW EASY THIS HAS BEEN FOR YOU SO FAR?
STEP TWO WON'T BE AS KIND. PRECISION TIMING AND TEAMWORK ARE CRUCIAL TO OUR SUCCESS. BUT BY DAWN, GOTHAM WILL LIE IN FIERY RUIN.

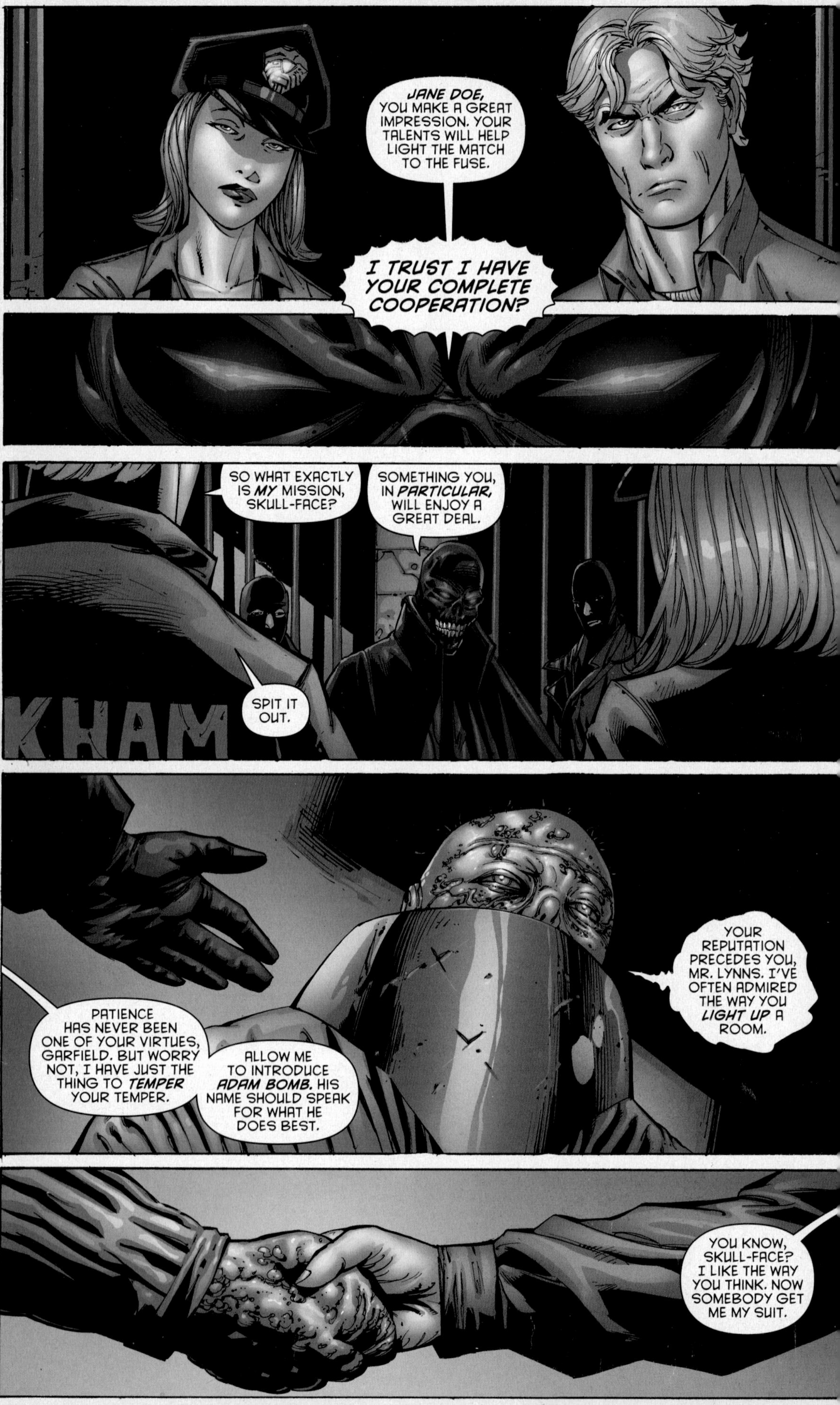
JANE DOE, YOU MAKE A GREAT IMPRESSION. YOUR TALENTS WILL HELP LIGHT THE MATCH TO THE FUSE.
I TRUST I HAVE YOUR COMPLETE COOPERATION?
SO WHAT EXACTLY IS MY MISSION, SKULL-FACE?
SOMETHING YOU, IN PARTICULAR, WILL ENJOY A GREAT DEAL.
SPIT IT OUT.
KHAM
YOUR REPUTATION PRECEDES YOU, MR. LYNNS. I'VE OFTEN ADMIRED THE WAY YOU LIGHT UP A ROOM.
PATIENCE HAS NEVER BEEN ONE OF YOUR VIRTUES, GARFIELD. BUT WORRY NOT, I HAVE JUST THE THING TO TEMPER YOUR TEMPER.
ALLOW ME TO INTRODUCE ADAM BOMB. HIS NAME SHOULD SPEAK FOR WHAT HE DOES BEST.
YOU KNOW, SKULL-FACE? I LIKE THE WAY YOU THINK. NOW SOMEBODY GET ME MY SUIT.

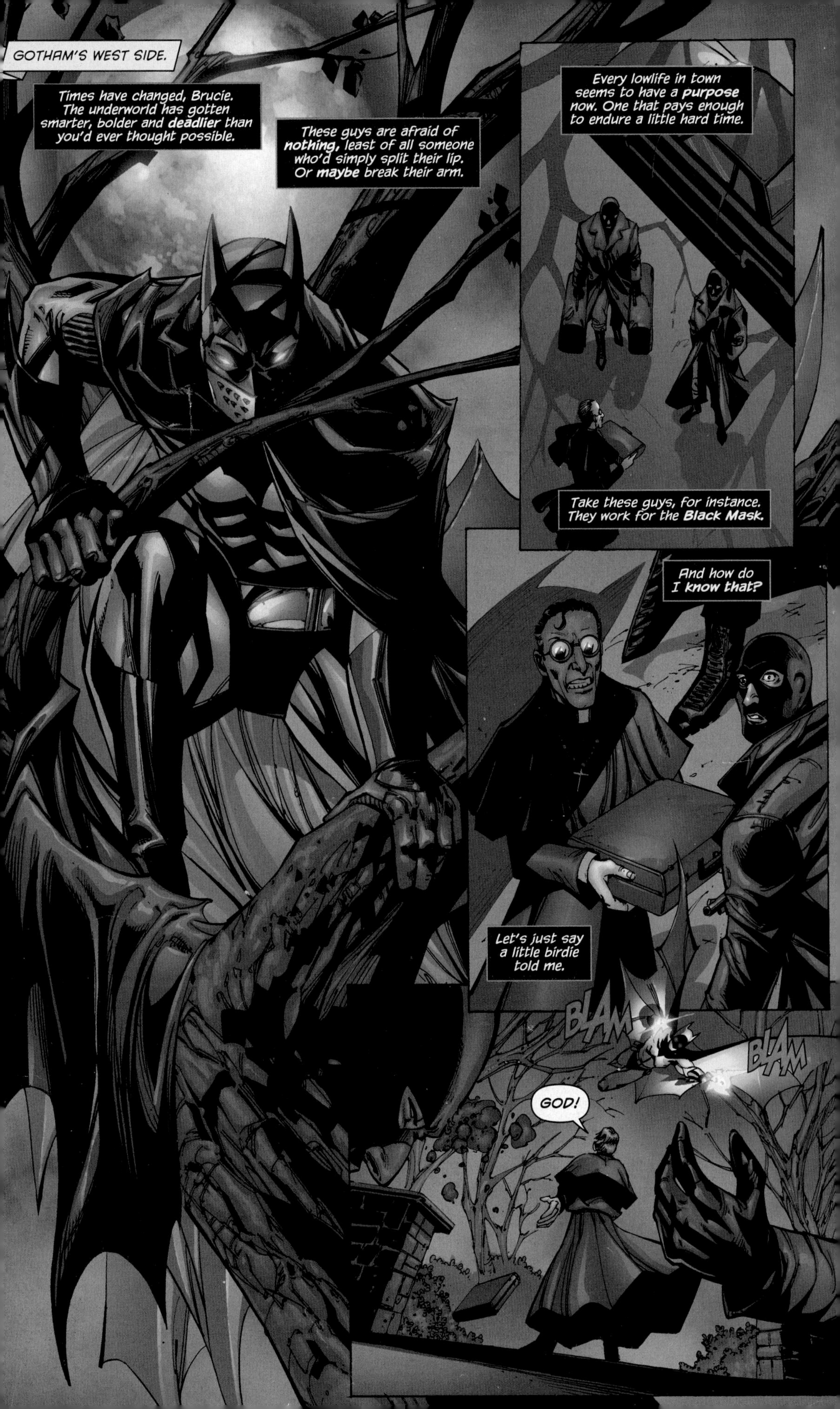
GOTHAM'S WEST SIDE.
Times have changed, Brucie. The underworld has gotten smarter, bolder and deadlier than you'd ever thought possible.
These guys are afraid of nothing, least of all someone who'd simply split their lip. Or maybe break their arm.
Every lowlife in town seems to have a purpose now. One that pays enough to endure a little hard time.
Take these guys, for instance. They work for the Black Mask.
And how do I know that?
Let's just say a little birdie told me.
BLAM
BLAM
GOD!

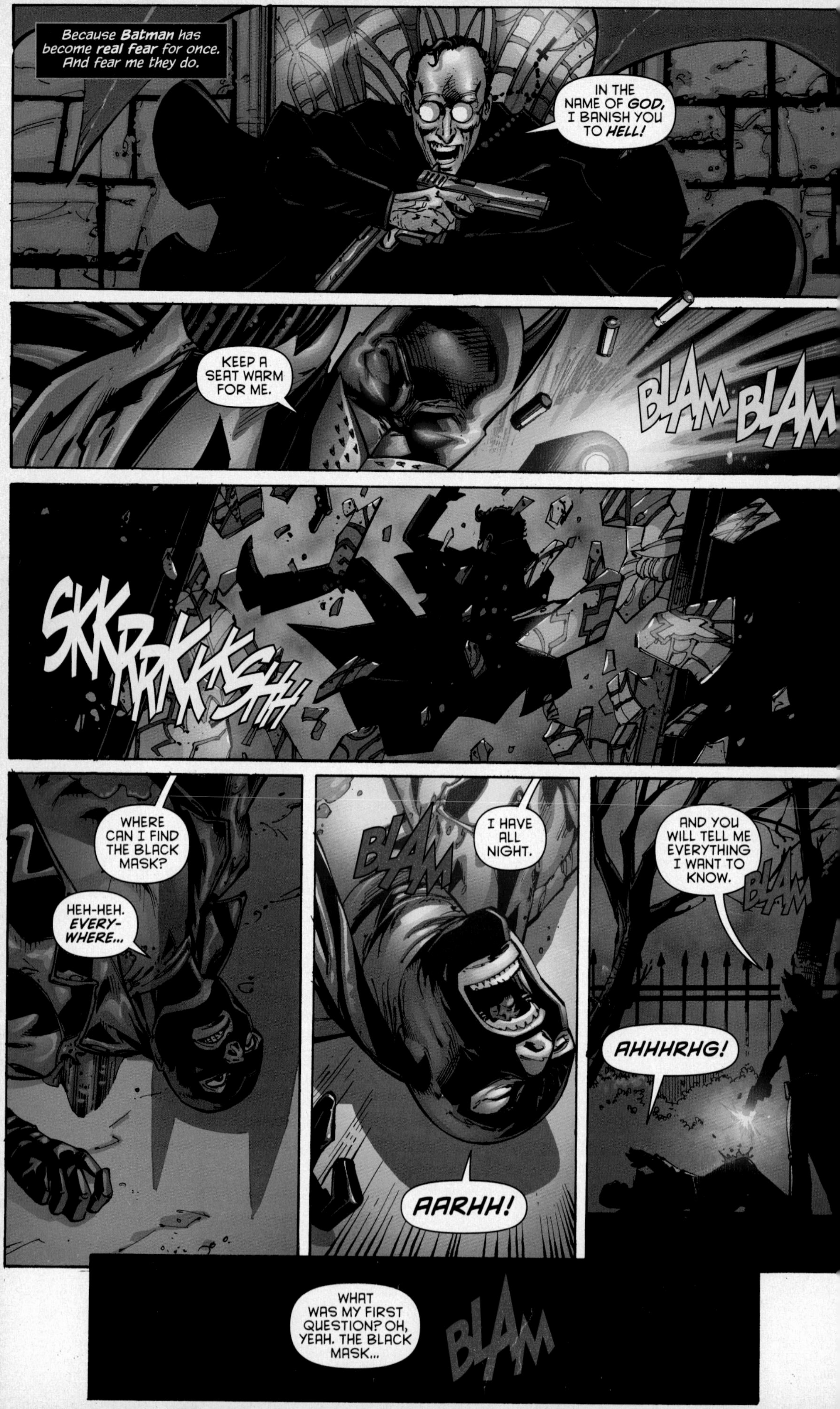
Because Batman has become real fear for once. And fear me they do.
IN THE NAME OF GOD, I BANISH YOU TO HELL!
KEEP A SEAT WARM FOR ME.
BLAM BLAM
SKKRRKKKSHH
WHERE CAN I FIND THE BLACK MASK?
HEH-HEH. EVERY-WHERE...
BLAM
I HAVE ALL NIGHT.
AARHH!
AND YOU WILL TELL ME EVERYTHING I WANT TO KNOW.
BLAM
AHHHRHG!
WHAT WAS MY FIRST QUESTION? OH, YEAH. THE BLACK MASK...
BLAM

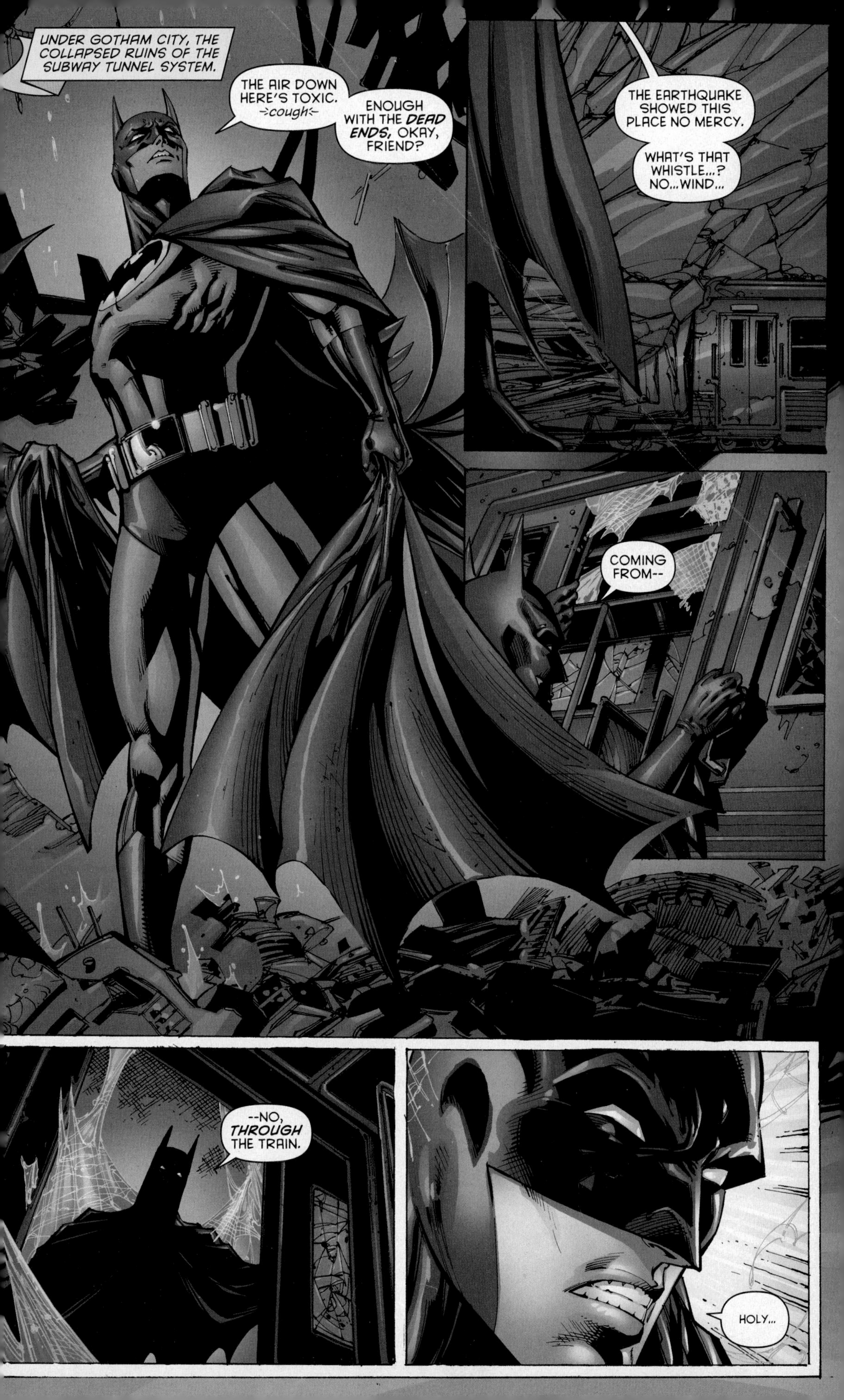

UNDER GOTHAM CITY, THE COLLAPSED RUINS OF THE SUBWAY TUNNEL SYSTEM.
THE AIR DOWN HERE'S TOXIC. *cough*
ENOUGH WITH THE DEAD ENDS, OKAY, FRIEND?
THE EARTHQUAKE SHOWED THIS PLACE NO MERCY.
WHAT'S THAT WHISTLE...? NO...WIND...
COMING FROM--
--NO, THROUGH THE TRAIN.
HOLY...

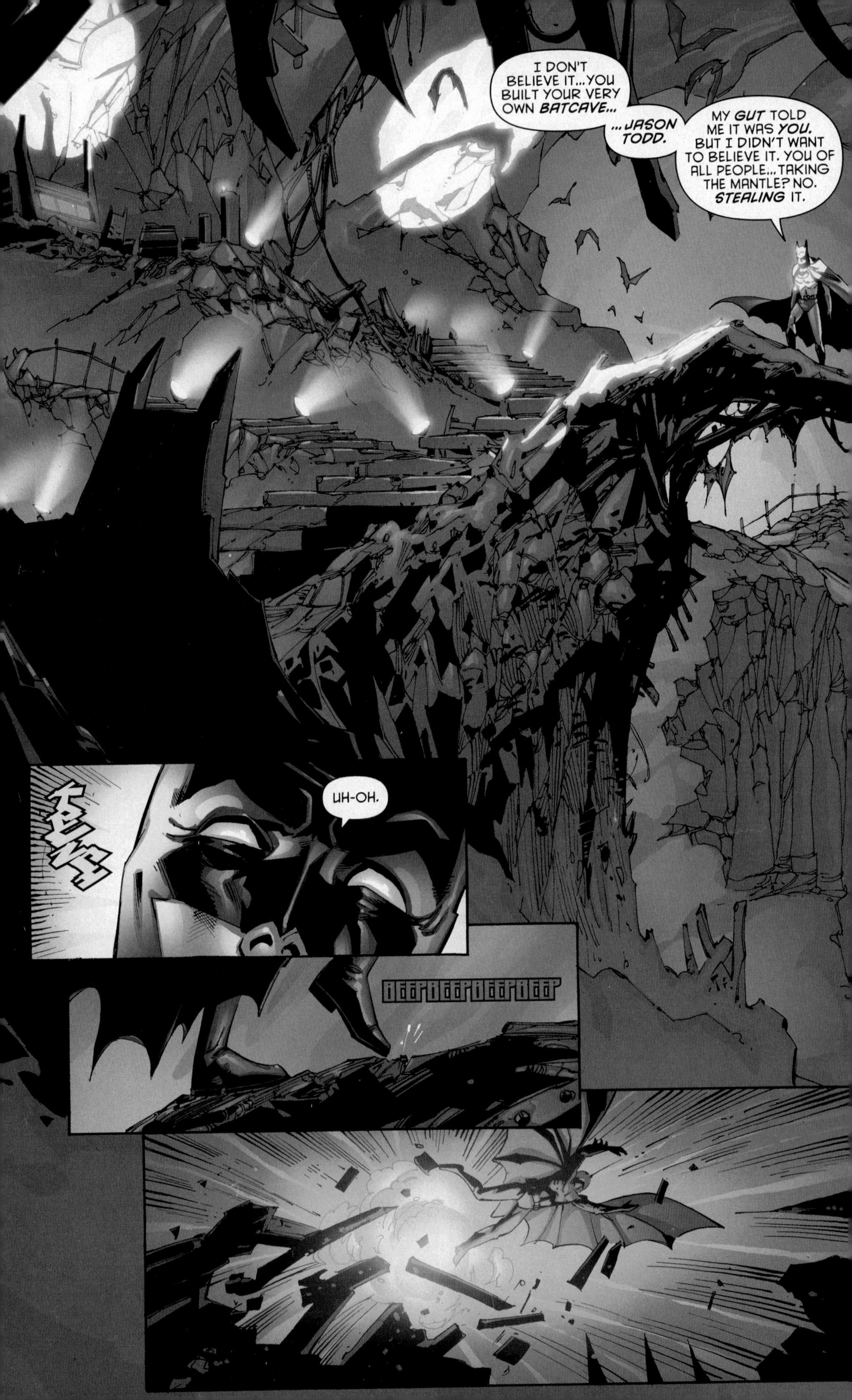
I DON'T BELIEVE IT...YOU BUILT YOUR VERY OWN *BATCAVE*...
...JASON TODD.
MY *GUT* TOLD ME IT WAS *YOU.* BUT I DIDN'T WANT TO BELIEVE IT. YOU OF ALL PEOPLE...TAKING THE MANTLE? NO. *STEALING* IT.
UH-OH.
BEEPBEEPBEEPBEEP

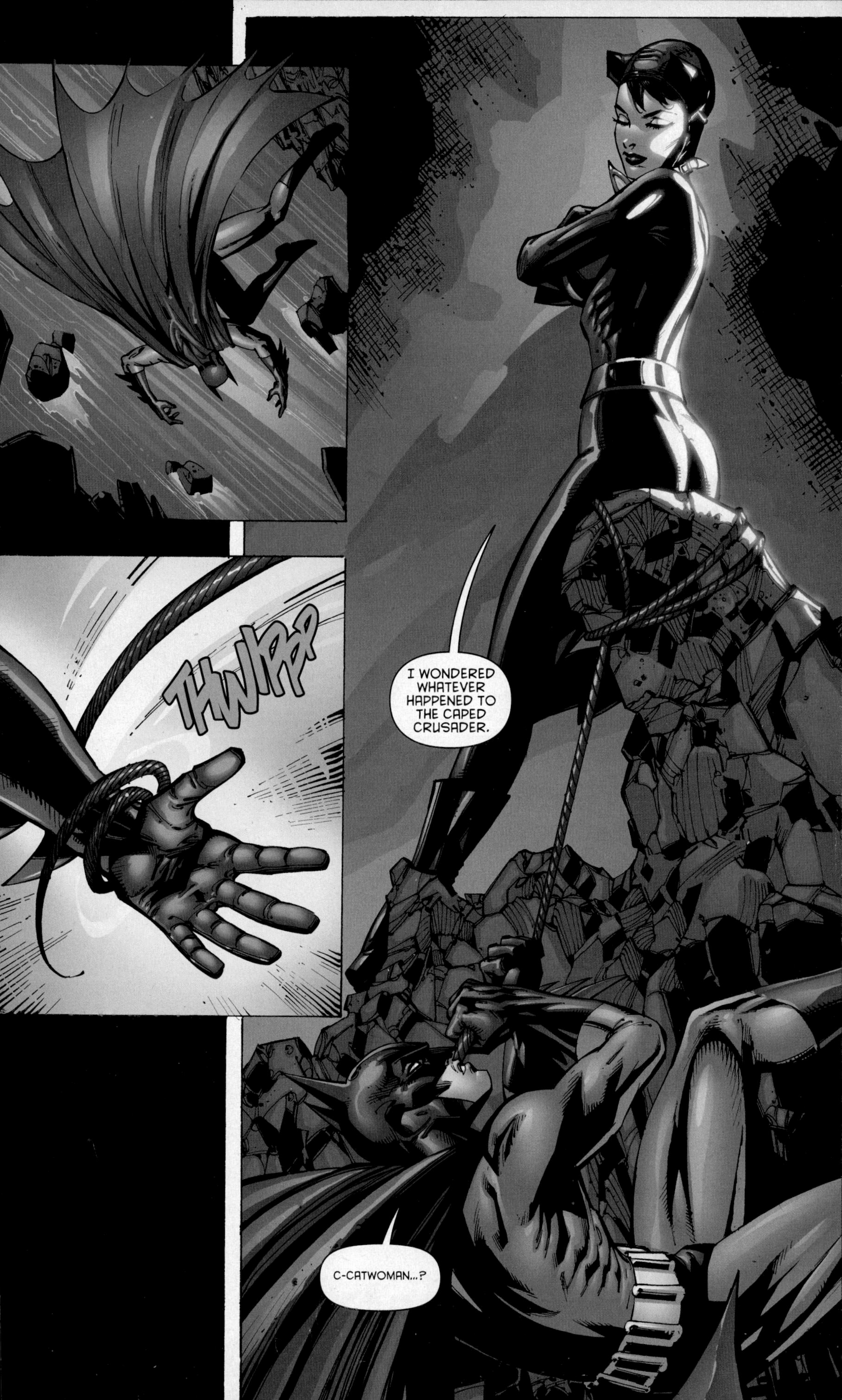
THWIPP
I WONDERED WHATEVER HAPPENED TO THE CAPED CRUSADER.
C-CATWOMAN...?

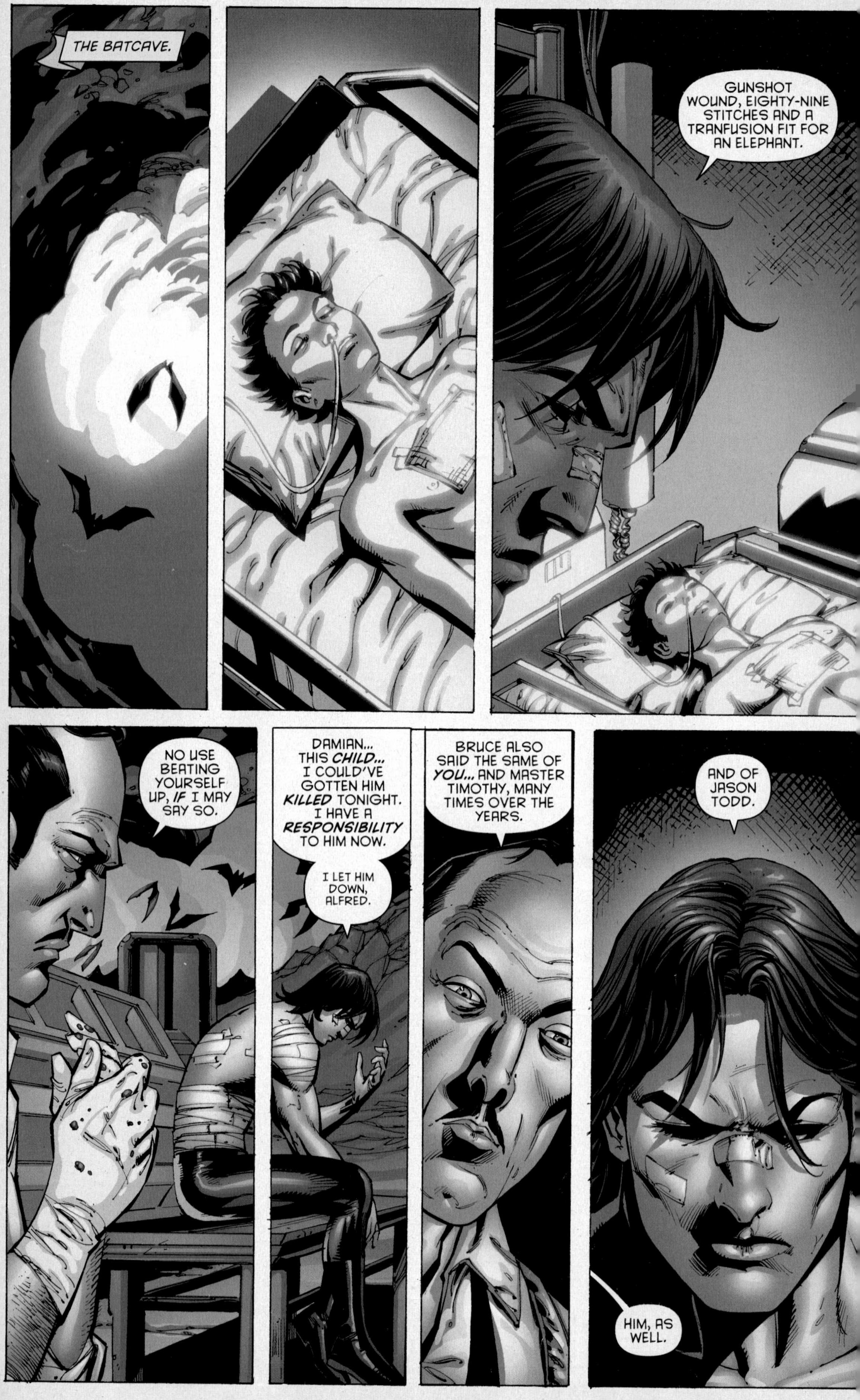

THE BATCAVE.
GUNSHOT WOUND, EIGHTY-NINE STITCHES AND A TRANFUSION FIT FOR AN ELEPHANT.
NO USE BEATING YOURSELF UP, *IF* I MAY SAY SO.
DAMIAN... THIS *CHILD*... I COULD'VE GOTTEN HIM *KILLED* TONIGHT. I HAVE A *RESPONSIBILITY* TO HIM NOW.
I LET HIM DOWN, ALFRED.
BRUCE ALSO SAID THE SAME OF *YOU*... AND MASTER TIMOTHY, MANY TIMES OVER THE YEARS.
AND OF JASON TODD.
HIM, AS WELL.

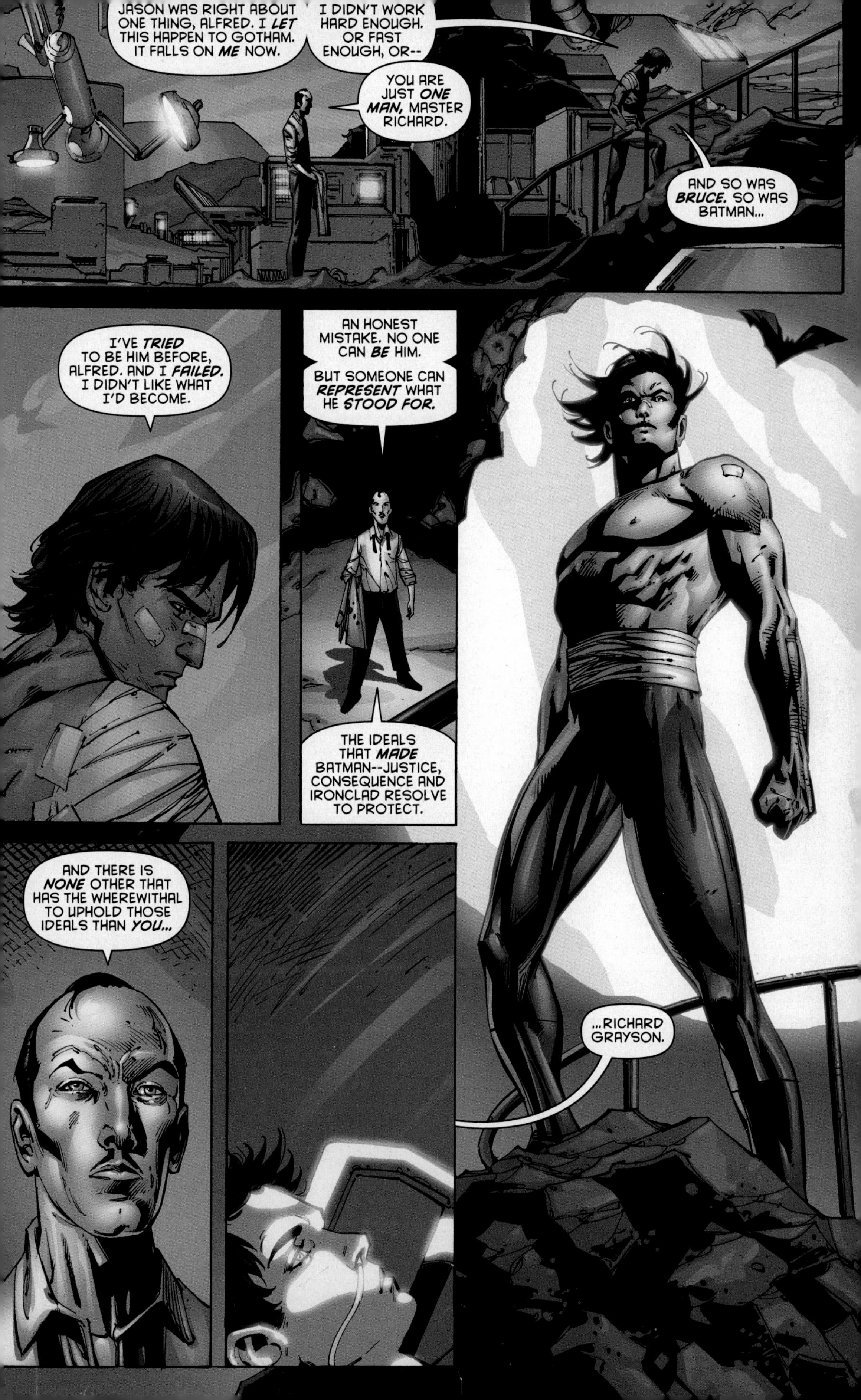
JASON WAS RIGHT ABOUT ONE THING, ALFRED. I LET THIS HAPPEN TO GOTHAM. IT FALLS ON ME NOW.
I DIDN'T WORK HARD ENOUGH. OR FAST ENOUGH, OR--
YOU ARE JUST ONE MAN, MASTER RICHARD.
AND SO WAS BRUCE. SO WAS BATMAN...
I'VE TRIED TO BE HIM BEFORE, ALFRED. AND I FAILED. I DIDN'T LIKE WHAT I'D BECOME.
AN HONEST MISTAKE. NO ONE CAN BE HIM.
BUT SOMEONE CAN REPRESENT WHAT HE STOOD FOR.
THE IDEALS THAT MADE BATMAN--JUSTICE, CONSEQUENCE AND IRONCLAD RESOLVE TO PROTECT.
AND THERE IS NONE OTHER THAT HAS THE WHEREWITHAL TO UPHOLD THOSE IDEALS THAN YOU...
...RICHARD GRAYSON.

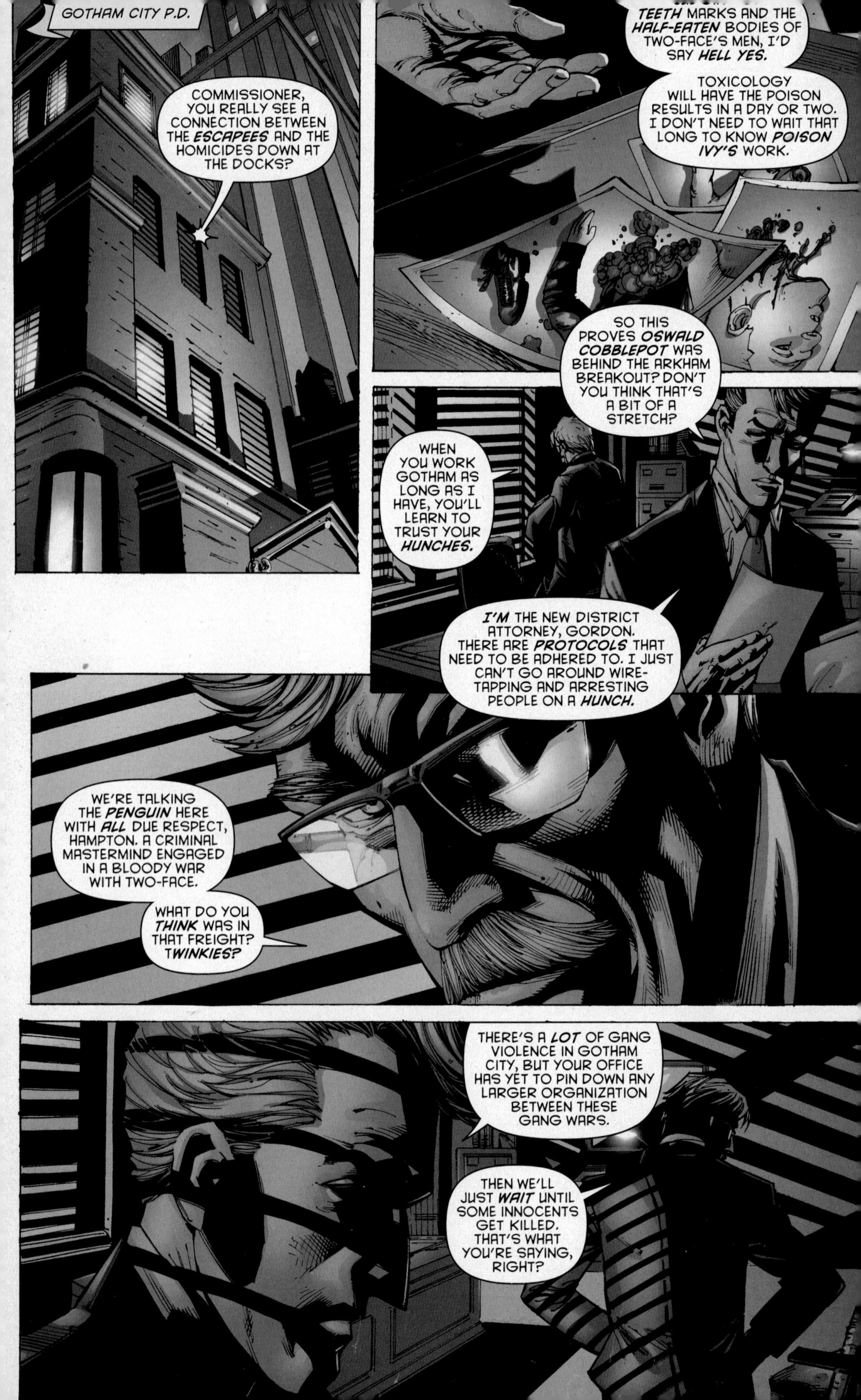
GOTHAM CITY P.D.
COMMISSIONER, YOU REALLY SEE A CONNECTION BETWEEN THE ESCAPEES AND THE HOMICIDES DOWN AT THE DOCKS?
TEETH MARKS AND THE HALF-EATEN BODIES OF TWO-FACE'S MEN, I'D SAY HELL YES.
TOXICOLOGY WILL HAVE THE POISON RESULTS IN A DAY OR TWO. I DON'T NEED TO WAIT THAT LONG TO KNOW POISON IVY'S WORK.
SO THIS PROVES OSWALD COBBLEPOT WAS BEHIND THE ARKHAM BREAKOUT? DON'T YOU THINK THAT'S A BIT OF A STRETCH?
WHEN YOU WORK GOTHAM AS LONG AS I HAVE, YOU'LL LEARN TO TRUST YOUR HUNCHES.
I'M THE NEW DISTRICT ATTORNEY, GORDON. THERE ARE PROTOCOLS THAT NEED TO BE ADHERED TO. I JUST CAN'T GO AROUND WIRE-TAPPING AND ARRESTING PEOPLE ON A HUNCH.
WE'RE TALKING THE PENGUIN HERE WITH ALL DUE RESPECT, HAMPTON. A CRIMINAL MASTERMIND ENGAGED IN A BLOODY WAR WITH TWO-FACE.
WHAT DO YOU THINK WAS IN THAT FREIGHT? TWINKIES?
THERE'S A LOT OF GANG VIOLENCE IN GOTHAM CITY, BUT YOUR OFFICE HAS YET TO PIN DOWN ANY LARGER ORGANIZATION BETWEEN THESE GANG WARS.
THEN WE'LL JUST WAIT UNTIL SOME INNOCENTS GET KILLED. THAT'S WHAT YOU'RE SAYING, RIGHT?

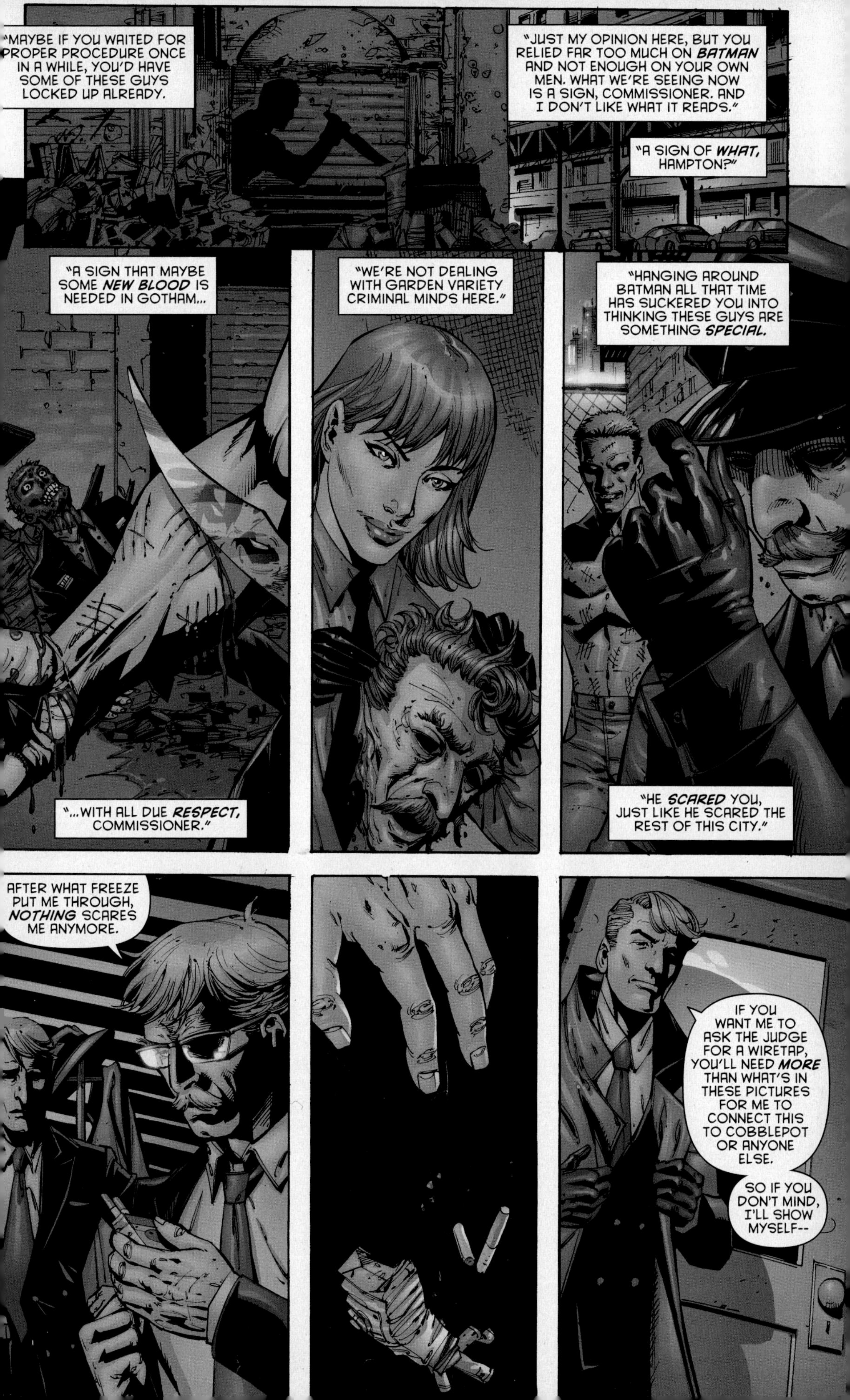
"MAYBE IF YOU WAITED FOR PROPER PROCEDURE ONCE IN A WHILE, YOU'D HAVE SOME OF THESE GUYS LOCKED UP ALREADY.
"JUST MY OPINION HERE, BUT YOU RELIED FAR TOO MUCH ON BATMAN AND NOT ENOUGH ON YOUR OWN MEN. WHAT WE'RE SEEING NOW IS A SIGN, COMMISSIONER. AND I DON'T LIKE WHAT IT READS."
"A SIGN OF WHAT, HAMPTON?"
"A SIGN THAT MAYBE SOME NEW BLOOD IS NEEDED IN GOTHAM...
"...WITH ALL DUE RESPECT, COMMISSIONER."
"WE'RE NOT DEALING WITH GARDEN VARIETY CRIMINAL MINDS HERE."
"HANGING AROUND BATMAN ALL THAT TIME HAS SUCKERED YOU INTO THINKING THESE GUYS ARE SOMETHING SPECIAL.
"HE SCARED YOU, JUST LIKE HE SCARED THE REST OF THIS CITY."
AFTER WHAT FREEZE PUT ME THROUGH, NOTHING SCARES ME ANYMORE.
IF YOU WANT ME TO ASK THE JUDGE FOR A WIRETAP, YOU'LL NEED MORE THAN WHAT'S IN THESE PICTURES FOR ME TO CONNECT THIS TO COBBLEPOT OR ANYONE ELSE.
SO IF YOU DON'T MIND, I'LL SHOW MYSELF--

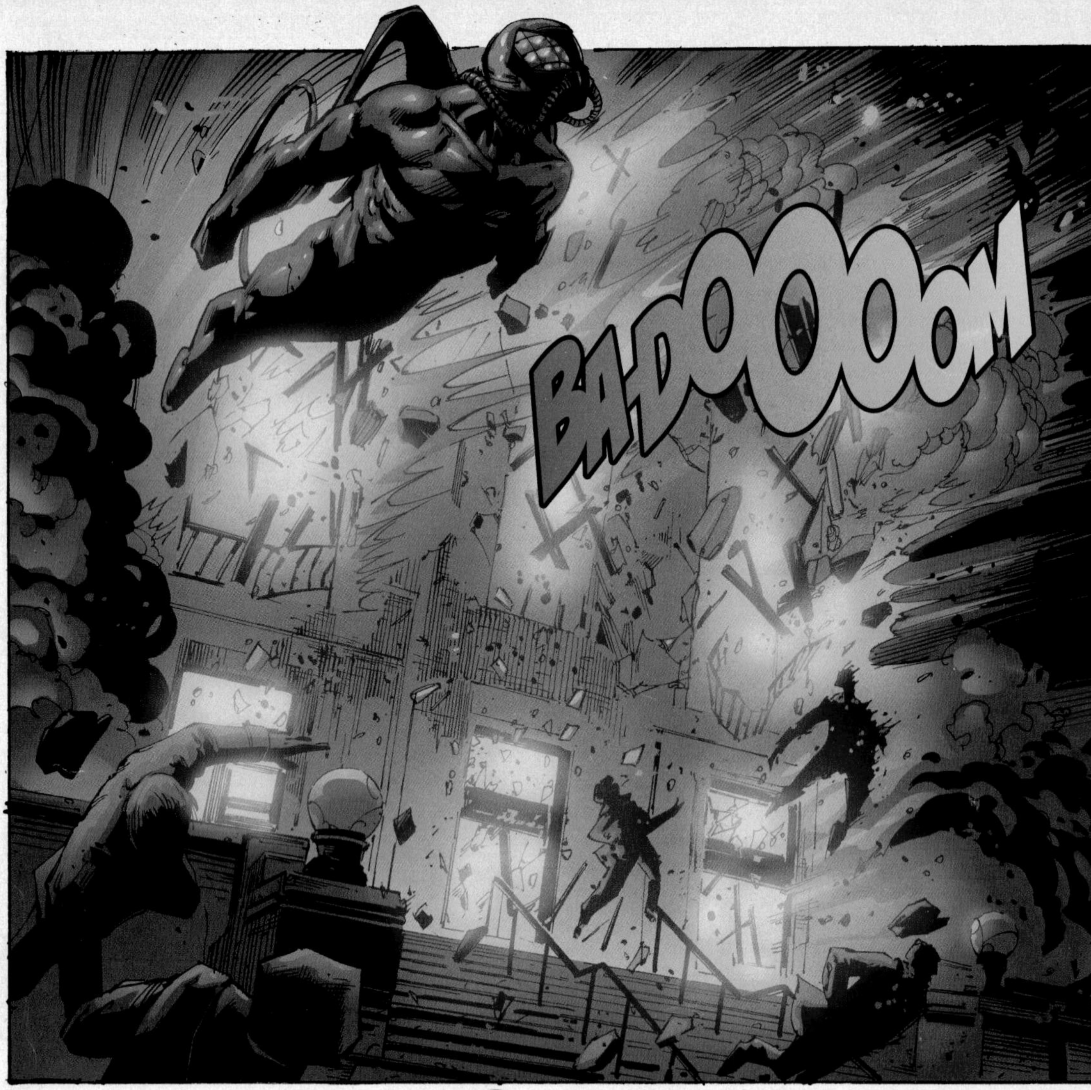
BA-DOOOOOM

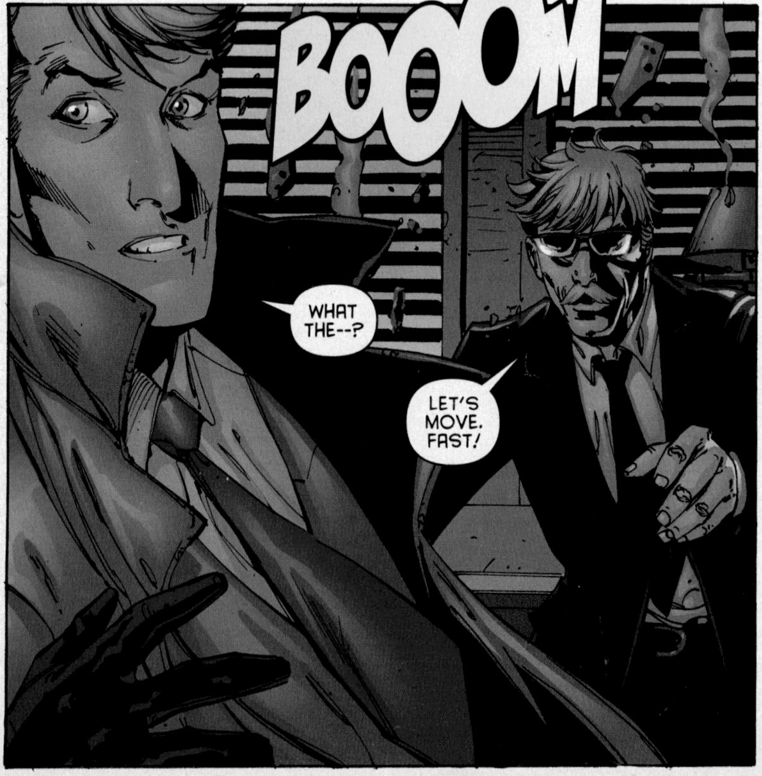
BOOOM
WHAT THE--?
LET'S MOVE. FAST!

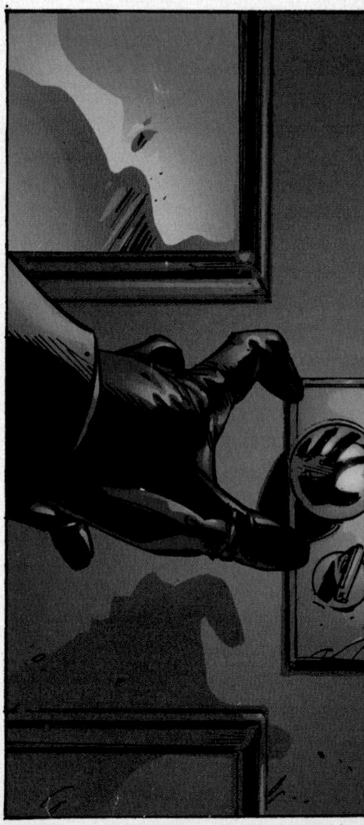

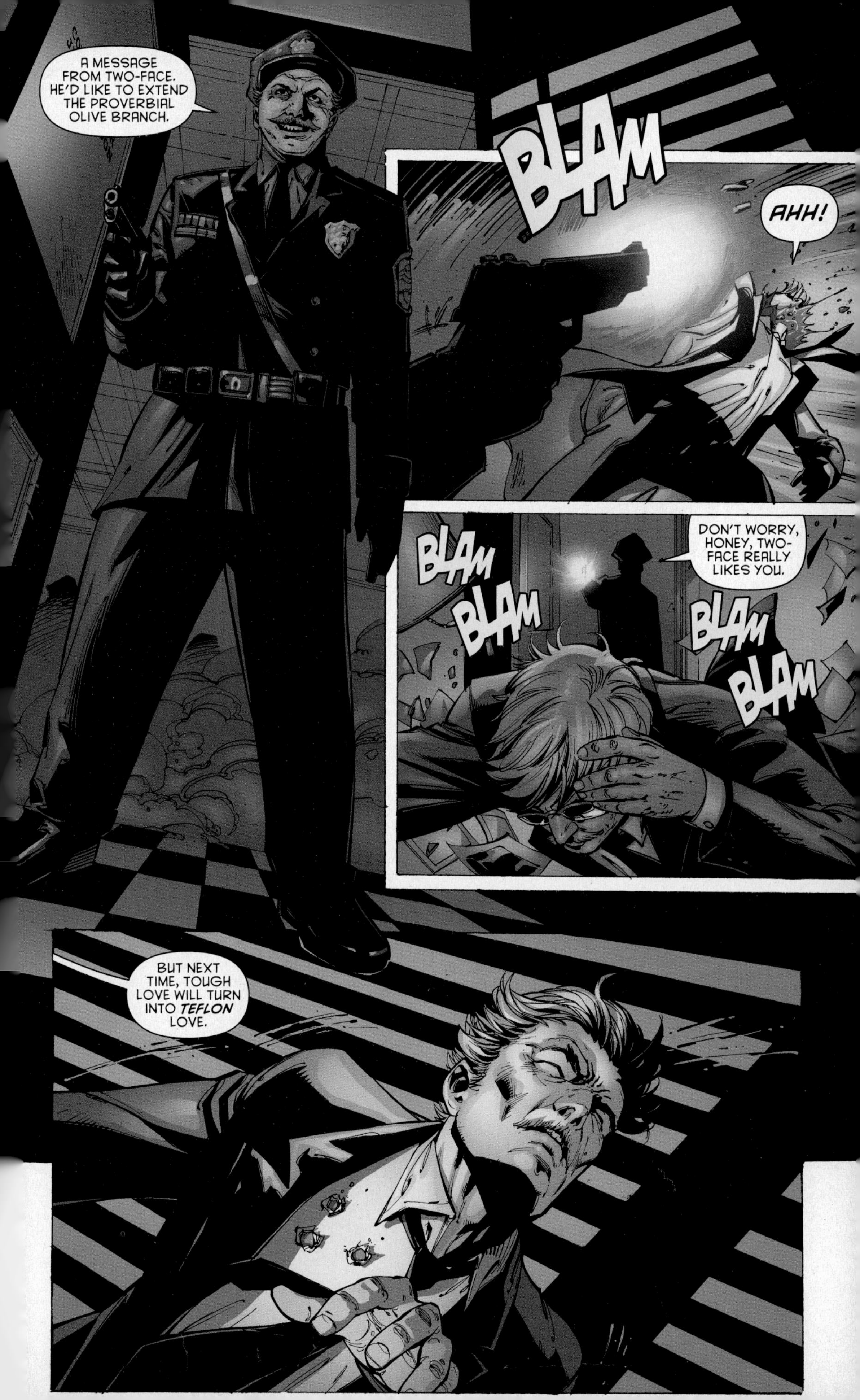
A MESSAGE FROM TWO-FACE. HE'D LIKE TO EXTEND THE PROVERBIAL OLIVE BRANCH.
BLAM
AHH!
BLAM
BLAM
DON'T WORRY, HONEY, TWO-FACE REALLY LIKES YOU.
BLAM
BLAM
BUT NEXT TIME, TOUGH LOVE WILL TURN INTO *TEFLON* LOVE.

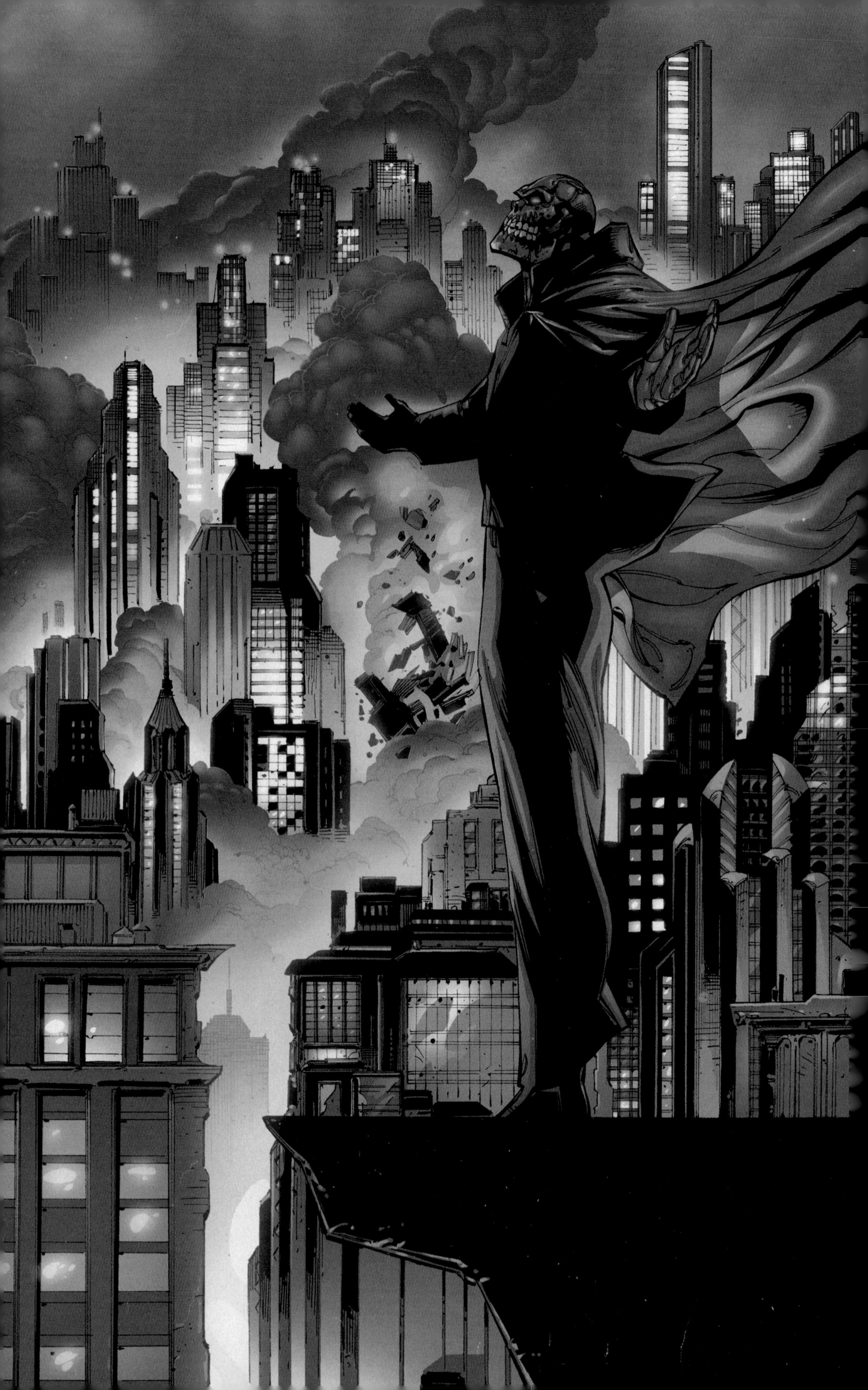

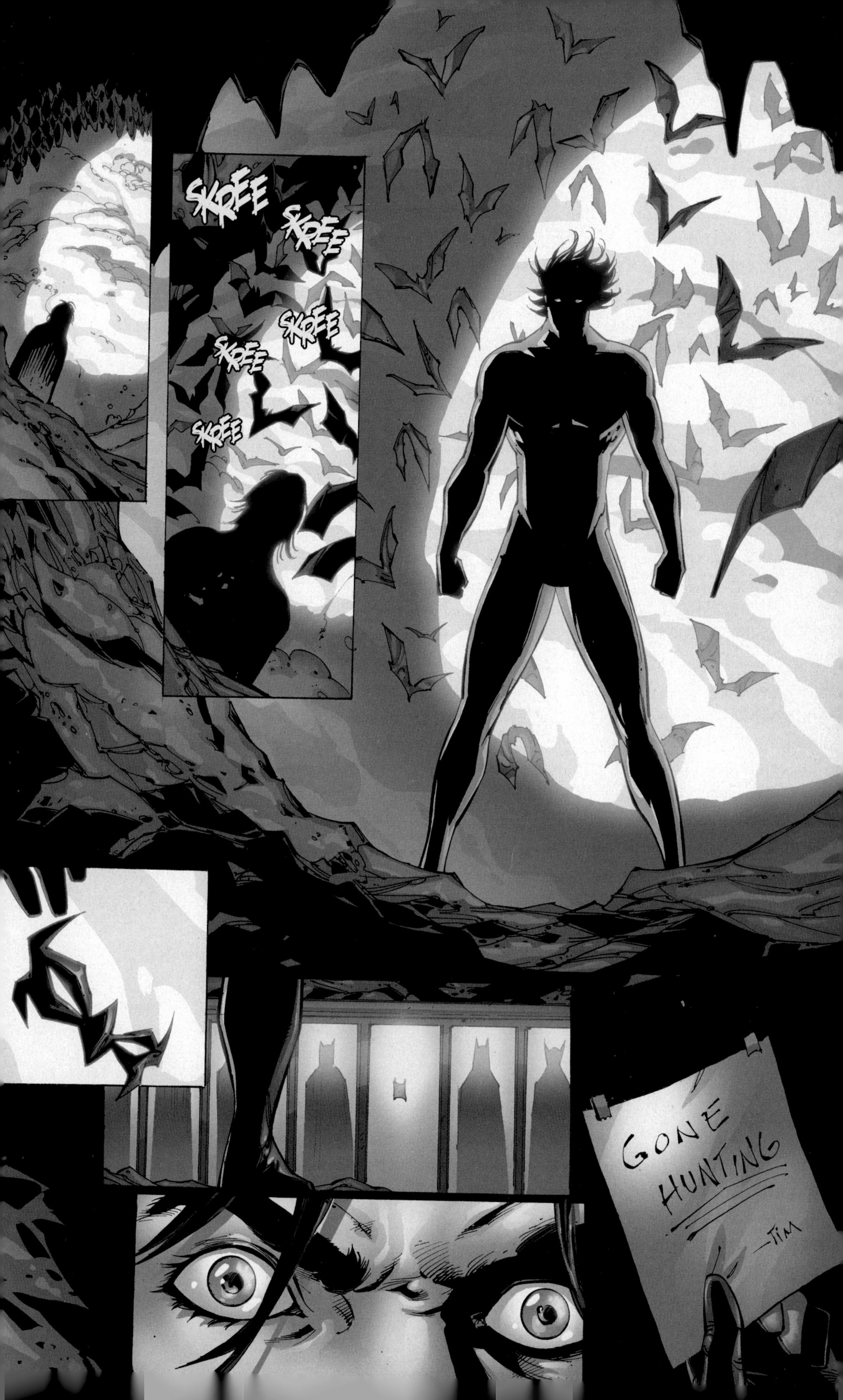
SKREE
SKREE
SKREE
SKREE
SKREE
GONE HUNTING
—TIM

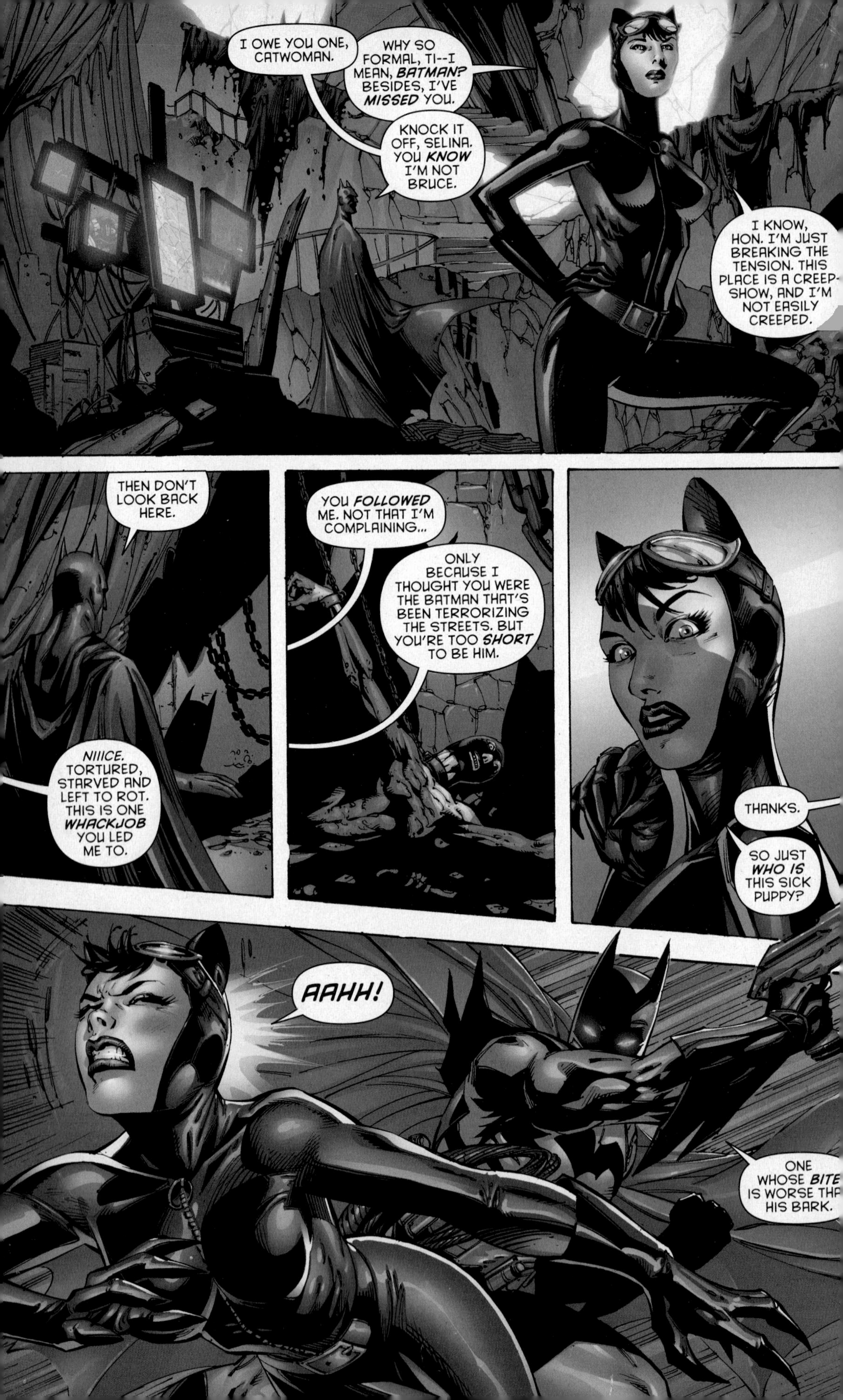
I OWE YOU ONE, CATWOMAN.
WHY SO FORMAL, TI--I MEAN, BATMAN? BESIDES, I'VE MISSED YOU.
KNOCK IT OFF, SELINA. YOU KNOW I'M NOT BRUCE.
I KNOW, HON. I'M JUST BREAKING THE TENSION. THIS PLACE IS A CREEP-SHOW, AND I'M NOT EASILY CREEPED.
THEN DON'T LOOK BACK HERE.
NIIICE. TORTURED, STARVED AND LEFT TO ROT. THIS IS ONE WHACKJOB YOU LED ME TO.
YOU FOLLOWED ME. NOT THAT I'M COMPLAINING...
ONLY BECAUSE I THOUGHT YOU WERE THE BATMAN THAT'S BEEN TERRORIZING THE STREETS. BUT YOU'RE TOO SHORT TO BE HIM.
THANKS.
SO JUST WHO IS THIS SICK PUPPY?
AAHH!
ONE WHOSE BITE IS WORSE THA HIS BARK.

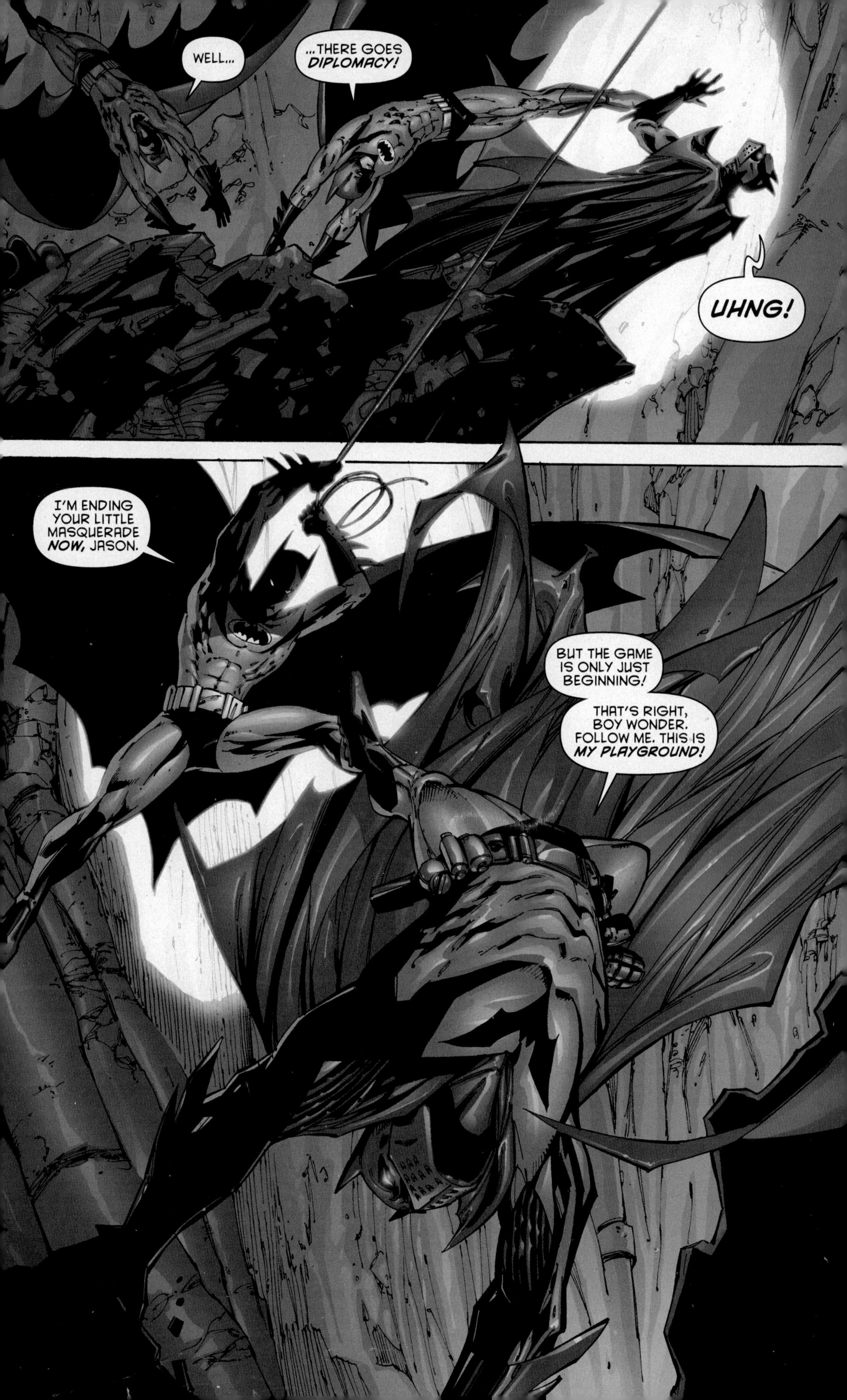
WELL...
...THERE GOES DIPLOMACY!
UHNG!
I'M ENDING YOUR LITTLE MASQUERADE NOW, JASON.
BUT THE GAME IS ONLY JUST BEGINNING!
THAT'S RIGHT, BOY WONDER. FOLLOW ME. THIS IS MY PLAYGROUND!

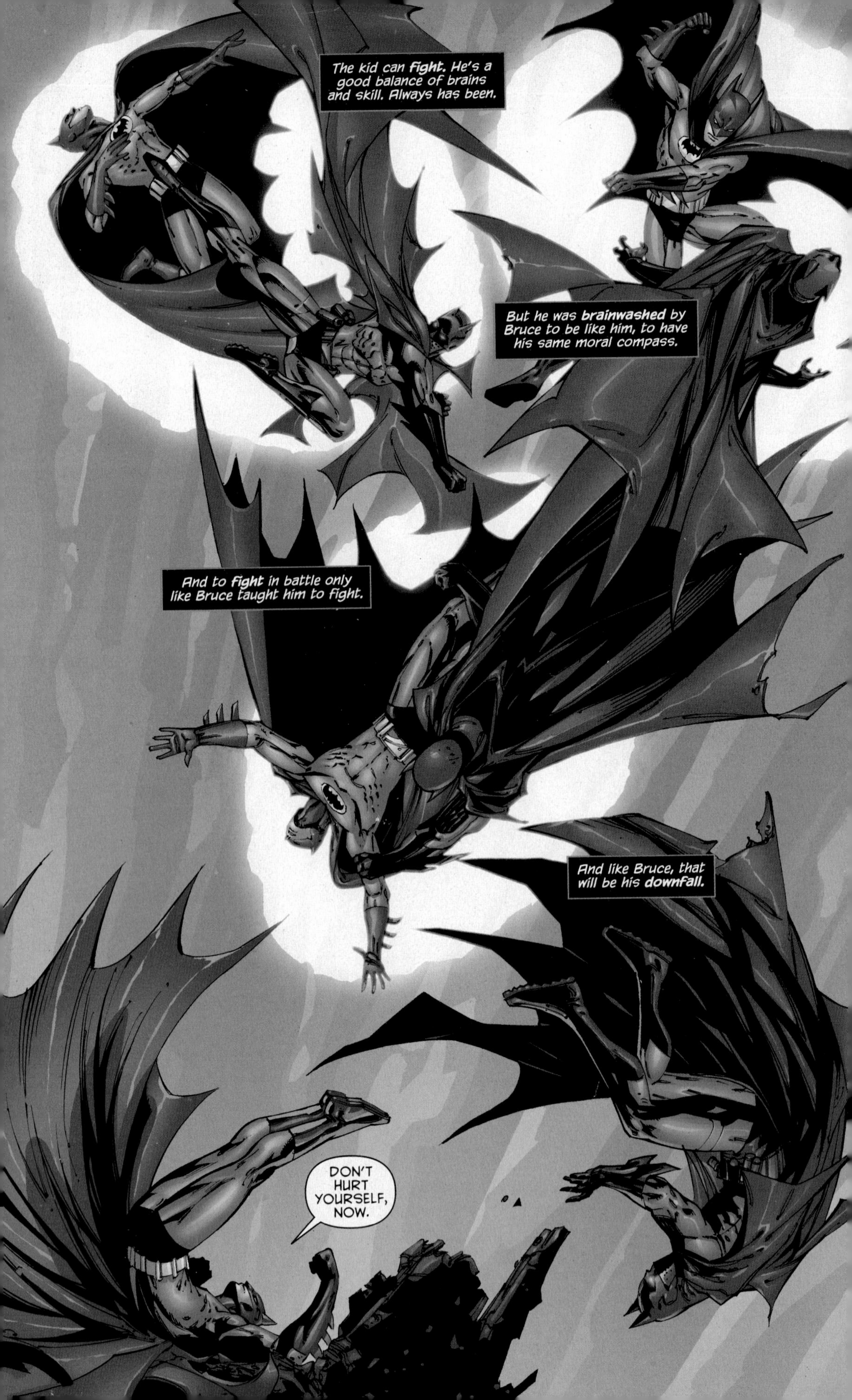
The kid can fight. He's a good balance of brains and skill. Always has been.
But he was brainwashed by Bruce to be like him, to have his same moral compass.
And to fight in battle only like Bruce taught him to fight.
And like Bruce, that will be his downfall.
DON'T HURT YOURSELF, NOW.

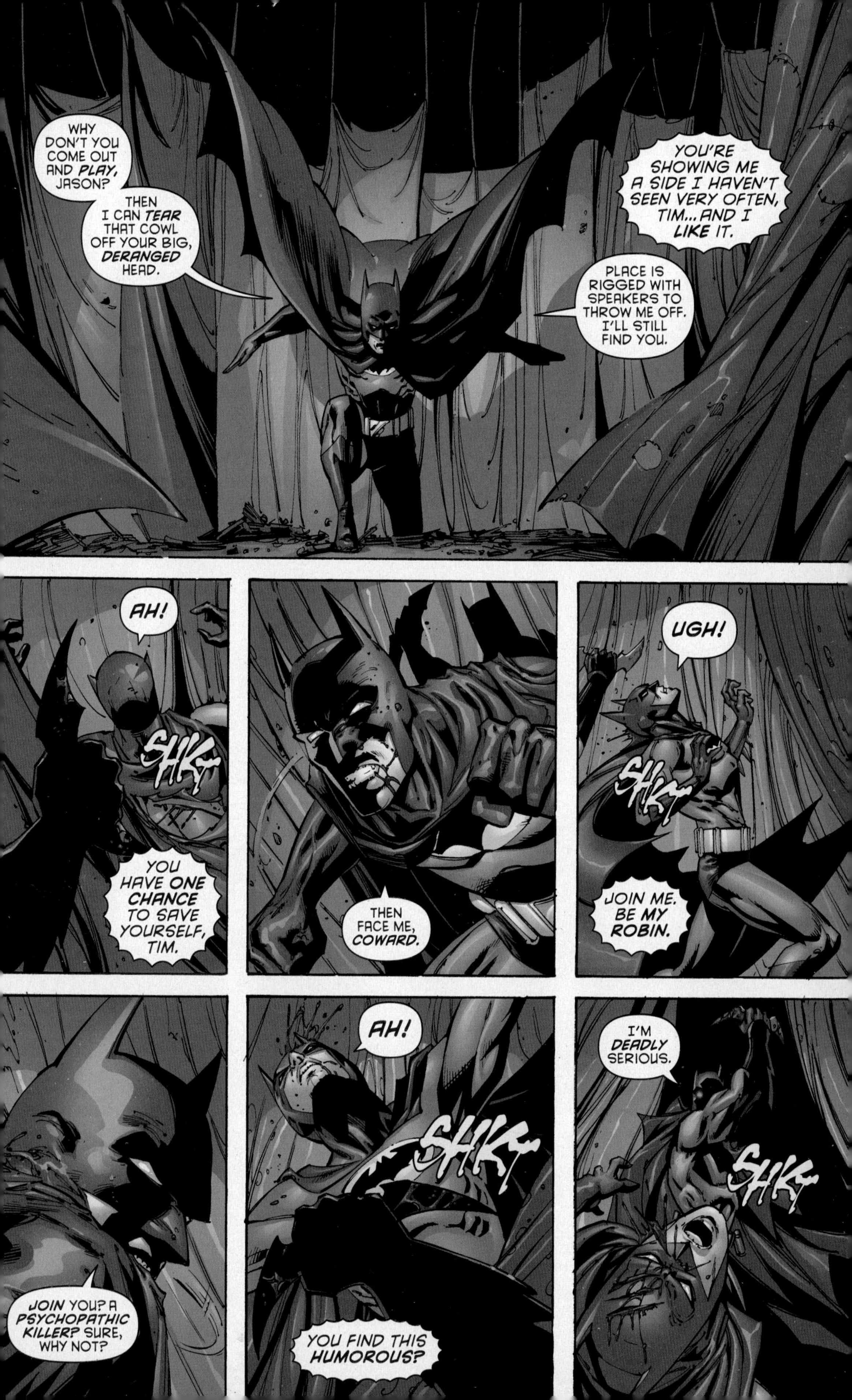
WHY DON'T YOU COME OUT AND PLAY, JASON?
THEN I CAN TEAR THAT COWL OFF YOUR BIG, DERANGED HEAD.
YOU'RE SHOWING ME A SIDE I HAVEN'T SEEN VERY OFTEN, TIM... AND I LIKE IT.
PLACE IS RIGGED WITH SPEAKERS TO THROW ME OFF. I'LL STILL FIND YOU.
AH!
SHK
YOU HAVE ONE CHANCE TO SAVE YOURSELF, TIM.
THEN FACE ME, COWARD.
UGH!
SHK
JOIN ME. BE MY ROBIN.
JOIN YOU? A PSYCHOPATHIC KILLER? SURE, WHY NOT?
AH!
SHK
YOU FIND THIS HUMOROUS?
I'M DEADLY SERIOUS.
SHK

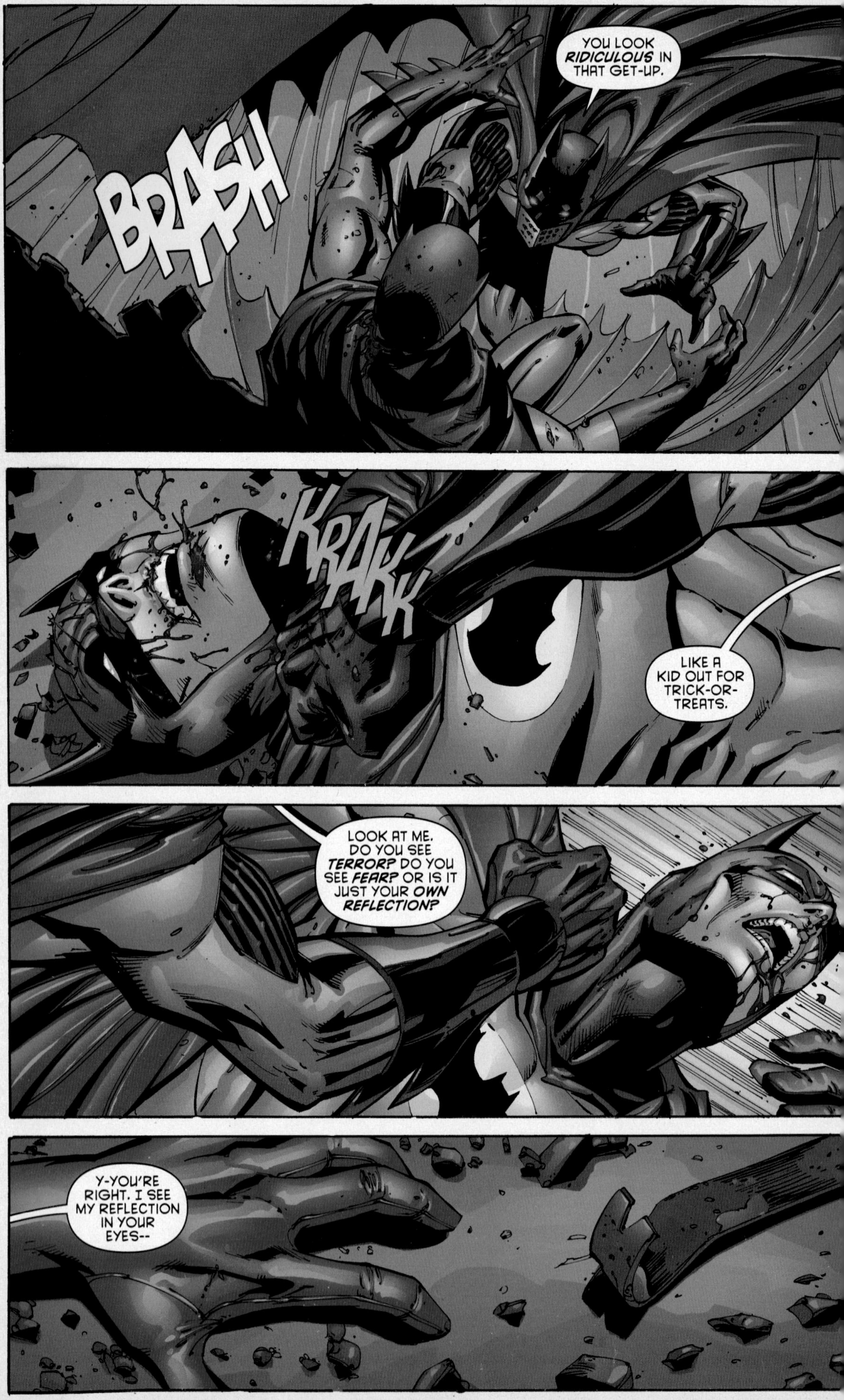
YOU LOOK RIDICULOUS IN THAT GET-UP.
BRASH
KRAKK
LIKE A KID OUT FOR TRICK-OR-TREATS.
LOOK AT ME. DO YOU SEE TERROR? DO YOU SEE FEAR? OR IS IT JUST YOUR OWN REFLECTION?
Y-YOU'RE RIGHT. I SEE MY REFLECTION IN YOUR EYES--

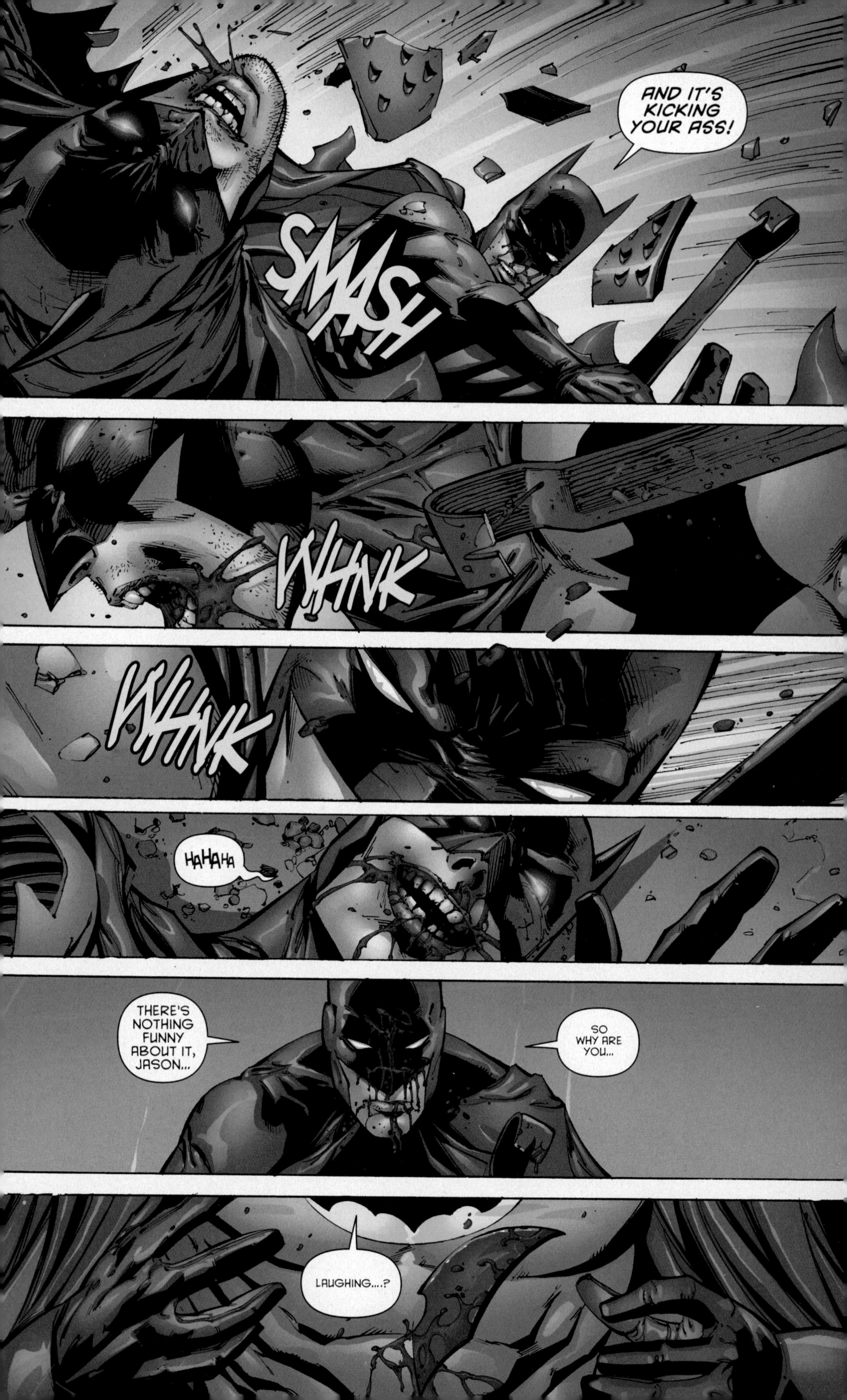
AND IT'S KICKING YOUR ASS!
SMASH
WHNK
WHNK
HAHAHA
THERE'S NOTHING FUNNY ABOUT IT, JASON...
SO WHY ARE YOU...
LAUGHING....?

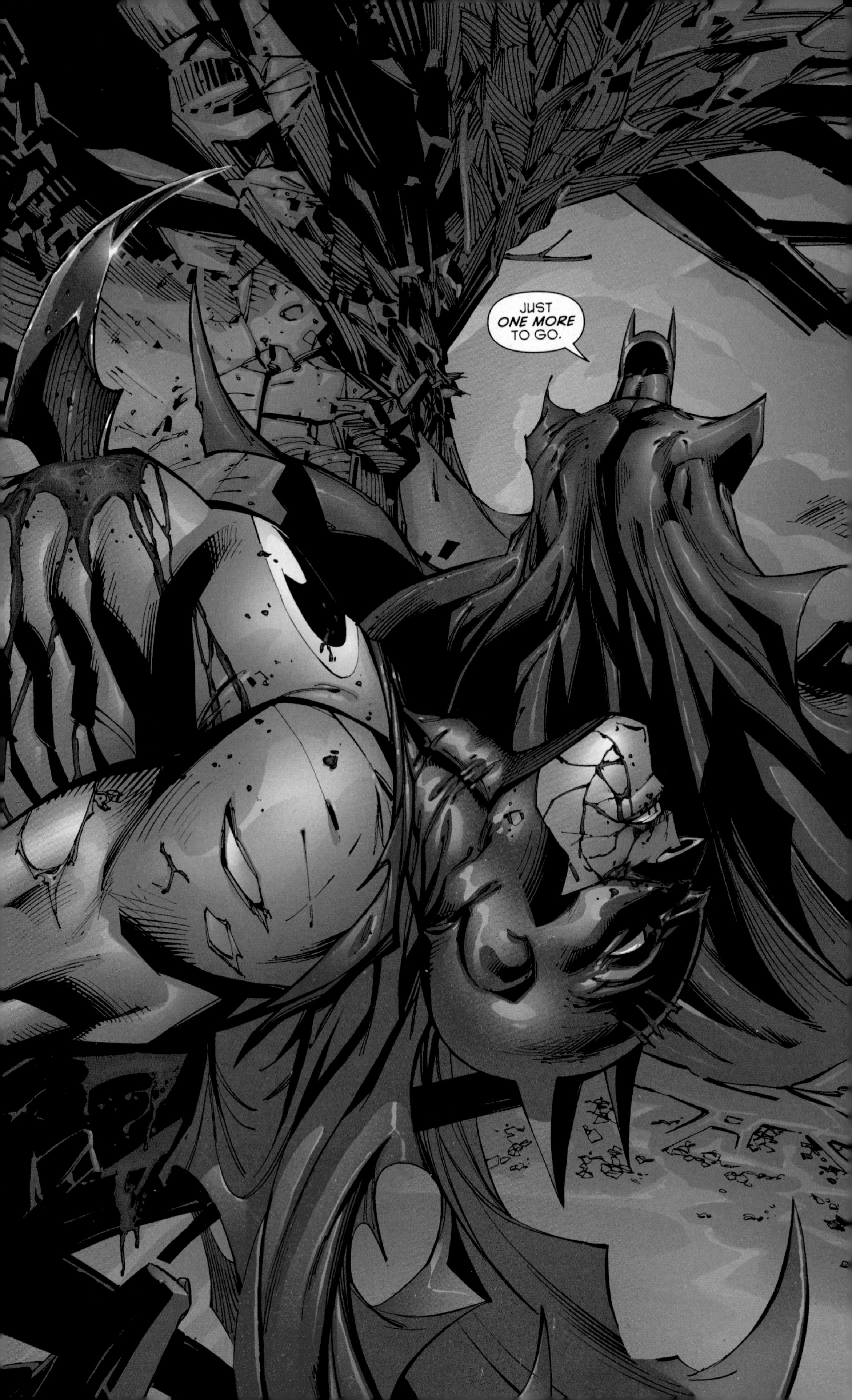
JUST *ONE MORE* TO GO.

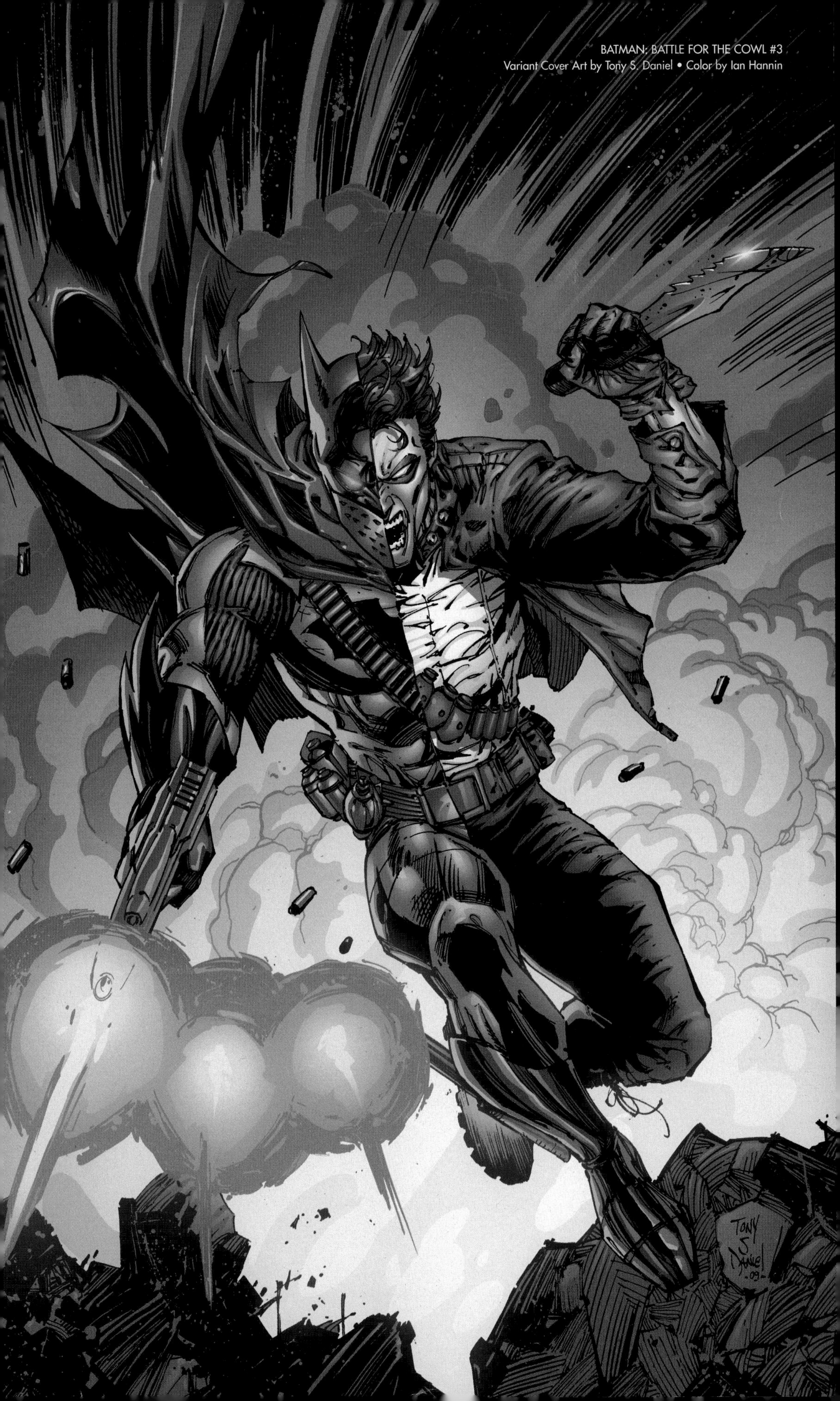

BATMAN: BATTLE FOR THE COWL #3
Variant Cover Art by Tony S. Daniel • Color by Ian Hannin

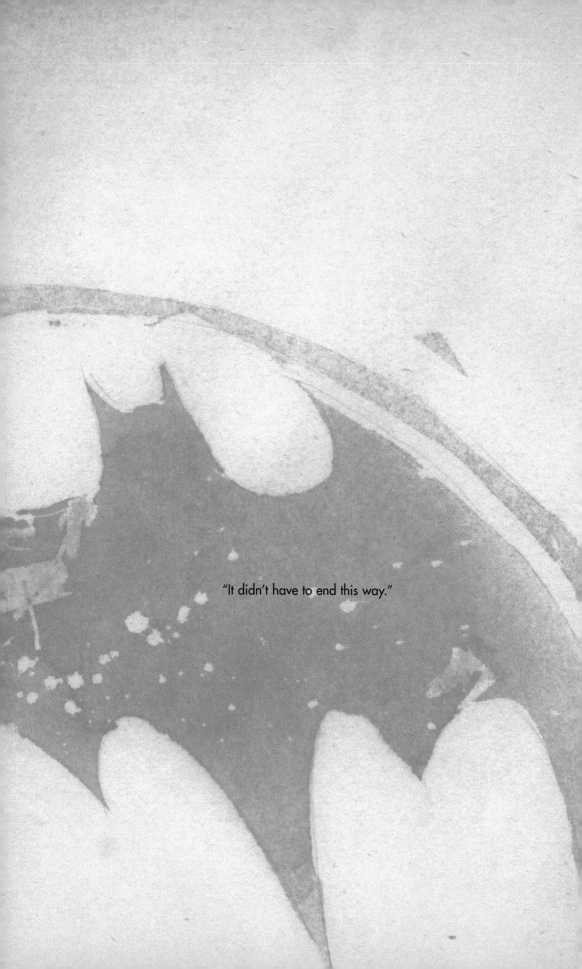

"It didn't have to end this way."

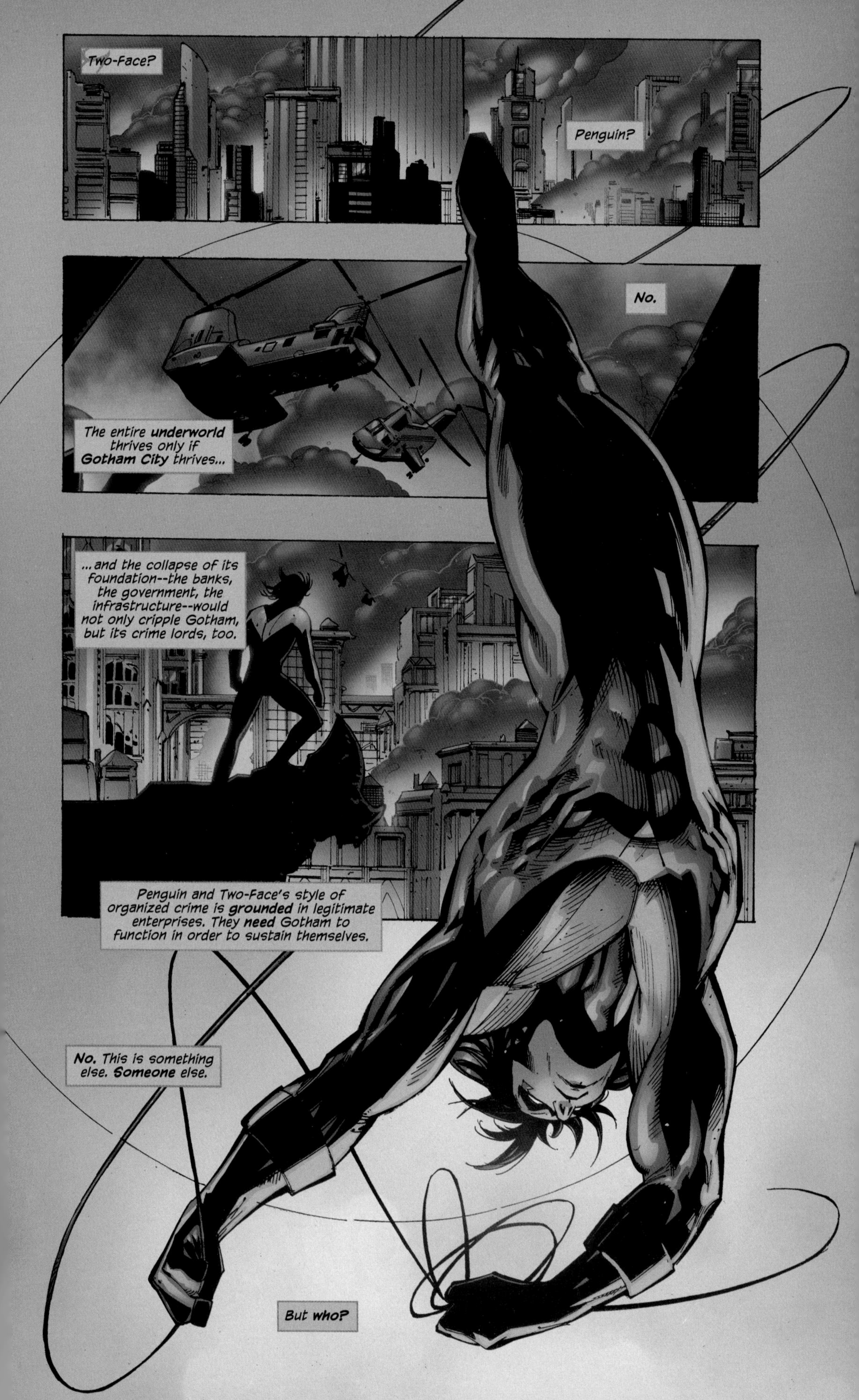

Two-Face?
Penguin?
No.
The entire underworld thrives only if Gotham City thrives...
...and the collapse of its foundation--the banks, the government, the infrastructure--would not only cripple Gotham, but its crime lords, too.
Penguin and Two-Face's style of organized crime is grounded in legitimate enterprises. They need Gotham to function in order to sustain themselves.
No. This is something else. Someone else.
But who?

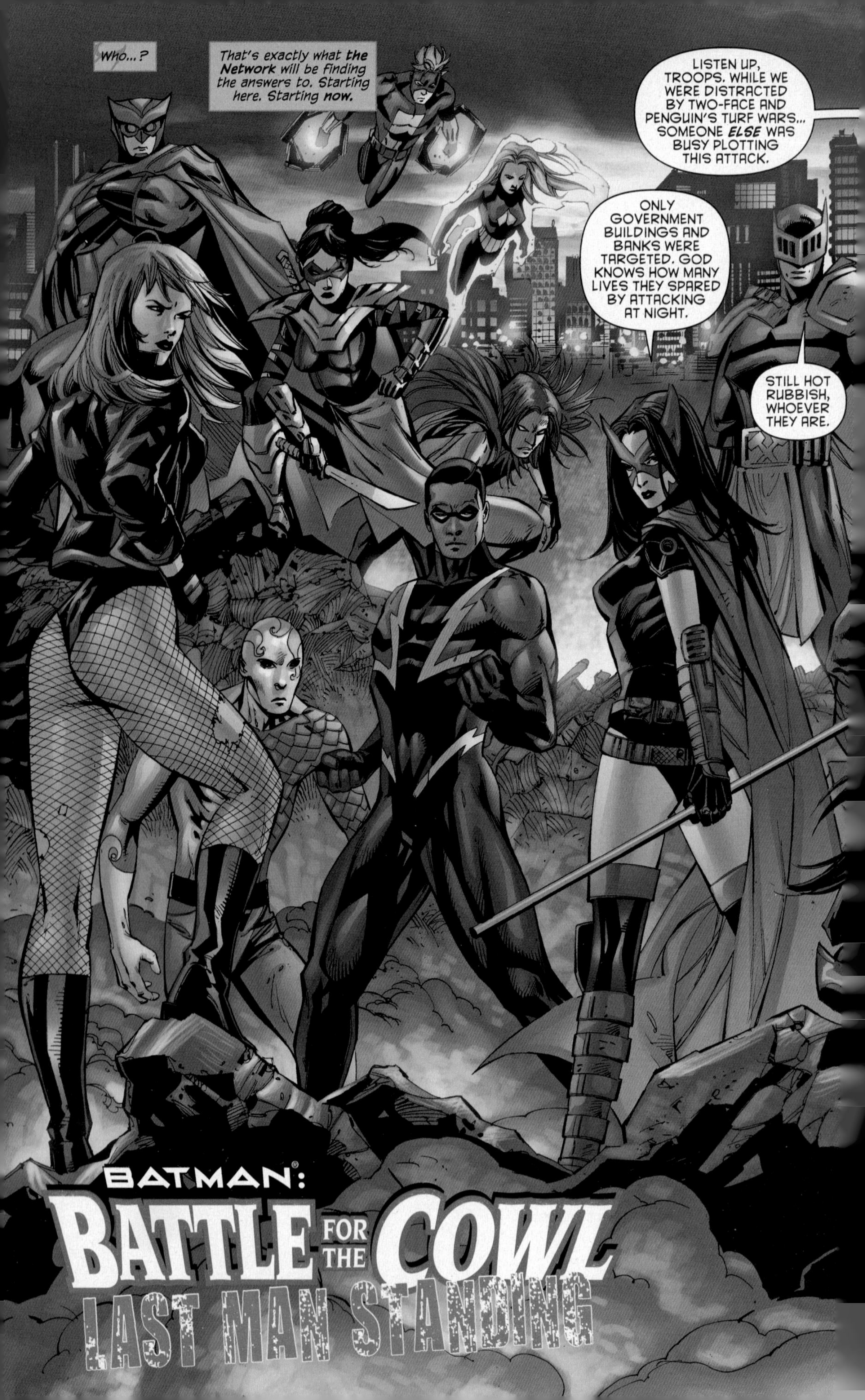
Who...?
That's exactly what the Network will be finding the answers to. Starting here. Starting now.
LISTEN UP, TROOPS. WHILE WE WERE DISTRACTED BY TWO-FACE AND PENGUIN'S TURF WARS... SOMEONE ELSE WAS BUSY PLOTTING THIS ATTACK.
ONLY GOVERNMENT BUILDINGS AND BANKS WERE TARGETED. GOD KNOWS HOW MANY LIVES THEY SPARED BY ATTACKING AT NIGHT.
STILL HOT RUBBISH, WHOEVER THEY ARE.
BATMAN®:
BATTLE FOR THE COWL
LAST MAN STANDING

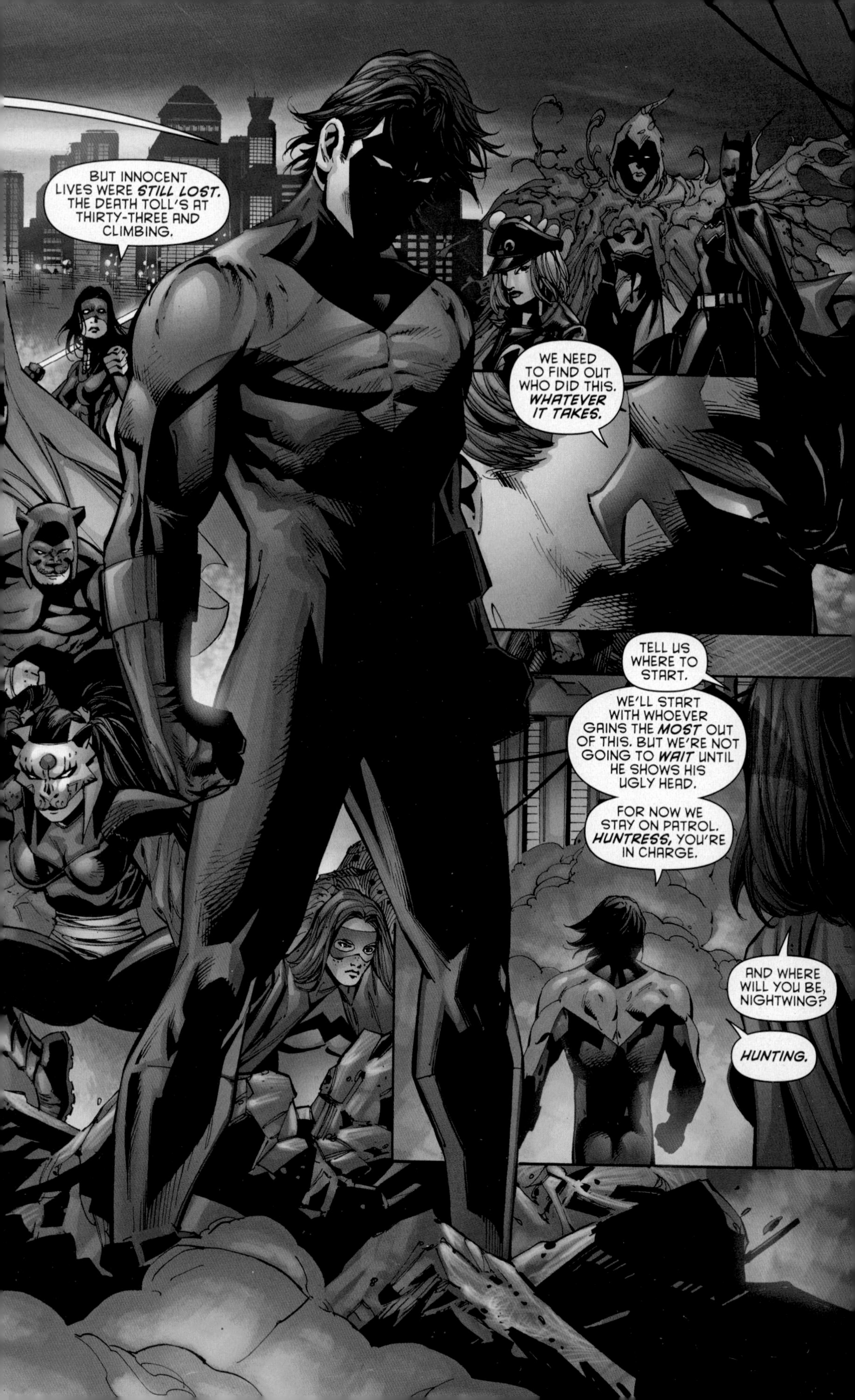
BUT INNOCENT LIVES WERE STILL LOST. THE DEATH TOLL'S AT THIRTY-THREE AND CLIMBING.
WE NEED TO FIND OUT WHO DID THIS. WHATEVER IT TAKES.
TELL US WHERE TO START.
WE'LL START WITH WHOEVER GAINS THE MOST OUT OF THIS. BUT WE'RE NOT GOING TO WAIT UNTIL HE SHOWS HIS UGLY HEAD.
FOR NOW WE STAY ON PATROL. HUNTRESS, YOU'RE IN CHARGE.
AND WHERE WILL YOU BE, NIGHTWING?
HUNTING.

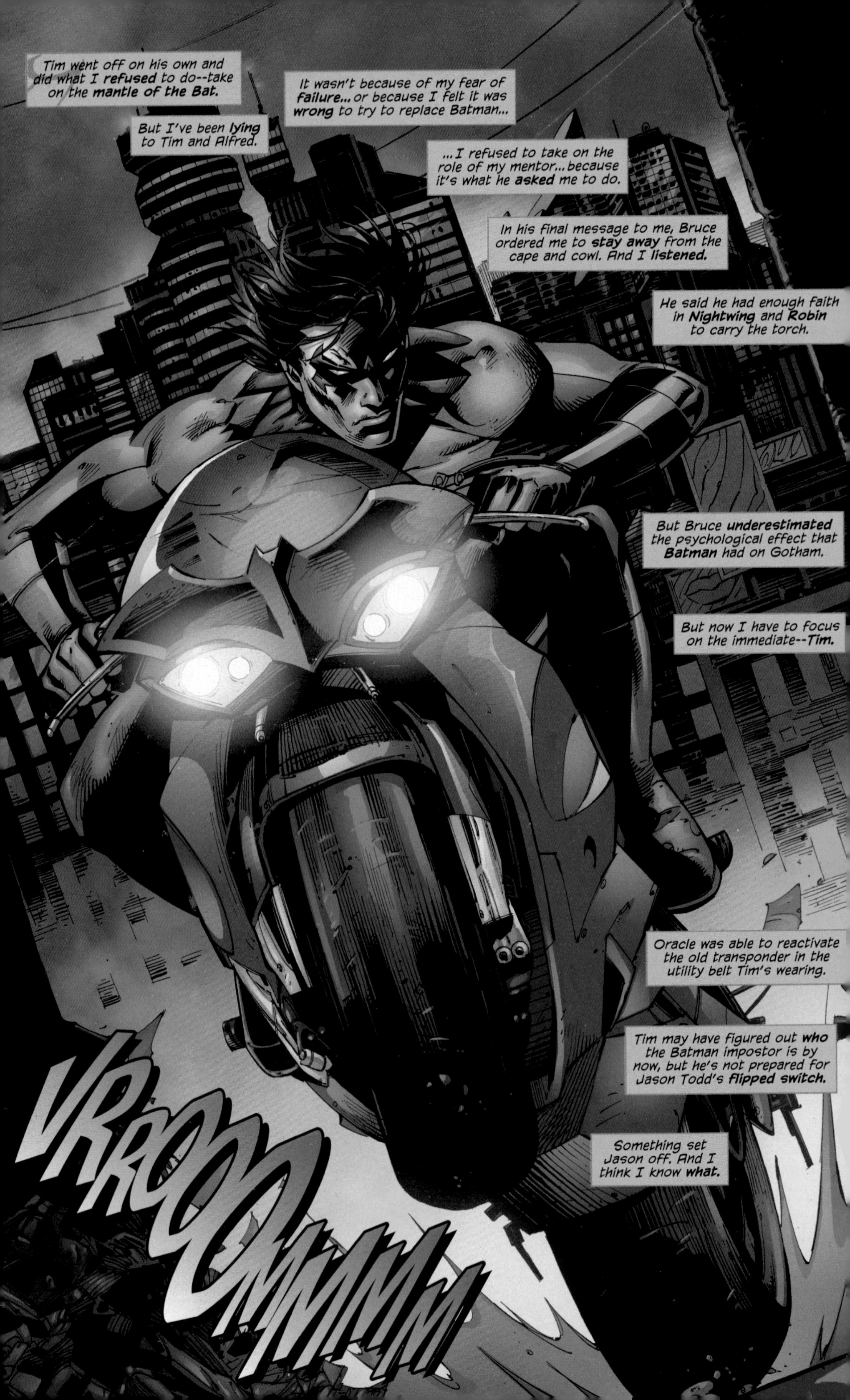
Tim went off on his own and did what I refused to do--take on the mantle of the Bat.
But I've been lying to Tim and Alfred.
It wasn't because of my fear of failure... or because I felt it was wrong to try to replace Batman...
...I refused to take on the role of my mentor... because it's what he asked me to do.
In his final message to me, Bruce ordered me to stay away from the cape and cowl. And I listened.
He said he had enough faith in Nightwing and Robin to carry the torch.
But Bruce underestimated the psychological effect that Batman had on Gotham.
But now I have to focus on the immediate--Tim.
Oracle was able to reactivate the old transponder in the utility belt Tim's wearing.
Tim may have figured out who the Batman impostor is by now, but he's not prepared for Jason Todd's flipped switch.
Something set Jason off. And I think I know what.
VRROOOMMMMM

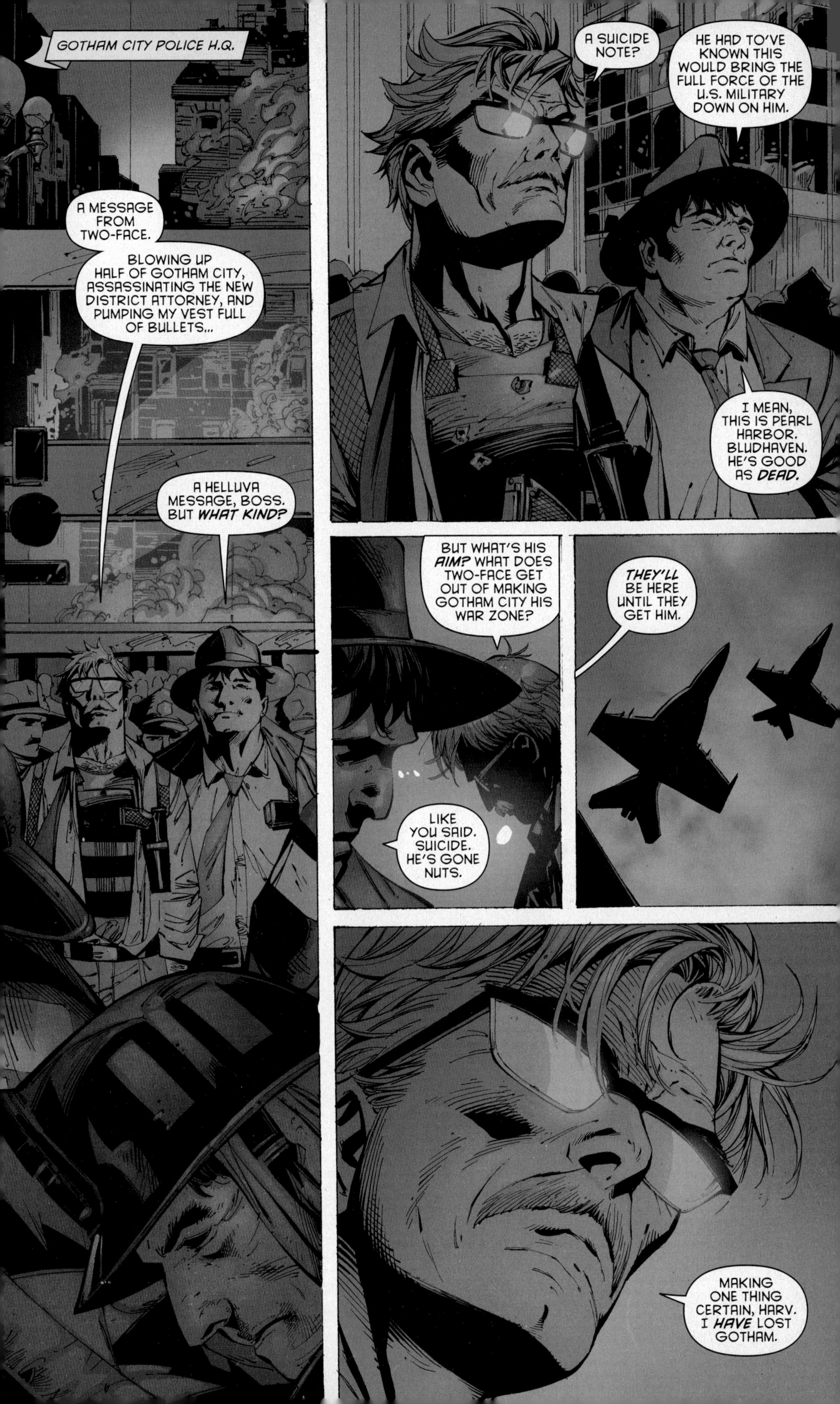
GOTHAM CITY POLICE H.Q.
A MESSAGE FROM TWO-FACE.
BLOWING UP HALF OF GOTHAM CITY, ASSASSINATING THE NEW DISTRICT ATTORNEY, AND PUMPING MY VEST FULL OF BULLETS...
A HELLUVA MESSAGE, BOSS. BUT WHAT KIND?
A SUICIDE NOTE?
HE HAD TO'VE KNOWN THIS WOULD BRING THE FULL FORCE OF THE U.S. MILITARY DOWN ON HIM.
I MEAN, THIS IS PEARL HARBOR. BLUDHAVEN. HE'S GOOD AS DEAD.
BUT WHAT'S HIS AIM? WHAT DOES TWO-FACE GET OUT OF MAKING GOTHAM CITY HIS WAR ZONE?
LIKE YOU SAID. SUICIDE. HE'S GONE NUTS.
THEY'LL BE HERE UNTIL THEY GET HIM.
MAKING ONE THING CERTAIN, HARV. I HAVE LOST GOTHAM.

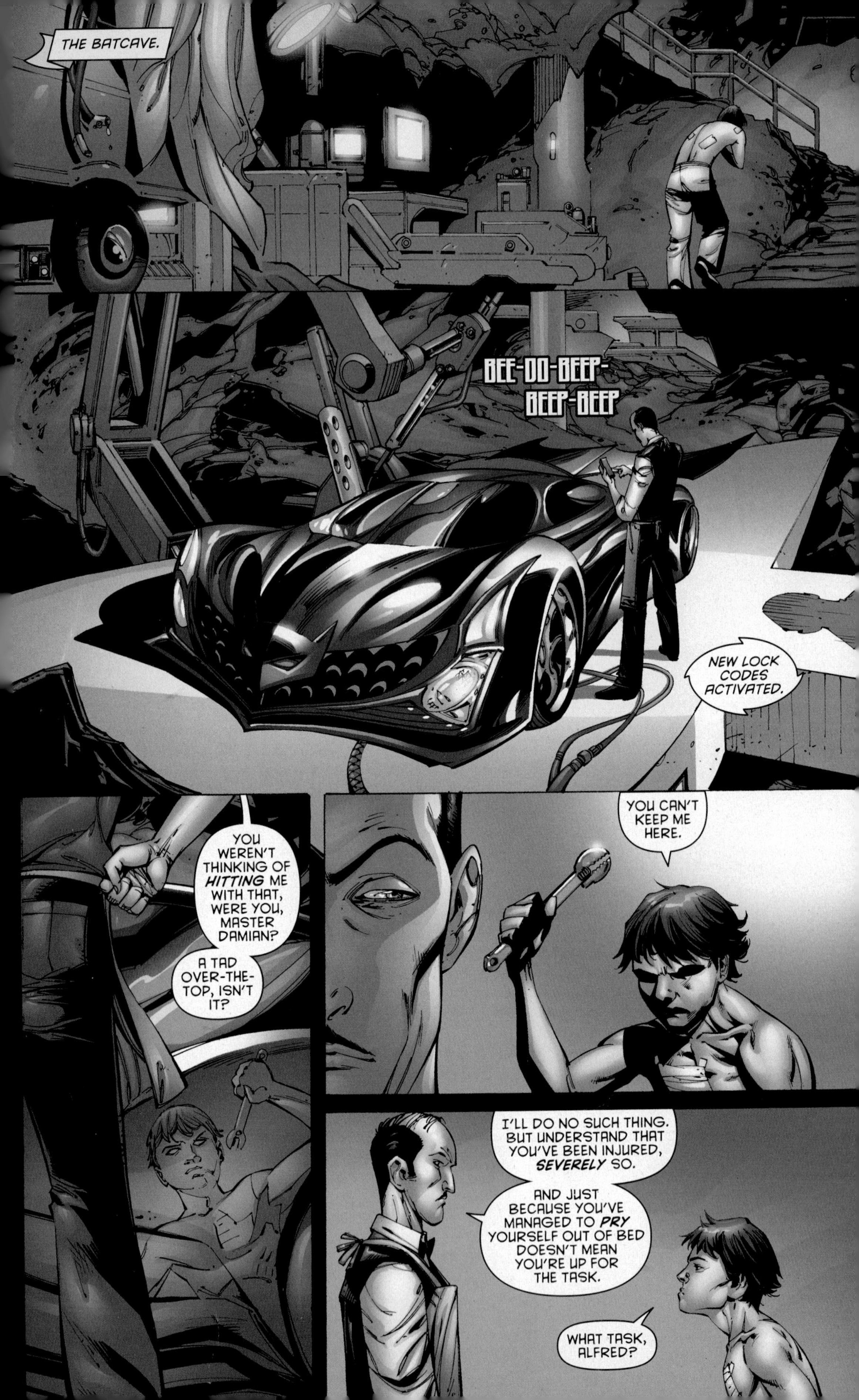
THE BATCAVE.
BEE-DO-BEEP-BEEP-BEEP
NEW LOCK CODES ACTIVATED.
YOU WEREN'T THINKING OF HITTING ME WITH THAT, WERE YOU, MASTER DAMIAN?
A TAD OVER-THE-TOP, ISN'T IT?
YOU CAN'T KEEP ME HERE.
I'LL DO NO SUCH THING. BUT UNDERSTAND THAT YOU'VE BEEN INJURED, SEVERELY SO.
AND JUST BECAUSE YOU'VE MANAGED TO PRY YOURSELF OUT OF BED DOESN'T MEAN YOU'RE UP FOR THE TASK.
WHAT TASK, ALFRED?

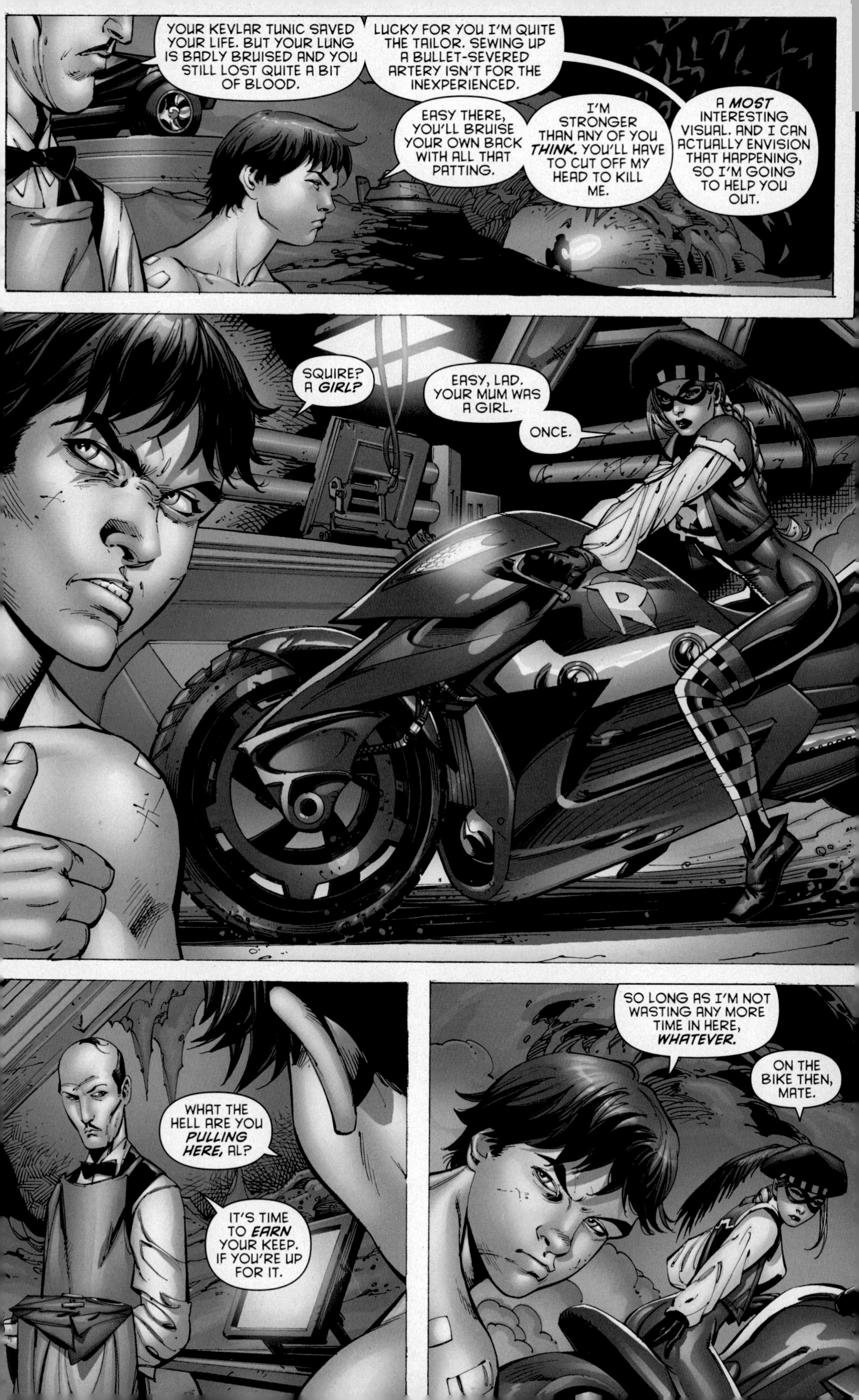
YOUR KEVLAR TUNIC SAVED YOUR LIFE. BUT YOUR LUNG IS BADLY BRUISED AND YOU STILL LOST QUITE A BIT OF BLOOD.
LUCKY FOR YOU I'M QUITE THE TAILOR. SEWING UP A BULLET-SEVERED ARTERY ISN'T FOR THE INEXPERIENCED.
EASY THERE, YOU'LL BRUISE YOUR OWN BACK WITH ALL THAT PATTING.
I'M STRONGER THAN ANY OF YOU *THINK.* YOU'LL HAVE TO CUT OFF MY HEAD TO KILL ME.
A *MOST* INTERESTING VISUAL. AND I CAN ACTUALLY ENVISION THAT HAPPENING, SO I'M GOING TO HELP YOU OUT.
SQUIRE? A *GIRL?*
EASY, LAD. YOUR MUM WAS A GIRL.
ONCE.
WHAT THE HELL ARE YOU *PULLING HERE,* AL?
IT'S TIME TO *EARN* YOUR KEEP. IF YOU'RE UP FOR IT.
SO LONG AS I'M NOT WASTING ANY MORE TIME IN HERE, *WHATEVER.*
ON THE BIKE THEN, MATE.

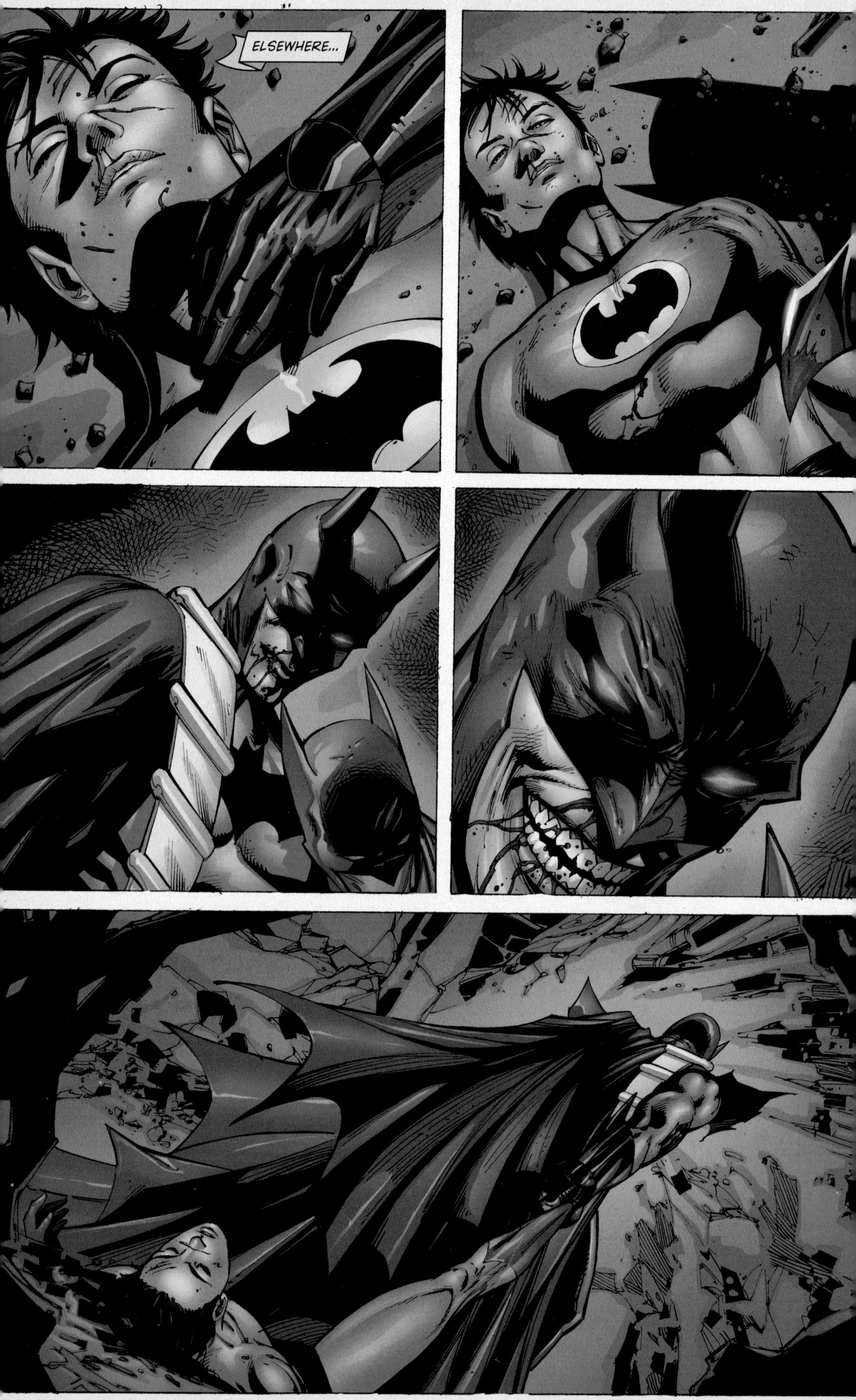
ELSEWHERE...

THIS IS VICKI VALE REPORTING LIVE WITH BREAKING NEWS FROM THE 52ND BLOCK OF BRIDGE STREET--

--WHERE ARMY BLACKHAWKS ARE BATTERING A SUSPECTED TWO-FACE STRONGHOLD.

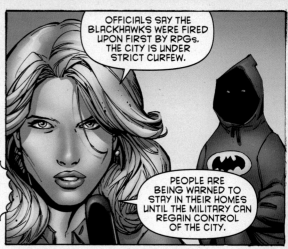

OFFICIALS SAY THE BLACKHAWKS WERE FIRED UPON FIRST BY RPGs. THE CITY IS UNDER STRICT CURFEW.

PEOPLE ARE BEING WARNED TO STAY IN THEIR HOMES UNTIL THE MILITARY CAN REGAIN CONTROL OF THE CITY.

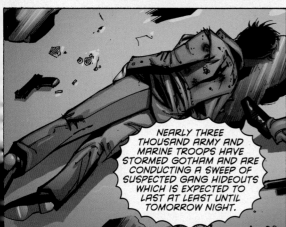

NEARLY THREE THOUSAND ARMY AND MARINE TROOPS HAVE STORMED GOTHAM AND ARE CONDUCTING A SWEEP OF SUSPECTED GANG HIDEOUTS WHICH IS EXPECTED TO LAST AT LEAST UNTIL TOMORROW NIGHT.

THE TARGETS OF THE RAIDS? HARVEY DENT, A.K.A. TWO-FACE, AND HIS ARCH ENEMY, OSWALD COBBLEPOT--

--A.K.A. THE PENGUIN. BOTH ENGAGED IN A BLOODY STREET WAR FOR CONTROL OF GOTHAM'S UNDERWORLD.

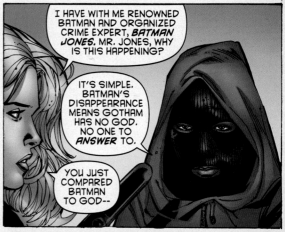

I HAVE WITH ME RENOWNED BATMAN AND ORGANIZED CRIME EXPERT, *BATMAN JONES.* MR. JONES, WHY IS THIS HAPPENING?

IT'S SIMPLE. BATMAN'S DISAPPEARANCE MEANS GOTHAM HAS NO GOD. NO ONE TO *ANSWER* TO.

YOU JUST COMPARED BATMAN TO GOD--

ISN'T IT CLEAR THAT BATMAN ISN'T JUST A *MAN?* HE'S FEAR, HE'S CONSEQUENCE, HE'S RETRIBUTION... I CAN GO ON.

THIS IS JUST THE *BEGINNING,* IF YOU ASK M--

CLK

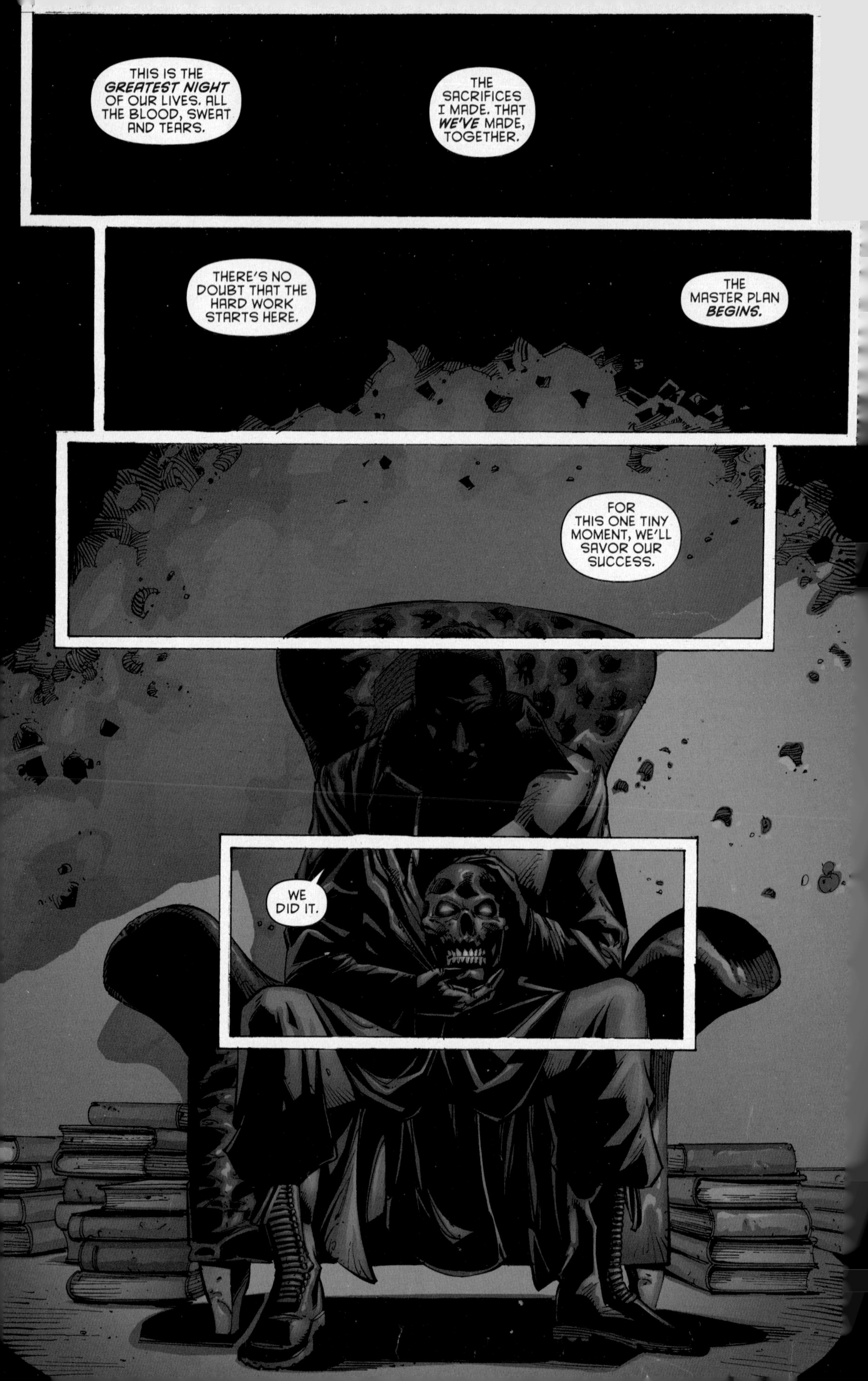
THIS IS THE GREATEST NIGHT OF OUR LIVES. ALL THE BLOOD, SWEAT AND TEARS.
THE SACRIFICES I MADE. THAT WE'VE MADE, TOGETHER.
THERE'S NO DOUBT THAT THE HARD WORK STARTS HERE.
THE MASTER PLAN BEGINS.
FOR THIS ONE TINY MOMENT, WE'LL SAVOR OUR SUCCESS.
WE DID IT.

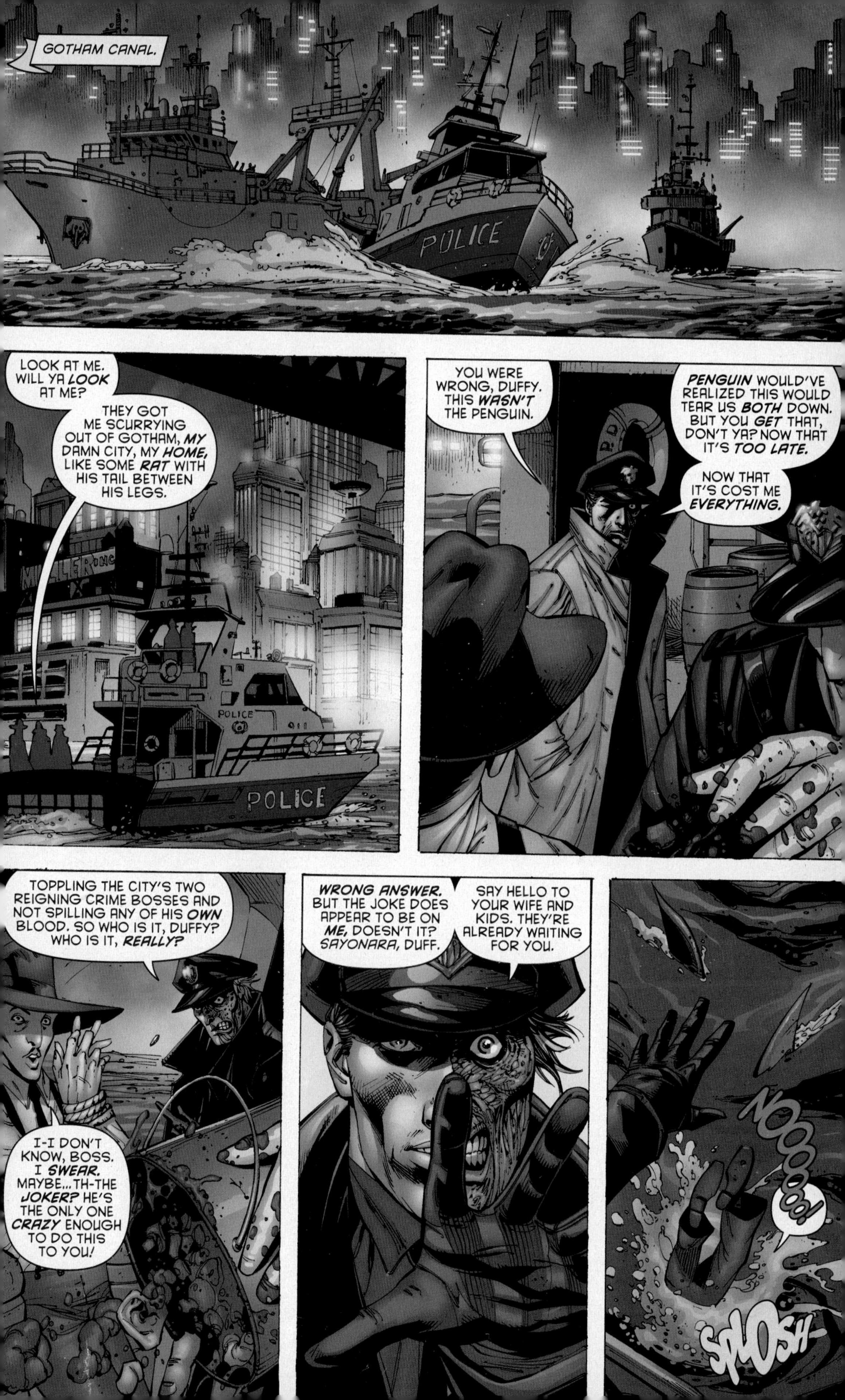
GOTHAM CANAL.
LOOK AT ME. WILL YA LOOK AT ME?
THEY GOT ME SCURRYING OUT OF GOTHAM, MY DAMN CITY, MY HOME, LIKE SOME RAT WITH HIS TAIL BETWEEN HIS LEGS.
YOU WERE WRONG, DUFFY. THIS WASN'T THE PENGUIN.
PENGUIN WOULD'VE REALIZED THIS WOULD TEAR US BOTH DOWN. BUT YOU GET THAT, DON'T YA? NOW THAT IT'S TOO LATE.
NOW THAT IT'S COST ME EVERYTHING.
TOPPLING THE CITY'S TWO REIGNING CRIME BOSSES AND NOT SPILLING ANY OF HIS OWN BLOOD. SO WHO IS IT, DUFFY? WHO IS IT, REALLY?
I-I DON'T KNOW, BOSS. I SWEAR. MAYBE...TH-THE JOKER? HE'S THE ONLY ONE CRAZY ENOUGH TO DO THIS TO YOU!
WRONG ANSWER. BUT THE JOKE DOES APPEAR TO BE ON ME, DOESN'T IT? SAYONARA, DUFF.
SAY HELLO TO YOUR WIFE AND KIDS. THEY'RE ALREADY WAITING FOR YOU.
NOOOOOOO!
SPLOSH

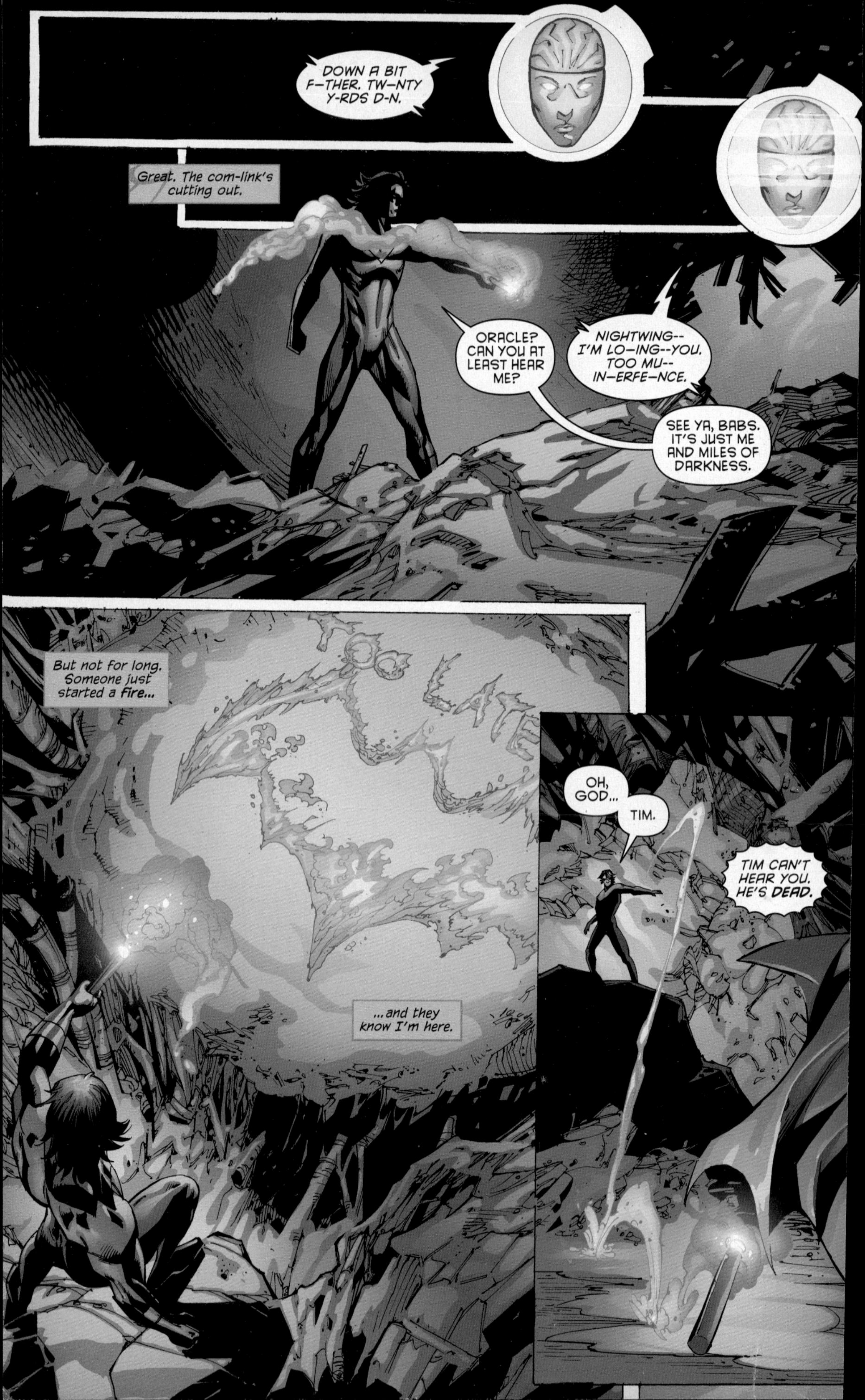
DOWN A BIT F—THER. TW—NTY Y-RDS D-N.
Great. The com-link's cutting out.
ORACLE? CAN YOU AT LEAST HEAR ME?
NIGHTWING-- I'M LO-ING--YOU. TOO MU-- IN-ERFE-NCE.
SEE YA, BABS. IT'S JUST ME AND MILES OF DARKNESS.
But not for long. Someone just started a *fire*...
TOO LATE
...and they know I'm here.
OH, GOD...
TIM.
TIM CAN'T HEAR YOU. HE'S *DEAD*.

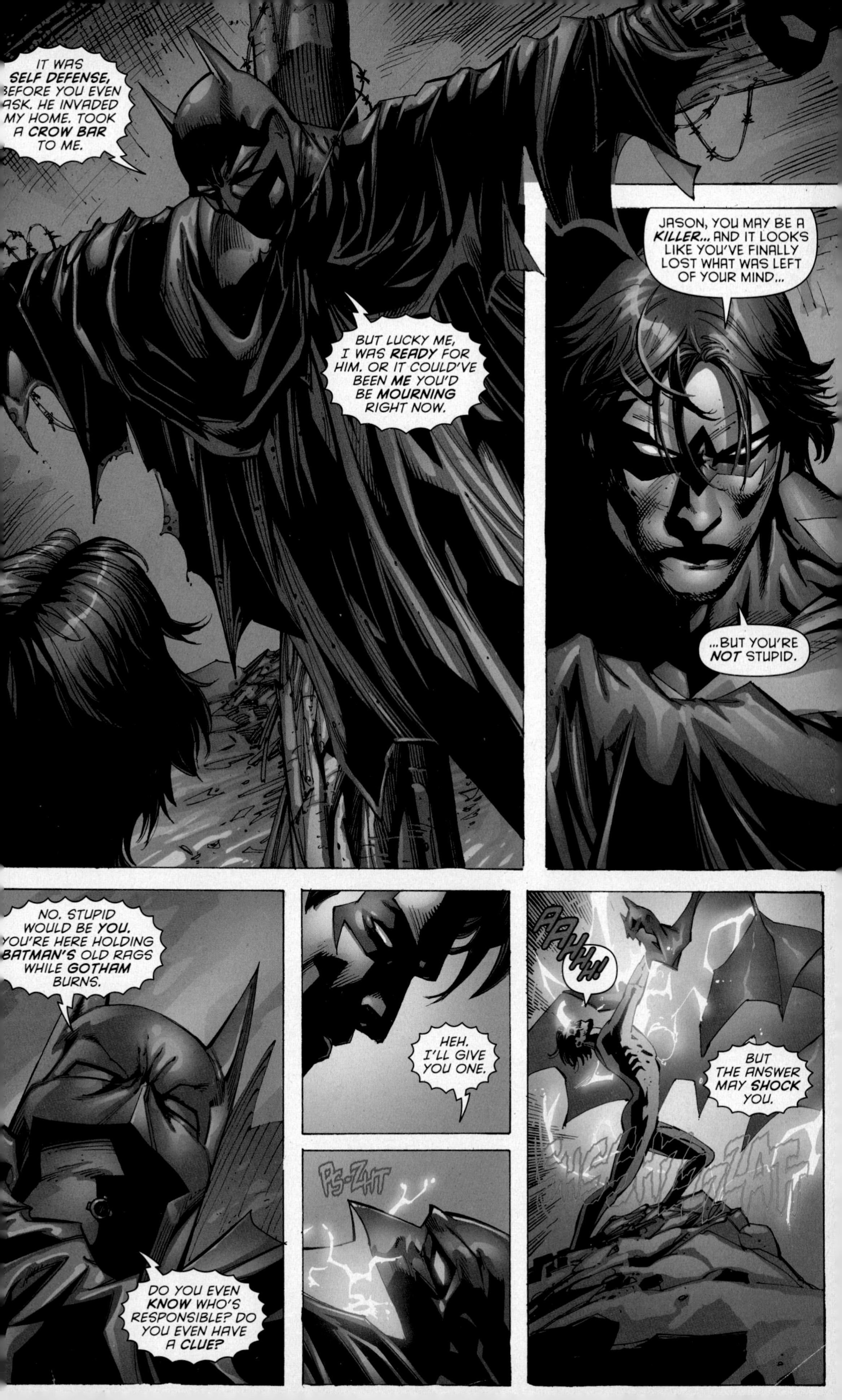
IT WAS SELF DEFENSE, BEFORE YOU EVEN ASK. HE INVADED MY HOME. TOOK A CROW BAR TO ME.
BUT LUCKY ME, I WAS READY FOR HIM. OR IT COULD'VE BEEN ME YOU'D BE MOURNING RIGHT NOW.
JASON, YOU MAY BE A KILLER... AND IT LOOKS LIKE YOU'VE FINALLY LOST WHAT WAS LEFT OF YOUR MIND...
...BUT YOU'RE NOT STUPID.
NO. STUPID WOULD BE YOU. YOU'RE HERE HOLDING BATMAN'S OLD RAGS WHILE GOTHAM BURNS.
DO YOU EVEN KNOW WHO'S RESPONSIBLE? DO YOU EVEN HAVE A CLUE?
HEH. I'LL GIVE YOU ONE.
PS-ZHT
AAHHH!
BUT THE ANSWER MAY SHOCK YOU.

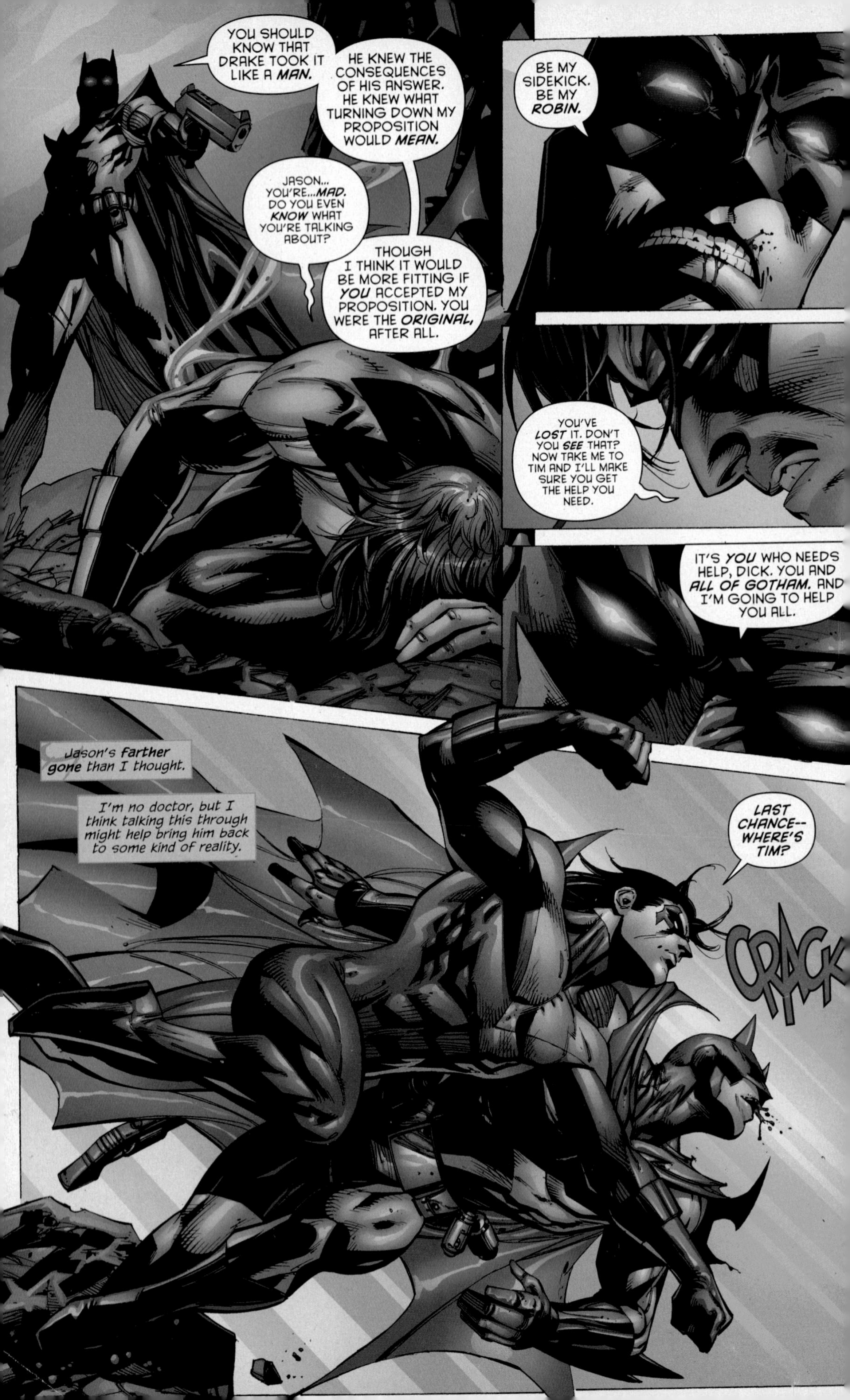

YOU SHOULD KNOW THAT DRAKE TOOK IT LIKE A *MAN.*
HE KNEW THE CONSEQUENCES OF HIS ANSWER. HE KNEW WHAT TURNING DOWN MY PROPOSITION WOULD *MEAN.*
JASON... YOU'RE...*MAD.* DO YOU EVEN *KNOW* WHAT YOU'RE TALKING ABOUT?
THOUGH I THINK IT WOULD BE MORE FITTING IF *YOU* ACCEPTED MY PROPOSITION. YOU WERE THE *ORIGINAL,* AFTER ALL.
BE MY SIDEKICK. BE MY *ROBIN.*
YOU'VE *LOST* IT. DON'T YOU *SEE* THAT? NOW TAKE ME TO TIM AND I'LL MAKE SURE YOU GET THE HELP YOU NEED.
IT'S *YOU* WHO NEEDS HELP, DICK. YOU AND *ALL OF GOTHAM.* AND I'M GOING TO HELP YOU ALL.
Jason's **farther gone** than I thought.
I'm no doctor, but I think talking this through might help bring him back to some kind of reality.
LAST CHANCE-- WHERE'S TIM?
CRACK

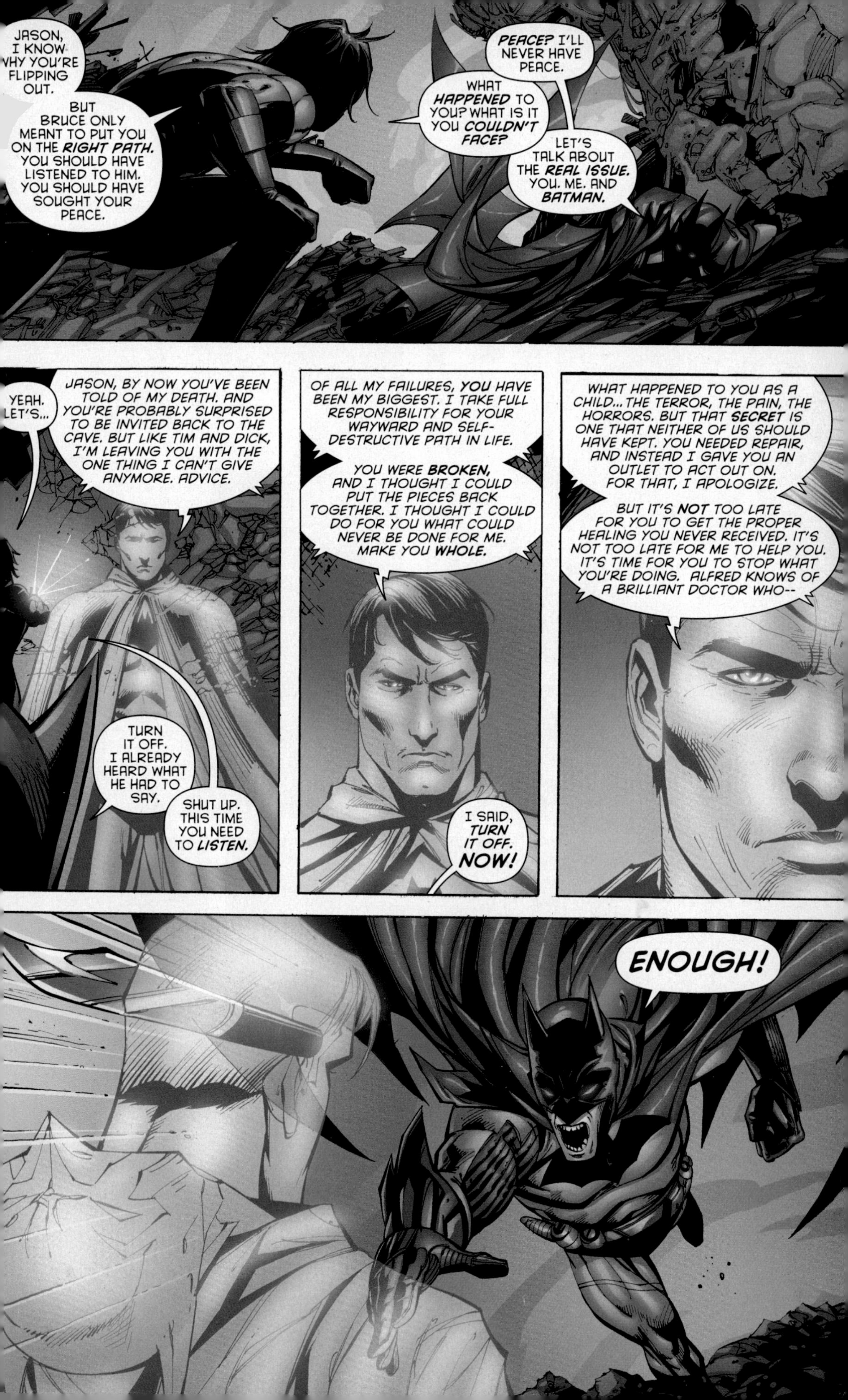

JASON, I KNOW WHY YOU'RE FLIPPING OUT.
BUT BRUCE ONLY MEANT TO PUT YOU ON THE RIGHT PATH. YOU SHOULD HAVE LISTENED TO HIM. YOU SHOULD HAVE SOUGHT YOUR PEACE.
PEACE? I'LL NEVER HAVE PEACE.
WHAT HAPPENED TO YOU? WHAT IS IT YOU COULDN'T FACE?
LET'S TALK ABOUT THE REAL ISSUE. YOU. ME. AND BATMAN.
YEAH. LET'S...
JASON, BY NOW YOU'VE BEEN TOLD OF MY DEATH. AND YOU'RE PROBABLY SURPRISED TO BE INVITED BACK TO THE CAVE. BUT LIKE TIM AND DICK, I'M LEAVING YOU WITH THE ONE THING I CAN'T GIVE ANYMORE. ADVICE.
TURN IT OFF. I ALREADY HEARD WHAT HE HAD TO SAY.
SHUT UP. THIS TIME YOU NEED TO LISTEN.
OF ALL MY FAILURES, YOU HAVE BEEN MY BIGGEST. I TAKE FULL RESPONSIBILITY FOR YOUR WAYWARD AND SELF-DESTRUCTIVE PATH IN LIFE.
YOU WERE BROKEN, AND I THOUGHT I COULD PUT THE PIECES BACK TOGETHER. I THOUGHT I COULD DO FOR YOU WHAT COULD NEVER BE DONE FOR ME. MAKE YOU WHOLE.
I SAID, TURN IT OFF. NOW!
WHAT HAPPENED TO YOU AS A CHILD... THE TERROR, THE PAIN, THE HORRORS. BUT THAT SECRET IS ONE THAT NEITHER OF US SHOULD HAVE KEPT. YOU NEEDED REPAIR, AND INSTEAD I GAVE YOU AN OUTLET TO ACT OUT ON. FOR THAT, I APOLOGIZE.
BUT IT'S NOT TOO LATE FOR YOU TO GET THE PROPER HEALING YOU NEVER RECEIVED. IT'S NOT TOO LATE FOR ME TO HELP YOU. IT'S TIME FOR YOU TO STOP WHAT YOU'RE DOING. ALFRED KNOWS OF A BRILLIANT DOCTOR WHO--
ENOUGH!

TWO HUNDRED FEET BELOW GOTHAM...

CAN'T'CHA KEEP UP, BOY?

IT'S YOUR *MOUTH* I CAN'T KEEP UP WITH.

I'LL BELIEVE IT WHEN I *DON'T* HEAR IT. LET'S GET ON WITH IT.

I'M SURE NIGHTWING COULD USE A HAND FINDING ROBIN. THIS WAY, THEN.

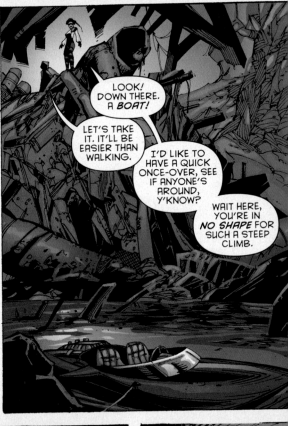

LOOK! DOWN THERE. A *BOAT!*

LET'S TAKE IT. IT'LL BE EASIER THAN WALKING.

I'D LIKE TO HAVE A QUICK ONCE-OVER, SEE IF ANYONE'S AROUND, Y'KNOW?

WAIT HERE, YOU'RE IN *NO SHAPE* FOR SUCH A STEEP CLIMB.

WHO DIED AND MADE *YOU* MY BOSS?

MY GPS DID. ORACLE PINPOINTED NIGHTWING'S LAST COM-LINK FOR ME.

BESIDES, YOU'RE THE GIMPY ONE, AND WE'D BE A RIGHT FRIGHTFUL SIGHT TAKING *YOUR* LEAD.

I'LL GIVE YOU "GIMPY".

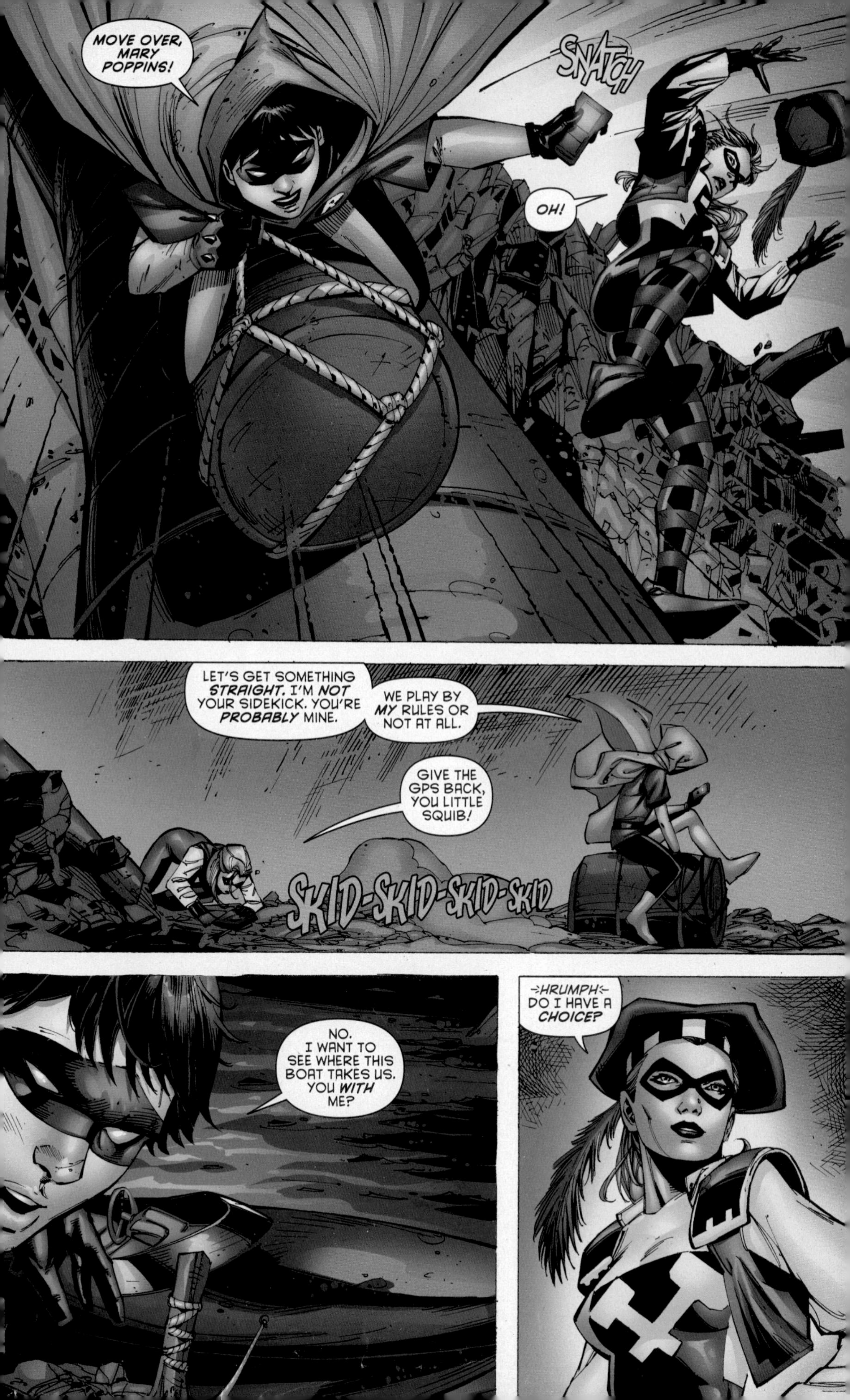
MOVE OVER, MARY POPPINS!
SNATCH
OH!
LET'S GET SOMETHING STRAIGHT. I'M NOT YOUR SIDEKICK. YOU'RE PROBABLY MINE.
WE PLAY BY MY RULES OR NOT AT ALL.
GIVE THE GPS BACK, YOU LITTLE SQUIB!
SKID-SKID-SKID-SKID
NO. I WANT TO SEE WHERE THIS BOAT TAKES US. YOU WITH ME?
>HRUMPH< DO I HAVE A CHOICE?

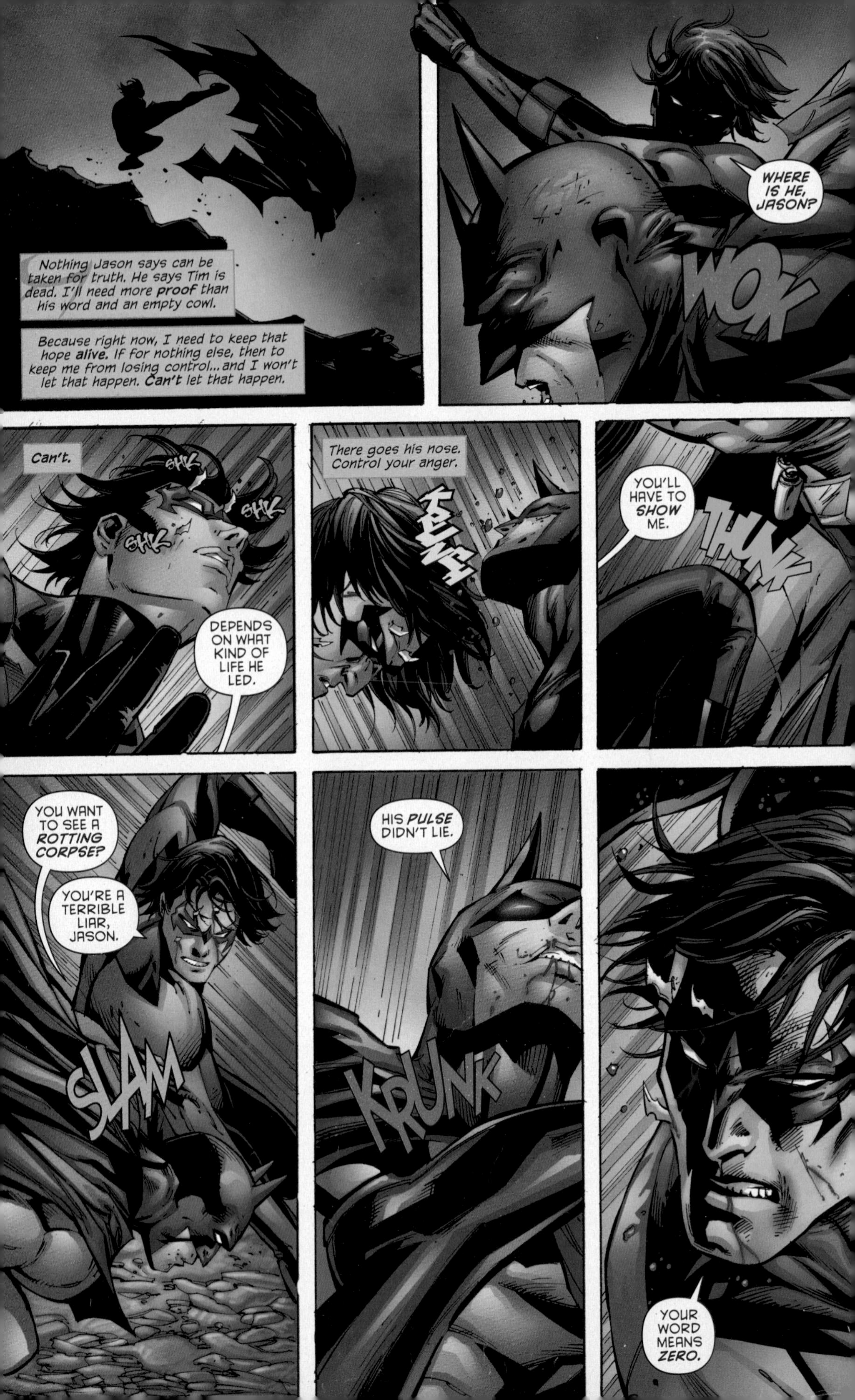

Nothing Jason says can be taken for truth. He says Tim is dead. I'll need more proof than his word and an empty cowl.
Because right now, I need to keep that hope alive. If for nothing else, then to keep me from losing control...and I won't let that happen. Can't let that happen.
WHERE IS HE, JASON?
WOK
Can't.
SHK
SHK
SHK
DEPENDS ON WHAT KIND OF LIFE HE LED.
There goes his nose. Control your anger.
YOU'LL HAVE TO SHOW ME.
THUNK
YOU WANT TO SEE A ROTTING CORPSE?
YOU'RE A TERRIBLE LIAR, JASON.
SLAM
HIS PULSE DIDN'T LIE.
KRUNK
YOUR WORD MEANS ZERO.

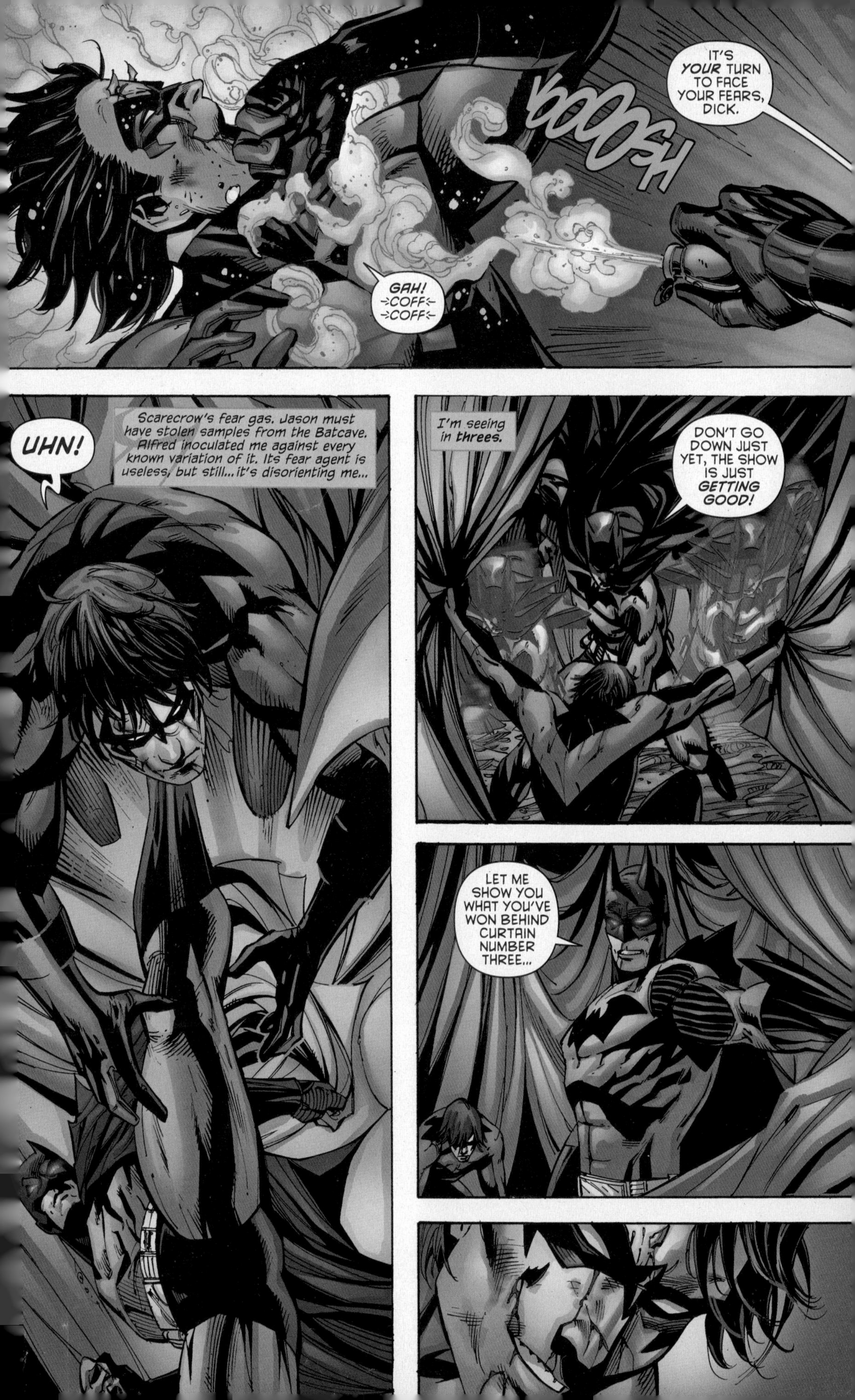
IT'S *YOUR* TURN TO FACE YOUR FEARS, DICK.
VOOOOSH
GAH! COFF COFF
UHN!
Scarecrow's fear gas. Jason must have stolen samples from the Batcave. Alfred inoculated me against every known variation of it. Its fear agent is useless, but still...it's disorienting me...
I'm seeing in **threes.**
DON'T GO DOWN JUST YET, THE SHOW IS JUST *GETTING GOOD!*
LET ME SHOW YOU WHAT YOU'VE WON BEHIND CURTAIN NUMBER THREE...

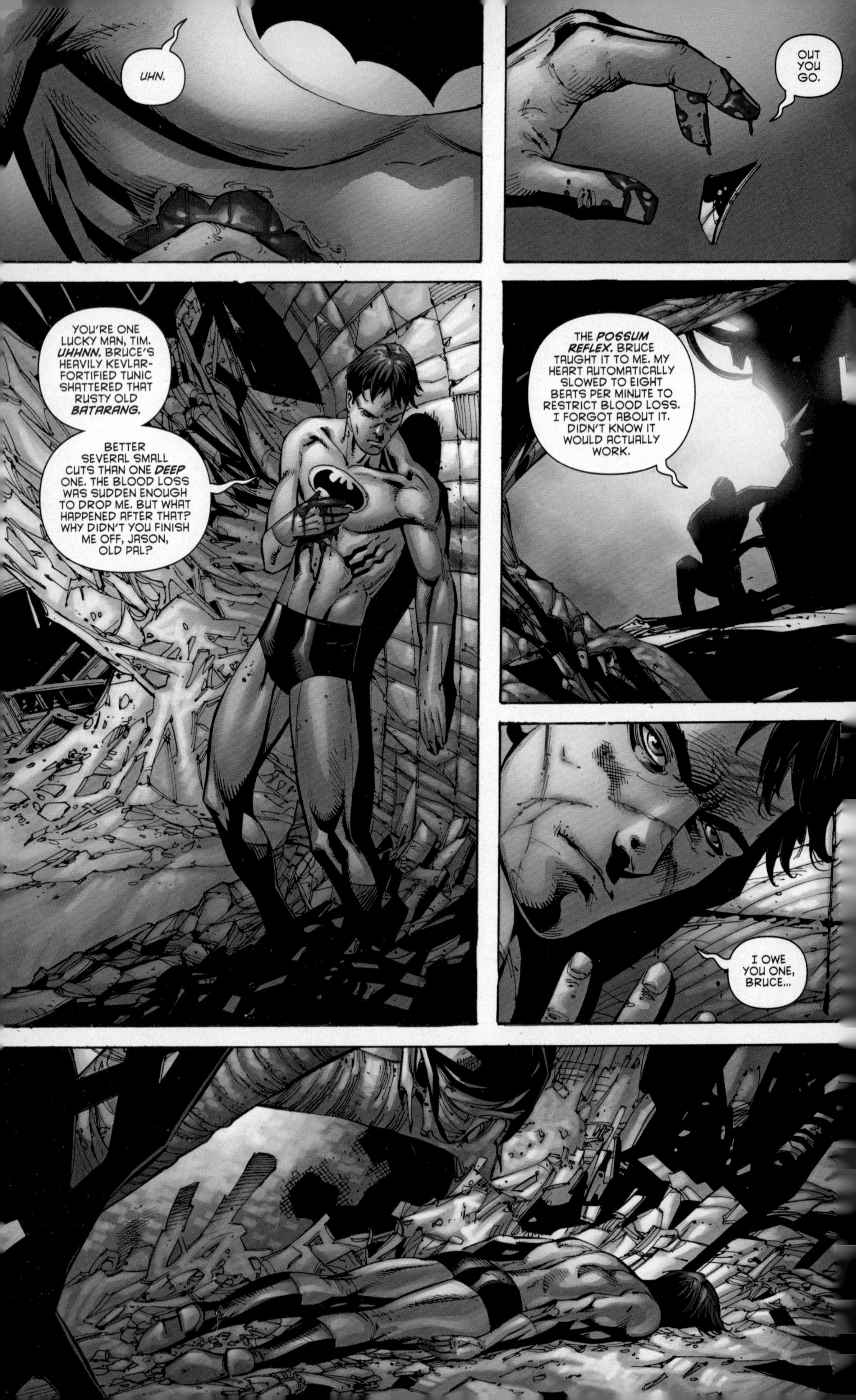

UHN.
OUT YOU GO.
YOU'RE ONE LUCKY MAN, TIM. *UHHNN.* BRUCE'S HEAVILY KEVLAR-FORTIFIED TUNIC SHATTERED THAT RUSTY OLD *BATARANG.*
BETTER SEVERAL SMALL CUTS THAN ONE *DEEP* ONE. THE BLOOD LOSS WAS SUDDEN ENOUGH TO DROP ME. BUT WHAT HAPPENED AFTER THAT? WHY DIDN'T YOU FINISH ME OFF, JASON, OLD PAL?
THE *POSSUM REFLEX.* BRUCE TAUGHT IT TO ME. MY HEART AUTOMATICALLY SLOWED TO EIGHT BEATS PER MINUTE TO RESTRICT BLOOD LOSS. I FORGOT ABOUT IT. DIDN'T KNOW IT WOULD ACTUALLY WORK.
I OWE YOU ONE, BRUCE...

Bruce's last will and testament didn't go over well with Jason. Whatever traumatized him all those years ago was *buried deep.* Bruce dug it up, forcing Jason to deal with it. Tough love.

But Jason never could seek out another for help. Not even if it was *Bruce.*

IT'S OVER, JASON.

And whatever scab he formed over the years was unexpectedly *ripped off.* This is the only way Jason thinks he can heal. By overcompensating. Only now, he's too far gone. He's *self-destructing.*

KRUNK

YOU'RE RIGHT. IT *IS* OVER.

REST IN PEACE, DICK.

CLICK

Rigged. He'll flatten what's left of this place.

THOOM

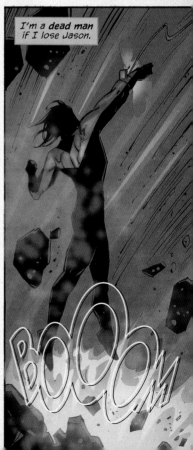

I'm a *dead man* if I lose Jason.

BOOOM

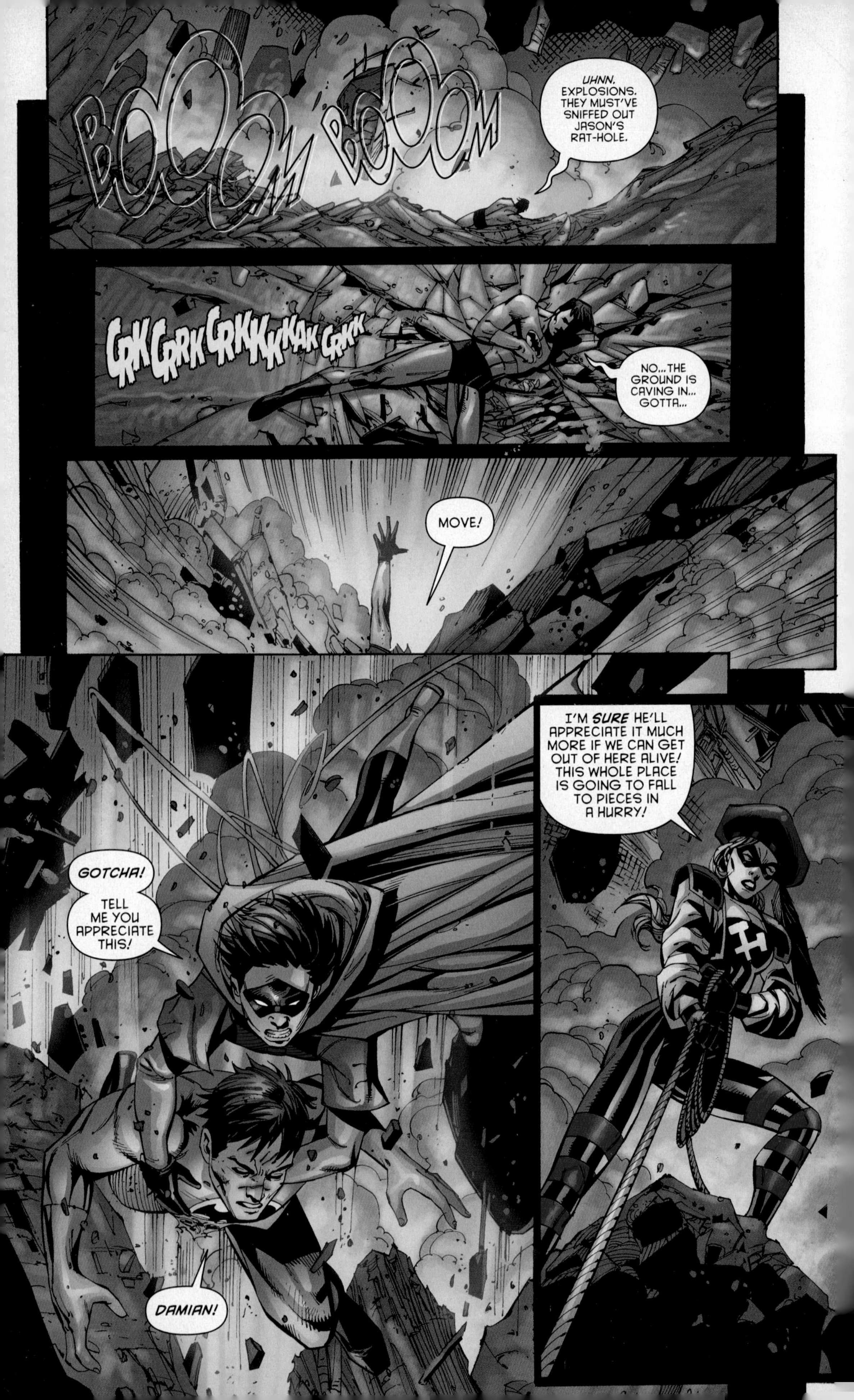
BOOOOM BOOOOM
UHNN. EXPLOSIONS. THEY MUST'VE SNIFFED OUT JASON'S RAT-HOLE.
GRK GRRK GRKKKKKAK GRKK
NO... THE GROUND IS CAVING IN... GOTTA...
MOVE!
GOTCHA!
TELL ME YOU APPRECIATE THIS!
I'M SURE HE'LL APPRECIATE IT MUCH MORE IF WE CAN GET OUT OF HERE ALIVE! THIS WHOLE PLACE IS GOING TO FALL TO PIECES IN A HURRY!
DAMIAN!

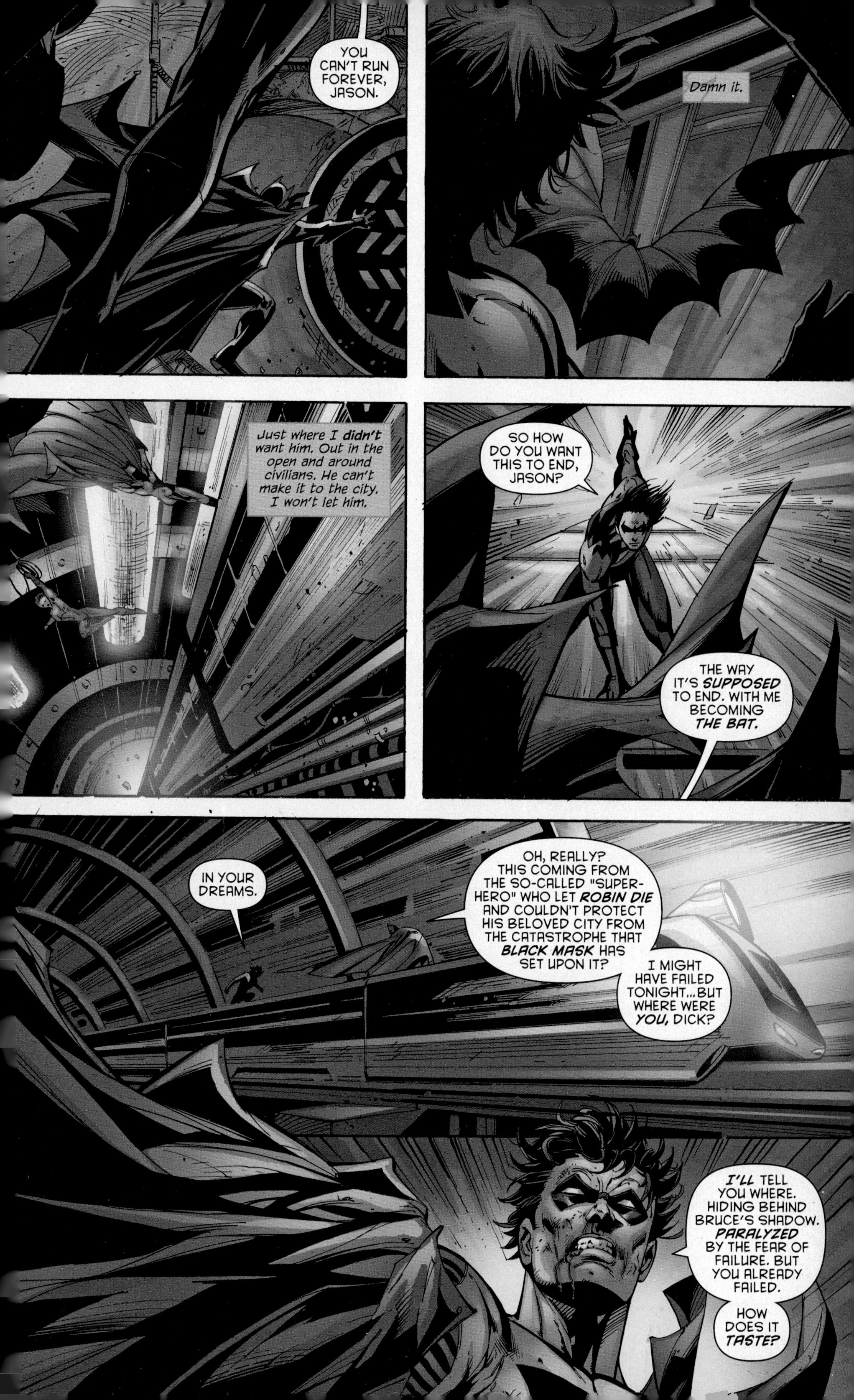
YOU CAN'T RUN FOREVER, JASON.
Damn it.
Just where I didn't want him. Out in the open and around civilians. He can't make it to the city. I won't let him.
SO HOW DO YOU WANT THIS TO END, JASON?
THE WAY IT'S SUPPOSED TO END. WITH ME BECOMING THE BAT.
IN YOUR DREAMS.
OH, REALLY? THIS COMING FROM THE SO-CALLED "SUPER-HERO" WHO LET ROBIN DIE AND COULDN'T PROTECT HIS BELOVED CITY FROM THE CATASTROPHE THAT BLACK MASK HAS SET UPON IT?
I MIGHT HAVE FAILED TONIGHT...BUT WHERE WERE YOU, DICK?
I'LL TELL YOU WHERE. HIDING BEHIND BRUCE'S SHADOW. PARALYZED BY THE FEAR OF FAILURE. BUT YOU ALREADY FAILED.
HOW DOES IT TASTE?

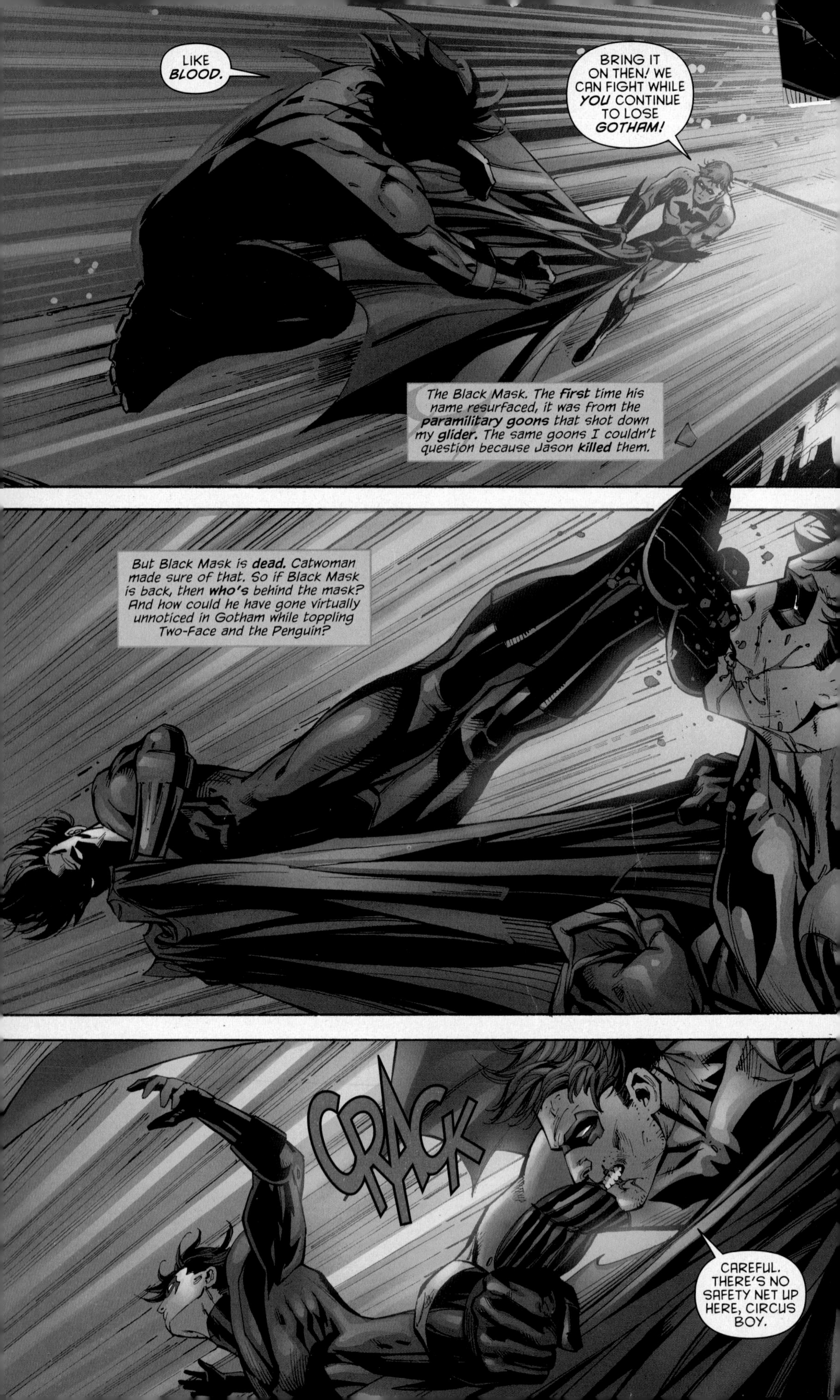
LIKE BLOOD.
BRING IT ON THEN! WE CAN FIGHT WHILE YOU CONTINUE TO LOSE GOTHAM!
The Black Mask. The first time his name resurfaced, it was from the paramilitary goons that shot down my glider. The same goons I couldn't question because Jason killed them.
But Black Mask is dead. Catwoman made sure of that. So if Black Mask is back, then who's behind the mask? And how could he have gone virtually unnoticed in Gotham while toppling Two-Face and the Penguin?
CRACK
CAREFUL. THERE'S NO SAFETY NET UP HERE, CIRCUS BOY.

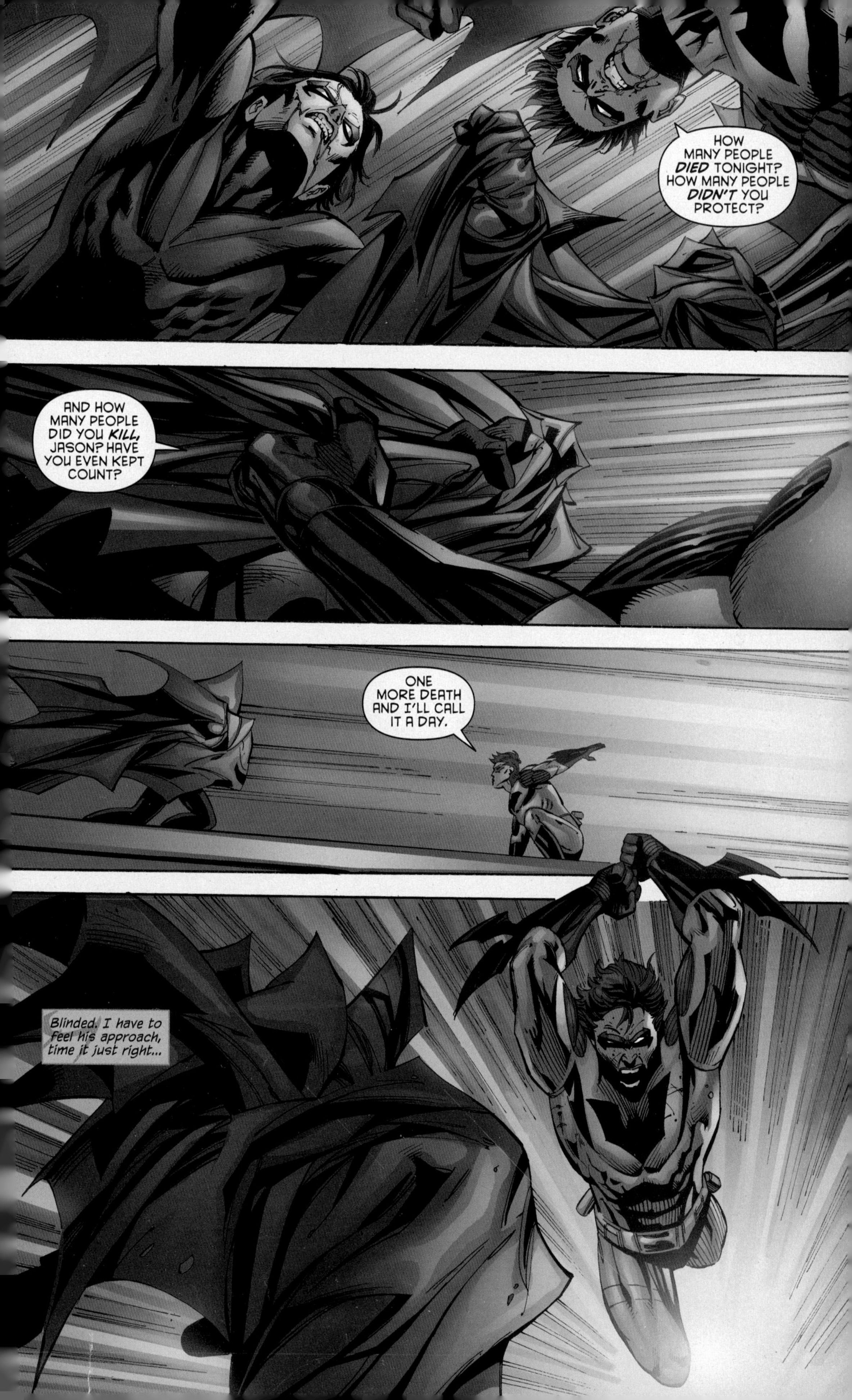
HOW MANY PEOPLE DIED TONIGHT? HOW MANY PEOPLE DIDN'T YOU PROTECT?
AND HOW MANY PEOPLE DID YOU KILL, JASON? HAVE YOU EVEN KEPT COUNT?
ONE MORE DEATH AND I'LL CALL IT A DAY.
Blinded. I have to feel his approach, time it just right...

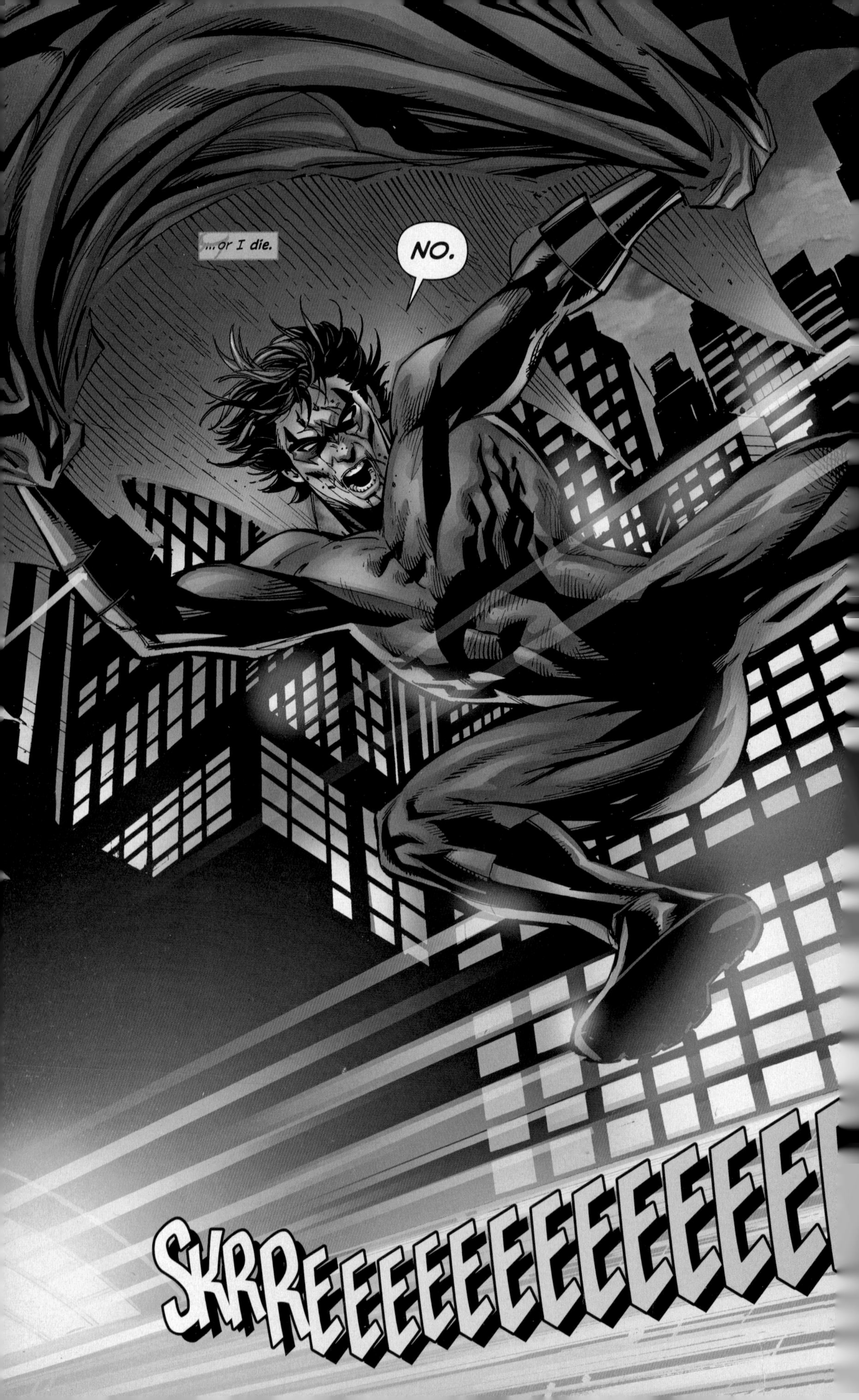
...or I die.
NO.
SKRREEEEEEEEEEEEEE

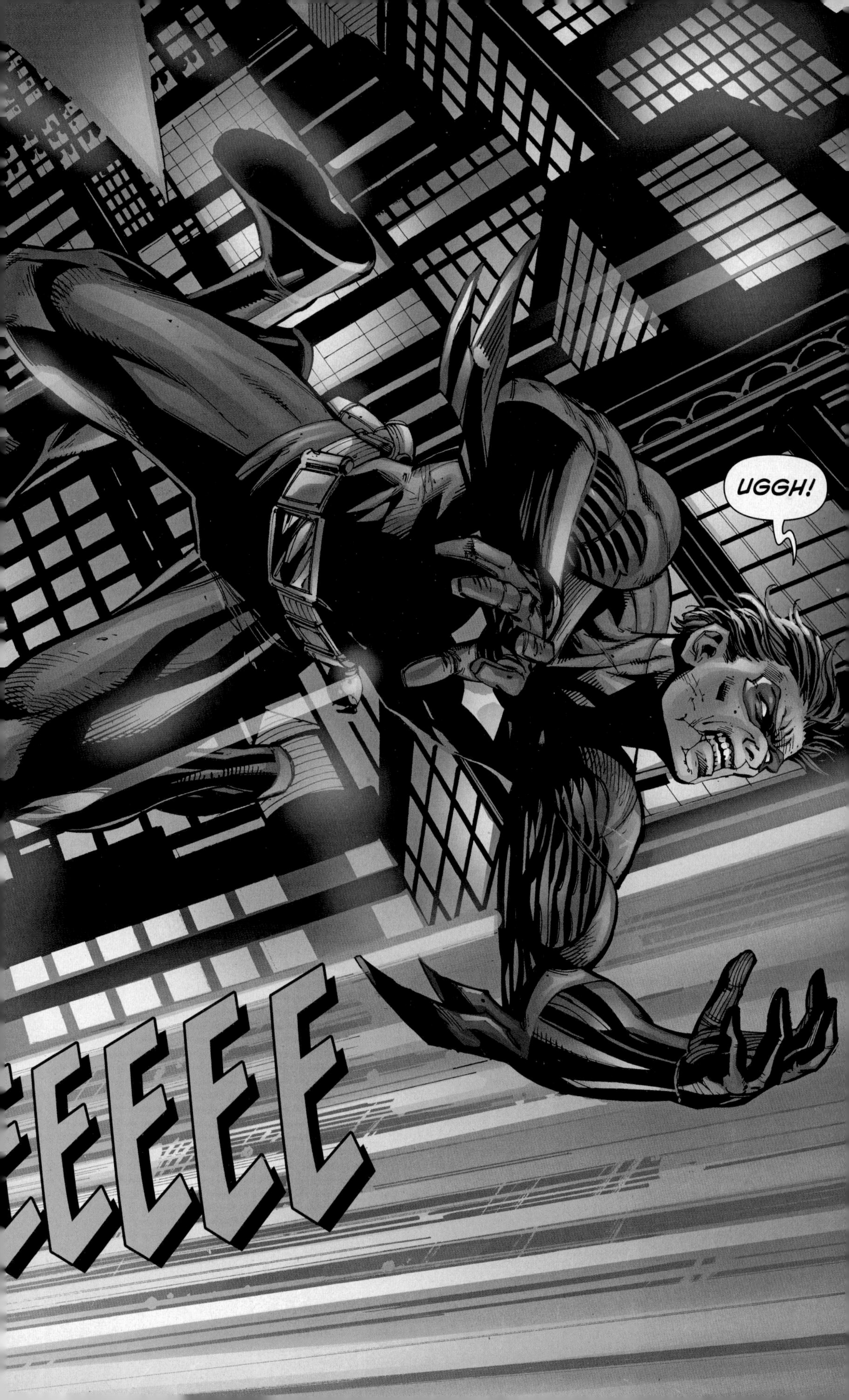
UGGH!
EEEEE

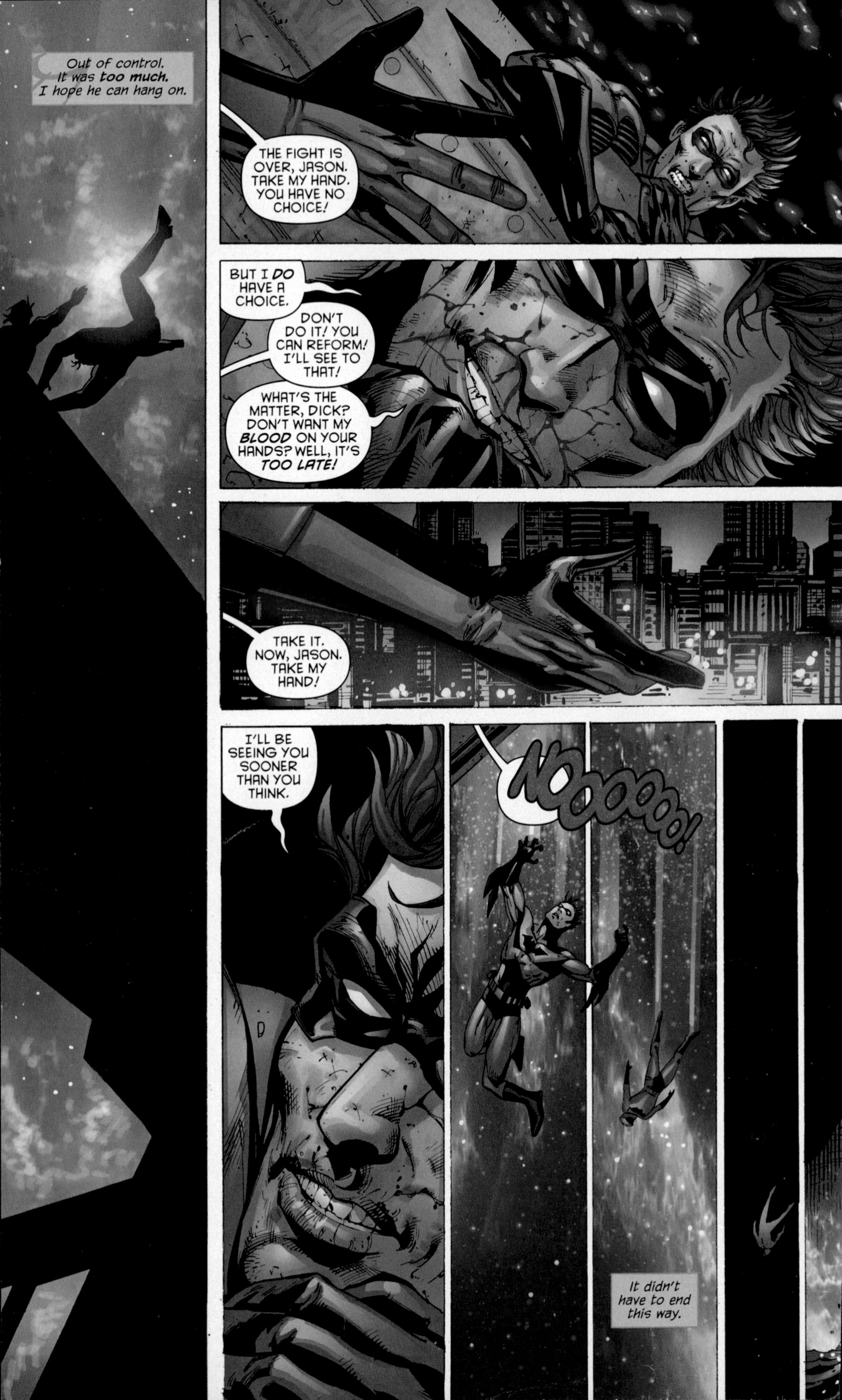
Out of control. It was too much. I hope he can hang on.
THE FIGHT IS OVER, JASON. TAKE MY HAND. YOU HAVE NO CHOICE!
BUT I DO HAVE A CHOICE.
DON'T DO IT! YOU CAN REFORM! I'LL SEE TO THAT!
WHAT'S THE MATTER, DICK? DON'T WANT MY BLOOD ON YOUR HANDS? WELL, IT'S TOO LATE!
TAKE IT. NOW, JASON. TAKE MY HAND!
I'LL BE SEEING YOU SOONER THAN YOU THINK.
NOOOOOO!
It didn't have to end this way.

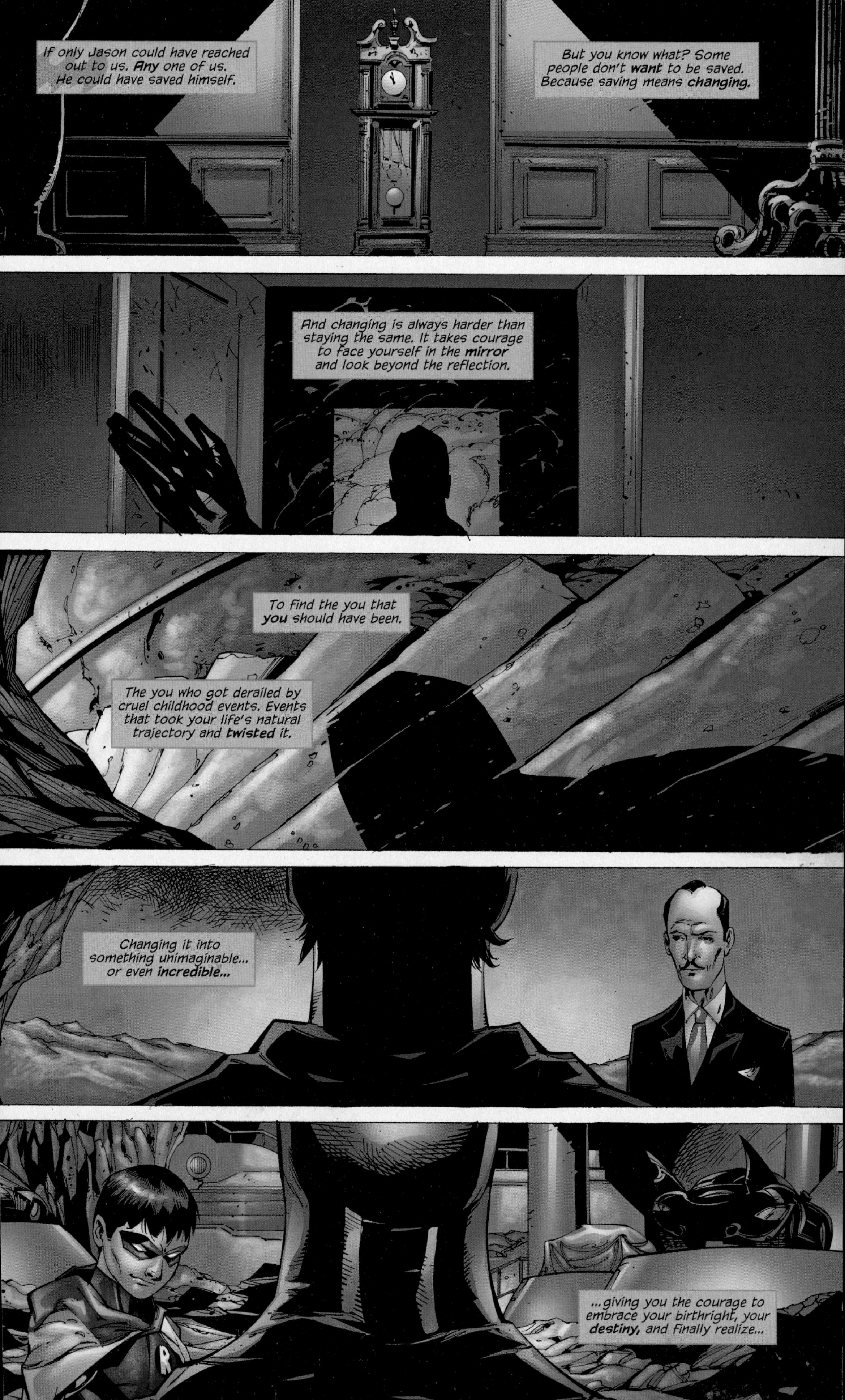
If only Jason could have reached out to us. Any one of us. He could have saved himself.
But you know what? Some people don't want to be saved. Because saving means changing.
And changing is always harder than staying the same. It takes courage to face yourself in the mirror and look beyond the reflection.
To find the you that you should have been.
The you who got derailed by cruel childhood events. Events that took your life's natural trajectory and twisted it.
Changing it into something unimaginable... or even incredible...
...giving you the courage to embrace your birthright, your destiny, and finally realize...

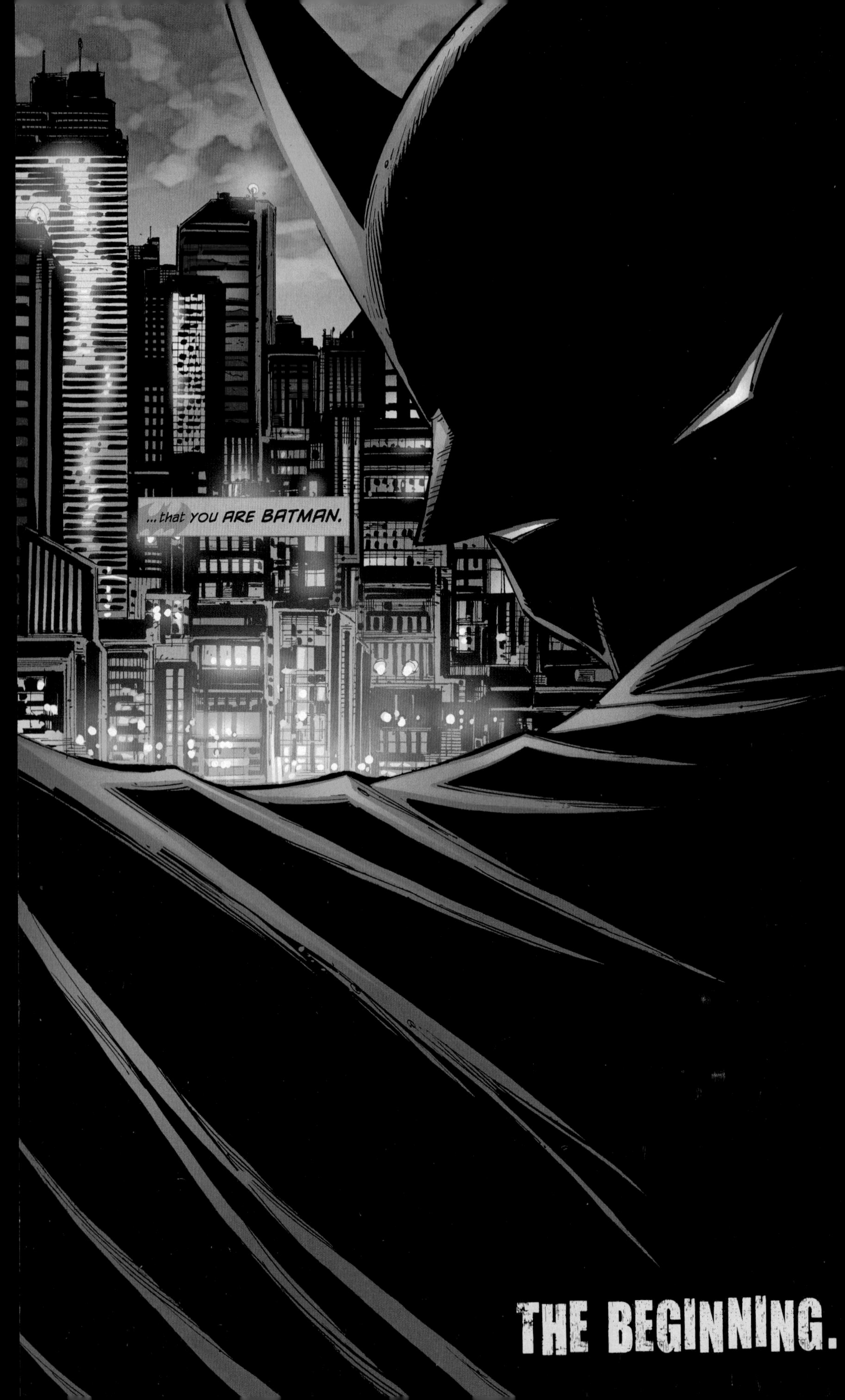
...that YOU ARE BATMAN.
THE BEGINNING.

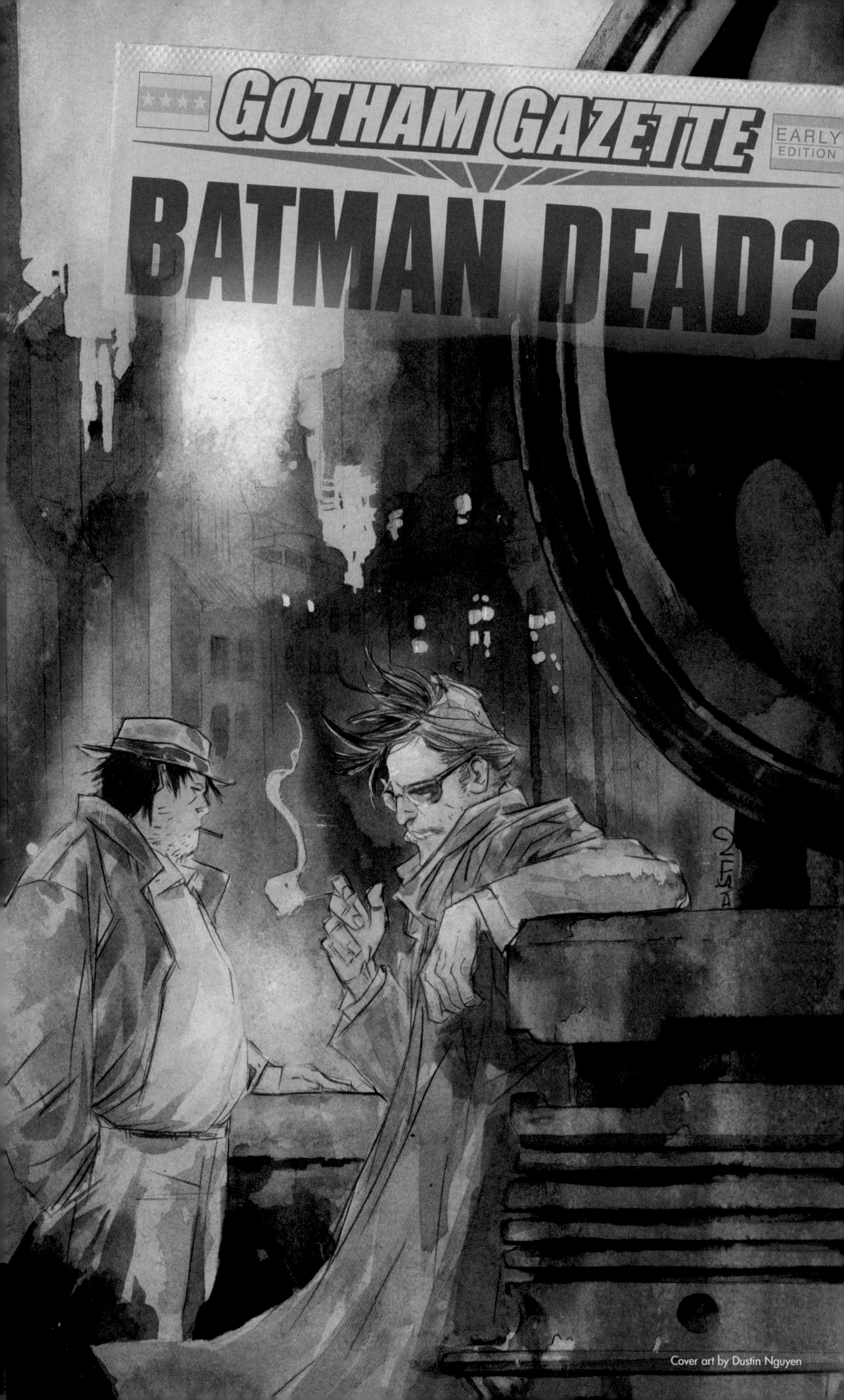
GOTHAM GAZETTE
EARLY EDITION
BATMAN DEAD?

Cover art by Dustin Nguyen

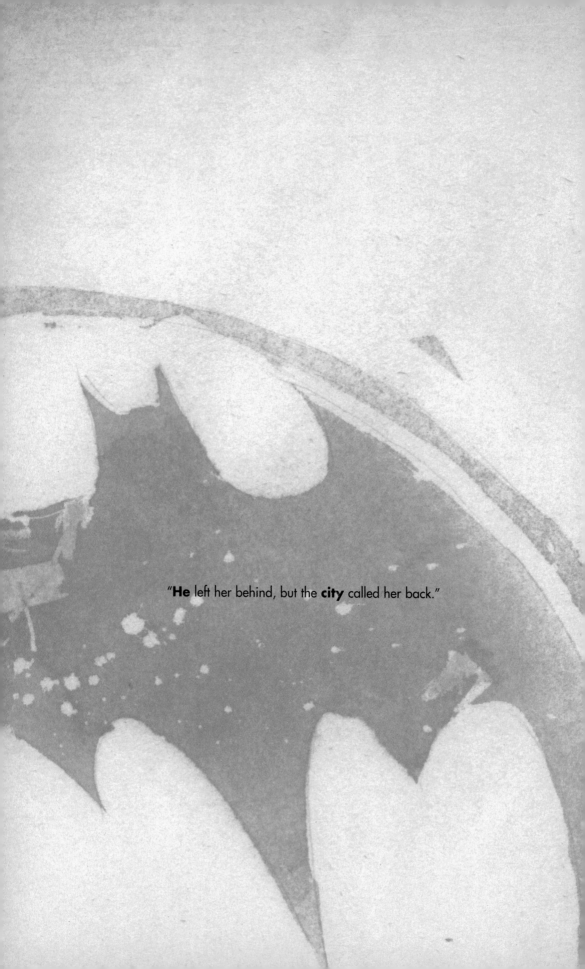

"**He** left her behind, but the **city** called her back."

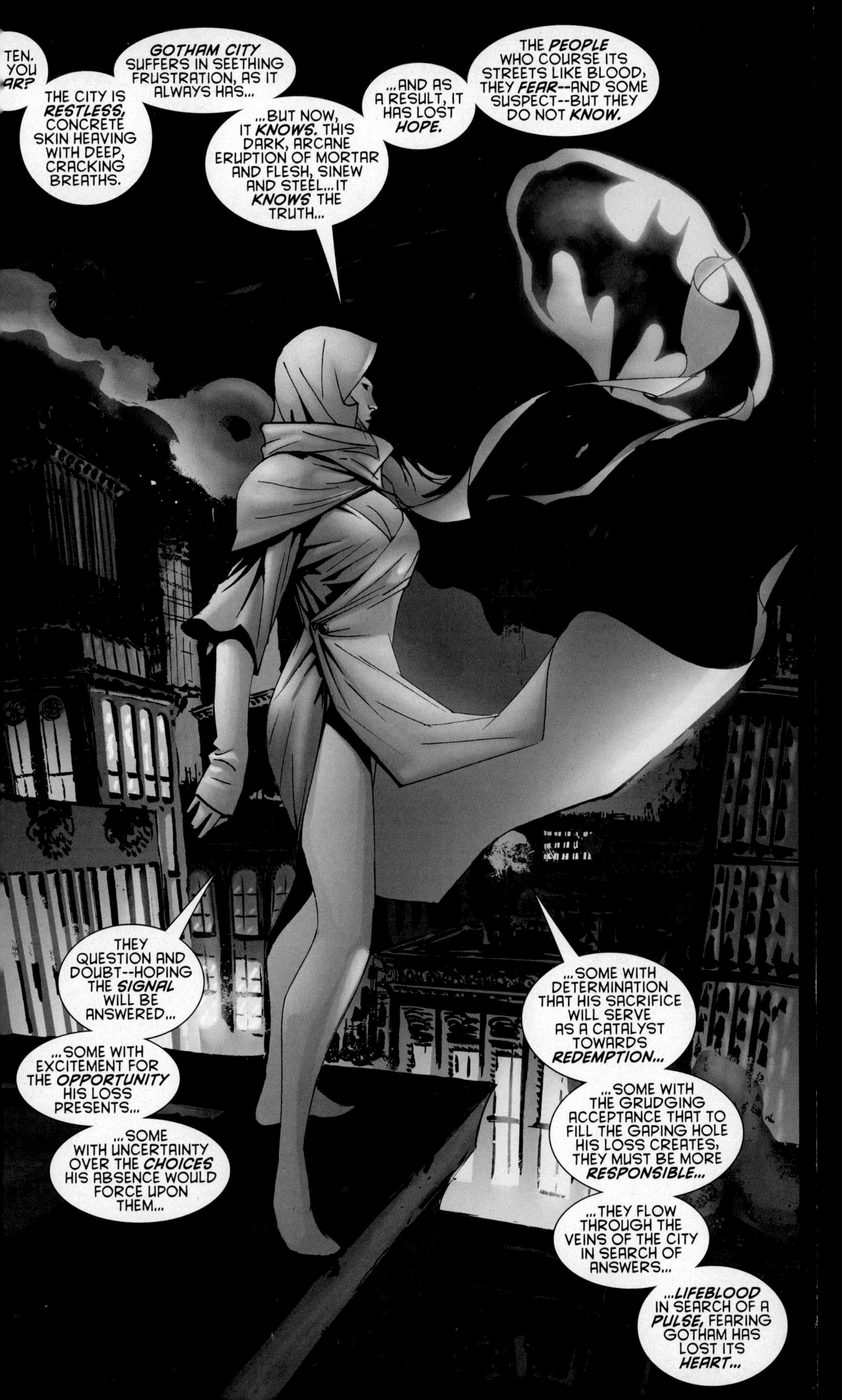
TEN. YOU AR?
GOTHAM CITY SUFFERS IN SEETHING FRUSTRATION, AS IT ALWAYS HAS...
THE CITY IS RESTLESS, CONCRETE SKIN HEAVING WITH DEEP, CRACKING BREATHS.
...BUT NOW, IT KNOWS. THIS DARK, ARCANE ERUPTION OF MORTAR AND FLESH, SINEW AND STEEL...IT KNOWS THE TRUTH...
...AND AS A RESULT, IT HAS LOST HOPE.
THE PEOPLE WHO COURSE ITS STREETS LIKE BLOOD, THEY FEAR--AND SOME SUSPECT--BUT THEY DO NOT KNOW.
THEY QUESTION AND DOUBT--HOPING THE SIGNAL WILL BE ANSWERED...
...SOME WITH EXCITEMENT FOR THE OPPORTUNITY HIS LOSS PRESENTS...
...SOME WITH UNCERTAINTY OVER THE CHOICES HIS ABSENCE WOULD FORCE UPON THEM...
...SOME WITH DETERMINATION THAT HIS SACRIFICE WILL SERVE AS A CATALYST TOWARDS REDEMPTION...
...SOME WITH THE GRUDGING ACCEPTANCE THAT TO FILL THE GAPING HOLE HIS LOSS CREATES, THEY MUST BE MORE RESPONSIBLE...
...THEY FLOW THROUGH THE VEINS OF THE CITY IN SEARCH OF ANSWERS...
...LIFEBLOOD IN SEARCH OF A PULSE, FEARING GOTHAM HAS LOST ITS HEART...

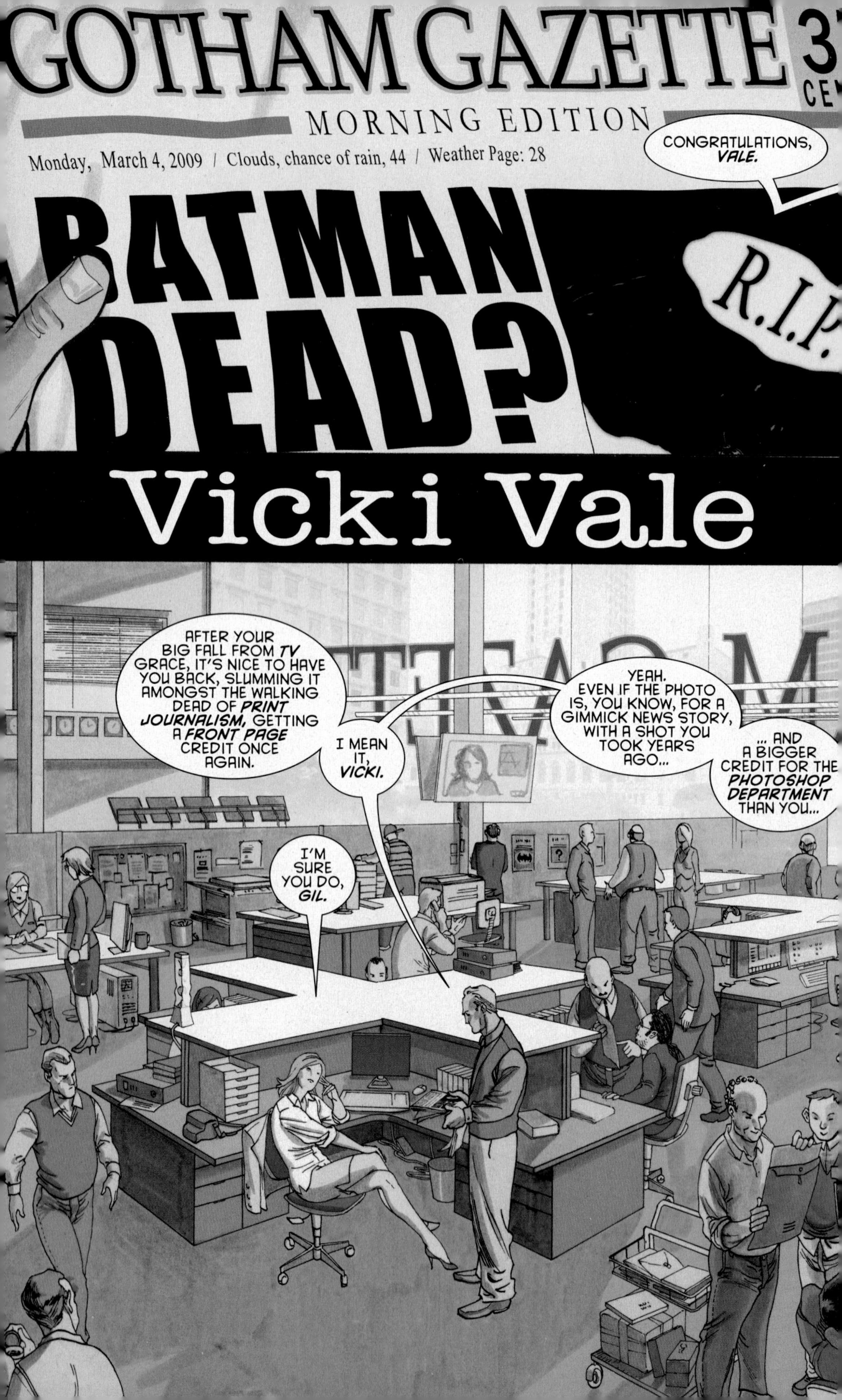

GOTHAM GAZETTE
MORNING EDITION
Monday, March 4, 2009 / Clouds, chance of rain, 44 / Weather Page: 28
BATMAN DEAD?
R.I.P.
CONGRATULATIONS, VALE.
Vicki Vale
AFTER YOUR BIG FALL FROM TV GRACE, IT'S NICE TO HAVE YOU BACK, SLUMMING IT AMONGST THE WALKING DEAD OF PRINT JOURNALISM, GETTING A FRONT PAGE CREDIT ONCE AGAIN.
I MEAN IT, VICKI.
YEAH. EVEN IF THE PHOTO IS, YOU KNOW, FOR A GIMMICK NEWS STORY, WITH A SHOT YOU TOOK YEARS AGO...
... AND A BIGGER CREDIT FOR THE PHOTOSHOP DEPARTMENT THAN YOU...
I'M SURE YOU DO, GIL.

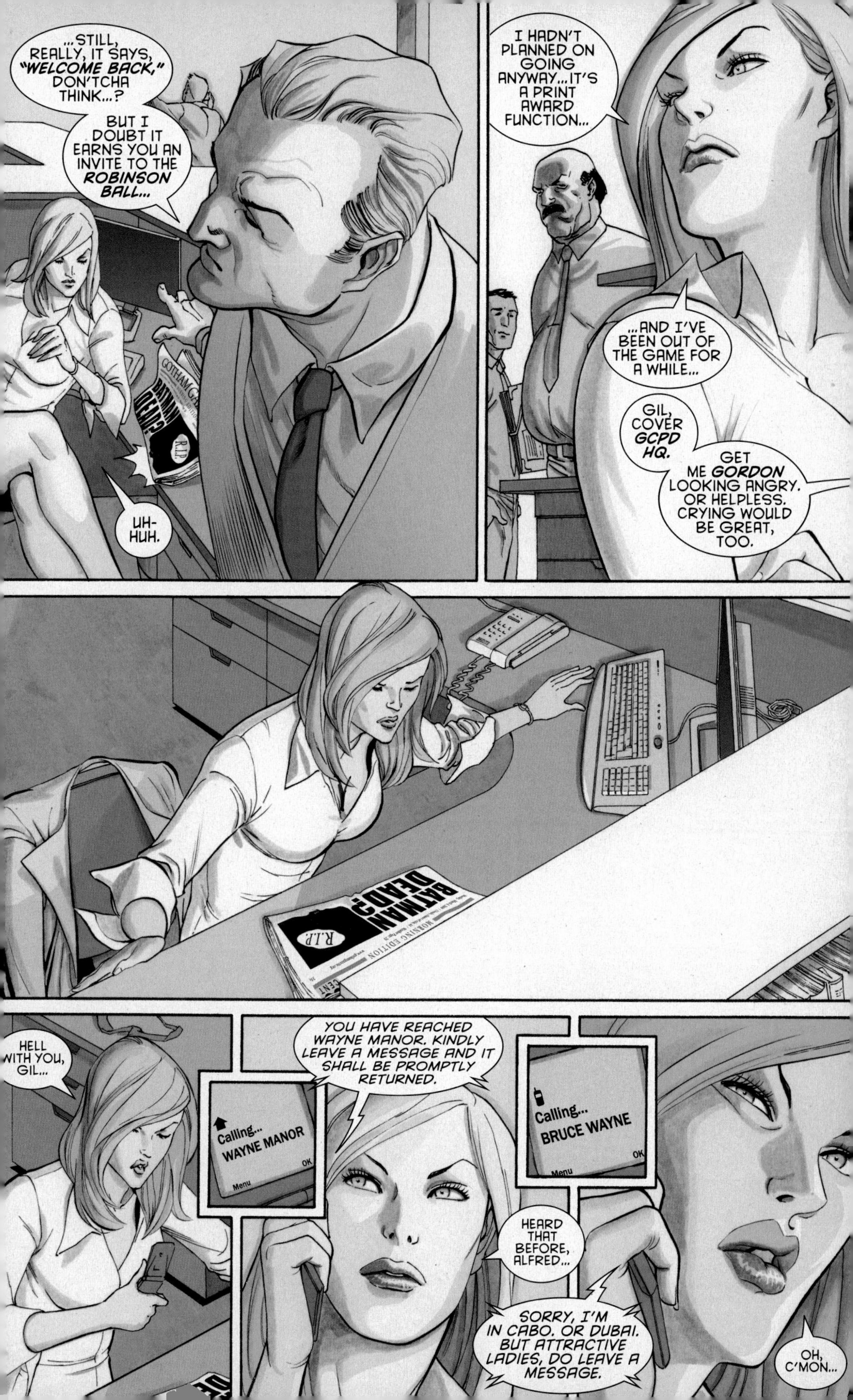
...STILL, REALLY, IT SAYS, "WELCOME BACK," DON'TCHA THINK...?
BUT I DOUBT IT EARNS YOU AN INVITE TO THE ROBINSON BALL...
UH-HUH.
I HADN'T PLANNED ON GOING ANYWAY...IT'S A PRINT AWARD FUNCTION...
...AND I'VE BEEN OUT OF THE GAME FOR A WHILE...
GIL, COVER GCPD HQ.
GET ME GORDON LOOKING ANGRY. OR HELPLESS. CRYING WOULD BE GREAT, TOO.
BATMAN DEAD?
R.I.P.
MORNING EDITION
HELL WITH YOU, GIL...
YOU HAVE REACHED WAYNE MANOR. KINDLY LEAVE A MESSAGE AND IT SHALL BE PROMPTLY RETURNED.
Calling... WAYNE MANOR
Menu
OK
HEARD THAT BEFORE, ALFRED...
Calling... BRUCE WAYNE
Menu
OK
SORRY, I'M IN CABO. OR DUBAI. BUT ATTRACTIVE LADIES, DO LEAVE A MESSAGE.
OH, C'MON...

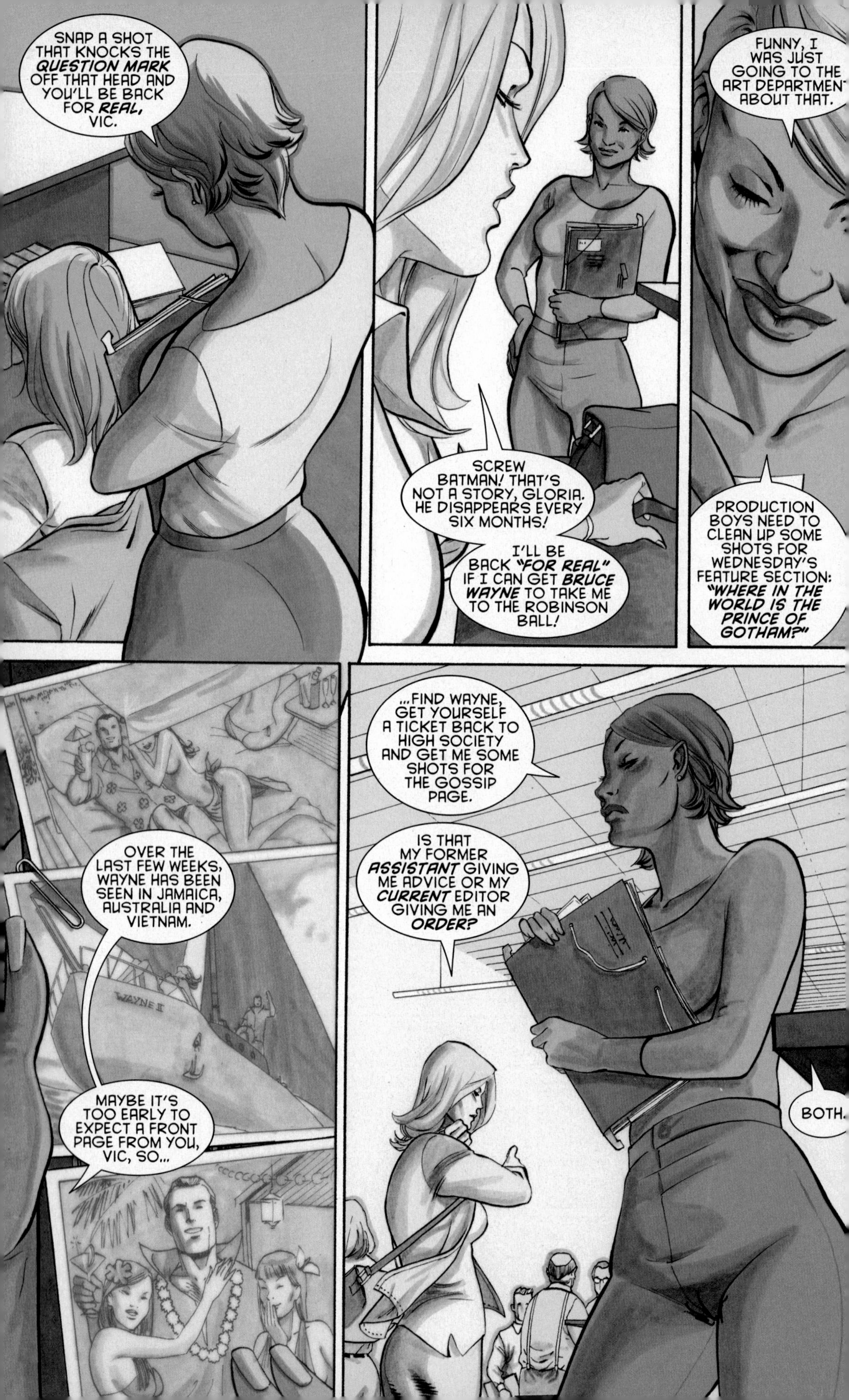

SNAP A SHOT THAT KNOCKS THE *QUESTION MARK* OFF THAT HEAD AND YOU'LL BE BACK FOR *REAL,* VIC.
SCREW BATMAN! THAT'S NOT A STORY, GLORIA. HE DISAPPEARS EVERY SIX MONTHS!
I'LL BE BACK *"FOR REAL"* IF I CAN GET *BRUCE WAYNE* TO TAKE ME TO THE ROBINSON BALL!
FUNNY, I WAS JUST GOING TO THE ART DEPARTMENT ABOUT THAT.
PRODUCTION BOYS NEED TO CLEAN UP SOME SHOTS FOR WEDNESDAY'S FEATURE SECTION: *"WHERE IN THE WORLD IS THE PRINCE OF GOTHAM?"*
OVER THE LAST FEW WEEKS, WAYNE HAS BEEN SEEN IN JAMAICA, AUSTRALIA AND VIETNAM.
WAYNE II
MAYBE IT'S TOO EARLY TO EXPECT A FRONT PAGE FROM YOU, VIC, SO...
...FIND WAYNE, GET YOURSELF A TICKET BACK TO HIGH SOCIETY AND GET ME SOME SHOTS FOR THE GOSSIP PAGE.
IS THAT MY FORMER *ASSISTANT* GIVING ME ADVICE OR MY *CURRENT* EDITOR GIVING ME AN *ORDER?*
BOTH.

She starts her search where Wayne had last been seen in Gotham--

--acting in ways that were excessive even by *his* usual standards.

Which led her to reacquaint herself with Wayne Enterprises C.E.O. *Lucius Fox*--

--whose ability to prevaricate for his Chairman was still like silk in motion.

She went to his home, but the butler, *Alfred*, did not answer.

And the gate security code had been changed.

A source at Gotham Airport sent her Wayne's charter jet itinerary.

WAYNE ENTERPR.
Leave
WAYNE, BRUCE
VIETNAM
Depart: 10:45pm
Arrive: 11:54pm
2 stops
Change Airline. Time between flights: 6hr 46min
Depart: 6:49am
Arrive: 8:55am
U.S.
Change planes. Time between flights: 2hr 6min

But a computer glitch corrupted the file.

She spent her first day in a very long time thinking like a journalist.

It terrified her because it was also the first day in a very long time she had felt *alive*.

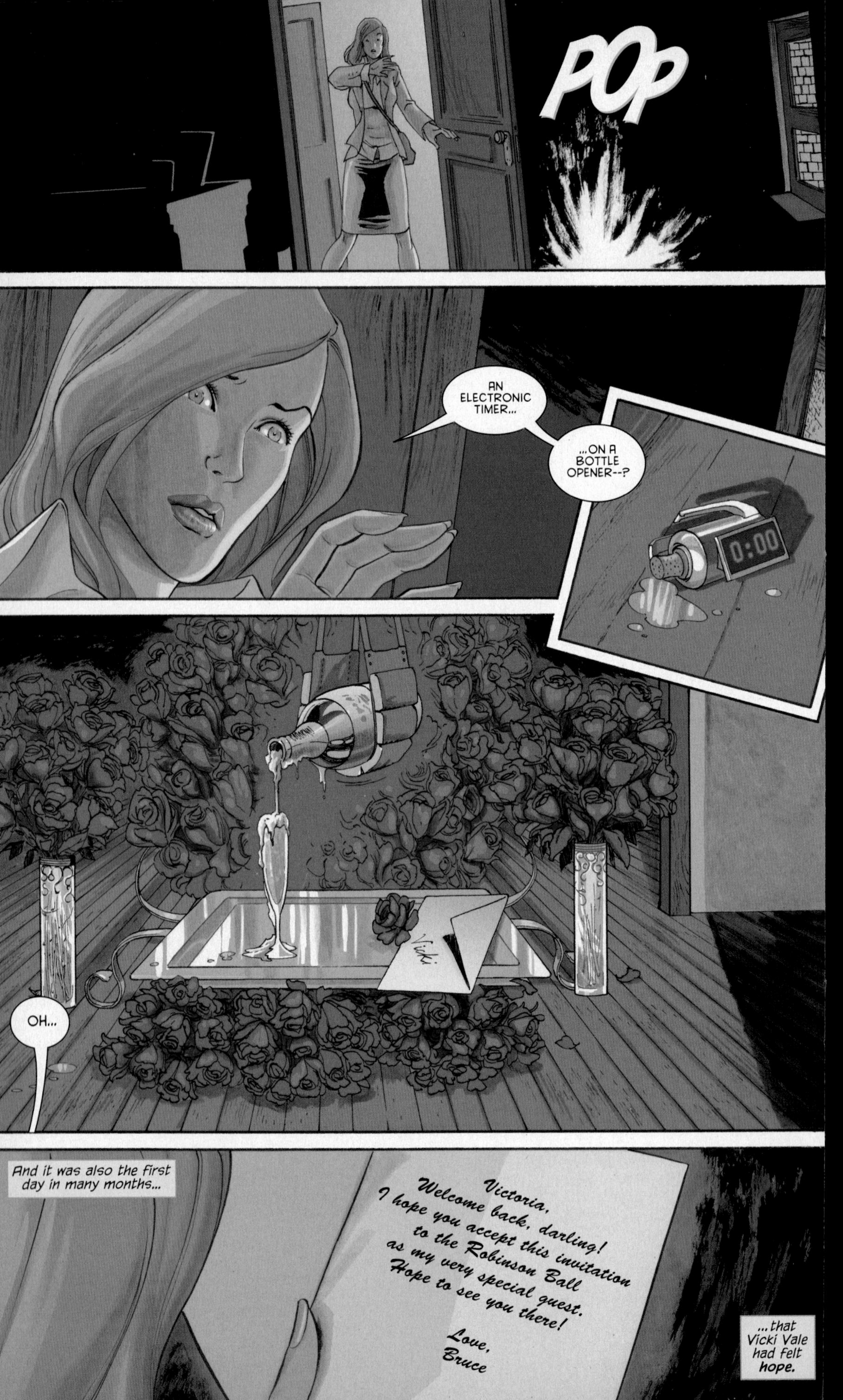
POP
AN ELECTRONIC TIMER...
...ON A BOTTLE OPENER--?
0:00
OH...
Vicki
And it was also the first day in many months...
Victoria,
Welcome back, darling!
I hope you accept this invitation
to the Robinson Ball
as my very special guest.
Hope to see you there!
Love,
Bruce
...that Vicki Vale had felt hope.

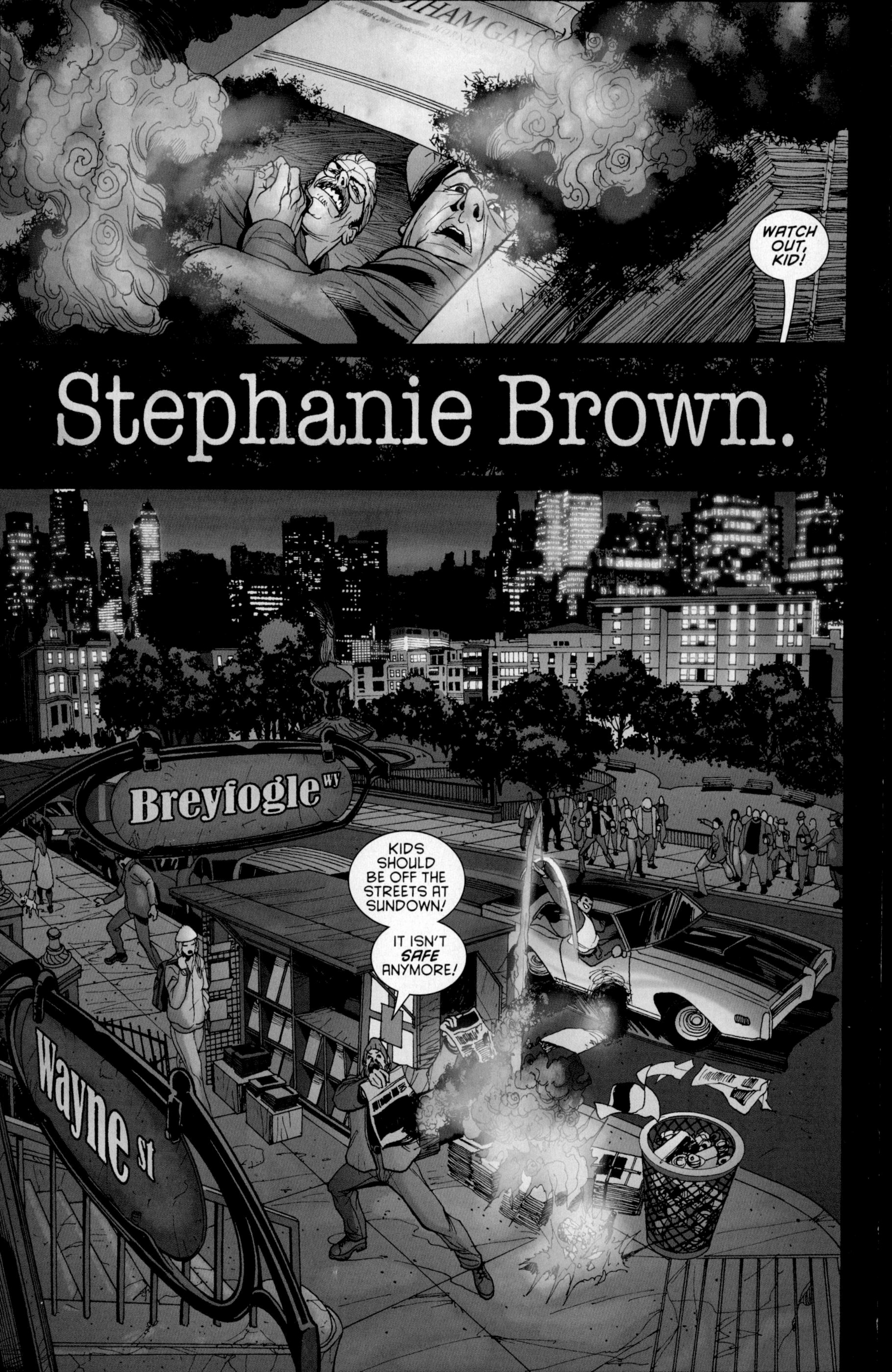
WATCH OUT, KID!
Stephanie Brown.
Breyfogle wy
KIDS SHOULD BE OFF THE STREETS AT SUNDOWN!
IT ISN'T SAFE ANYMORE!
Wayne st

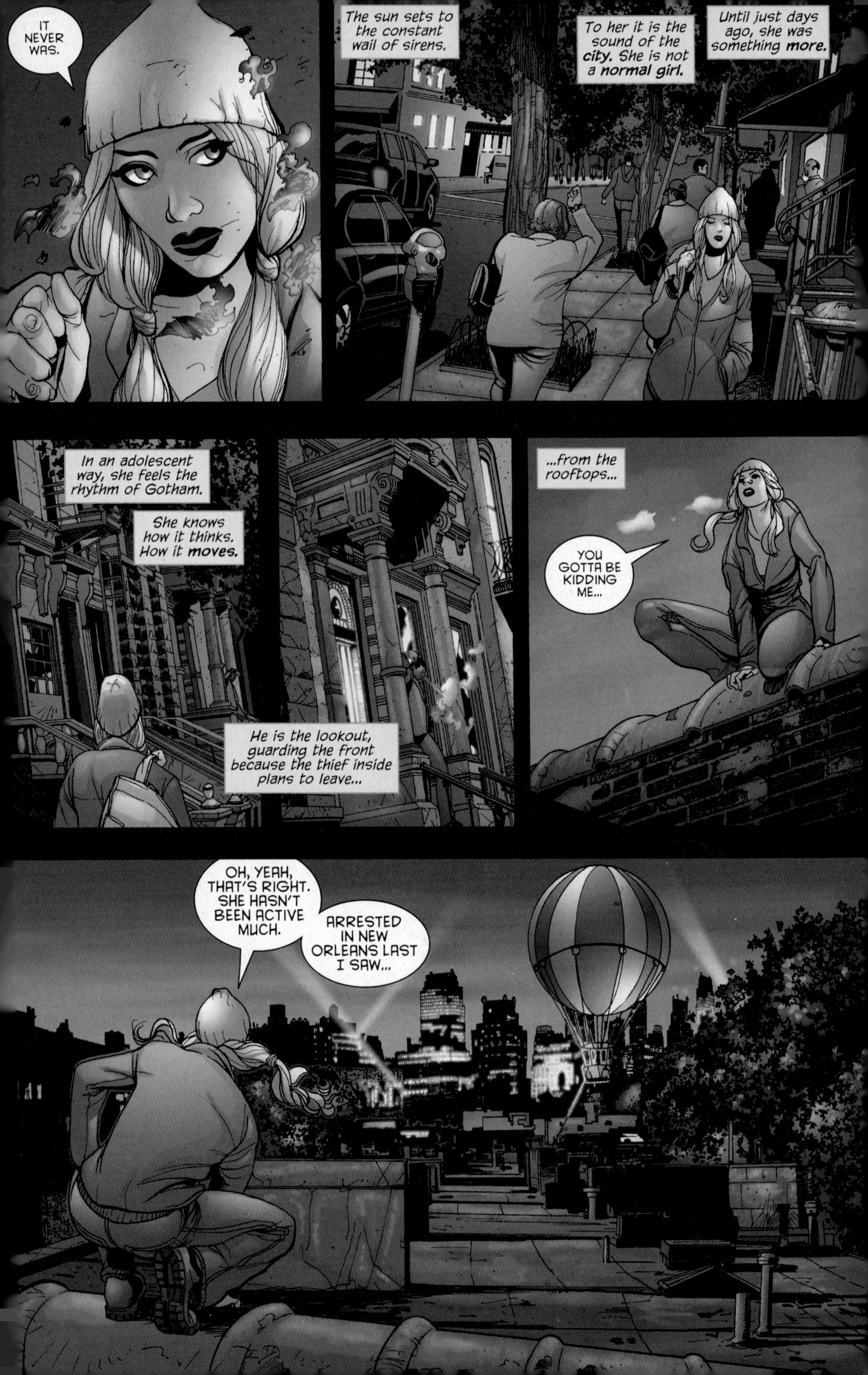
IT NEVER WAS.
The sun sets to the constant wail of sirens.
To her it is the sound of the city. She is not a normal girl.
Until just days ago, she was something more.
In an adolescent way, she feels the rhythm of Gotham.
She knows how it thinks. How it moves.
He is the lookout, guarding the front because the thief inside plans to leave...
...from the rooftops...
YOU GOTTA BE KIDDING ME...
OH, YEAH, THAT'S RIGHT. SHE HASN'T BEEN ACTIVE MUCH.
ARRESTED IN NEW ORLEANS LAST I SAW...

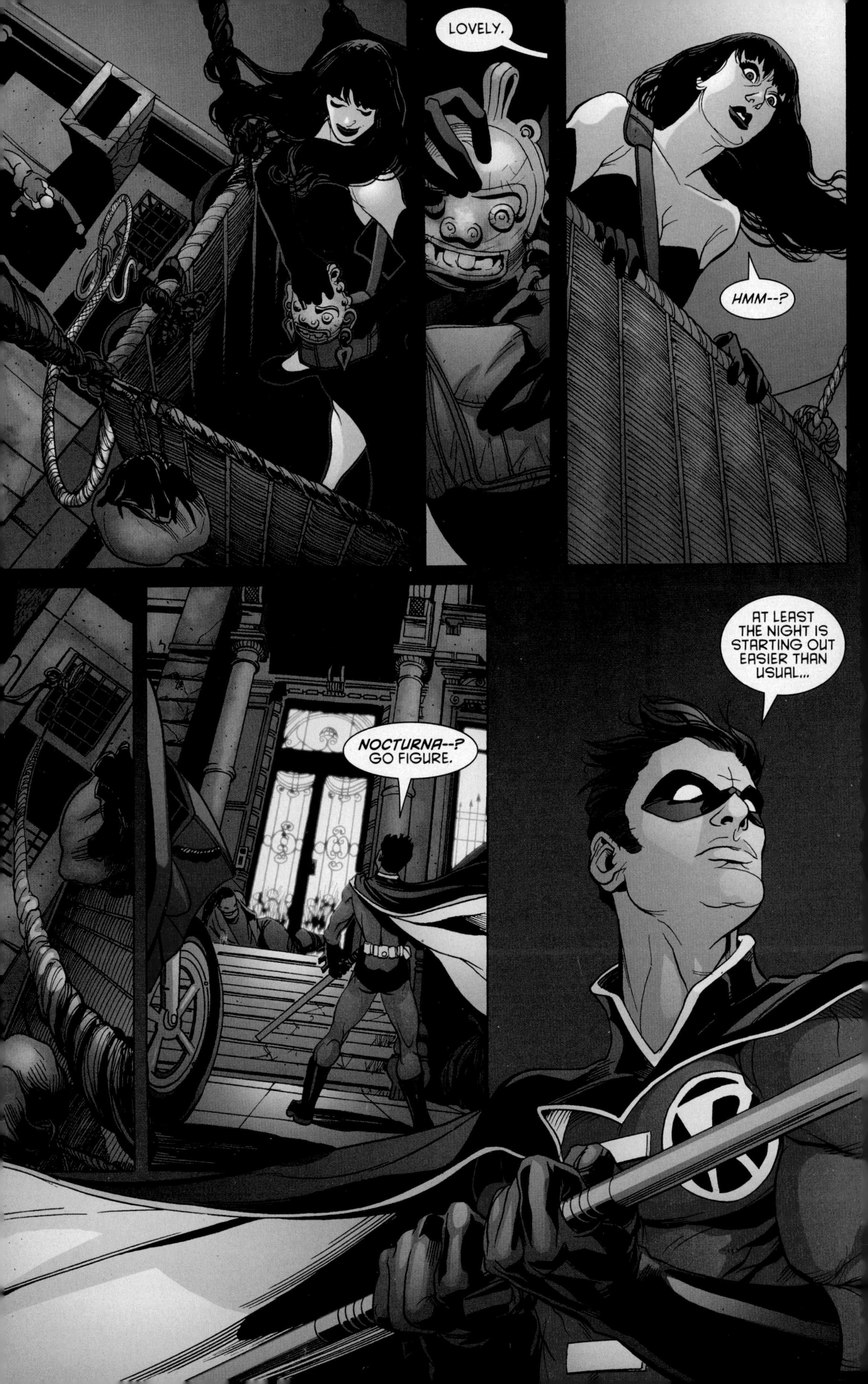
LOVELY.
HMM--?
NOCTURNA--? GO FIGURE.
AT LEAST THE NIGHT IS STARTING OUT EASIER THAN USUAL...

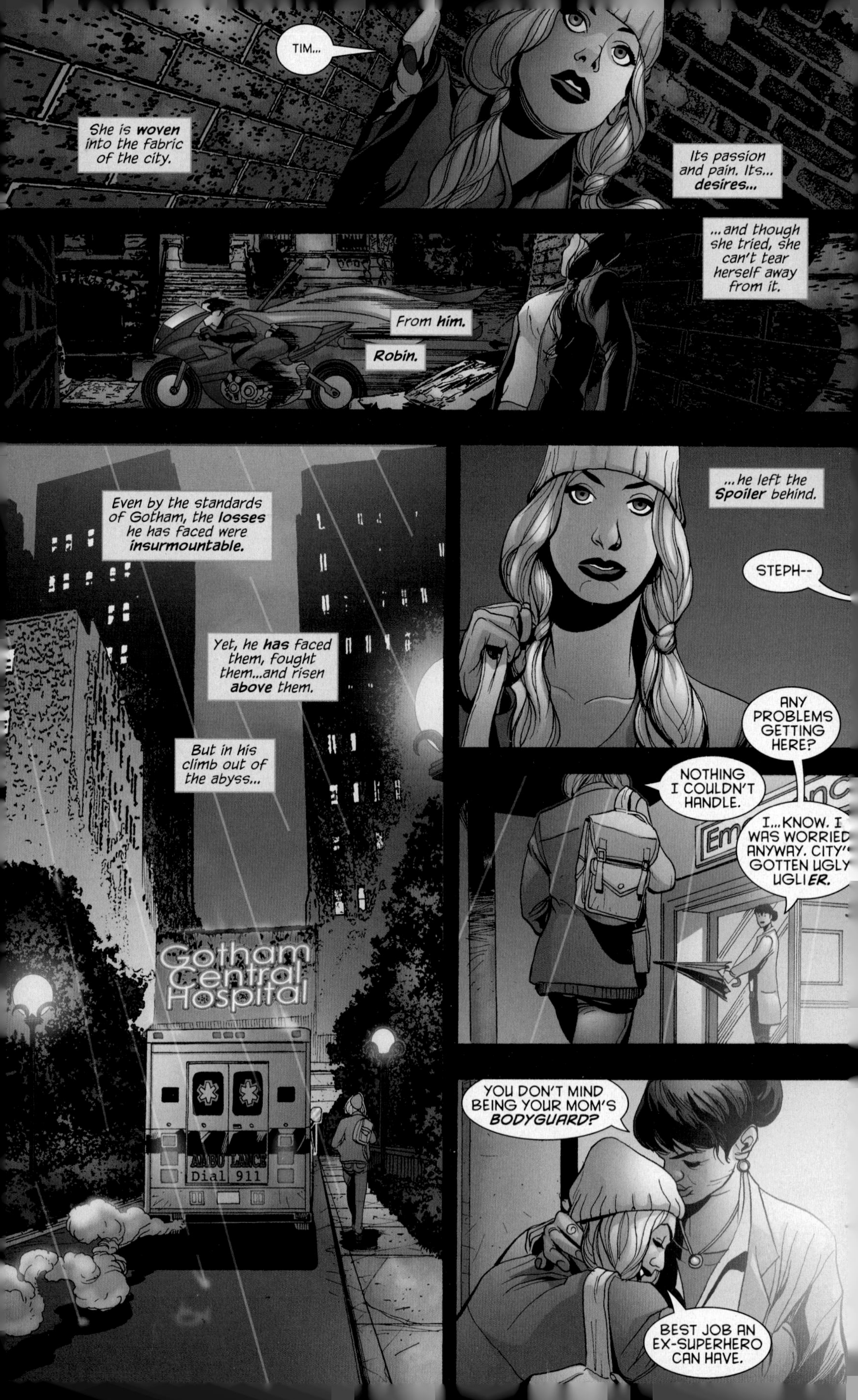
TIM...
She is woven into the fabric of the city.
Its passion and pain. Its... desires...
...and though she tried, she can't tear herself away from it.
From him.
Robin.
Even by the standards of Gotham, the losses he has faced were insurmountable.
Yet, he has faced them, fought them...and risen above them.
But in his climb out of the abyss...
Gotham Central Hospital
AMBULANCE
Dial 911
...he left the Spoiler behind.
STEPH--
ANY PROBLEMS GETTING HERE?
NOTHING I COULDN'T HANDLE.
I...KNOW. I WAS WORRIED ANYWAY. CITY'S GOTTEN UGLY UGLIER.
YOU DON'T MIND BEING YOUR MOM'S BODYGUARD?
BEST JOB AN EX-SUPERHERO CAN HAVE.

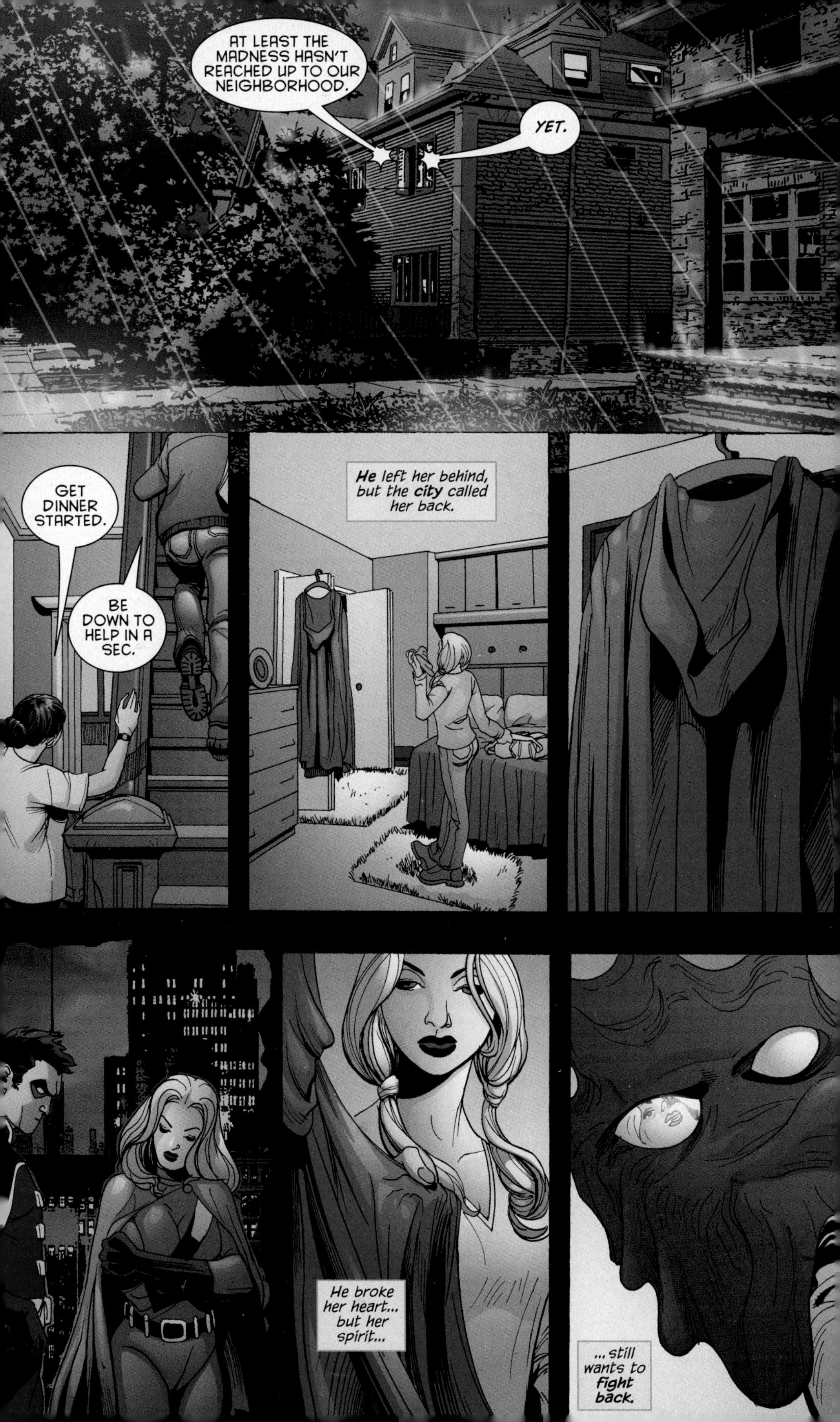
AT LEAST THE MADNESS HASN'T REACHED UP TO OUR NEIGHBORHOOD.
YET.
GET DINNER STARTED.
BE DOWN TO HELP IN A SEC.
He left her behind, but the city called her back.
He broke her heart... but her spirit...
...still wants to fight back.

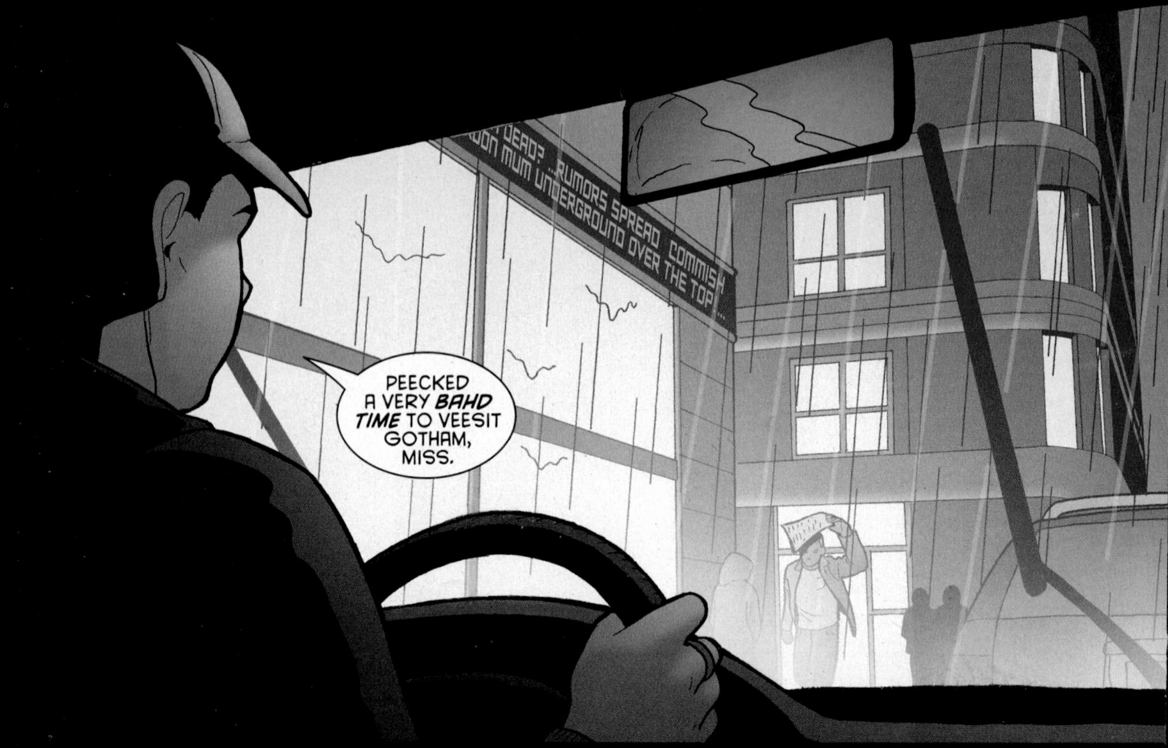
DEAD?...RUMORS SPREAD COMMISH
DON MUM UNDERGROUND OVER THE TOP!...
PEECKED A VERY BAHD TIME TO VEESIT GOTHAM, MISS.

Leslie Thompkins

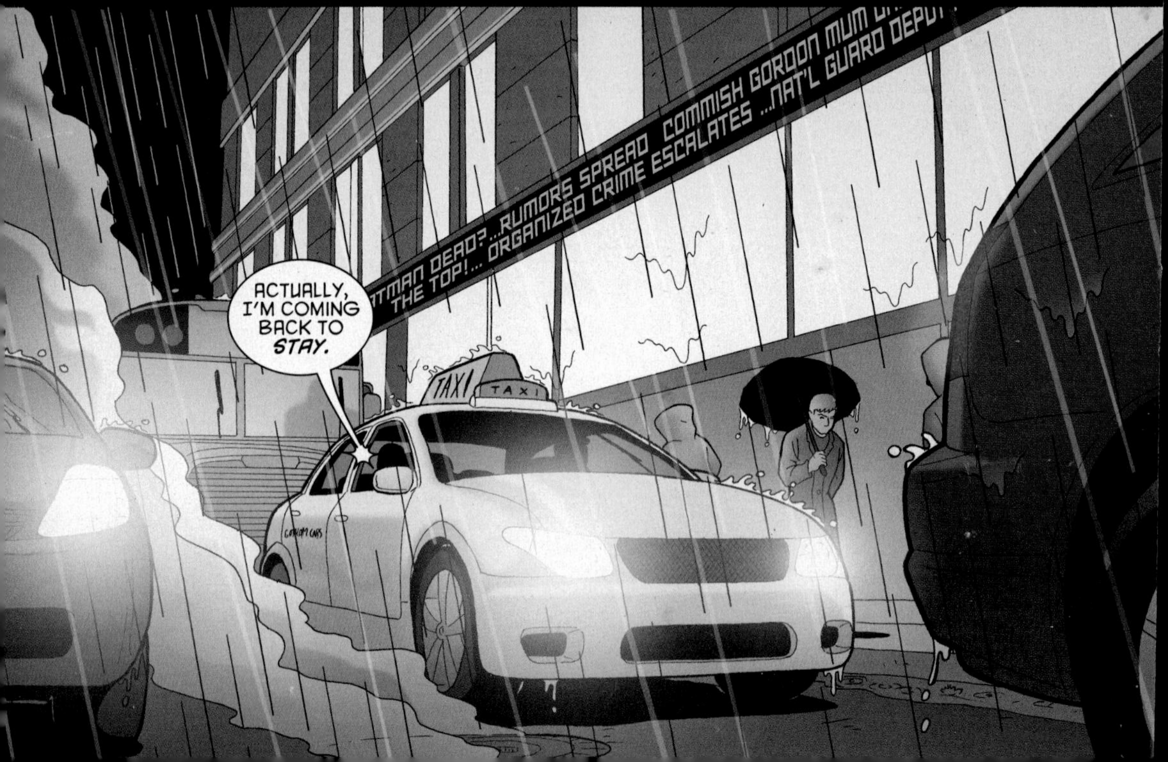
TMAN DEAD?...RUMORS SPREAD COMMISH GORDON MUM UN
THE TOP!... ORGANIZED CRIME ESCALATES ...NAT'L GUARD DEPU
ACTUALLY, I'M COMING BACK TO STAY.
TAXI

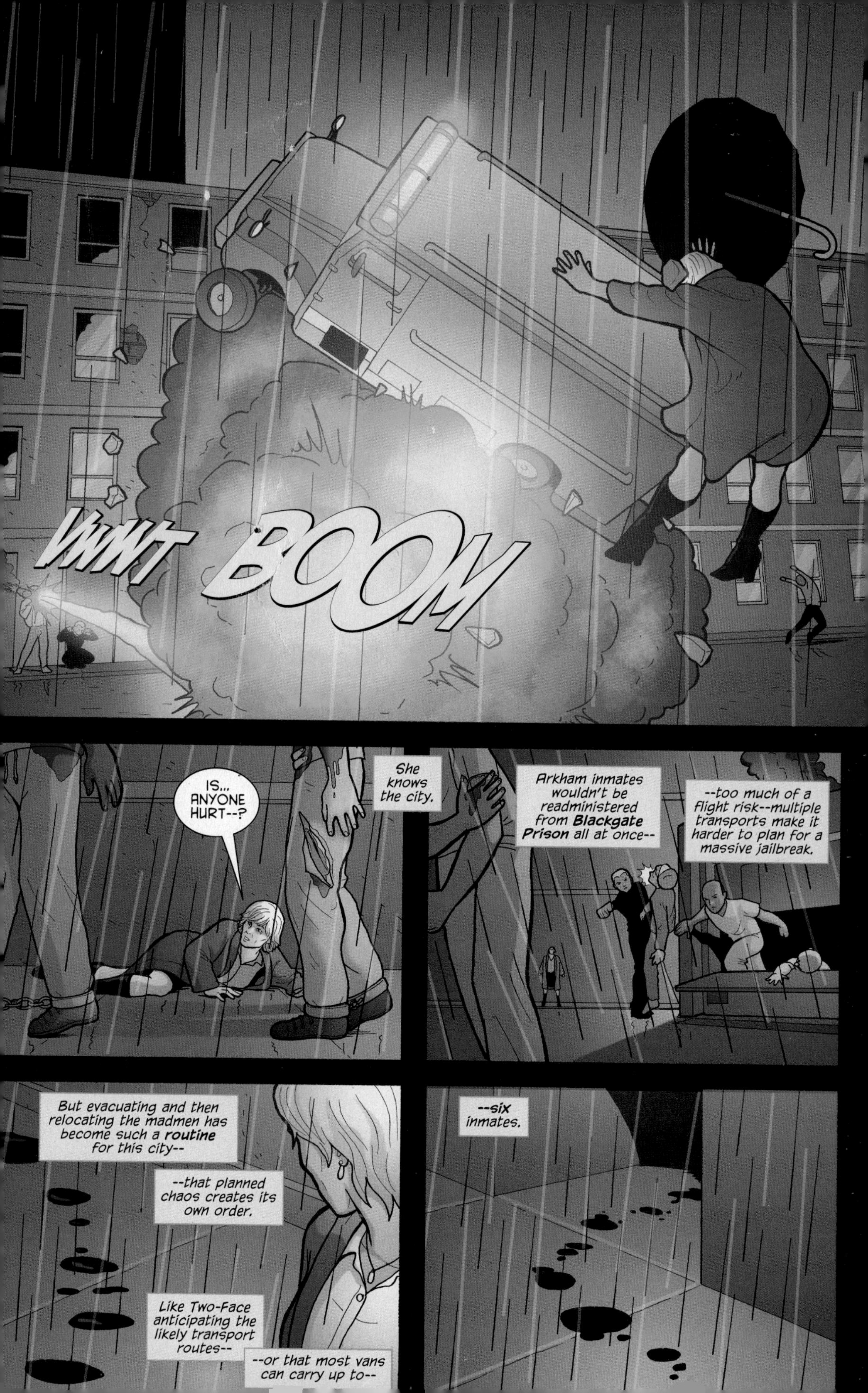
VWWT BOOM
IS... ANYONE HURT--?
She knows the city.
Arkham inmates wouldn't be readministered from Blackgate Prison all at once--
--too much of a flight risk--multiple transports make it harder to plan for a massive jailbreak.
But evacuating and then relocating the madmen has become such a routine for this city--
--that planned chaos creates its own order.
Like Two-Face anticipating the likely transport routes--
--or that most vans can carry up to--
--six inmates.

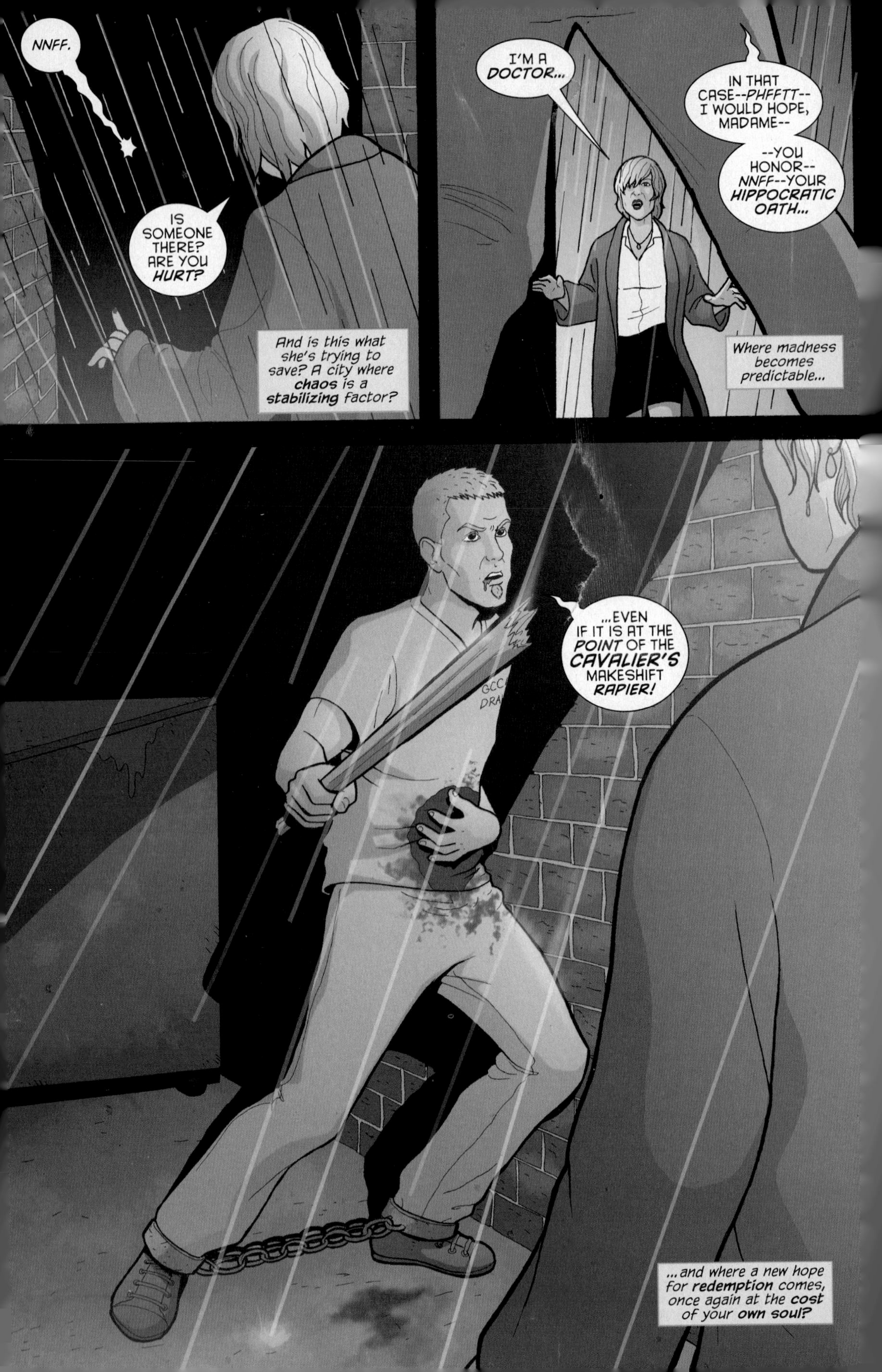
NNFF.
IS SOMEONE THERE? ARE YOU HURT?
And is this what she's trying to save? A city where chaos is a stabilizing factor?
I'M A DOCTOR...
IN THAT CASE--PHFFTT--I WOULD HOPE, MADAME--
--YOU HONOR--NNFF--YOUR HIPPOCRATIC OATH...
Where madness becomes predictable...
...EVEN IF IT IS AT THE POINT OF THE CAVALIER'S MAKESHIFT RAPIER!
...and where a new hope for redemption comes, once again at the cost of your own soul?

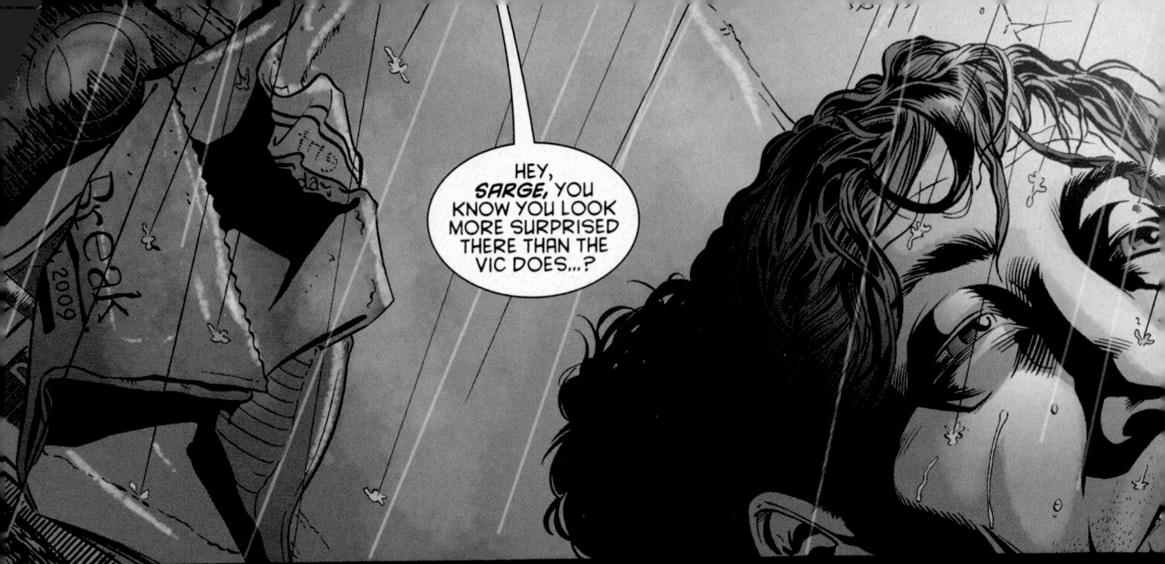
HEY, SARGE, YOU KNOW YOU LOOK MORE SURPRISED THERE THAN THE VIC DOES...?

Harvey Bullock

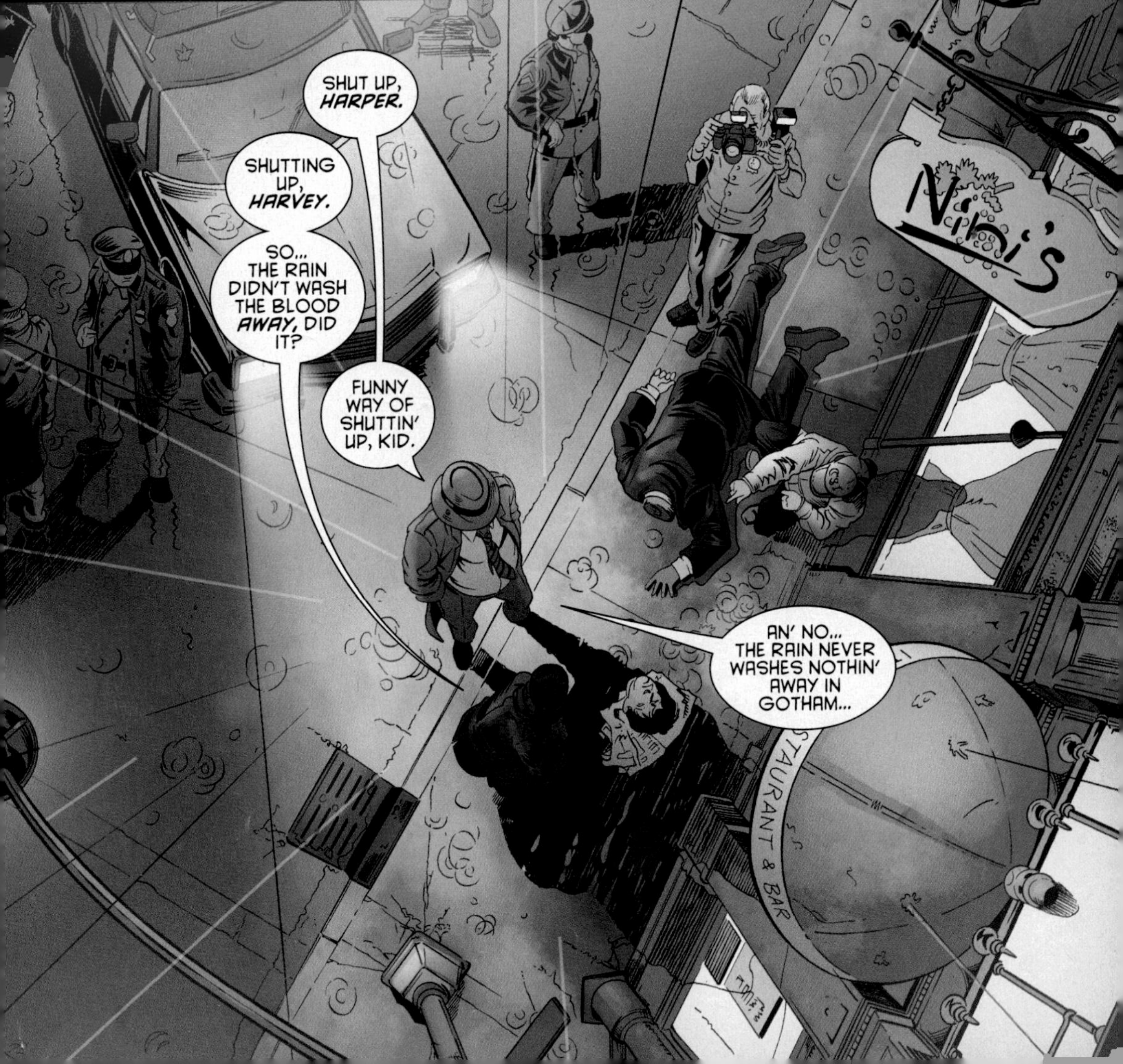
SHUT UP, HARPER.
SHUTTING UP, HARVEY.
SO... THE RAIN DIDN'T WASH THE BLOOD AWAY, DID IT?
FUNNY WAY OF SHUTTIN' UP, KID.
Nini's
AN' NO... THE RAIN NEVER WASHES NOTHIN' AWAY IN GOTHAM...
STAURANT & BAR

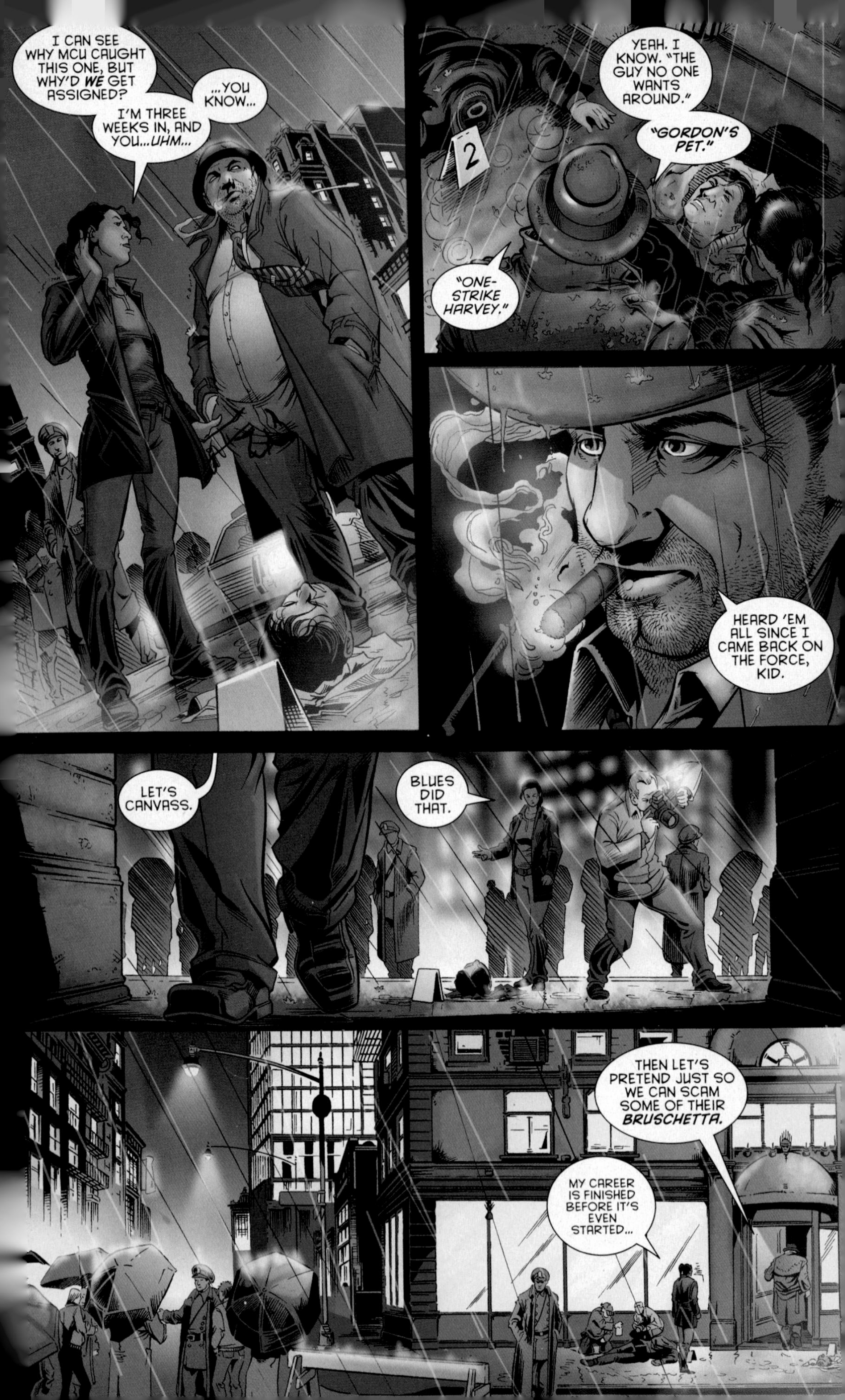
I CAN SEE WHY MCU CAUGHT THIS ONE, BUT WHY'D *WE* GET ASSIGNED?
I'M THREE WEEKS IN, AND YOU...*UHM*...
...YOU KNOW...
YEAH. I KNOW. "THE GUY NO ONE WANTS AROUND."
"GORDON'S PET."
"ONE-STRIKE HARVEY."
HEARD 'EM ALL SINCE I CAME BACK ON THE FORCE, KID.
LET'S CANVASS.
BLUES DID THAT.
THEN LET'S PRETEND JUST SO WE CAN SCAM SOME OF THEIR *BRUSCHETTA.*
MY CAREER IS FINISHED BEFORE IT'S EVEN STARTED...

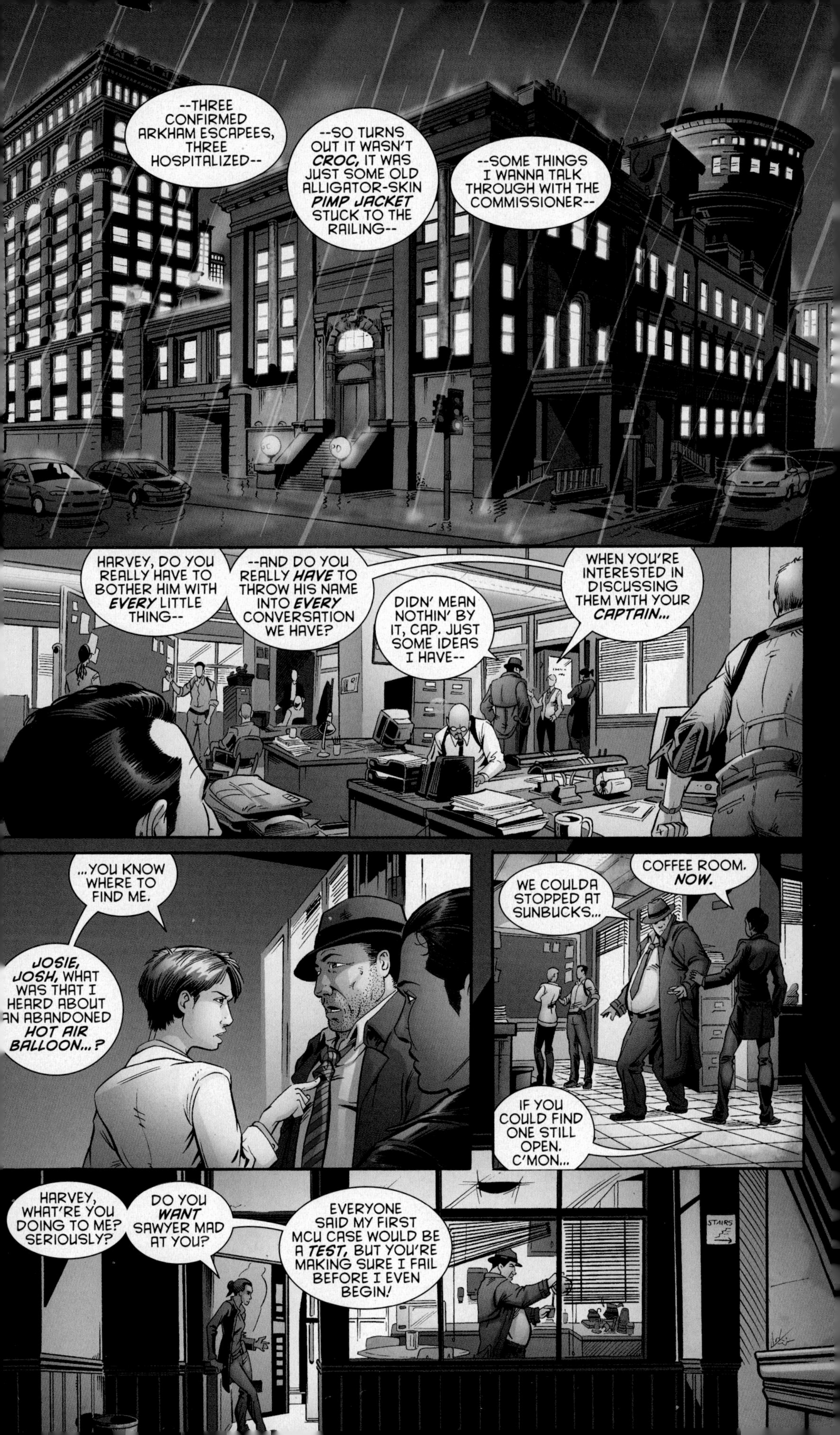
--THREE CONFIRMED ARKHAM ESCAPEES, THREE HOSPITALIZED--
--SO TURNS OUT IT WASN'T CROC, IT WAS JUST SOME OLD ALLIGATOR-SKIN PIMP JACKET STUCK TO THE RAILING--
--SOME THINGS I WANNA TALK THROUGH WITH THE COMMISSIONER--
HARVEY, DO YOU REALLY HAVE TO BOTHER HIM WITH EVERY LITTLE THING--
--AND DO YOU REALLY HAVE TO THROW HIS NAME INTO EVERY CONVERSATION WE HAVE?
DIDN' MEAN NOTHIN' BY IT, CAP. JUST SOME IDEAS I HAVE--
WHEN YOU'RE INTERESTED IN DISCUSSING THEM WITH YOUR CAPTAIN...
...YOU KNOW WHERE TO FIND ME.
JOSIE, JOSH, WHAT WAS THAT I HEARD ABOUT AN ABANDONED HOT AIR BALLOON...?
COFFEE ROOM. NOW.
WE COULDA STOPPED AT SUNBUCKS...
IF YOU COULD FIND ONE STILL OPEN. C'MON...
HARVEY, WHAT'RE YOU DOING TO ME? SERIOUSLY?
DO YOU WANT SAWYER MAD AT YOU?
EVERYONE SAID MY FIRST MCU CASE WOULD BE A TEST, BUT YOU'RE MAKING SURE I FAIL BEFORE I EVEN BEGIN!
STAIRS

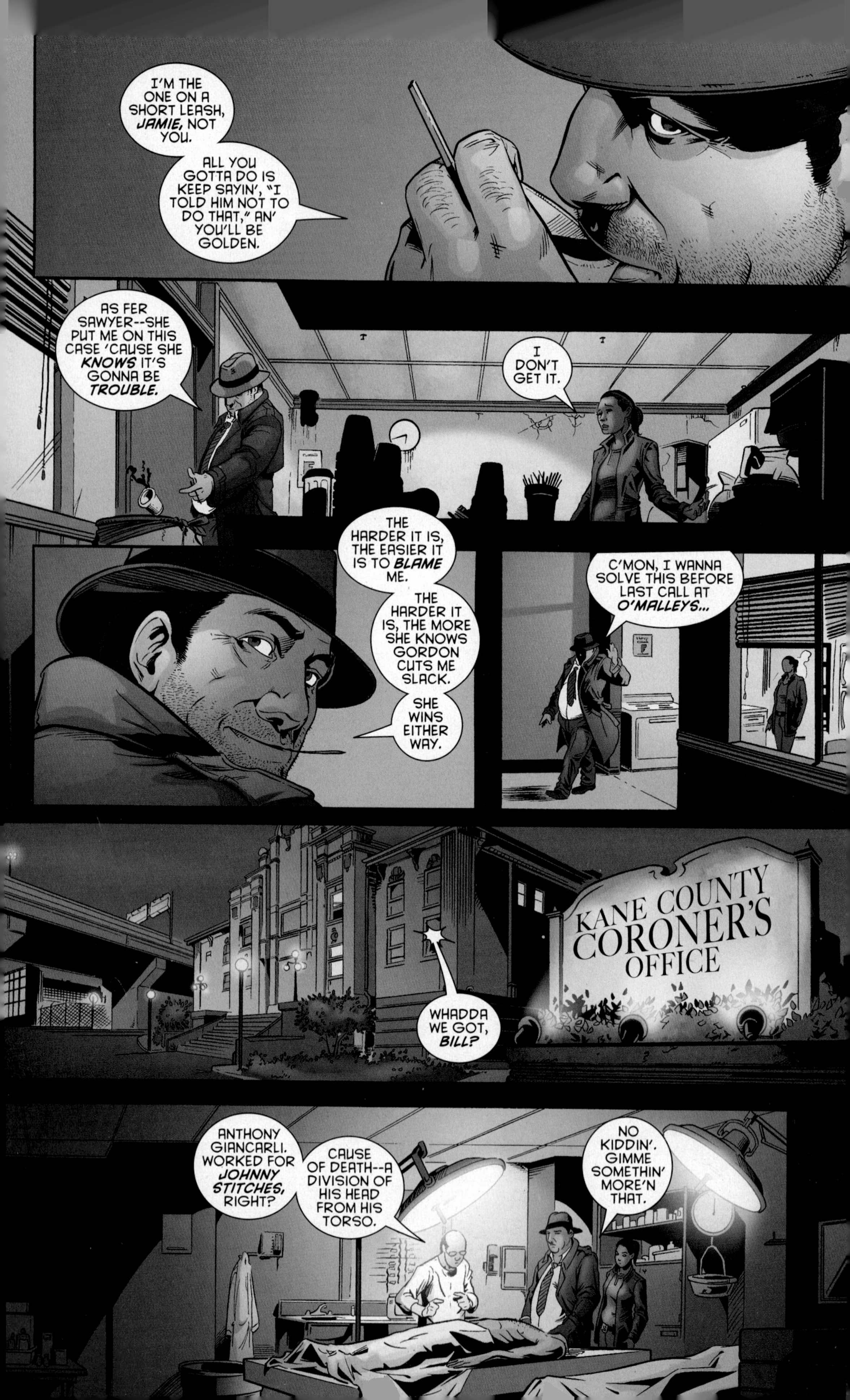

I'M THE ONE ON A SHORT LEASH, JAMIE, NOT YOU.
ALL YOU GOTTA DO IS KEEP SAYIN', "I TOLD HIM NOT TO DO THAT," AN' YOU'LL BE GOLDEN.
AS FER SAWYER--SHE PUT ME ON THIS CASE 'CAUSE SHE KNOWS IT'S GONNA BE TROUBLE.
I DON'T GET IT.
THE HARDER IT IS, THE EASIER IT IS TO BLAME ME.
THE HARDER IT IS, THE MORE SHE KNOWS GORDON CUTS ME SLACK.
SHE WINS EITHER WAY.
C'MON, I WANNA SOLVE THIS BEFORE LAST CALL AT O'MALLEYS...
KANE COUNTY CORONER'S OFFICE
WHADDA WE GOT, BILL?
ANTHONY GIANCARLI. WORKED FOR JOHNNY STITCHES, RIGHT?
CAUSE OF DEATH--A DIVISION OF HIS HEAD FROM HIS TORSO.
NO KIDDIN'. GIMME SOMETHIN' MORE'N THAT.

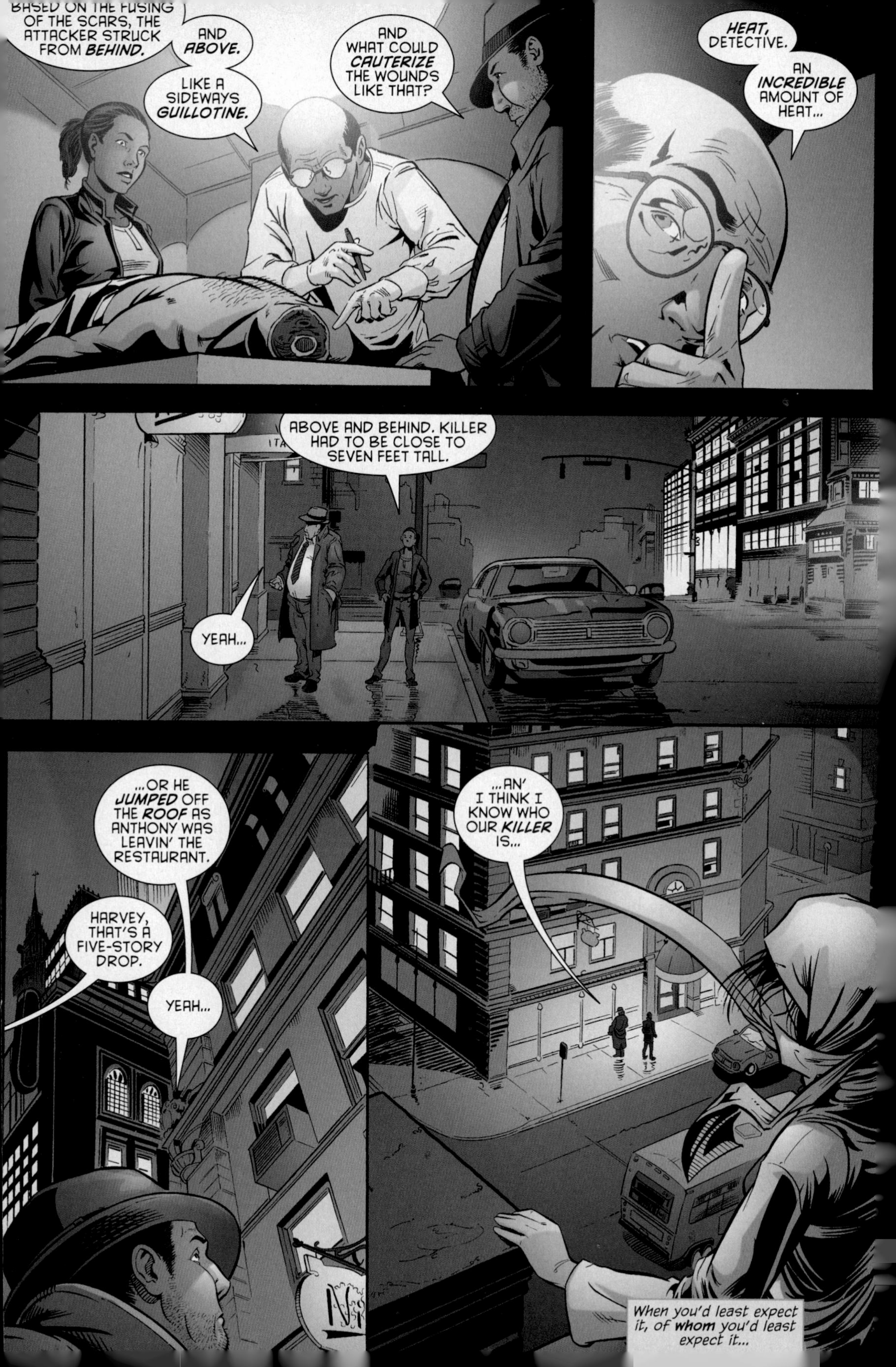
BASED ON THE FUSING OF THE SCARS, THE ATTACKER STRUCK FROM BEHIND.
AND ABOVE.
LIKE A SIDEWAYS GUILLOTINE.
AND WHAT COULD CAUTERIZE THE WOUNDS LIKE THAT?
HEAT, DETECTIVE.
AN INCREDIBLE AMOUNT OF HEAT...
ABOVE AND BEHIND. KILLER HAD TO BE CLOSE TO SEVEN FEET TALL.
YEAH...
...OR HE JUMPED OFF THE ROOF AS ANTHONY WAS LEAVIN' THE RESTAURANT.
HARVEY, THAT'S A FIVE-STORY DROP.
YEAH...
...AN' I THINK I KNOW WHO OUR KILLER IS...
When you'd least expect it, of whom you'd least expect it...

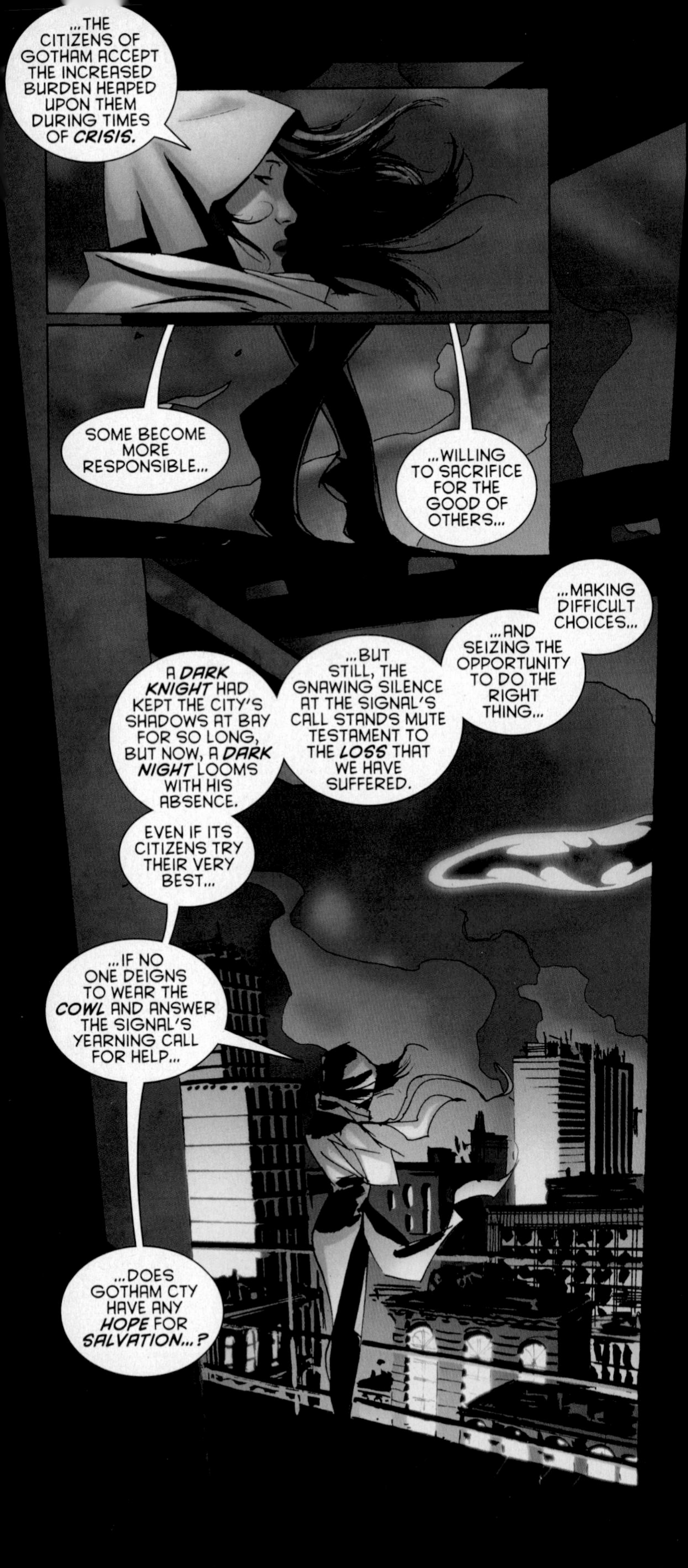
...THE CITIZENS OF GOTHAM ACCEPT THE INCREASED BURDEN HEAPED UPON THEM DURING TIMES OF CRISIS.
SOME BECOME MORE RESPONSIBLE...
...WILLING TO SACRIFICE FOR THE GOOD OF OTHERS...
...MAKING DIFFICULT CHOICES...
...AND SEIZING THE OPPORTUNITY TO DO THE RIGHT THING...
...BUT STILL, THE GNAWING SILENCE AT THE SIGNAL'S CALL STANDS MUTE TESTAMENT TO THE LOSS THAT WE HAVE SUFFERED.
A DARK KNIGHT HAD KEPT THE CITY'S SHADOWS AT BAY FOR SO LONG, BUT NOW, A DARK NIGHT LOOMS WITH HIS ABSENCE.
EVEN IF ITS CITIZENS TRY THEIR VERY BEST...
...IF NO ONE DEIGNS TO WEAR THE COWL AND ANSWER THE SIGNAL'S YEARNING CALL FOR HELP...
...DOES GOTHAM CTY HAVE ANY HOPE FOR SALVATION...?

GOTHAM GAZETTE
BATMAN DEAD?

Written By
Fabian Nicieza

The Veil
Art by
Dustin Nguyen

Vicki Vale
Art by
Guillem March

Stephanie Brown
Art by
ChrisCross

Leslie Thompkins
Art by
Jamie McKelvie

Harvey Bullock
Art by
Alex Konat
And
Mark McKenna

Letters by
Swands

Colors by
Guy Major (pgs 103, 109-124),
Guillem March (pgs 104-108)

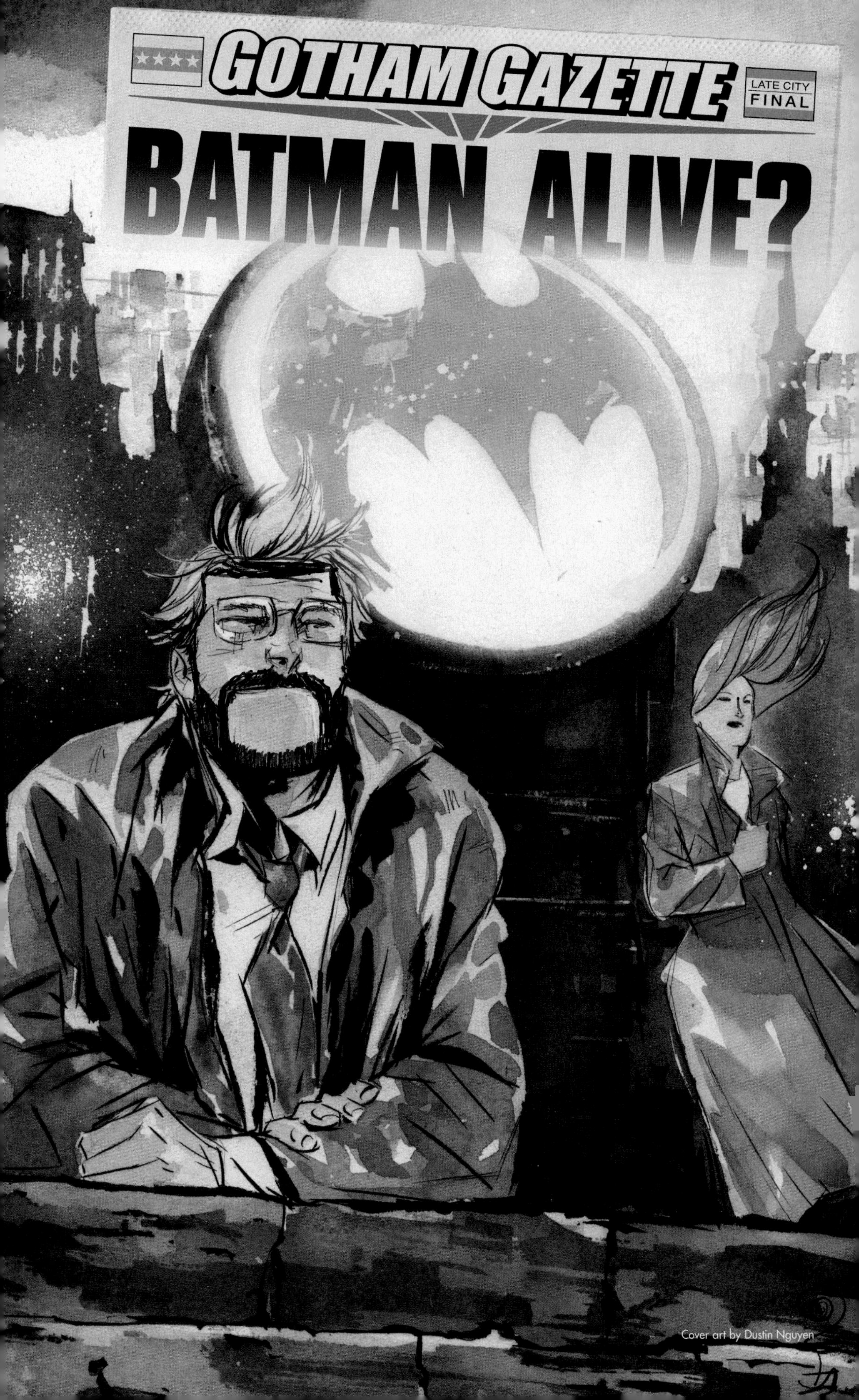
GOTHAM GAZETTE
LATE CITY FINAL
BATMAN ALIVE?
Cover art by Dustin Nguyen

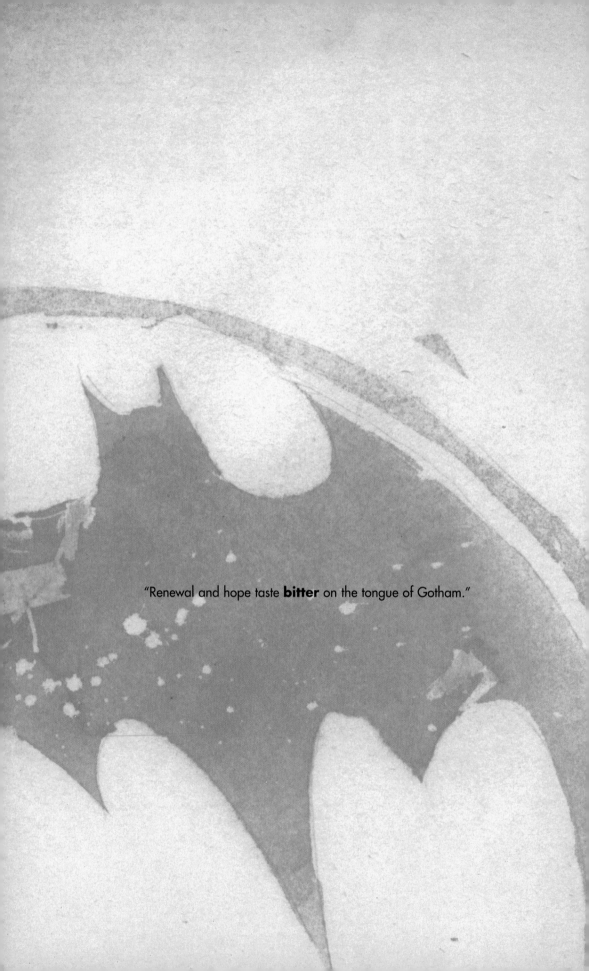

"Renewal and hope taste **bitter** on the tongue of Gotham."

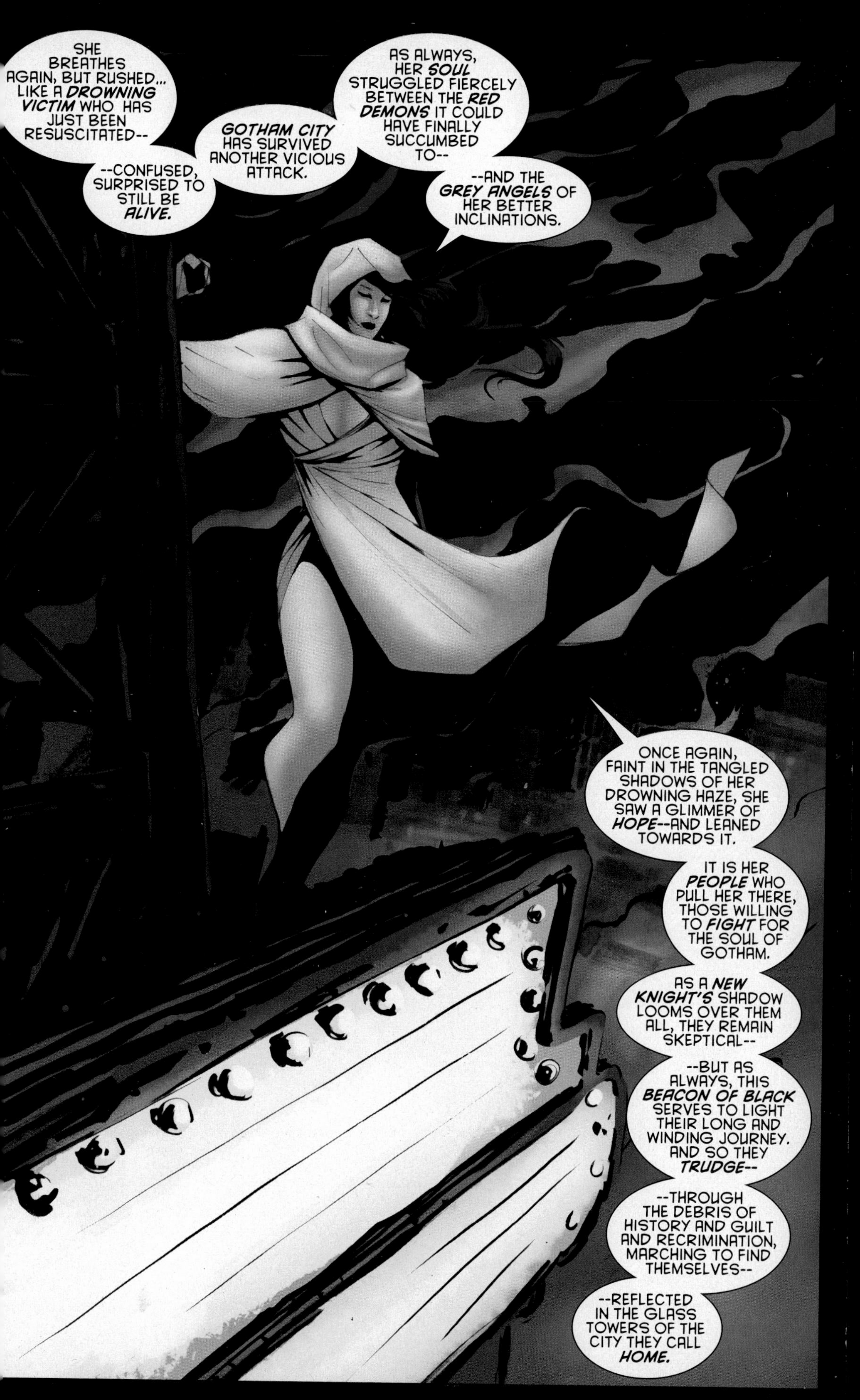

SHE BREATHES AGAIN, BUT RUSHED... LIKE A *DROWNING VICTIM* WHO HAS JUST BEEN RESUSCITATED--
--CONFUSED, SURPRISED TO STILL BE *ALIVE.*
GOTHAM CITY HAS SURVIVED ANOTHER VICIOUS ATTACK.
AS ALWAYS, HER *SOUL* STRUGGLED FIERCELY BETWEEN THE *RED DEMONS* IT COULD HAVE FINALLY SUCCUMBED TO--
--AND THE *GREY ANGELS* OF HER BETTER INCLINATIONS.
ONCE AGAIN, FAINT IN THE TANGLED SHADOWS OF HER DROWNING HAZE, SHE SAW A GLIMMER OF *HOPE*--AND LEANED TOWARDS IT.
IT IS HER *PEOPLE* WHO PULL HER THERE, THOSE WILLING TO *FIGHT* FOR THE SOUL OF GOTHAM.
AS A *NEW KNIGHT'S* SHADOW LOOMS OVER THEM ALL, THEY REMAIN SKEPTICAL--
--BUT AS ALWAYS, THIS *BEACON OF BLACK* SERVES TO LIGHT THEIR LONG AND WINDING JOURNEY. AND SO THEY *TRUDGE*--
--THROUGH THE DEBRIS OF HISTORY AND GUILT AND RECRIMINATION, MARCHING TO FIND THEMSELVES--
--REFLECTED IN THE GLASS TOWERS OF THE CITY THEY CALL *HOME.*

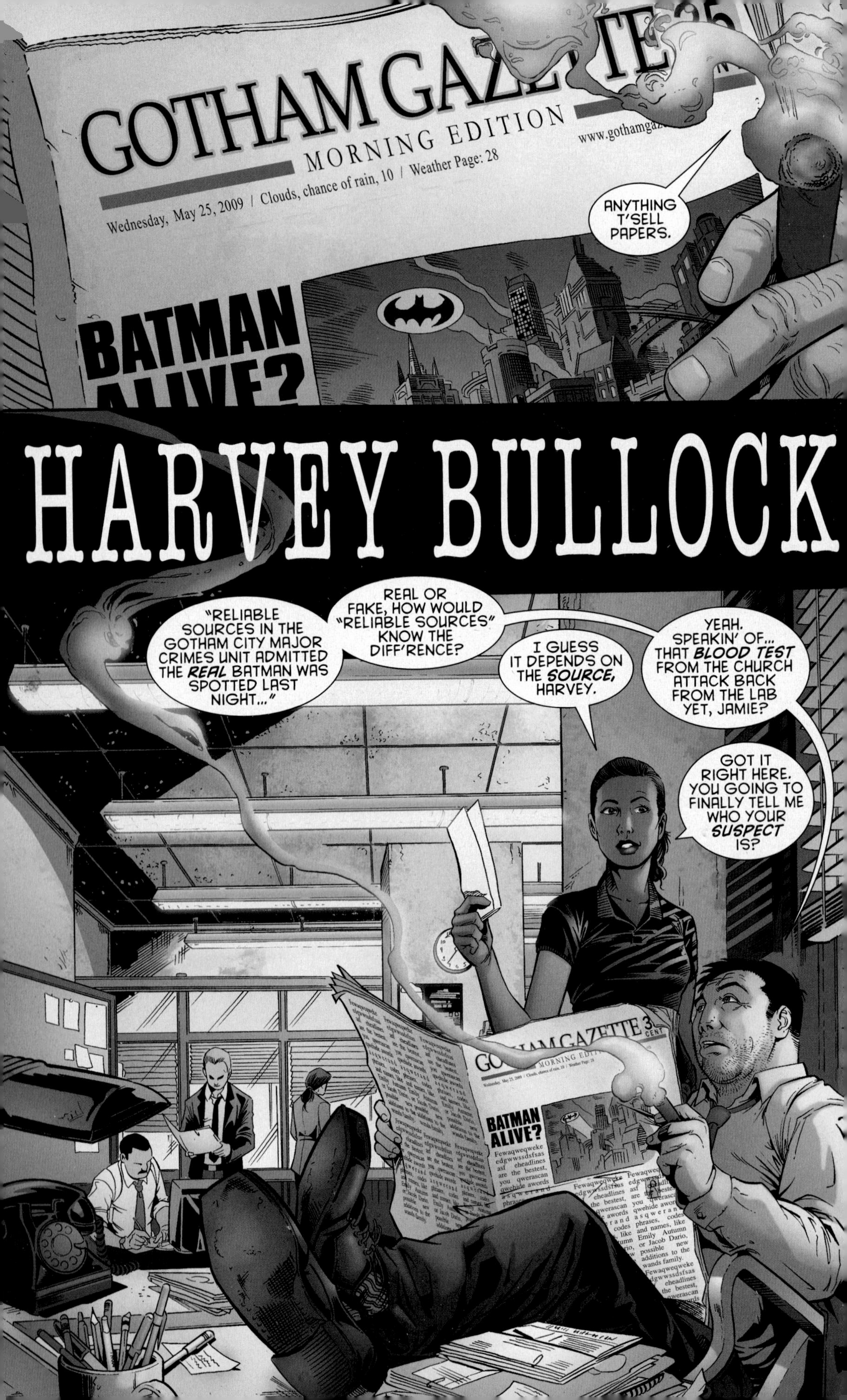
GOTHAM GAZETTE 25
MORNING EDITION
www.gothamgaz
Wednesday, May 25, 2009 / Clouds, chance of rain, 10 / Weather Page: 28
ANYTHING T'SELL PAPERS.
BATMAN ALIVE?
HARVEY BULLOCK
"RELIABLE SOURCES IN THE GOTHAM CITY MAJOR CRIMES UNIT ADMITTED THE *REAL* BATMAN WAS SPOTTED LAST NIGHT..."
REAL OR FAKE, HOW WOULD "RELIABLE SOURCES" KNOW THE DIFF'RENCE?
I GUESS IT DEPENDS ON THE *SOURCE,* HARVEY.
YEAH. SPEAKIN' OF... THAT *BLOOD TEST* FROM THE CHURCH ATTACK BACK FROM THE LAB YET, JAMIE?
GOT IT RIGHT HERE. YOU GOING TO FINALLY TELL ME WHO YOUR *SUSPECT* IS?
GOTHAM GAZETTE
BATMAN ALIVE?

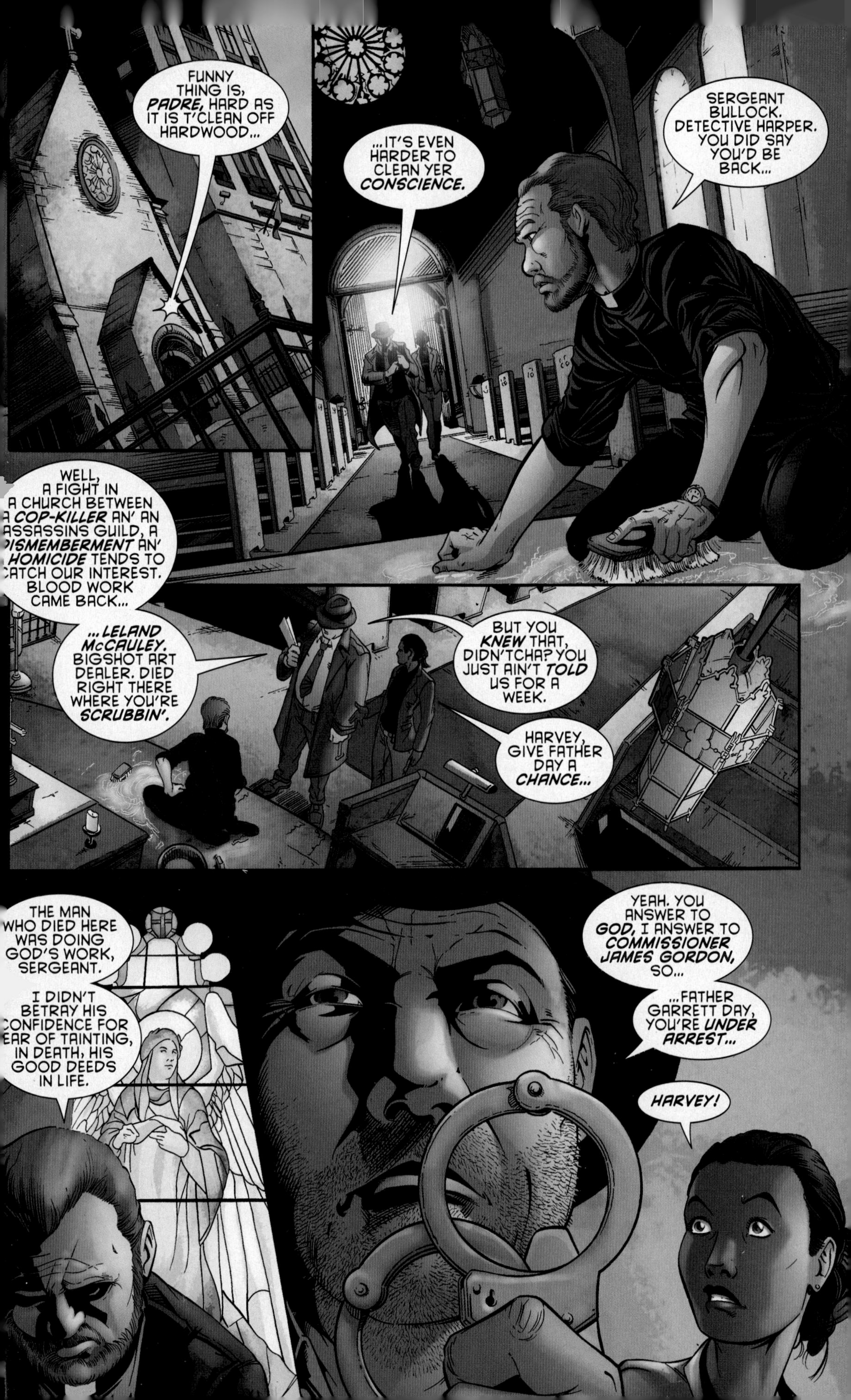
FUNNY THING IS, PADRE, HARD AS IT IS T'CLEAN OFF HARDWOOD...
...IT'S EVEN HARDER TO CLEAN YER CONSCIENCE.
SERGEANT BULLOCK. DETECTIVE HARPER. YOU DID SAY YOU'D BE BACK...
WELL, A FIGHT IN A CHURCH BETWEEN A COP-KILLER AN' AN ASSASSINS GUILD, A DISMEMBERMENT AN' HOMICIDE TENDS TO CATCH OUR INTEREST. BLOOD WORK CAME BACK...
...LELAND McCAULEY. BIGSHOT ART DEALER. DIED RIGHT THERE WHERE YOU'RE SCRUBBIN'.
BUT YOU KNEW THAT, DIDN'TCHA? YOU JUST AIN'T TOLD US FOR A WEEK.
HARVEY, GIVE FATHER DAY A CHANCE...
THE MAN WHO DIED HERE WAS DOING GOD'S WORK, SERGEANT.
I DIDN'T BETRAY HIS CONFIDENCE FOR FEAR OF TAINTING, IN DEATH, HIS GOOD DEEDS IN LIFE.
YEAH. YOU ANSWER TO GOD, I ANSWER TO COMMISSIONER JAMES GORDON, SO...
...FATHER GARRETT DAY, YOU'RE UNDER ARREST...
HARVEY!

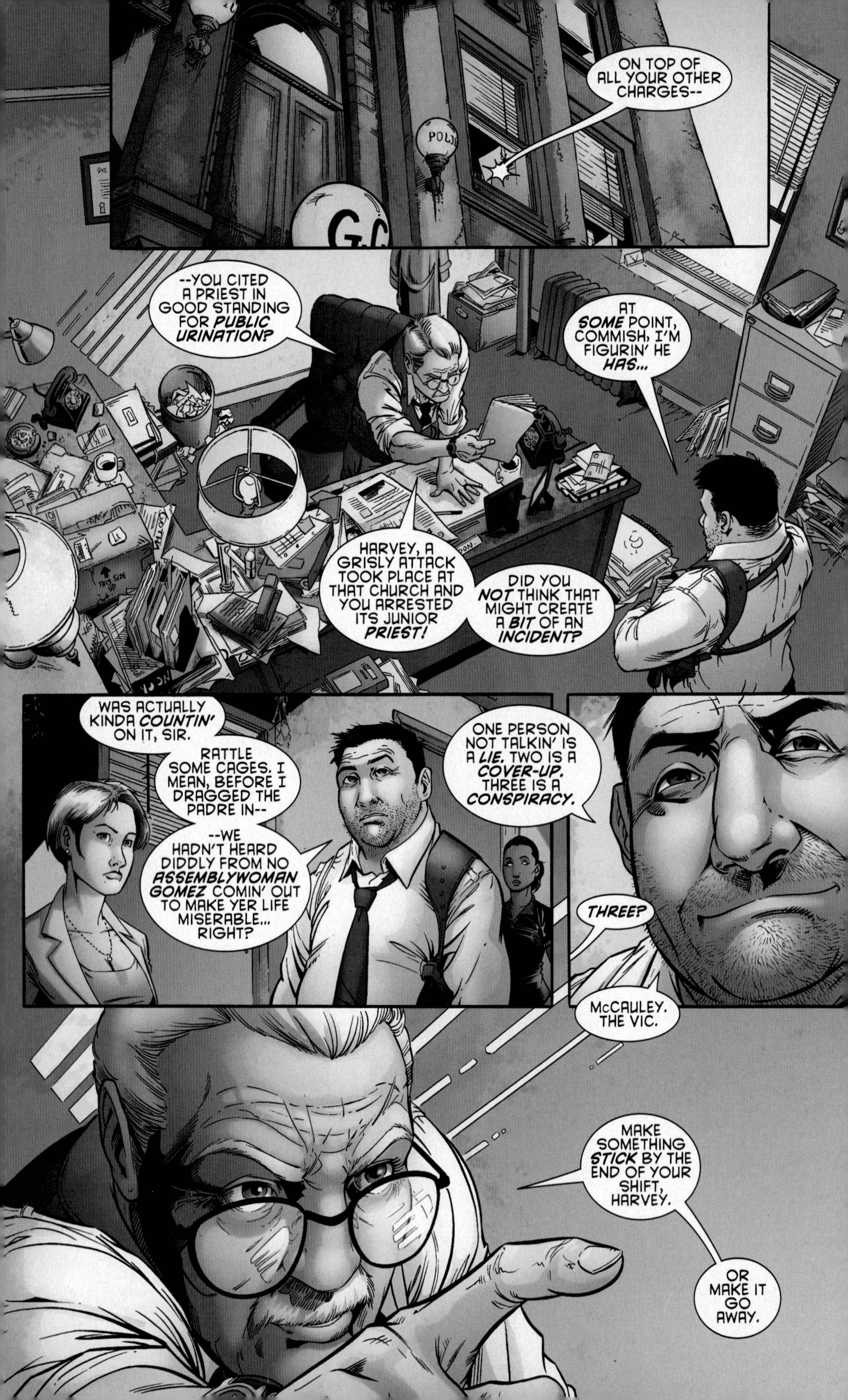
ON TOP OF ALL YOUR OTHER CHARGES--
POLI
G.C.
--YOU CITED A PRIEST IN GOOD STANDING FOR PUBLIC URINATION?
AT SOME POINT, COMMISH, I'M FIGURIN' HE HAS...
HARVEY, A GRISLY ATTACK TOOK PLACE AT THAT CHURCH AND YOU ARRESTED ITS JUNIOR PRIEST!
DID YOU NOT THINK THAT MIGHT CREATE A BIT OF AN INCIDENT?
THIS SIDE UP
WAS ACTUALLY KINDA COUNTIN' ON IT, SIR.
RATTLE SOME CAGES. I MEAN, BEFORE I DRAGGED THE PADRE IN--
--WE HADN'T HEARD DIDDLY FROM NO ASSEMBLYWOMAN GOMEZ COMIN' OUT TO MAKE YER LIFE MISERABLE... RIGHT?
ONE PERSON NOT TALKIN' IS A LIE. TWO IS A COVER-UP. THREE IS A CONSPIRACY.
THREE?
McCAULEY. THE VIC.
MAKE SOMETHING STICK BY THE END OF YOUR SHIFT, HARVEY.
OR MAKE IT GO AWAY.

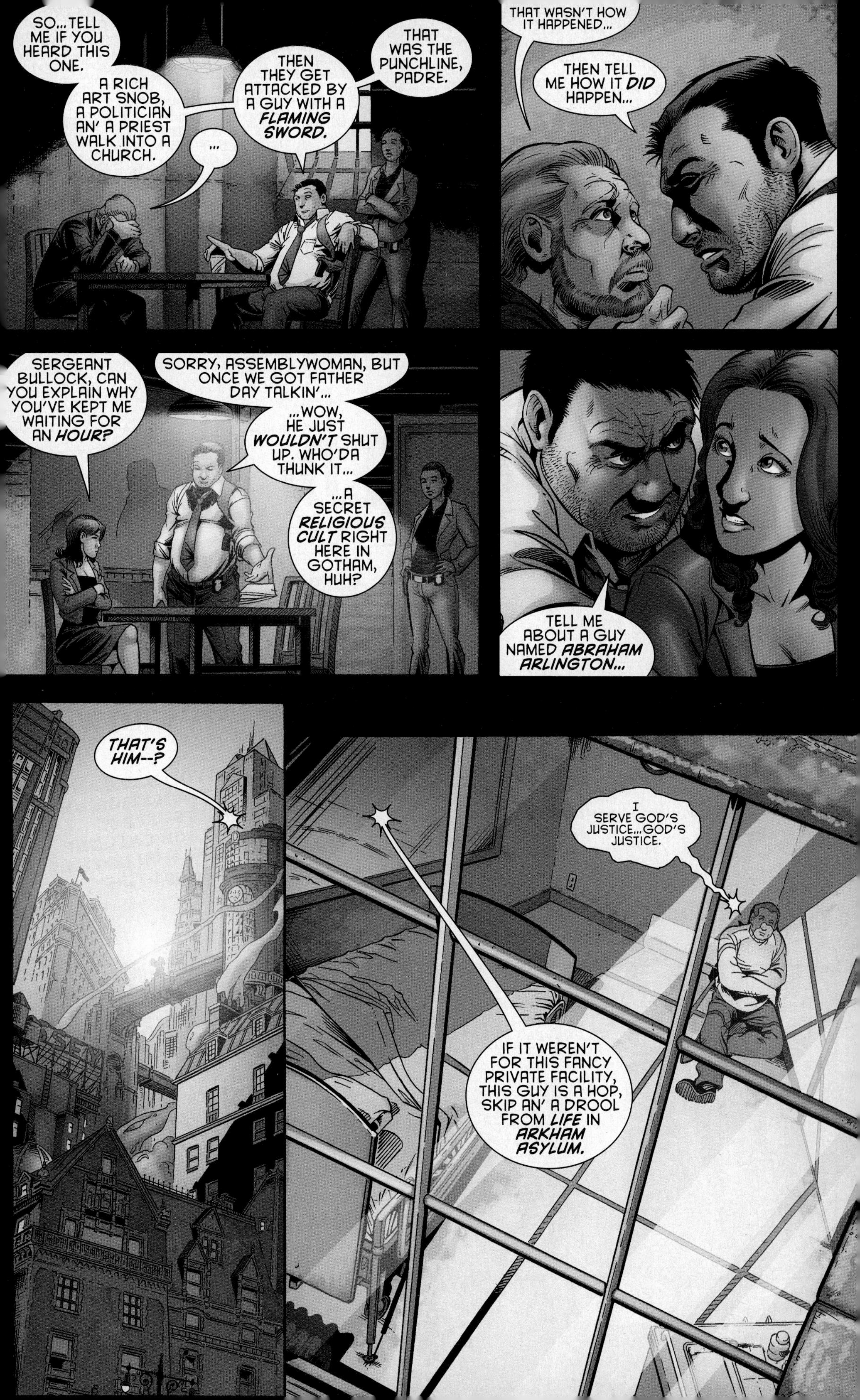
SO... TELL ME IF YOU HEARD THIS ONE.
A RICH ART SNOB, A POLITICIAN AN' A PRIEST WALK INTO A CHURCH.
...
THEN THEY GET ATTACKED BY A GUY WITH A FLAMING SWORD.
THAT WAS THE PUNCHLINE, PADRE.
THAT WASN'T HOW IT HAPPENED...
THEN TELL ME HOW IT DID HAPPEN...
SERGEANT BULLOCK, CAN YOU EXPLAIN WHY YOU'VE KEPT ME WAITING FOR AN HOUR?
SORRY, ASSEMBLYWOMAN, BUT ONCE WE GOT FATHER DAY TALKIN'...
...WOW, HE JUST WOULDN'T SHUT UP. WHO'DA THUNK IT...
...A SECRET RELIGIOUS CULT RIGHT HERE IN GOTHAM, HUH?
TELL ME ABOUT A GUY NAMED ABRAHAM ARLINGTON...
THAT'S HIM--?
I SERVE GOD'S JUSTICE...GOD'S JUSTICE.
IF IT WEREN'T FOR THIS FANCY PRIVATE FACILITY, THIS GUY IS A HOP, SKIP AN' A DROOL FROM LIFE IN ARKHAM ASYLUM.

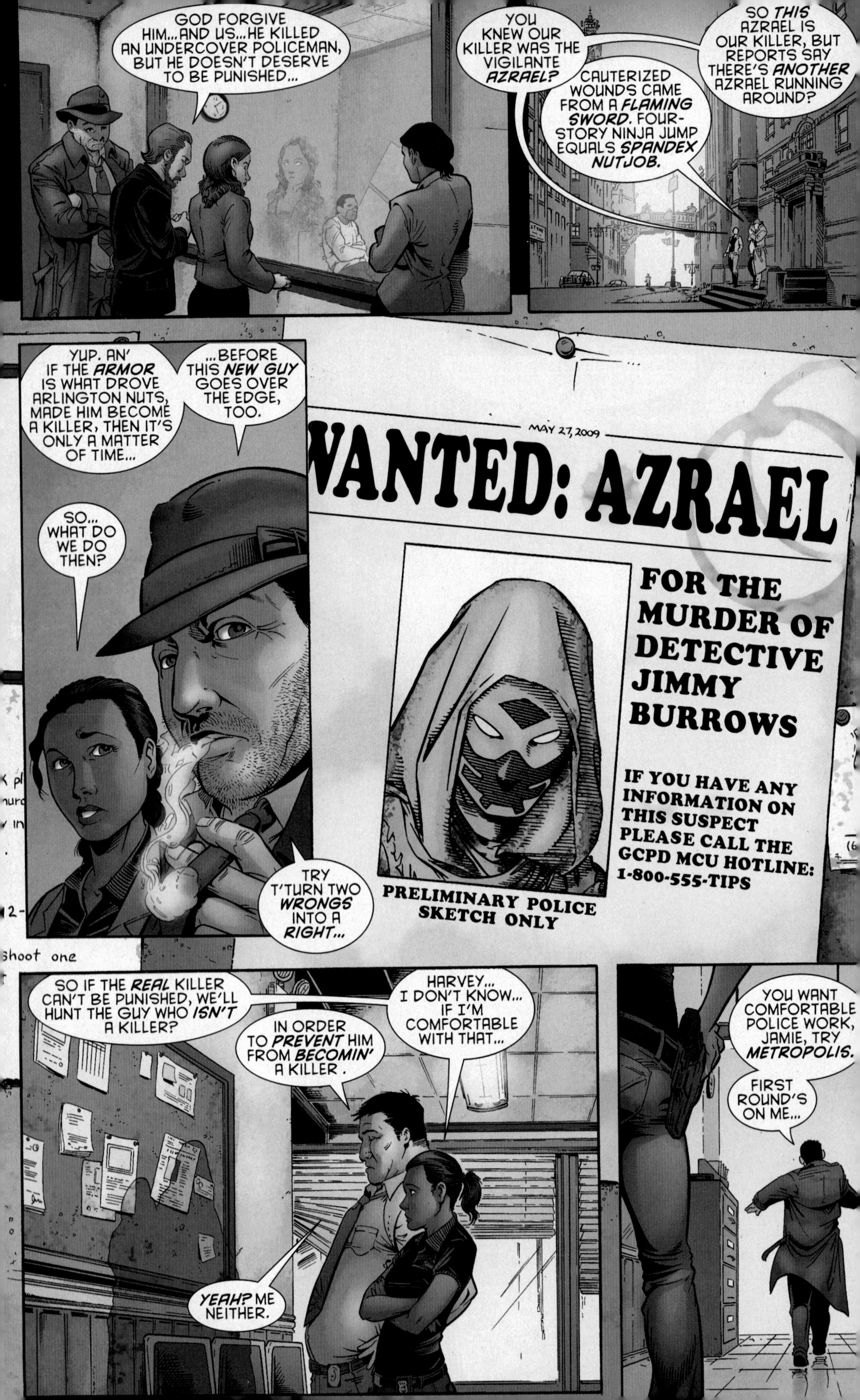
GOD FORGIVE HIM...AND US...HE KILLED AN UNDERCOVER POLICEMAN, BUT HE DOESN'T DESERVE TO BE PUNISHED...
YOU KNEW OUR KILLER WAS THE VIGILANTE AZRAEL?
CAUTERIZED WOUNDS CAME FROM A FLAMING SWORD. FOUR-STORY NINJA JUMP EQUALS SPANDEX NUTJOB.
SO THIS AZRAEL IS OUR KILLER, BUT REPORTS SAY THERE'S ANOTHER AZRAEL RUNNING AROUND?
YUP. AN' IF THE ARMOR IS WHAT DROVE ARLINGTON NUTS, MADE HIM BECOME A KILLER, THEN IT'S ONLY A MATTER OF TIME...
...BEFORE THIS NEW GUY GOES OVER THE EDGE, TOO.
SO... WHAT DO WE DO THEN?
TRY T'TURN TWO WRONGS INTO A RIGHT...
MAY 27, 2009
WANTED: AZRAEL
FOR THE MURDER OF DETECTIVE JIMMY BURROWS
IF YOU HAVE ANY INFORMATION ON THIS SUSPECT PLEASE CALL THE GCPD MCU HOTLINE: 1-800-555-TIPS
PRELIMINARY POLICE SKETCH ONLY
SO IF THE REAL KILLER CAN'T BE PUNISHED, WE'LL HUNT THE GUY WHO ISN'T A KILLER?
IN ORDER TO PREVENT HIM FROM BECOMIN' A KILLER .
HARVEY... I DON'T KNOW... IF I'M COMFORTABLE WITH THAT...
YEAH? ME NEITHER.
YOU WANT COMFORTABLE POLICE WORK, JAMIE, TRY METROPOLIS.
FIRST ROUND'S ON ME...

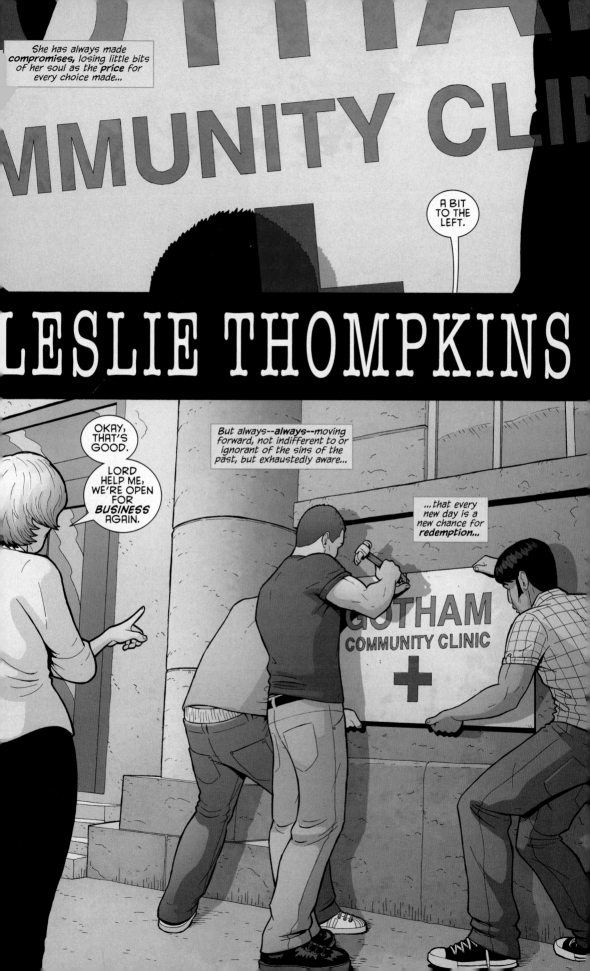

She has always made *compromises*, losing little bits of her soul as the *price* for every choice made...

A BIT TO THE LEFT.

LESLIE THOMPKINS

OKAY, THAT'S GOOD.

LORD HELP ME, WE'RE OPEN FOR *BUSINESS* AGAIN.

But always--*always*--moving forward, not indifferent to or ignorant of the sins of the past, but exhaustedly aware...

...that every new day is a new chance for *redemption*...

GOTHAM COMMUNITY CLINIC

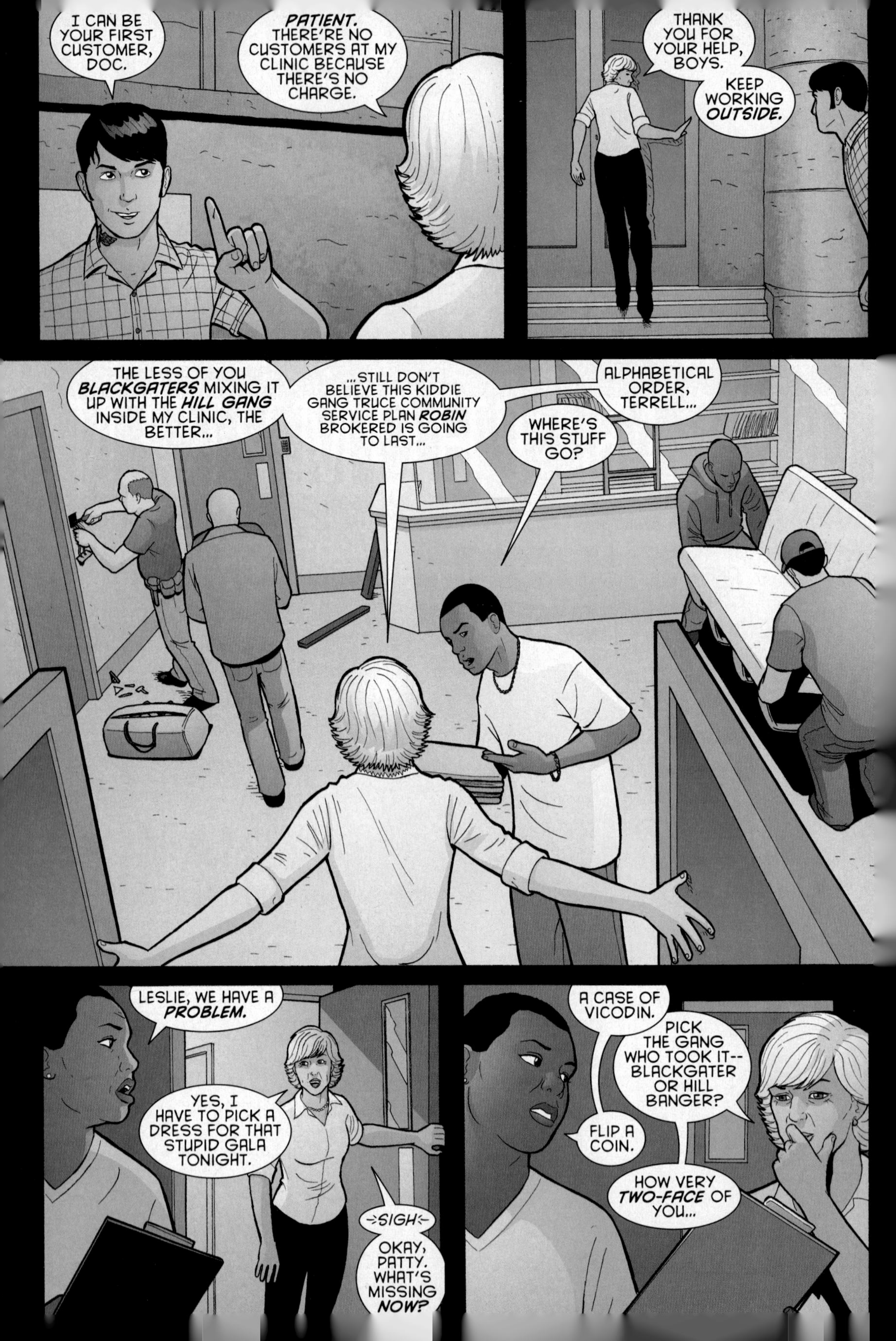
I CAN BE YOUR FIRST CUSTOMER, DOC.
PATIENT. THERE'RE NO CUSTOMERS AT MY CLINIC BECAUSE THERE'S NO CHARGE.
THANK YOU FOR YOUR HELP, BOYS.
KEEP WORKING OUTSIDE.
THE LESS OF YOU BLACKGATERS MIXING IT UP WITH THE HILL GANG INSIDE MY CLINIC, THE BETTER...
...STILL DON'T BELIEVE THIS KIDDIE GANG TRUCE COMMUNITY SERVICE PLAN ROBIN BROKERED IS GOING TO LAST...
ALPHABETICAL ORDER, TERRELL...
WHERE'S THIS STUFF GO?
LESLIE, WE HAVE A PROBLEM.
YES, I HAVE TO PICK A DRESS FOR THAT STUPID GALA TONIGHT.
-SIGH-
OKAY, PATTY. WHAT'S MISSING NOW?
A CASE OF VICODIN.
PICK THE GANG WHO TOOK IT-- BLACKGATER OR HILL BANGER?
FLIP A COIN.
HOW VERY TWO-FACE OF YOU...

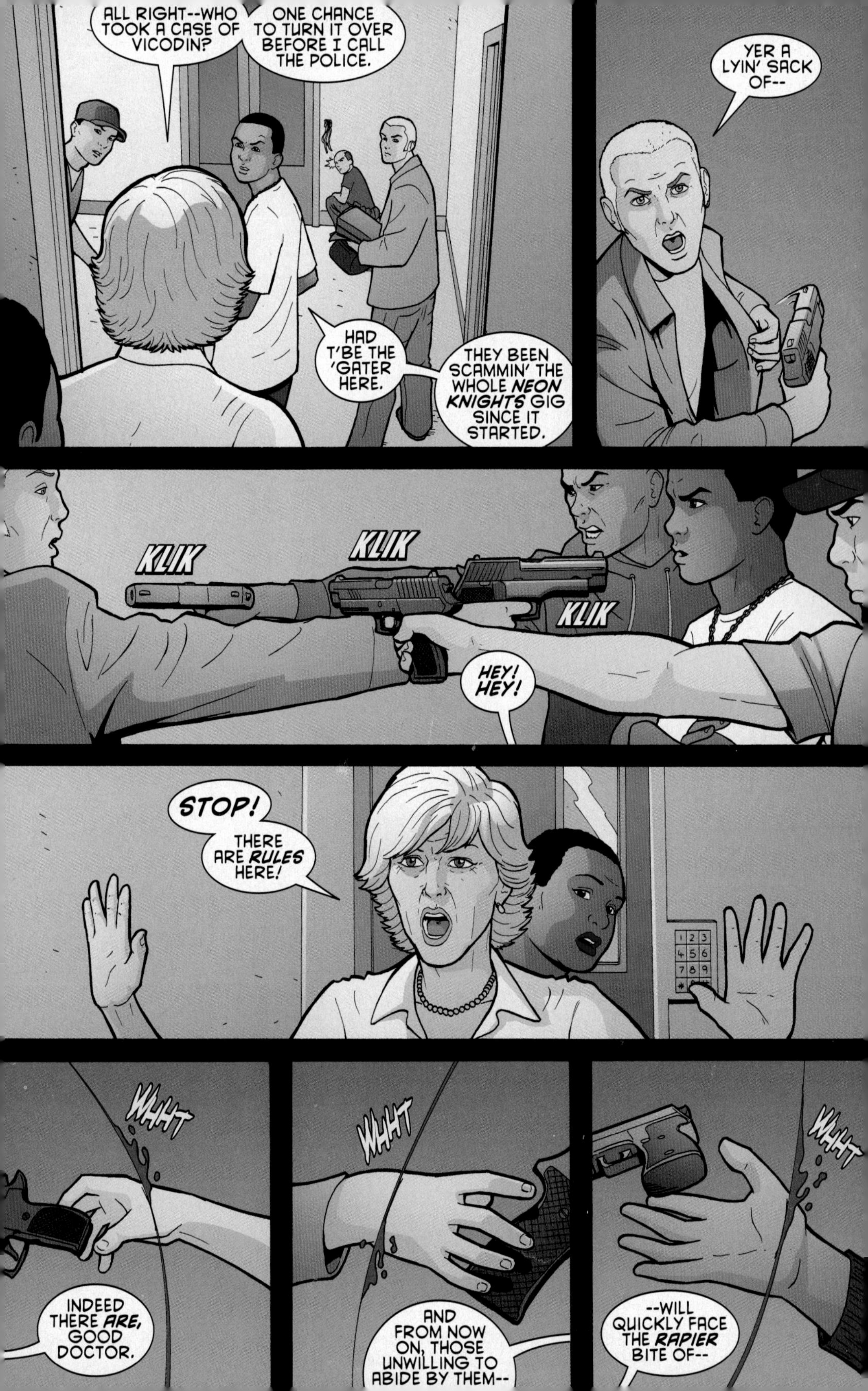
ALL RIGHT--WHO TOOK A CASE OF VICODIN?
ONE CHANCE TO TURN IT OVER BEFORE I CALL THE POLICE.
HAD T'BE THE 'GATER HERE.
THEY BEEN SCAMMIN' THE WHOLE NEON KNIGHTS GIG SINCE IT STARTED.
YER A LYIN' SACK OF--
KLIK
KLIK
KLIK
HEY! HEY!
STOP!
THERE ARE RULES HERE!
WHHT
INDEED THERE ARE, GOOD DOCTOR.
WHHT
AND FROM NOW ON, THOSE UNWILLING TO ABIDE BY THEM--
WHHT
--WILL QUICKLY FACE THE RAPIER BITE OF--

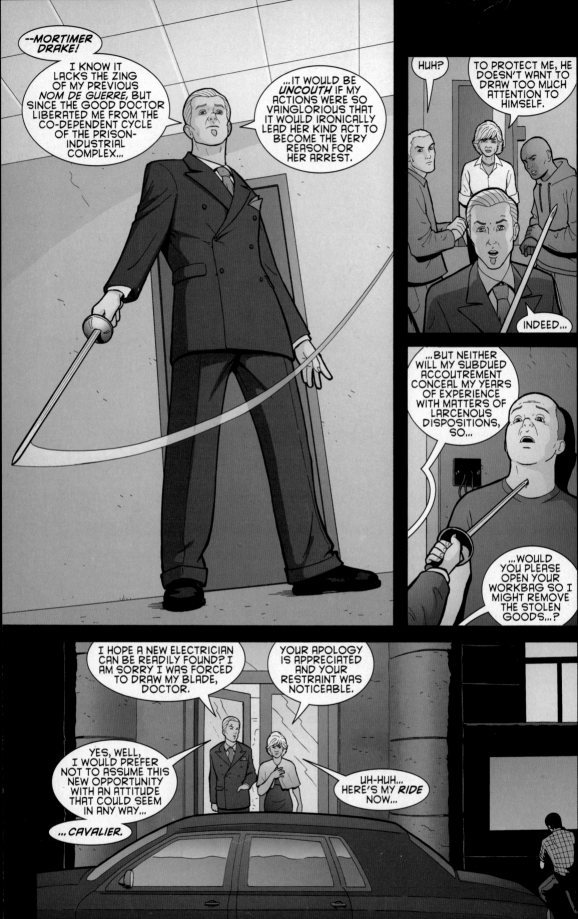

--MORTIMER DRAKE!

I KNOW IT LACKS THE ZING OF MY PREVIOUS *NOM DE GUERRE*, BUT SINCE THE GOOD DOCTOR LIBERATED ME FROM THE CO-DEPENDENT CYCLE OF THE PRISON-INDUSTRIAL COMPLEX...

...IT WOULD BE *UNCOUTH* IF MY ACTIONS WERE SO VAINGLORIOUS THAT IT WOULD IRONICALLY LEAD HER KIND ACT TO BECOME THE VERY REASON FOR HER ARREST.

HUH?

TO PROTECT ME, HE DOESN'T WANT TO DRAW TOO MUCH ATTENTION TO HIMSELF.

INDEED...

...BUT NEITHER WILL MY SUBDUED ACCOUTREMENT CONCEAL MY YEARS OF EXPERIENCE WITH MATTERS OF LARCENOUS DISPOSITIONS, SO...

...WOULD YOU PLEASE OPEN YOUR WORKBAG SO I MIGHT REMOVE THE STOLEN GOODS...?

I HOPE A NEW ELECTRICIAN CAN BE READILY FOUND? I AM SORRY I WAS FORCED TO DRAW MY BLADE, DOCTOR.

YOUR APOLOGY IS APPRECIATED AND YOUR RESTRAINT WAS NOTICEABLE.

YES, WELL, I WOULD PREFER NOT TO ASSUME THIS NEW OPPORTUNITY WITH AN ATTITUDE THAT COULD SEEM IN ANY WAY...

...CAVALIER.

UH-HUH... HERE'S MY *RIDE* NOW...

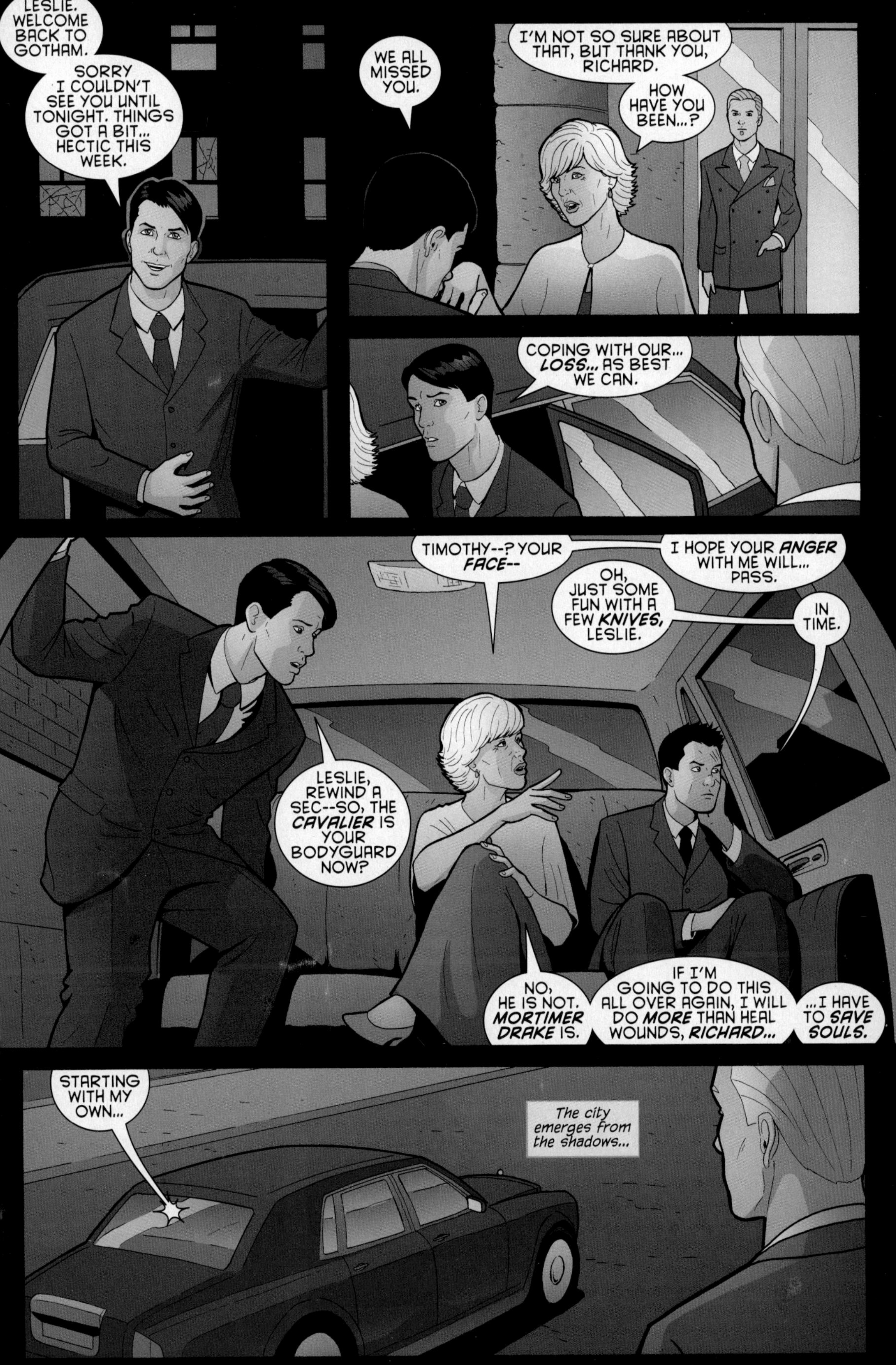
LESLIE. WELCOME BACK TO GOTHAM.
SORRY I COULDN'T SEE YOU UNTIL TONIGHT. THINGS GOT A BIT... HECTIC THIS WEEK.
WE ALL MISSED YOU.
I'M NOT SO SURE ABOUT THAT, BUT THANK YOU, RICHARD.
HOW HAVE YOU BEEN...?
COPING WITH OUR... LOSS... AS BEST WE CAN.
TIMOTHY--? YOUR FACE--
OH, JUST SOME FUN WITH A FEW KNIVES, LESLIE.
I HOPE YOUR ANGER WITH ME WILL... PASS.
IN TIME.
LESLIE, REWIND A SEC--SO, THE CAVALIER IS YOUR BODYGUARD NOW?
NO, HE IS NOT. MORTIMER DRAKE IS.
IF I'M GOING TO DO THIS ALL OVER AGAIN, I WILL DO MORE THAN HEAL WOUNDS, RICHARD...
...I HAVE TO SAVE SOULS.
STARTING WITH MY OWN...
The city emerges from the shadows...

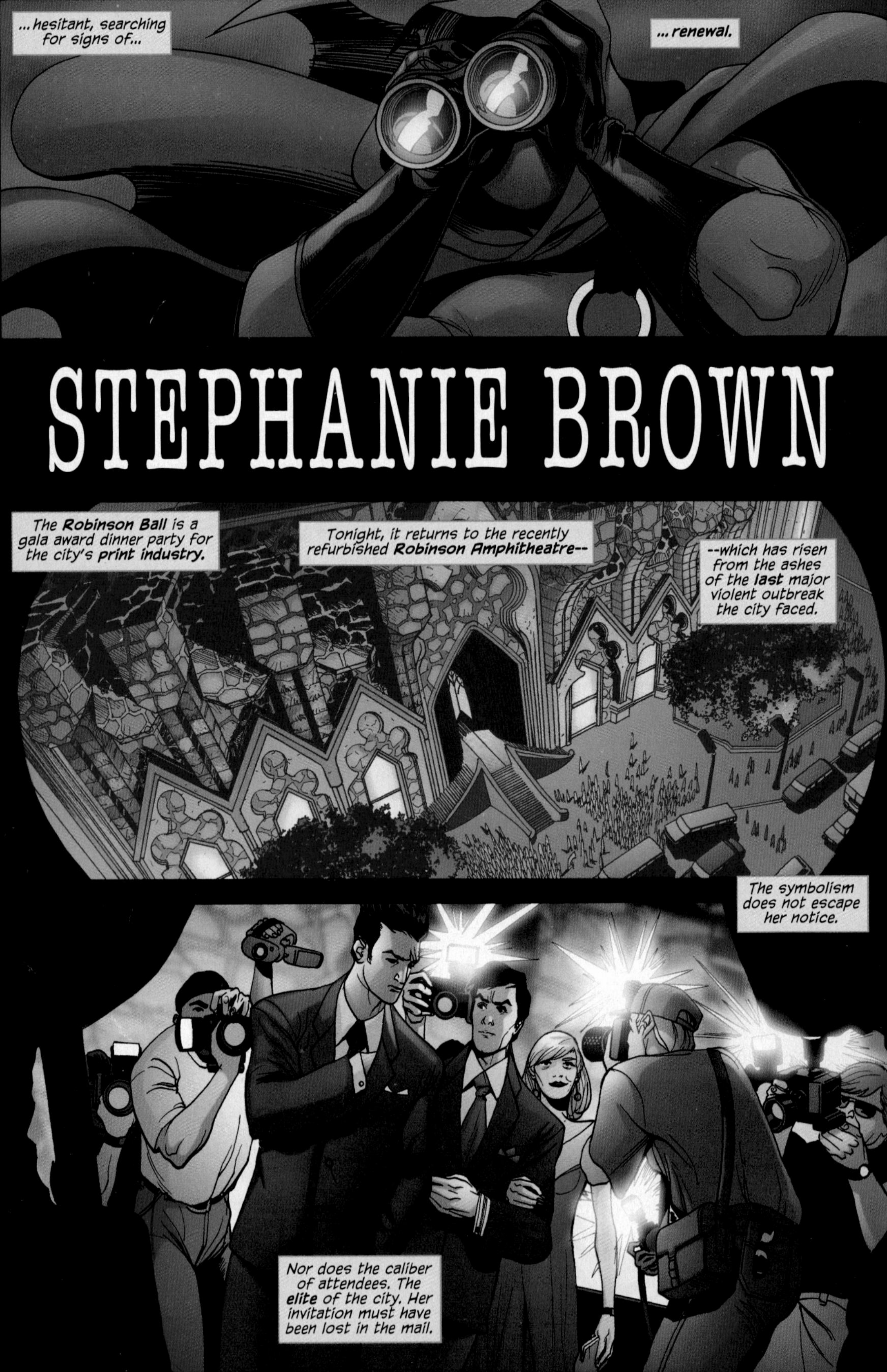
...hesitant, searching for signs of...
...renewal.
STEPHANIE BROWN
The Robinson Ball is a gala award dinner party for the city's print industry.
Tonight, it returns to the recently refurbished Robinson Amphitheatre--
--which has risen from the ashes of the last major violent outbreak the city faced.
The symbolism does not escape her notice.
Nor does the caliber of attendees. The elite of the city. Her invitation must have been lost in the mail.

Bruce Wayne, who is rumored to make his reappearance at the ball tonight.

Dick Grayson, Wayne's older ward. Stephanie knows them as **Robin** and **Nightwing**.

Although those identities may now be...outmoded.

And the woman...

Dr. Leslie Thompkins, who faked Stephanie's **death** over a year ago and took her to **Africa**.

She's back. And starting over.

Like they **all** seem to.

Like **Barbara Gordon**, who serves as the organizational Oracle for the superhero community.

They all come back for the same reason they left.

Because of the city--

--and its love for **second chances**--

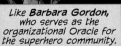

NOCTURNA, AGAIN?

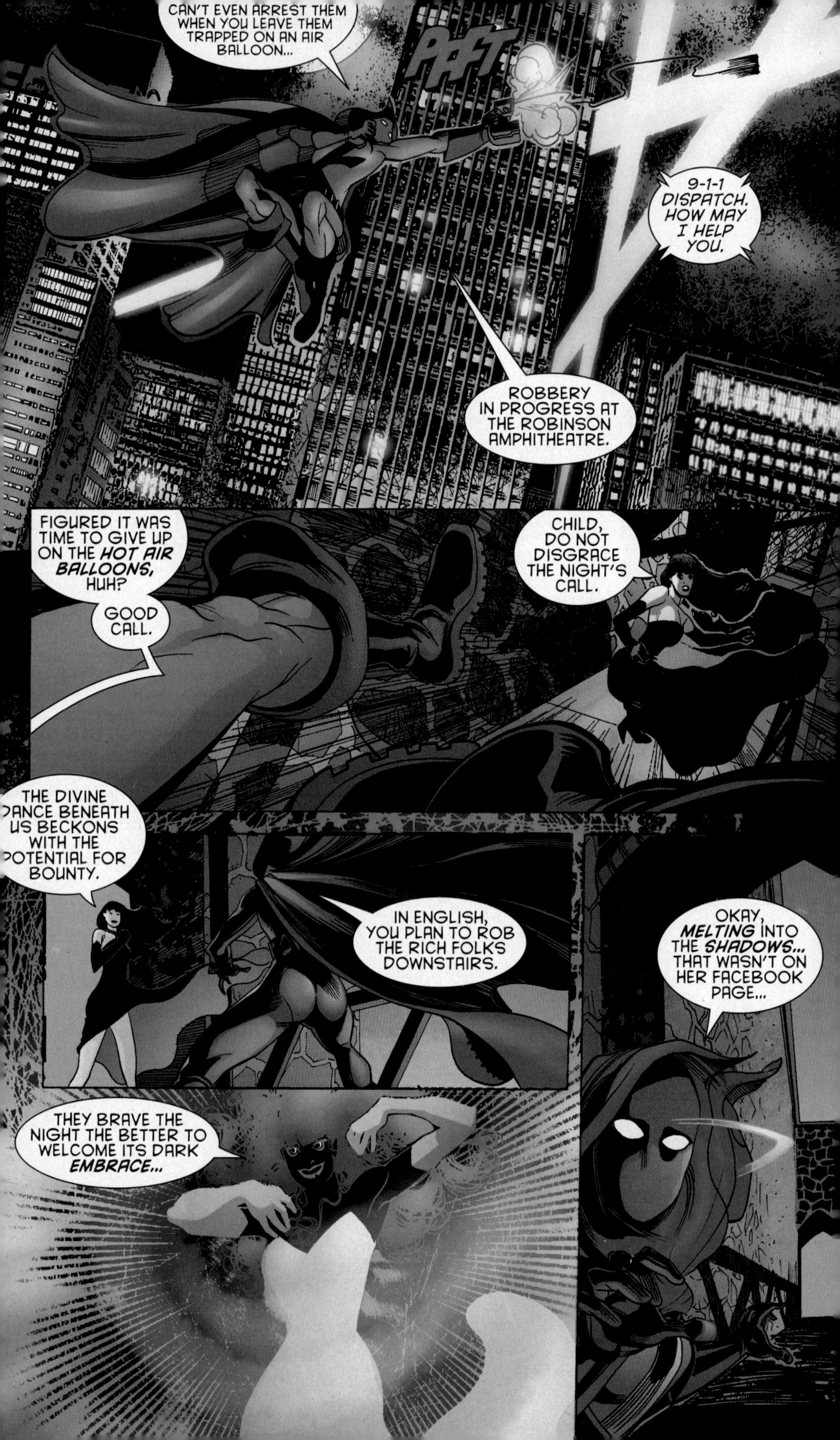
CAN'T EVEN ARREST THEM WHEN YOU LEAVE THEM TRAPPED ON AN AIR BALLOON...
PAFT
9-1-1 DISPATCH. HOW MAY I HELP YOU.
ROBBERY IN PROGRESS AT THE ROBINSON AMPHITHEATRE.
FIGURED IT WAS TIME TO GIVE UP ON THE *HOT AIR BALLOONS,* HUH?
GOOD CALL.
CHILD, DO NOT DISGRACE THE NIGHT'S CALL.
THE DIVINE DANCE BENEATH US BECKONS WITH THE POTENTIAL FOR BOUNTY.
IN ENGLISH, YOU PLAN TO ROB THE RICH FOLKS DOWNSTAIRS.
OKAY, *MELTING* INTO THE *SHADOWS...* THAT WASN'T ON HER FACEBOOK PAGE...
THEY BRAVE THE NIGHT THE BETTER TO WELCOME ITS DARK *EMBRACE...*

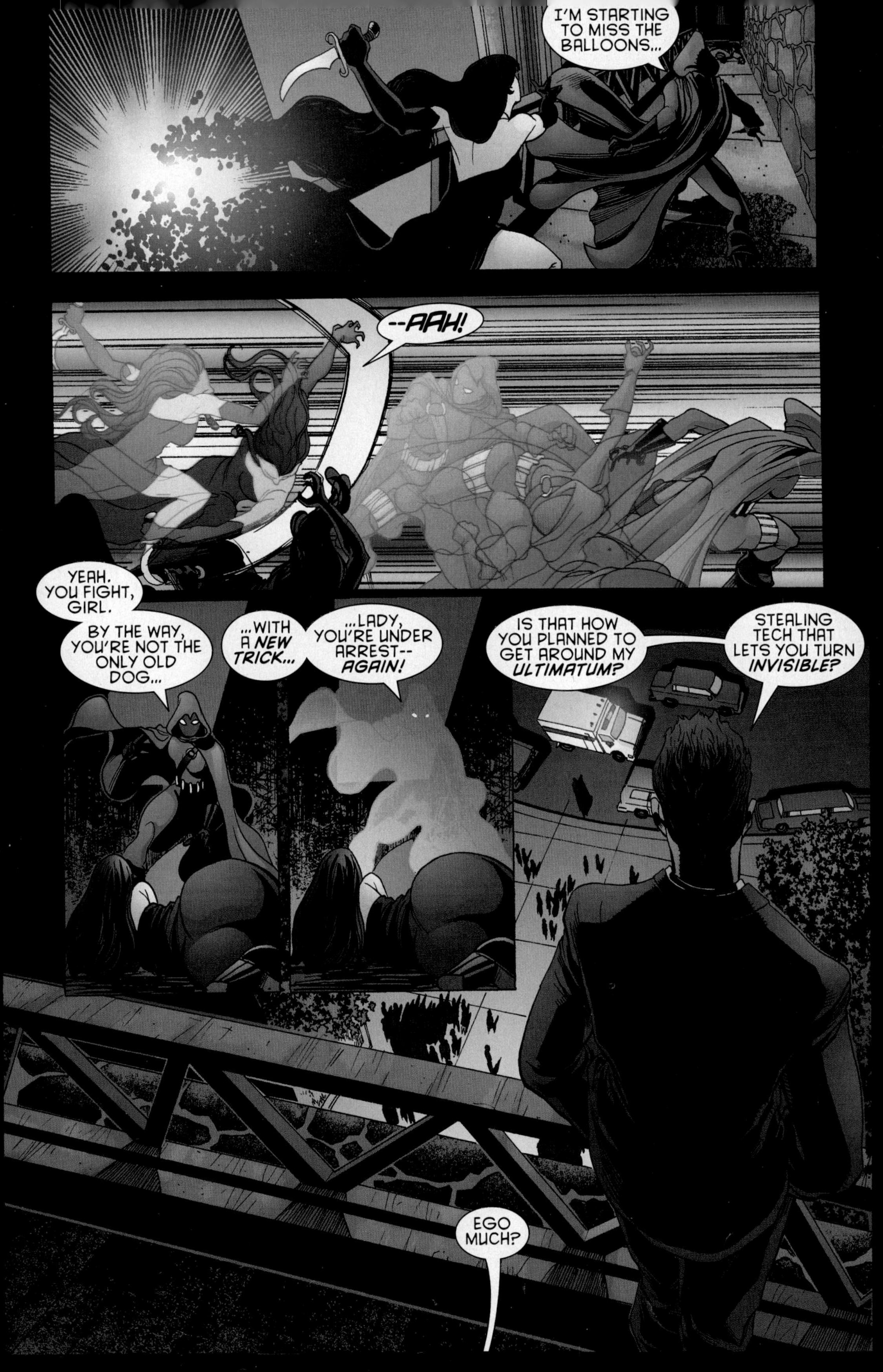
I'M STARTING TO MISS THE BALLOONS...
--AAH!
YEAH. YOU FIGHT, GIRL.
BY THE WAY, YOU'RE NOT THE ONLY OLD DOG...
...WITH A NEW TRICK...
...LADY, YOU'RE UNDER ARREST--AGAIN!
IS THAT HOW YOU PLANNED TO GET AROUND MY ULTIMATUM?
STEALING TECH THAT LETS YOU TURN INVISIBLE?
EGO MUCH?

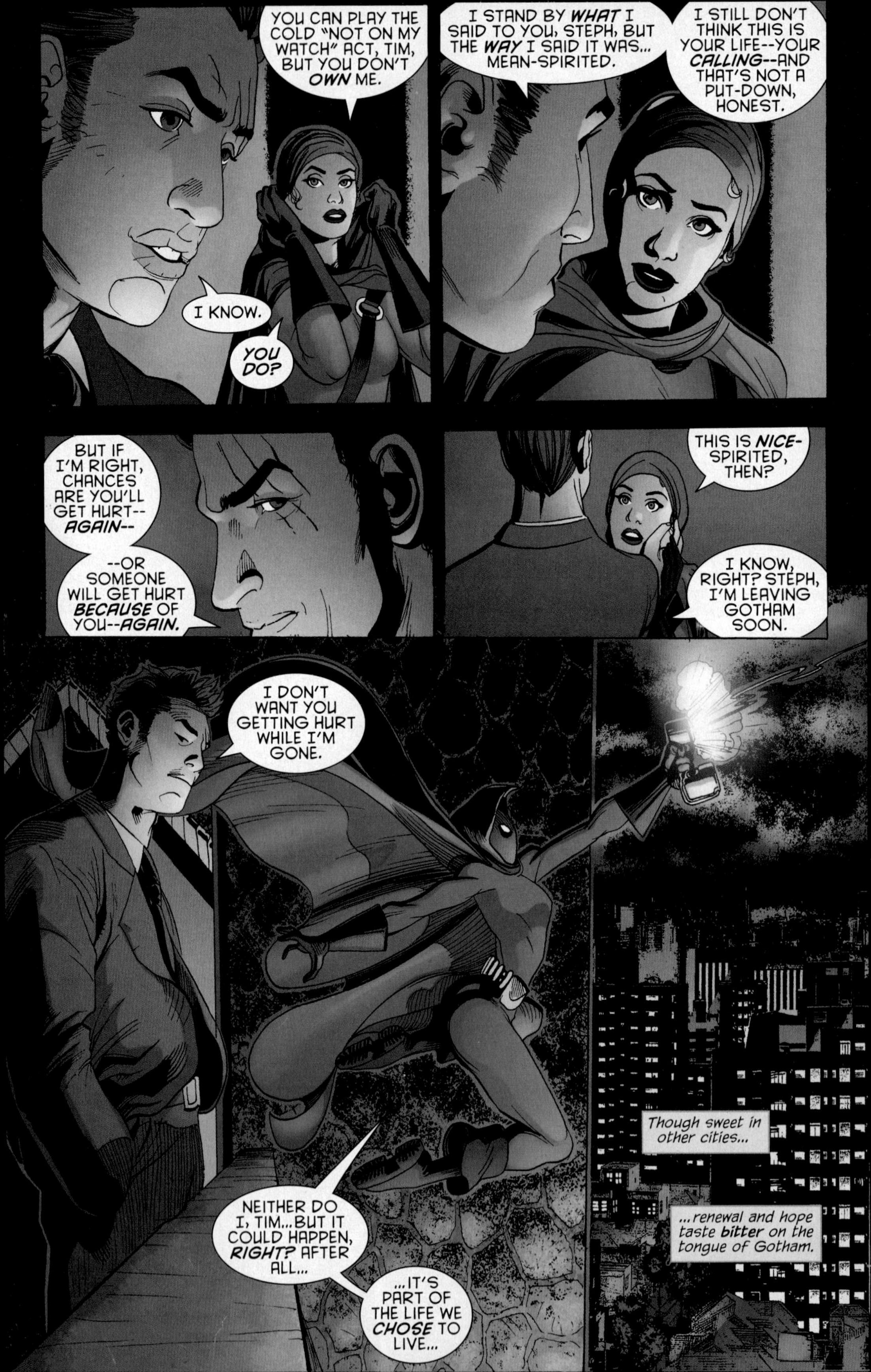
YOU CAN PLAY THE COLD "NOT ON MY WATCH" ACT, TIM, BUT YOU DON'T OWN ME.
I KNOW.
YOU DO?
I STAND BY WHAT I SAID TO YOU, STEPH, BUT THE WAY I SAID IT WAS... MEAN-SPIRITED.
I STILL DON'T THINK THIS IS YOUR LIFE--YOUR CALLING--AND THAT'S NOT A PUT-DOWN, HONEST.
BUT IF I'M RIGHT, CHANCES ARE YOU'LL GET HURT--AGAIN--
--OR SOMEONE WILL GET HURT BECAUSE OF YOU--AGAIN.
THIS IS NICE-SPIRITED, THEN?
I KNOW, RIGHT? STEPH, I'M LEAVING GOTHAM SOON.
I DON'T WANT YOU GETTING HURT WHILE I'M GONE.
NEITHER DO I, TIM...BUT IT COULD HAPPEN, RIGHT? AFTER ALL...
...IT'S PART OF THE LIFE WE CHOSE TO LIVE...
Though sweet in other cities...
...renewal and hope taste bitter on the tongue of Gotham.

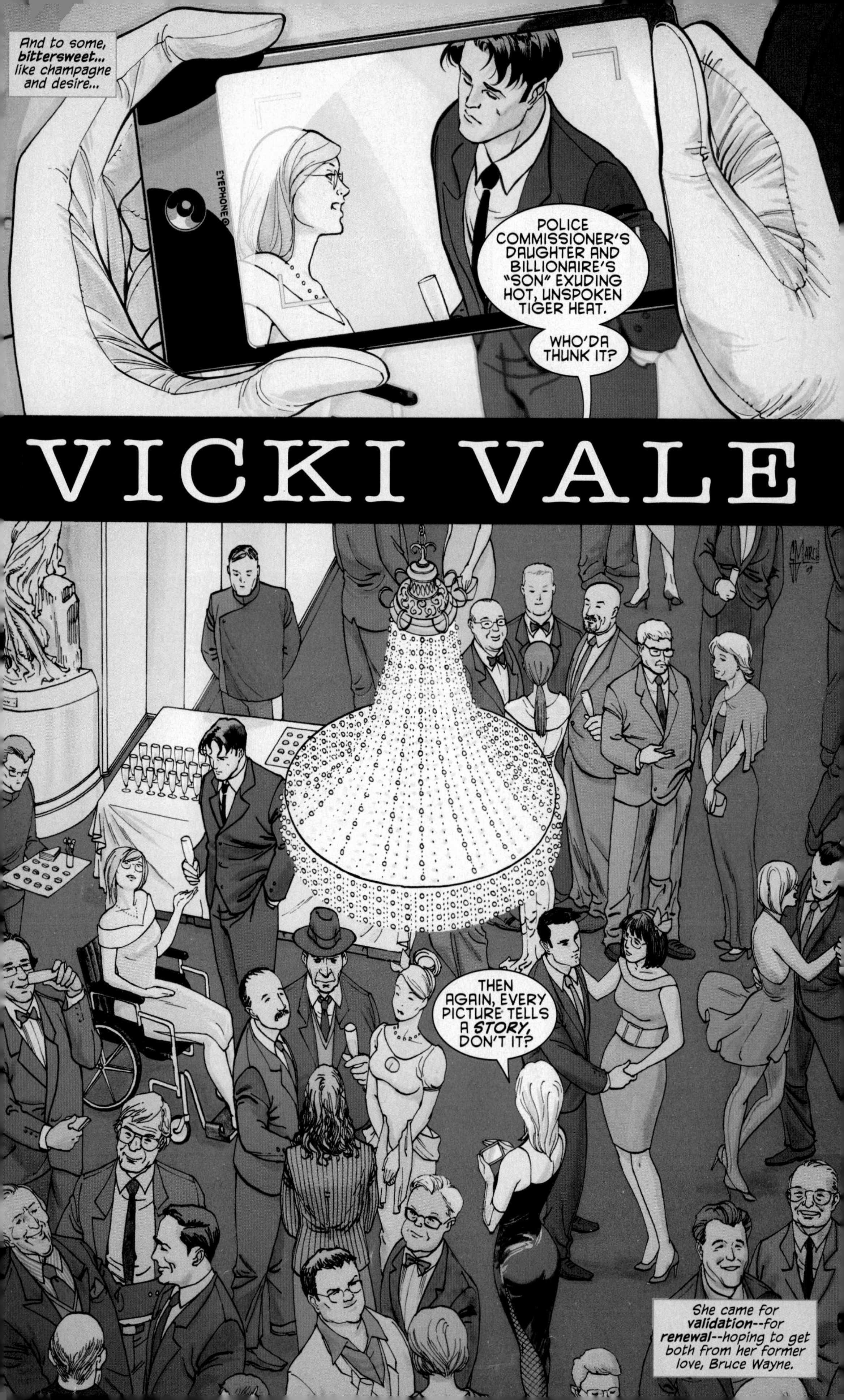
And to some, **bittersweet...** like champagne and desire...
EYEPHONE©
POLICE COMMISSIONER'S DAUGHTER AND BILLIONAIRE'S "SON" EXUDING HOT, UNSPOKEN TIGER HEAT.
WHO'DA THUNK IT?
VICKI VALE
THEN AGAIN, EVERY PICTURE TELLS A *STORY,* DON'T IT?
She came for **validation**--for **renewal**--hoping to get both from her former love, Bruce Wayne.

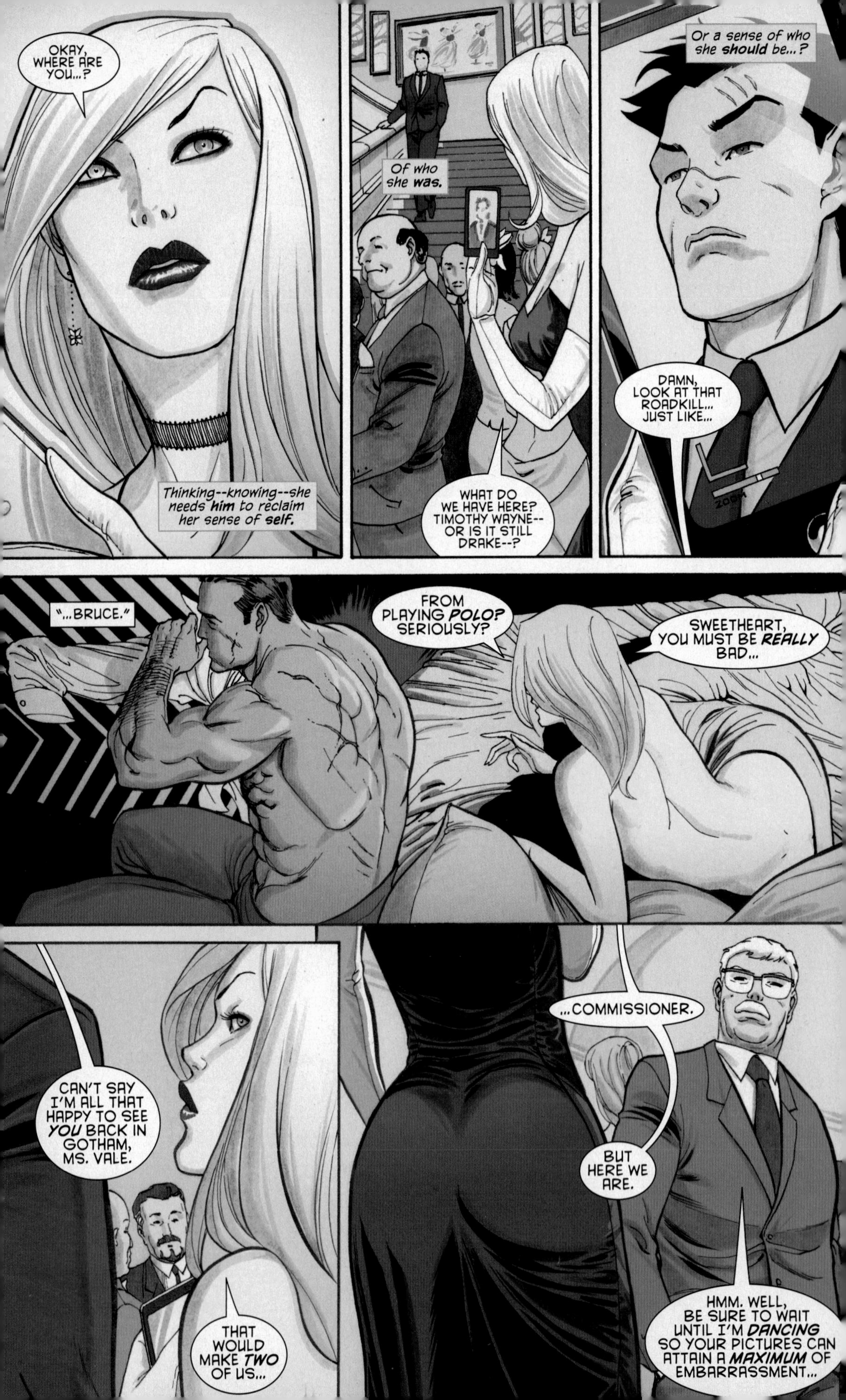
OKAY, WHERE ARE YOU...?
Thinking--knowing--she needs him to reclaim her sense of self.
Of who she was.
WHAT DO WE HAVE HERE? TIMOTHY WAYNE-- OR IS IT STILL DRAKE--?
Or a sense of who she should be...?
DAMN, LOOK AT THAT ROADKILL... JUST LIKE...
"...BRUCE."
FROM PLAYING POLO? SERIOUSLY?
SWEETHEART, YOU MUST BE REALLY BAD...
CAN'T SAY I'M ALL THAT HAPPY TO SEE YOU BACK IN GOTHAM, MS. VALE.
THAT WOULD MAKE TWO OF US...
...COMMISSIONER.
BUT HERE WE ARE.
HMM. WELL, BE SURE TO WAIT UNTIL I'M DANCING SO YOUR PICTURES CAN ATTAIN A MAXIMUM OF EMBARRASSMENT...

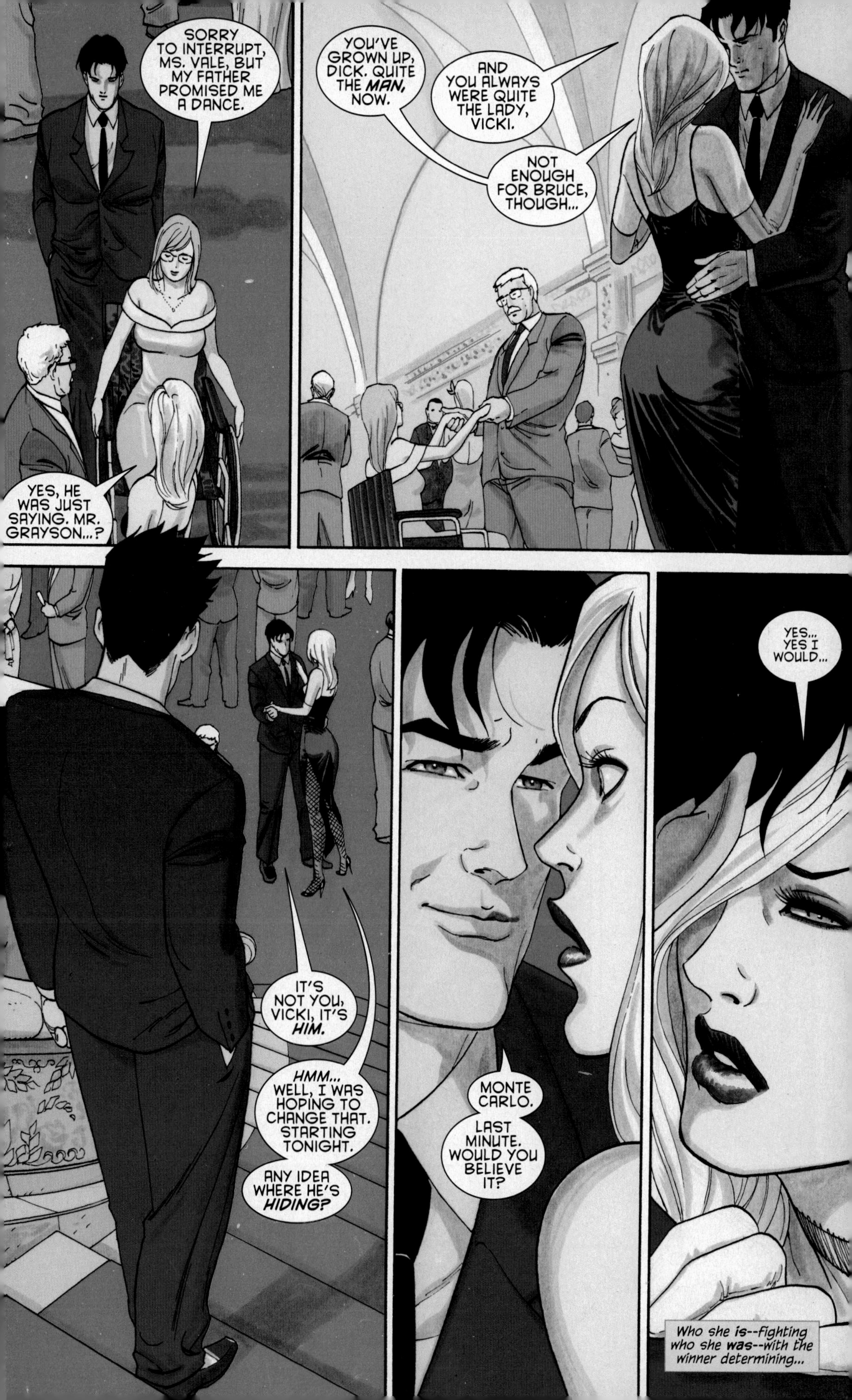
SORRY TO INTERRUPT, MS. VALE, BUT MY FATHER PROMISED ME A DANCE.
YES, HE WAS JUST SAYING. MR. GRAYSON...?
YOU'VE GROWN UP, DICK. QUITE THE *MAN,* NOW.
AND YOU ALWAYS WERE QUITE THE LADY, VICKI.
NOT ENOUGH FOR BRUCE, THOUGH...
IT'S NOT YOU, VICKI, IT'S *HIM.*
HMM... WELL, I WAS HOPING TO CHANGE THAT. STARTING TONIGHT.
ANY IDEA WHERE HE'S *HIDING?*
MONTE CARLO.
LAST MINUTE. WOULD YOU BELIEVE IT?
YES... YES I WOULD...
Who she **is**--*fighting who she* **was**--*with the winner determining...*

...who she will be.

Relationships in Gotham are so odd, she thinks.

What forces some people apart...

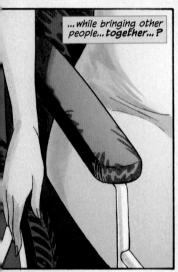

...while bringing other people...together...?

GOTHAM G[...]
MORNING EDITION
Thursday / Rain, 64 / Weather Page: 26

COMMISH DAUGHTER PARALYZED!

NO...

YES...

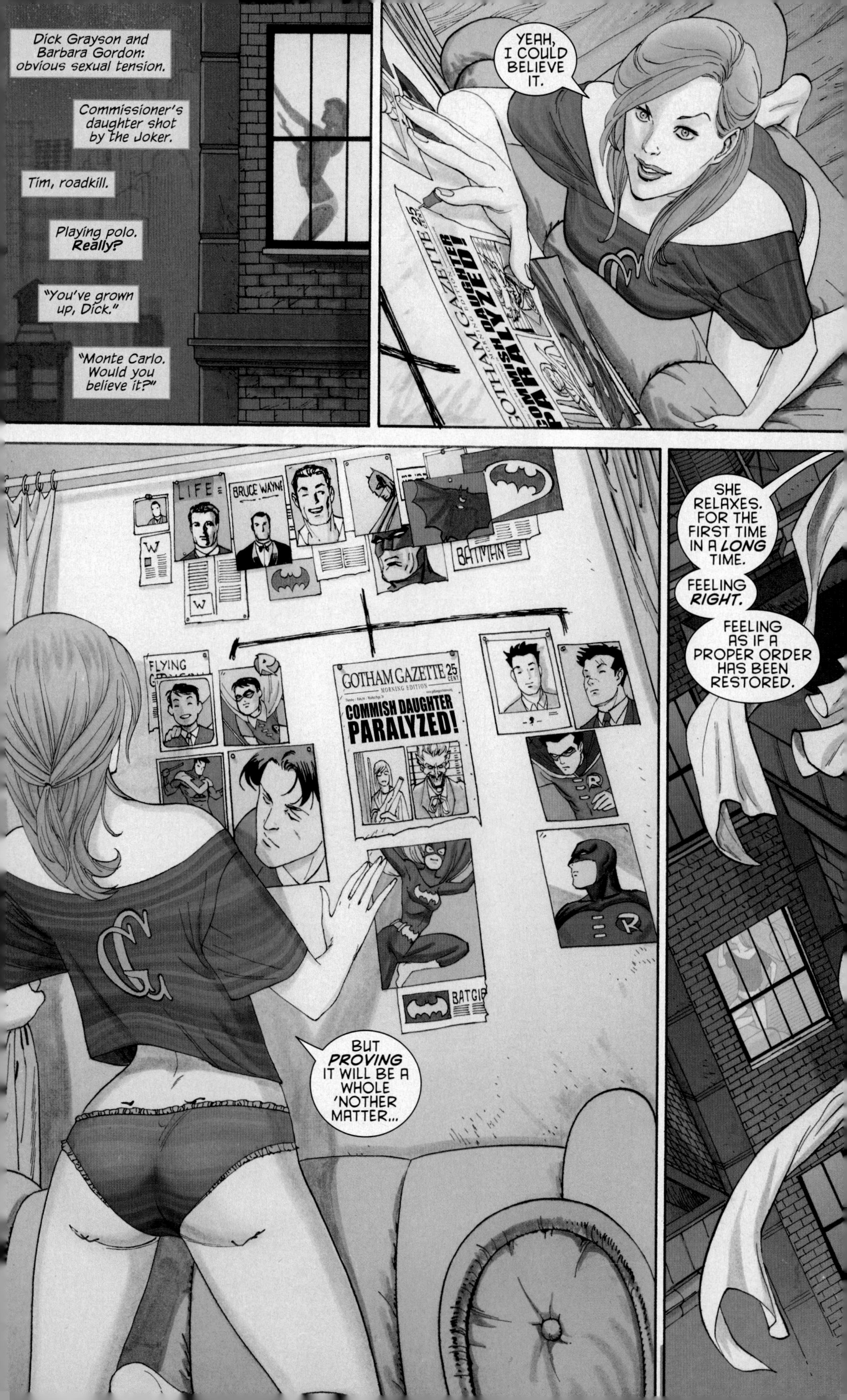
Dick Grayson and Barbara Gordon: obvious sexual tension.
Commissioner's daughter shot by the Joker.
Tim, roadkill.
Playing polo. *Really?*
"You've grown up, Dick."
"Monte Carlo. Would you believe it?"
YEAH, I COULD BELIEVE IT.
GOTHAM GAZETTE
COMMISH DAUGHTER PARALYZED!
LIFE
BRUCE WAYNE
BATMAN
GOTHAM GAZETTE 25 CENT
MORNING EDITION
COMMISH DAUGHTER PARALYZED!
BUT *PROVING* IT WILL BE A WHOLE 'NOTHER MATTER...
SHE RELAXES. FOR THE FIRST TIME IN A *LONG* TIME.
FEELING *RIGHT*.
FEELING AS IF A PROPER ORDER HAS BEEN RESTORED.

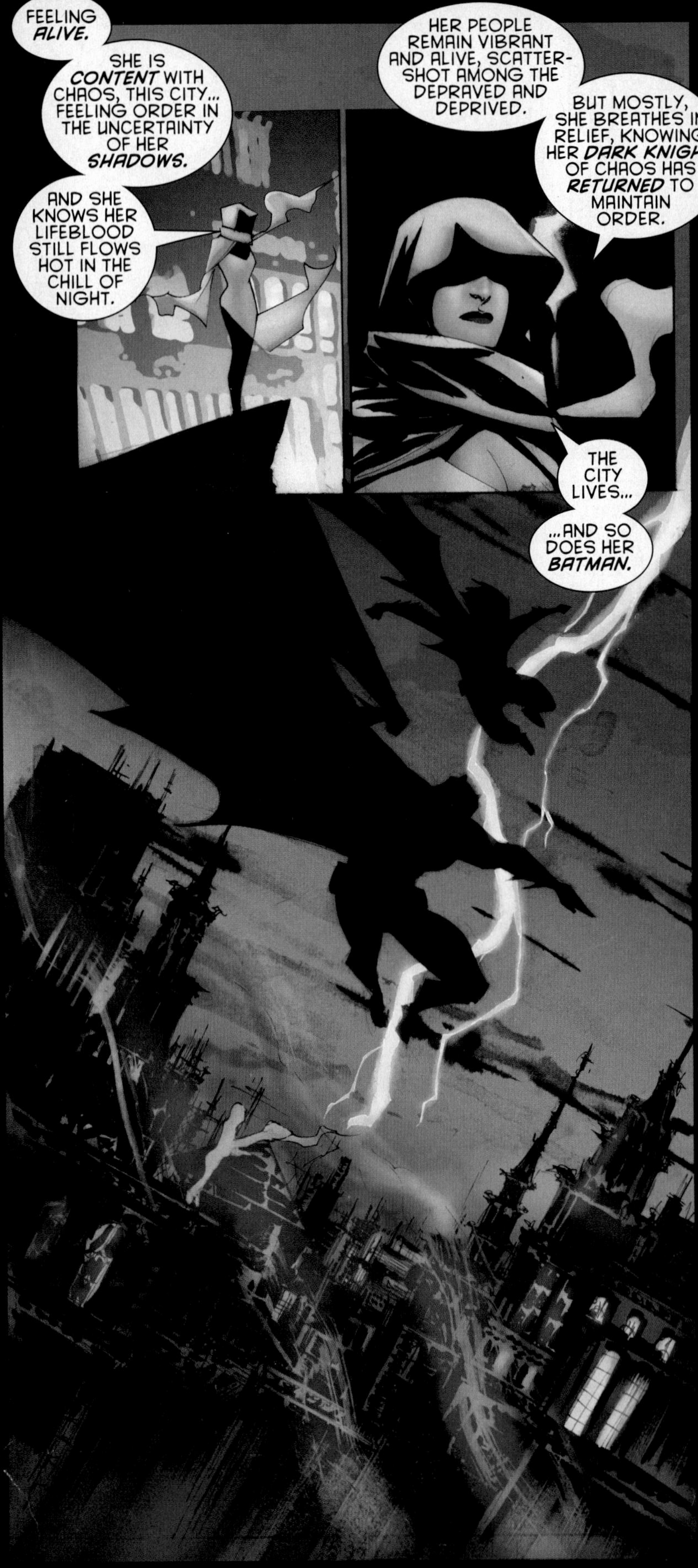
FEELING *ALIVE.*
SHE IS *CONTENT* WITH CHAOS, THIS CITY... FEELING ORDER IN THE UNCERTAINTY OF HER *SHADOWS.*
AND SHE KNOWS HER LIFEBLOOD STILL FLOWS HOT IN THE CHILL OF NIGHT.
HER PEOPLE REMAIN VIBRANT AND ALIVE, SCATTER-SHOT AMONG THE DEPRAVED AND DEPRIVED.
BUT MOSTLY, SHE BREATHES IN RELIEF, KNOWING HER *DARK KNIGHT* OF CHAOS HAS *RETURNED* TO MAINTAIN ORDER.
THE CITY LIVES...
...AND SO DOES HER *BATMAN.*

GOTHAM GAZETTE
BATMAN ALIVE?

Written By
Fabian Nicieza

The Veil
Art by
Dustin Nguyen

Vicki Vale
Art by
Guillem March

Stephanie Brown
Art by
ChrisCross

Leslie Thompkins
Art by
Jamie McKelvie

Harvey Bullock
Art by
Alex Konat &
Mark McKenna

Steve Wands
Letters

Colors by
Guy Major
(pgs 127-142,148)
Guillem March
(pgs 143-147)

Building the Network

Cover art and pencils by Tony S. Daniel

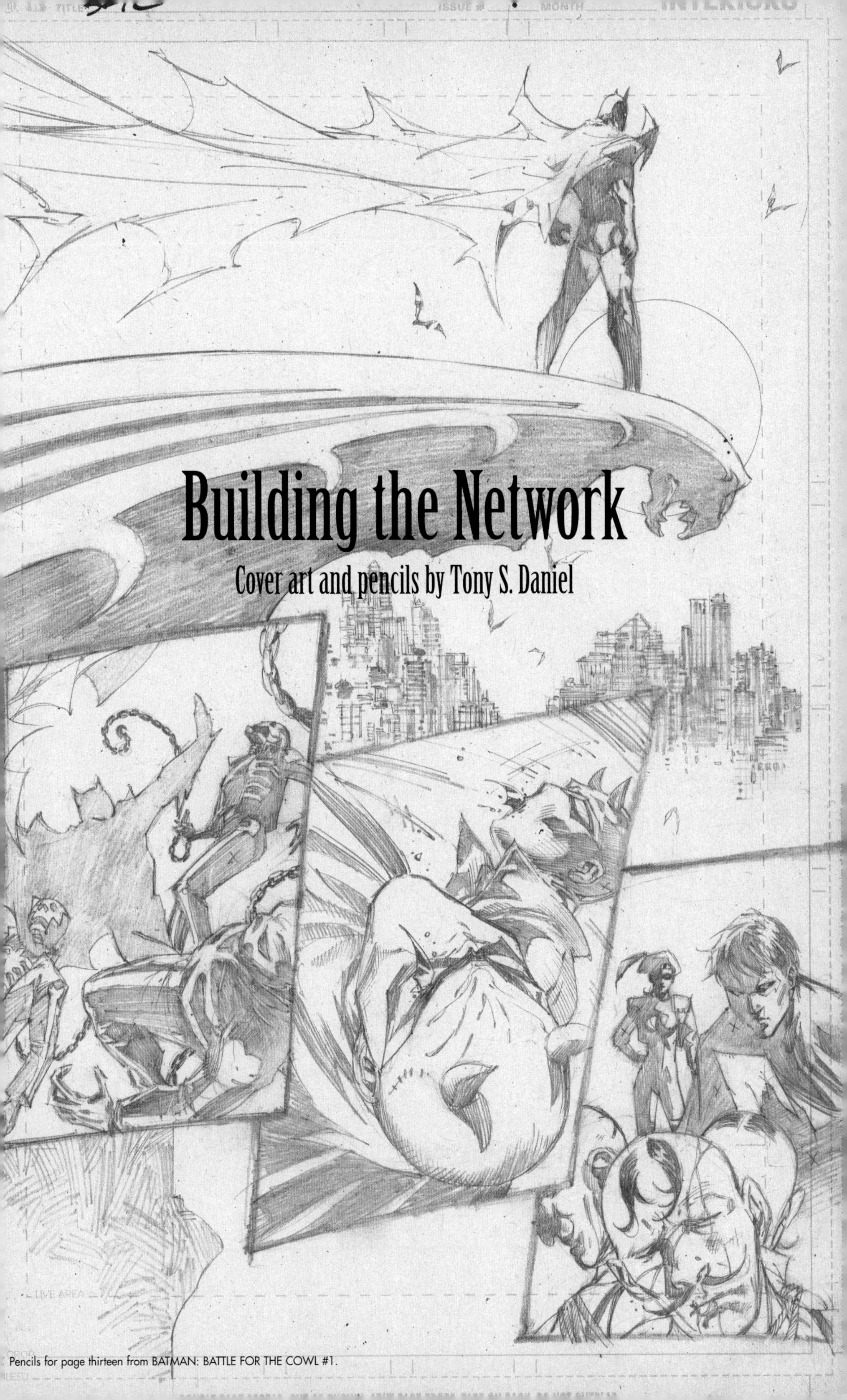

Pencils for page thirteen from BATMAN: BATTLE FOR THE COWL #1.

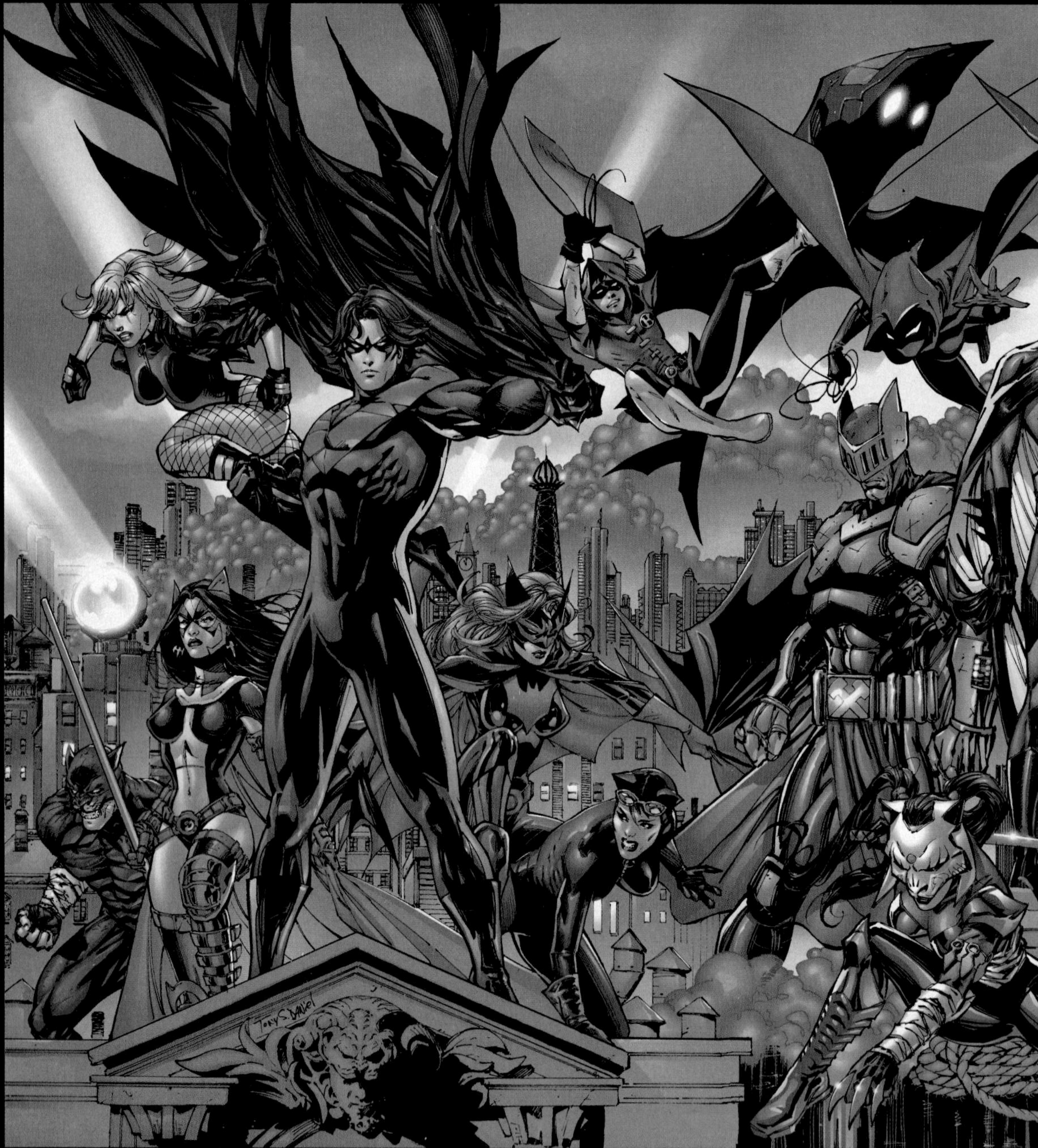
Tony S. Daniel

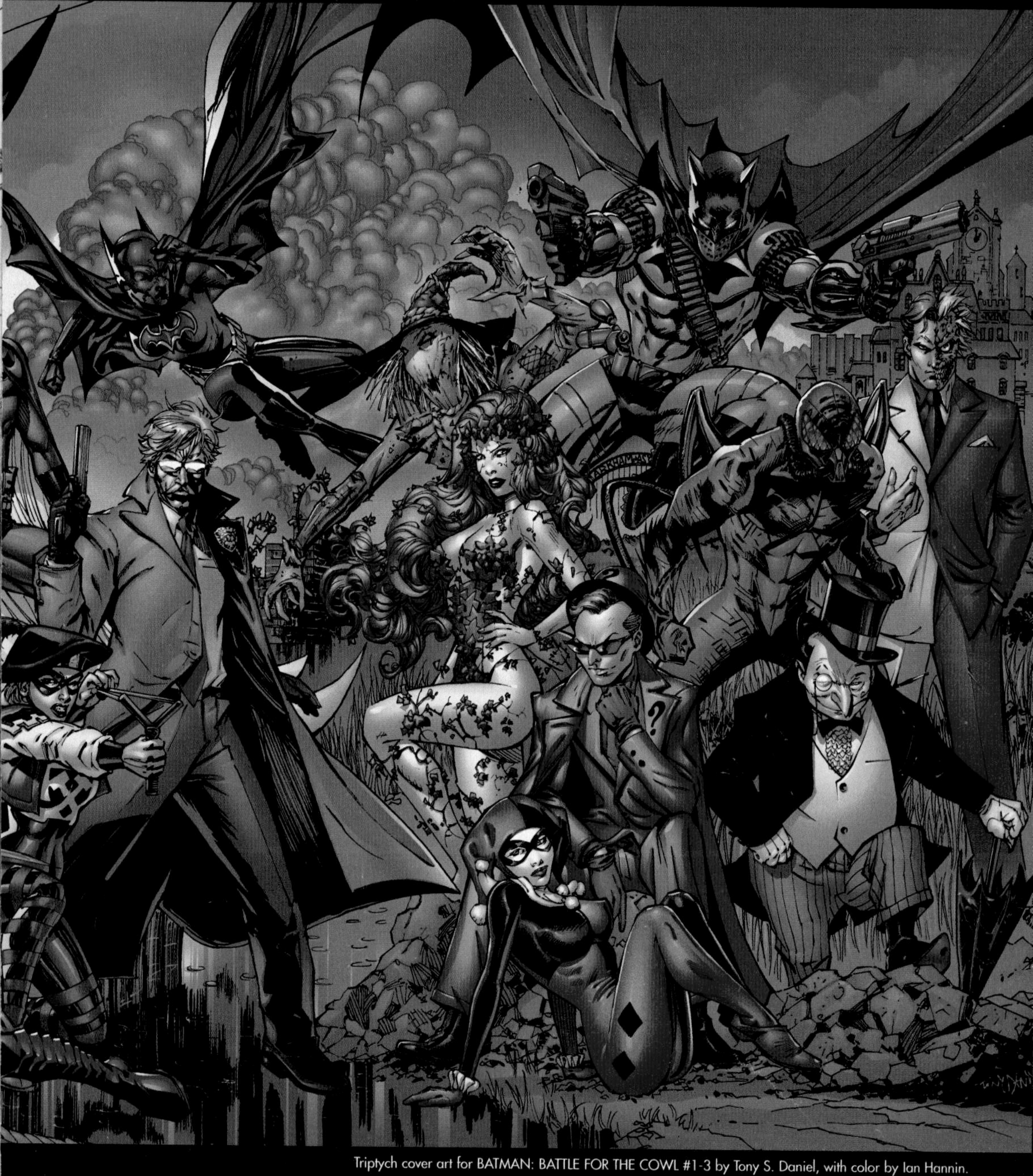

Triptych cover art for BATMAN: BATTLE FOR THE COWL #1-3 by Tony S. Daniel, with color by Ian Hannin.

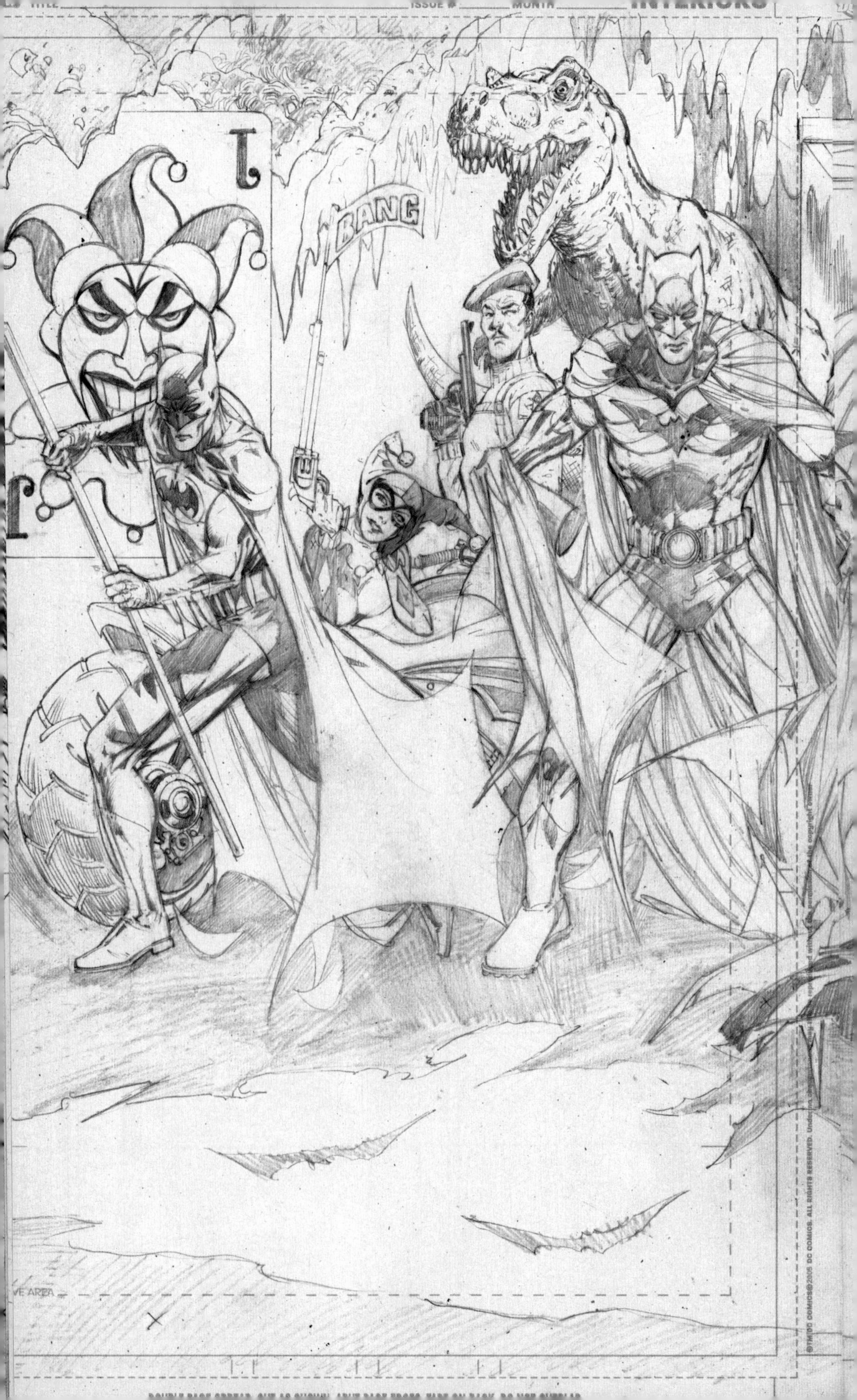
BANG

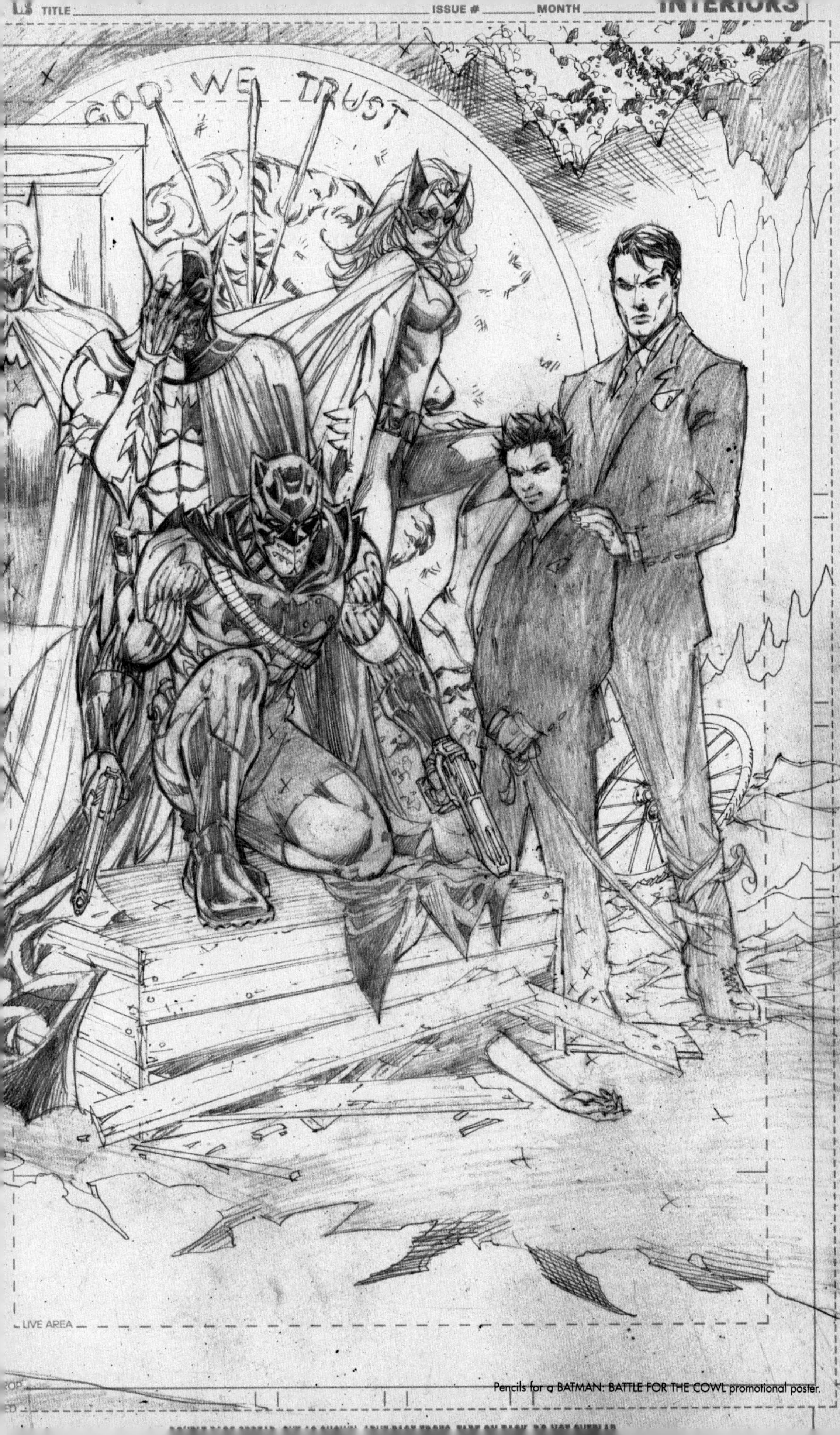
TITLE
ISSUE #
MONTH
INTERIORS
GOD WE TRUST
LIVE AREA

Pencils for a BATMAN: BATTLE FOR THE COWL promotional poster.

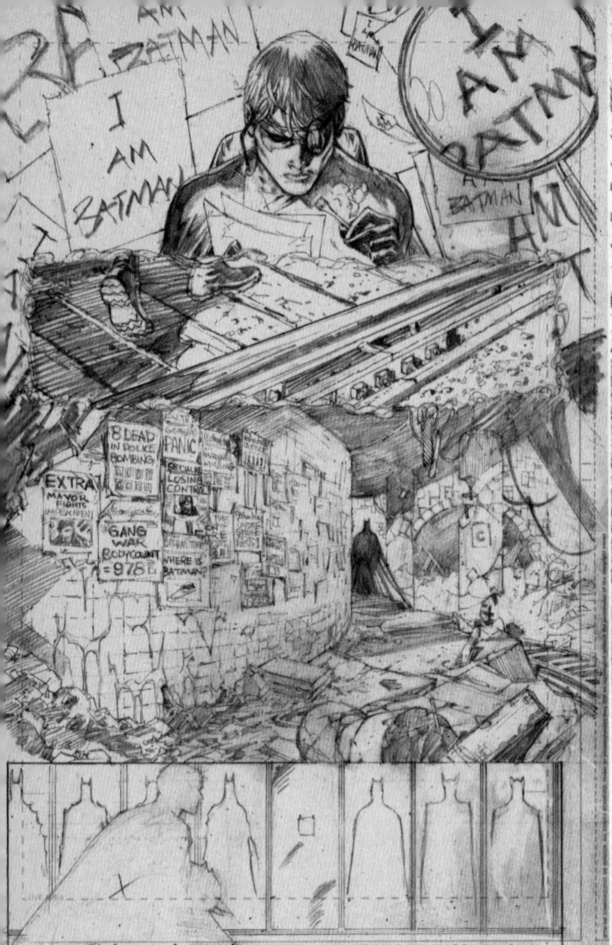
I AM BATMAN
I AM BATMAN
8 DEAD IN POLICE BOMBING
PANIC
LOSING CONTROL
WAYNE MISSING
EXTRA MAYOR FIGHTS IMPEACHMENT
GANG WAR BODYCOUNT =978
WHERE IS BATMAN?
UNDER SIEGE
Pencils for page fourteen from BATMAN: BATTLE FOR THE COWL #1.

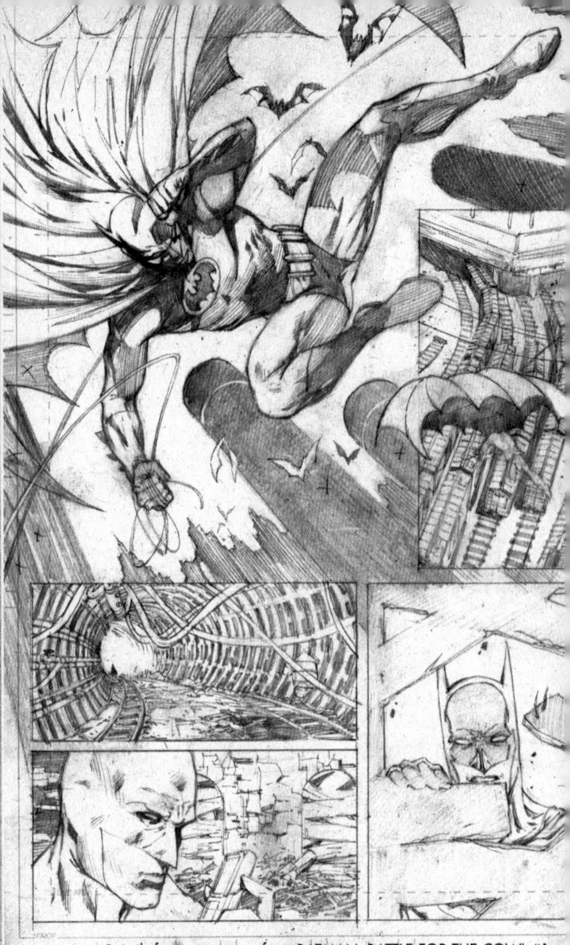
Pencils for page twenty from BATMAN: BATTLE FOR THE COWL #1.

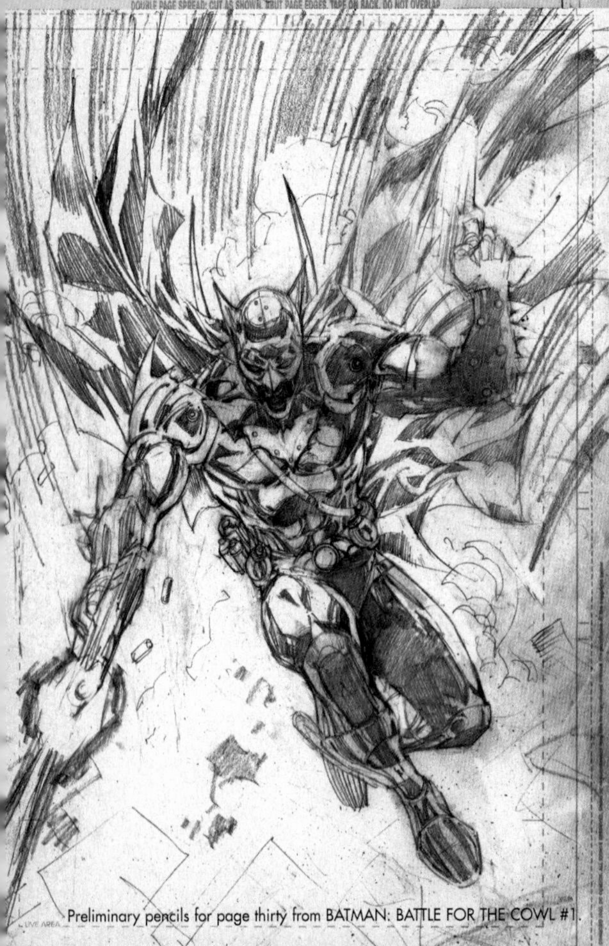
Preliminary pencils for page thirty from BATMAN: BATTLE FOR THE COWL #1.

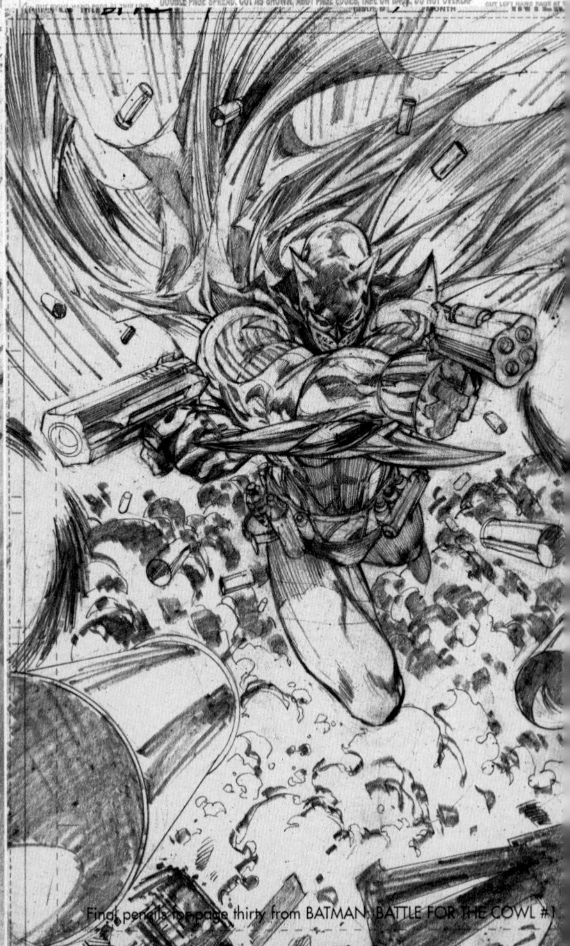
Final pencils for page thirty from BATMAN: BATTLE FOR THE COWL #1.